*The Past Is Not Dead*

# The Past Is Not Dead

Essays from the *Southern Quarterly*

Edited by Douglas B. Chambers, with Kenneth Watson

Foreword by Peggy Whitman Prenshaw

University Press of Mississippi for the *Southern Quarterly*
∾ Jackson

www.upress.state.ms.us

The University Press of Mississippi is a member of the Association of American University Presses.

First printing 2012

∞

Library of Congress Cataloging-in-Publication Data

The past is not dead : essays from the Southern quarterly / edited by Douglas B. Chambers, with Kenneth Watson ; foreword by Peggy Whitman Prenshaw.

    p. cm.

"A collection of [twenty-one representative] literary and historical essays that will mark the fiftieth anniversary of the Southern Quarterly ... (founded in 1962) dedicated to southern studies.... this essay collection features the best work published in the journal. Essays represent every decade of the journal's history. Topics range from historical essays ... to literary essays .... Important regional subjects ... are given special attention" —Publisher's note.

    Includes bibliographical references and index.

    ISBN 978-1-61703-303-2 (cloth : alk. paper) — ISBN 978-1-61703-304-9 (pbk. : alk. paper) — ISBN 978-1-61703-305-6 (ebook) 1. American literature—Southern States—History and criticism. 2. Southern States—In literature. 3. Southern States—History. 4. Southern States—Civilization. 5. Southern quarterly. I. Chambers, Douglas B., Ph. D. II. Watson, Kenneth. III. Southern quarterly.
PS261.P37 2012
814'.54080975—dc23                2011051685

British Library Cataloging-in-Publication Data available

# Contents

# Foreword

Rereading essays published during the years I edited the *Southern Quarterly* has reminded me of how much that work taught me about my profession—about southern studies, critical trends, about writing essays, and even about the relentless deadlines and budget worries imposed by a quarterly journal. Editing was the most demanding and intellectually rewarding work that I could have chosen for those years when I was leaving graduate school behind and making my way in academe. It pushed me well beyond the University of Southern Mississippi, connecting me with scholars nationally and internationally who were often doing work, as we say, "at the cutting edge" of the profession of letters.

An editor's job is surely manifold. In my case I began the job of editing as a junior professor in a regional university and with a journal hardly a decade old. The mission of *SoQ* was to encourage publishable research by the University of Southern Mississippi faculty. As an in-house publication dependent upon the essays sent my way, the journal content had no single focus and offered little incentive for professors ambitious to establish a professional identity wider than the university community. As I recall, I spent a lot of time in the first years persuading my senior colleagues to submit their work—and then more time diplomatically copyediting the manuscripts. I doubtless was more officious than was politically smart, but my earnest efforts generally won me their good grace.

What very early came to be obvious to everyone, including academic affairs vice president Charles Moorman and president Aubrey Lucas, was that the mission of the *Quarterly* gave little hope of increasing subscribers (no content focus), enhancing the reputations of the in-house scholars (little or no peer review), or, finally, extending the research and scholarly agenda of the university. As I recall, I proposed that the journal merge with the recently established *Mississippi Review*, perhaps reviving a nineteenth-century title, the *Southern Quarterly Review*. But the editor of the *Review* was committed to a magazine that focused upon poetry and fiction and thought the merger would be a lessening of that content. What I was most interested in was the expanding field of southern studies, and I thought a journal that broadly covered cultural studies of the South, specifically incorporating the visual, musical, architectural, folk, and popular arts with literary and historical study, would add to but not duplicate other publications that focused upon the South. In time, I found that coverage in the arts fields was significantly amplified by interviews with artists, and eventually the inclusion of such interviews, as well as those with writers, came to be a familiar feature of the journal's contents.

My persuasive and diplomatic skills were tested in the larger field as I contacted many scholars for submissions of their work, for service as peer reviewers, and for editing special issues or, more often, special features. I was especially committed to following the developing fields of feminist studies—and to publish female scholars whose work, broadly characterized as "southern" and "feminist," was a lively and exciting area of scholarship. Such issues as the winter 1979 Art and Feminism in the South, edited by Elsa Honig Fine and the two-issue Contemporary Southern Writers in 1983 were proud moments for me in this new direction. I remember that I was chastised in a letter to the editor for not identifying the contemporary writers in the titles of the two issues as "all women." Rather too smugly, I think now, I wrote back in a personal note that in a recent study of southern writers, all of whom were male, no mention was made in the title of that fact. I like to think that *SoQ* made a contribution to the broadening of southern studies by featuring women scholars as well as female artists. In some cases, early essays in the *Quarterly* led to book publications, an example of which is Kathryn Seidel's 1977 "The Southern Belle as an Antebellum Ideal," leading in 1985 to *The Southern Belle in the American Novel*.

The extension of southern studies to include the popular arts opened a vast area not widely covered in 1970s scholarly journals. University of Southern Mississippi professor Jac Tharpe edited Elvis: Images and Fancies, reprinted by the University Press of Mississippi in 1979, the first time that an issue of the journal, as I remember, was completely sold out. Tharpe was a gifted scholar who edited other well-received issues, such as the Walker Percy one. There were many at USM whose contribution to the *Southern Quarterly* was essential to its growth in reputation and circulation. Tom Richardson, a valued friend and board member, edited a fine issue on George Washington Cable. Jesse McKee, a colleague in the geography department, coedited with me A Sense of Place: Mississippi, a collection of papers and presentations given at a widely attended symposium at USM in 1978 and reprinted by the University Press of Mississippi. In the 1980s, managing editors Joycelyn Trigg and Cheryl Saunders, and later Stephen Young, who also served as editor for a period, were vital to our getting copy to the printer, meeting those relentless deadlines. Lola Norris was another whose work kept *SoQ* connected with its contributors, subscribers, and book publishers. Noel Polk's contributions as book editor and later as editor furthered still the reach and reputation of the *Quarterly*. In recent years, under the editorship of Douglas Chambers, *SoQ* has continued to thrive, offering memorable special features, fresh formats and designs, great covers, and overall a mature journal with a sure sense of the great breadth of "southern studies."

Reading Chambers's introduction and sitting down one afternoon to recall my years of editing the journal have made me realize how distant I am from that time. Recently I have written a study of southern women's autobiographies that should have prepared me for the realization that what one has of the past is the story we tell about it. There's no "recovering" the past. If it's not too self-congratulatory, I'm rather pleased with the story I'm reading and telling of my seventeen years as *SoQ* editor. The work educated and equipped me for a career that was greatly enhanced by the opportunity to read widely in contemporary scholarship, exposing me to developing trends in many areas of southern studies. I hope that the many others who have also contributed to the *Southern Quarterly*—as well as those who have been its readers over the past fifty years—will likewise find value and satisfaction in the work published in its pages.

PEGGY WHITMAN PRENSHAW
September 2011

# Acknowledgments

First and foremost, I thank the contributors for publishing with the *Southern Quarterly*. Peggy Whitman Prenshaw, *SoQ* editor from 1974 to 1991, deserves special recognition, and I am grateful for her foreword to this commemorative volume, and for her encouragement in general. I also appreciate my colleague Kenneth Watson, who served so ably as the journal's associate editor during my editorship (2005–2011), for his invaluable assistance. In producing this volume, I am proud to acknowledge the efforts of the *SoQ*'s several recent graduate assistants over the years: Jesse Kelley (2006–2007), now the digital resources librarian at Philander Smith College (Arkansas); Kyle Ainsworth (2008–2010), now the special collections librarian of the East Texas Research Center at Stephen F. Austin State University (Texas); and Elizabeth Simmons, who while serving as the *SoQ*'s graduate assistant in 2010–2011 worked her computer magic to rescue these published papers from the journal's bound reference collection. The journal's managing editor, Ann Branton, has always been a steady and reliable exemplar of professionalism, for which I am especially grateful. As editor it has been my privilege to work with her and her staff on the twenty-four journal issues we produced together. I wish to thank Craig Gill of the University Press of Mississippi for seeing the value in publishing this "best of" collection of essays, in honor of the journal's fiftieth anniversary, and Jerry Ward of Dillard University and Gwendolyn Midlo Hall of Michigan State University for their continuing encouragement and advice; and for their assistance I also thank my Southern Miss colleagues including Max Grivno, Andrew Haley, Philip C. Kolin, Joseph Navitsky (now at West Chester University), Maureen Ryan, and William K. Scarborough. Thanks also to the anonymous University Press of Mississippi manuscript reviewer, whose comments and criticisms improved the final draft. Any errors are my responsibility alone. As the *Southern Quarterly* approaches its golden jubilee, I dedicate this volume to the *past* and future editors of the journal.

# Introduction

## The *Southern Quarterly* and Southern Studies *The Voice of Humane Learning*

DOUGLAS B. CHAMBERS

In 1962 the University of Southern Mississippi established a scholarly journal, the *Southern Quarterly*. Having achieved its new designation as a university in February, and awarding its first doctoral degree that summer, in October the former Mississippi Southern College (which had been founded in 1910 as a state teacher's college) introduced the *Southern Quarterly* as "a scholarly journal of studies done in the humanities and social sciences by members of the faculty," and specifically as "a journal of articles grounded in research and scholarship rather than a magazine of book reviews, creative writings, or essays of mere opinion." The founding editor James L. Allen Jr. asserted, "the completely scholarly orientation and the broadly humanistic scope of our publication give it, we feel, its *raison d'etre* in an age of journalism increasingly characterized by magazines of opinion and review and in a social and academic age where technology and science threaten to overshadow all unless the voice of humane learning speaks out and makes itself heard."[1]

The development of the journal over the past fifty years mirrors the modern history of the University of Southern Mississippi. From its humble beginnings as a teacher-training college to its stated ambition under the college's fifth president William D. McCain (1955–1975) to grow into a "good" local university, to USM's aspirations in the 1980s and 1990s during the progressive "new South" presidency of Aubrey K. Lucas (1975–1996) to become a "distinguished" regional university, and the efforts since to make USM into a "national university for the Gulf South region"; all affected the course of development of this scholarly journal. From its beginnings under McCain as a modest in-house publishing venue to showcase the work of Southern Miss faculty, to its transformation under Lucas into an up-and-coming journal of southern studies published by USM, to its editorial drift as a mature journal in the 1990s and early 2000s, and then to crisis and revival in the first decade of the twenty-first century, the *Southern Quarterly* has always been a work in progress. Since the late 1970s, however, the journal has consistently been a distinctive, and eventually became a distinguished, journal of southern studies, and on the eve of its fiftieth anniversary it remains one of the oldest academic journals of southern studies in the U.S.

## "Southern"

Generally known as "Southern" and later as "Southern Miss," the college rose to university status and created a requisite scholarly journal as a direct result of the school's ambitious and energetic president, Dr. William D. McCain (1907–1993). A native Mississippian from the Delta, as a teenager in 1924 he had enlisted as a private in the Mississippi National Guard, served as an Army archivist in Italy during World War II, and remained a lifelong state guardsman, eventually rising to the rank of major general in the National Guard. During the Depression he earned a Ph.D. in history at Duke University (1935) and then worked as an assistant archivist at the National Archives in Washington, D.C. (1935–1937), before returning home as the director of the Mississippi Department of Archives and History (1938–1955) where he founded the *Journal of Mississippi History*.[2]

An unapologetic southern nationalist, Mississippi Dixiecrat, and arch-supporter of the then-segregated "southern way of life," McCain was a complicated son of the unreconstructed South who held closely to the Lost Cause and its lily-white romantic moonlight-and-magnolia view of southern history and culture, which he sought to preserve both practically and intellectually. Later characterized by a faculty critic as "a curious, complex man—a walking enigma," McCain was known to be coarse, and yet could be surprisingly sentimental. He was a humanities scholar who encouraged the sciences and technology as university president; an arch-white supremacist who eventually integrated Southern Miss in 1965 without public incident; and a man known for keeping his word who committed professional plagiarism (and was officially criticized by the American Historical Association in 1971). In short, McCain "was indeed a complex man, and he served in a complex age."[3]

In 1953, while state archivist, McCain refounded the moribund Sons of Confederate Veterans, revived their publication (the *Confederate Veteran*), and led the organization for the next four decades.[4] From 1953 to his death in 1993, McCain was the SCV's Adjutant-in-Chief, "a powerful administrative position that put him in charge of its day-to-day operations." He "deservedly is considered within the SCV as its true founder, [and] ran the organization with an iron fist until the late 1980s. A staunch segregationist opposed to civil rights, McCain was unwavering in his defense of the Confederacy and its politics."[5] The organization would eventually give an annual literary prize, name the library and the grounds at its national headquarters in Tennessee, and until 2005 maintain its incorporation in the state of Mississippi, in his honor.[6] As late as 2004, P. Charles Lunsford, a popular leader of the Old Guard white supremacist faction in the SCV (and the originator of the 1990s neo-Confederate slogan, "Heritage, Not Hate") which had just wrested control of the SCV back from post-McCain moderates, posted an email on the SCV website, extolling McCain as their inspiration:

> Those who say that the SCV has somehow changed in recent years are full of it. Our great mentor Gen. William D. McCain was a lifelong segregationist, never repenting until the day he died. Our CIC [Commander-in-Chief] during the early 1990s was Nathan Bedford Forrest II, and he simultaneously held the position of Grand Dragon of the KKK. So what?![7]

In 1955, Dr. McCain was appointed president of "Southern," where he famously promised at his inauguration to "keep the campus dusty or muddy with construction."[8] Though the state's college board had specifically warned the new president not to pursue efforts to turn "Southern" into a university, he immediately set himself to that herculean task. Two decades later, in a valedictory 1975 interview, McCain remembered that his goal from the beginning was "to take a small college and make a good university out of it."[9]

Over the following two decades of his presidency he kept that promise. "Southern" grew dramatically, from 3,000 students in 1955, to 5,000 students and 200 faculty in 1960, to 11,000 students and 470 full-time faculty by the time McCain retired in 1975. In the summer of 1962, Southern Miss awarded its first doctoral degree, in education; by 1972 the school offered terminal degrees in twenty-seven academic disciplines.[10] McCain had built or extensively renovated some thirty major buildings and other structures on campus (including at least ten new dormitories, the university library, the basketball coliseum, the football stadium, and a new fraternity row), established an undergraduate honors program (1965–1970), academic programs in polymer science and marine sciences (the latter at the university's newly developed Gulf Coast campus), reputable performing arts programs (including the Southern Playhouse theater and a comprehensive music program), and had achieved some distinction in intercollegiate sports (especially football and basketball).[11] Though the last years of his presidency (1968–1974) brought a series of administration scandals, which violated national standards of academic freedom and university governance resulting in generally low faculty morale, student unrest, and the threat of a negative review by the Southern Association of Colleges and Secondary Schools (SACS, the regional accreditation board), McCain had indeed boot-strapped the old Mississippi Southern College into a new "good" state university.[12]

Through the 1960s and early 1970s, as a ham-fisted old-style university president, McCain also continued his public advocacy of white supremacy and his ideological opposition to integration and civil rights in Mississippi and throughout the South. He publicly supported the pro-segregationist White Citizens' Council, was an occasional contributor to its monthly magazine *The Citizen*, including a strongly worded essay in September 1962 condemning as a threat to states' rights the federal actions to assist James Meredith after the recent violent anti-integration riots at the University of Mississippi, and was a prominent member of its speakers bureau.[13] He was also one of the principal founders of the WCC's youth division, the Patriotic American Youth, and as late as July 1972, President McCain sponsored a PAY forum at Southern Miss where he gave a public address.[14] In those tense times, McCain also worked closely with the Mississippi State Sovereignty Commission, including its extra-legal actions against Clyde Kennard (1927–1963), "a young, black, highly decorated Korean War veteran" and native and resident of Hattiesburg who applied three times to attend "Southern" (1956, 1958, 1959). Kennard was then twice arrested on trumped-up criminal charges, including the felony theft of five bags of chicken feed worth $25, for which he was sentenced in 1960 to seven years in the state penitentiary. Diagnosed with terminal cancer at Parchman, Kennard was denied medical treatment and put to hard labor, and then upon petition was given early release by arch-segregationist Governor Ross Barnett, before dying on July 4, 1963.[15] Just two years after Kennard's conviction, McCain's erstwhile friend and fellow Dixiecrat Governor Barnett, with the support of the state legislature, granted university status to "Southern," now officially renamed the University of Southern Mississippi on February 27, 1962.

In launching the *Southern Quarterly* later that year, President McCain put his personal stamp on his university's scholarly journal.[16] The inaugural editor explicitly recognized that the journal's founding constituted "the realization of a long-time dream of Dr. William D. McCain, President of the University of Southern Mississippi."[17] Establishing this new university journal no doubt was a dream come true for a professional historian, state archivist, and now university president, but also a neo-Confederate southern nationalist who had already founded one state scholarly journal as Dr. McCain, and quite another kind of literary magazine, the *Confederate Veteran*, as General McCain. One may see McCain's implicit influence in another explanatory point Professor Allen made in his inaugural editorial: "Those whose efforts and interests support *The Southern Quarterly* firmly feel that there is still a proper, necessary, and important place—in the world at large as well as in the academic world—for good, old-fashioned, solid scholarship."[18]

Allen concluded his introduction of the journal with an implicit challenge. He reminded all that the founding of the *Southern Quarterly* was not simply one of Southern's three "milestones" of 1962. In his view, and perhaps that of President McCain too, the journal was part and parcel of "the increasingly evident fact that Southern has come into full maturity as an institution of higher learning." In short, the success of the new scholarly journal would show that Southern Miss was a fully realized university and not one in name only:

> Actually, however, the relationship between these three milestones in the school's academic development—designation as a university, granting of doctoral degrees, and inauguration of our own scholarly publication—really goes much deeper than mere proximity in chronological sequence. For the latter two are unmistakable manifestations of the increasingly evident fact that Southern has come into full maturity as an institution of higher learning, that it has become an institution actively involved in all the broad academic and scholarly interests consonant with the name and state of university.[19]

## The *Southern Quarterly* as a Quarterly for "Southern"

The original purpose of the journal was precisely what it unabashedly advertised in its subtitle: "A Scholarly Journal of Studies in the Humanities and Social Sciences by the Faculty of the UNIVERSITY OF SOUTHERN MISSISSIPPI." It was to be a scholarly journal of, by, and presumably largely for "Southern." As Allen directly emphasized, the title itself "is intended to allude to the name of our school more than to regional interests."[20] Indeed for the first fifteen years, the *Southern Quarterly* was a modest in-house magazine for publishing scholarly work produced by Southern Miss faculty, on all subjects—southern or otherwise. It was administered by a twelve-member editorial board of notable Southern Miss faculty, with a revolving chairmanship, which included McCain who was specifically identified as "President of the University."[21] The founding members of the editorial board were some of the university's most prominent humanities professors of the day.[22]

The editor was officially termed the journal's "managing editor." Apparently it took President McCain several years to find a "managing editor" who was acceptable to his vision for the journal. The first two editors each lasted only a year apiece. James L. Allen Jr. was editor only for the first volume (1962–1963), and then abruptly disappeared from USM's history; by 1970 he was a visiting assistant professor in English at Stephen F. Austin State College, in Nacogdoches, Texas. The journal's second editor, Arthur H. DeRosier Jr. (d. 2008), then an associate professor of history who had been the journal's inaugural assistant editor under Allen, had come to Southern Miss from Michigan State and did not serve long, as he was "managing editor" only for the second volume (1963–1964). Clearly DeRosier had a flair for academic administration: he later was president of East Tennessee State University (1977–1987) and then of Rocky Mountain College (1987–2002). When DeRosier was promoted to "managing editor" in 1963, his new assistant editor was William H. Hatcher, a professor of political science. The following year at the start of Volume III (1964–1965), Hatcher was named "managing editor" and remained so for the next decade (through 1973), while also serving as department chair.[23]

Under Hatcher and his assistant editor Glenn T. Harper of the history department, who later was the longtime dean of the College of Liberal Arts,[24] the *Southern Quarterly* developed into just what President McCain had intended: an in-house journal to showcase the scholarly work of Southern Miss faculty. Regular contributors included the editor, the assistant editor, the editorial board members, and prominent administrators, often writing on their particular specialties.[25] In the 1970s, new humanities faculty were encouraged to publish in the journal too.[26]

From 1962 through the mid 1970s, the McCain era for both the university and its scholarly journal, the *Southern Quarterly* published some very good if necessarily randomly eclectic work, especially on Mississippi subjects. The geographers Arthell Kelley (1963, 1967, 1970) and Jesse O. McKee (1965, 1967, 1971, 1974) provided detailed studies of cultural and historical geography.[27] Senior faculty in history regularly contributed full scholarly essays, notably Arthur DeRosier (1962, 1964, 1965 [thrice]); John E. Gonzales (1963, 1966, 1969), who held the McCain Chair in History and was editor of the *Journal of Mississippi History* for three decades; and John Ray Skates (1967 [twice], 1970, 1972), who served as department chair from 1969 to 1980.[28] Others such as Charles Moorman and Wallace G. Kay (the first director of the Honors College, in the late 1970s), both in English, were prolific scholars who contributed essays almost annually and on a huge range of topics including popular culture.[29]

The journal's McCain era self-consciously sought to present "good, old-fashioned, solid scholarship." The journal averaged six or seven essays per issue, with a no-frills brown cover, and over 90 percent of the 353 scholarly essays published were by male faculty. For most of the period in fact, the gender imbalance was even more pronounced: of the thirty-two articles authored by female faculty, over one-third (twelve) were published in 1973–1975, the troubled last two years of McCain's presidency.[30] While eclectic, the topics covered were very traditional. There were only a few essays on women's studies, though the journal ran five articles on Choctaw topics and at least eleven on the Confederacy/states' rights. Although there were two articles in the mid 1960s touching on African American or African history, one was actually on "the foundation of Mississippi's racial policy" while the other focused on Commodore Matthew C. Perry.[31] It would not be until the 1970s that the *Southern Quarterly* would publish its first two bona fide articles on African American or African history, with one summary article on each subject: Roger Pearson on "Ancestor Worship in Sub-Saharan Africa" (1972), and Jesse O. McKee on "A Geographical Analysis of the Origin, Diffusion, and Spatial Distribution of the Black American in the United States" (1974).[32] No doubt the lily-white coverage of the journal's publications reflected the research interests of Southern Miss's faculty in that period and McCain's influence, just as the predominance of male authors reflected the fact that there were very few female professors at the university.

In Monte Piliawsky's (1982) scathing account of Southern Miss in the late 1960s and early 1970s, whose institutional cronyism and anti-intellectualism he characterized as the "Exit 13 syndrome," for the number of the nearest interstate highway exit, he also excoriated the *Southern Quarterly*, which was edited by his department chair in political science. Piliawsky denounced the parochialism and favoritism of the editor, the contributors, and the journal as a whole; to him it seemed that the journal had, under McCain's baleful influence, devolved by 1972 into an essentially anti-intellectual magazine for favored "Exit 13" toadies to publish otherwise unpublishable work. And perhaps it was, at least in part.[33]

## The *Southern Quarterly* and "A University for the New South"

Toward the end of McCain's tenure as president, late in the fall of 1973, the administration approved the appointment of a new "managing editor," a female professor no less. Peggy W. Prenshaw, a newly hired assistant professor in the English Department, was from Mississippi and studied Mississippi writers especially the work of Elizabeth Spencer (b. 1921). One imagines that her appointment was a breath of fresh air, particularly in the unhappy time that was Southern Miss in 1973–1974. Her first official issue was volume 12, number 3 (January 1974), which was a special issue, Teaching in the Humanities, guest-edited by Jesse F. McCartney, then-associate professor of English. In Prenshaw's first year as the journal's editor, however, the *Southern Quarterly* published eight articles by female faculty, and effectively broke the journal's informal color line by running Professor McKee's article on the Black American in the United States. Working within the old editorial structure, she also contributed a short article of "good, old-fashioned, solid scholarship" of her own entitled "A Review of the Modern Language Association Survey of Teacher Evaluation Procedures."[34] She also published an example of the New Criticism approach to studying southern literature by her young colleague David Berry on the poetry of James Dickey.[35] Things were looking up, for the journal as well as for the university.

Under pressure from both the state—Gov. William Waller, a racial moderate, had commissioned a select committee to study higher education in the state, and its 1974 report was critical of Southern Miss—and an impending SACS accreditation visit later that year, in 1974 General McCain announced his retirement, effective June 30, 1975.[36] His replacement, Dr. Aubrey K. Lucas, from State Line, Mississippi, was a full generation younger than General McCain and a product of "Southern." Having arrived as a freshman in 1953 when the school was still Mississippi Southern College, Lucas earned both BA and MA degrees and then went to Florida State University for his Ph.D.

(1966). He served Southern Miss as director of admissions, registrar, and dean of the graduate school before becoming president of Delta State College in 1971. His appointment was announced by the college board in October 1974, and he officially took office the first day of July 1975. In his inaugural address to the faculty, Dr. Lucas announced a new vision for Southern Miss: "We must set for ourselves no less a goal than to become a distinguished university. I believe that we can be, and I believe that we ought to serve notice on our competitors and our constituencies that we intend to be so." He stressed that his main goals were to encourage scholarship and to "nurture our faculty," including making them the highest paid in the state; to transform the existing university-wide undergraduate honors program into an Honors College, the better to recruit the state's best students; to strengthen the university library; and to reconcile the then-current conception of Southern Miss as "the career university"—with its emphasis on teaching for employment—with his vision of turning USM into a "distinguished university."[37] In short, Lucas's challenge was to take the "good" university to which Southern Miss had aspired since 1962, and make it into a "great" university. It would take ten years, but by 1985 Lucas achieved many of his original goals. The next ten-year SACS report, in 1985, praised the progress that USM had made under President Lucas, concluding that the university was then "poised for a giant step forward":

> . . . today the University is the largest . . . in Mississippi serving more than 13,000 . . . Quality of faculty and students enrolled is significantly moving the institution toward its goal of becoming a distinguished university. . . . [With] strong administrative and academic leadership and a positive campus morale . . . the framework . . . is clearly present.[38]

Whereas McCain, against formidable odds and by force of will, had built the hard infrastructure—university status, physical plant, rapid expansion—for a "good" local university in an age of change to which he never adapted personally, Lucas was a New South progressive temperamentally well-suited to the post–civil rights era. He invested in the soft infrastructure—centers of excellence, faculty morale and scholarship, diverse student learning opportunities—and collegial self-governance that are the hallmarks of a distinguished university. By 1988, USM was living up to its new institutional theme: "The University of the New South."[39]

With General McCain's retirement and the appointment of Dr. Lucas as president in 1975, important changes came quickly to the *Southern Quarterly*.

In volume 14 (1975–1976) Professor Prenshaw had two special issues punctuated by actual scholarly debate among the contributors: one on the poetry of John Donne (no. 3), and the other on the U.S. Bicentennial (no. 4). Both issues included revisionist—self-consciously new-fashioned—scholarship by younger faculty members. In the following year, with volume 15, Prenshaw set about reinventing the journal.

The first issue, October 1976, announced a major editorial reorganization, the first since the journal's founding fifteen years and a lifetime's experience earlier. This new editorial structure brought the journal in line with general academic standards, with an editor, an associate editor, and an advisory board, and thereby freed the *SoQ* from the temptations of editorial meddling by university administrators. Professor Prenshaw was declaring the journal's independence from administrative oversight of its content.

The choices that Prenshaw made are telling. She kept the journal's longtime assistant editor, Glenn T. Harper, from the McCain era.[40] But of the four advisory board members, three were faculty critics of the McCain administration at Southern Miss. One (John N. Burrus) had been an original editorial board member back in 1962, but apparently had fallen out of favor with McCain at some later point. Jesse F. McCartney was her more senior colleague in English, who had published a contrarian piece in the journal in defense of the humanities (1974), at the height of Southern Miss's flirtation with the job-training emphasis of the "career university"; a third, William M. Odom, was a newly hired junior foreign languages professor. And lastly, the fourth new advisory board member was none other than William K. Scarborough, the politically regressive but professionally gifted historian and exemplar of academic freedom, who had heroically survived McCain's attempts to fire him in 1968–1969 in the darkest days of the old "Exit 13 syndrome" at Southern Miss.[41]

In reforming the journal's editorial stance in 1976, Prenshaw went even further. She went against the inaugural 1962 mission statement by introducing scholarly book reviews, a major innovation for the *Southern Quarterly*. In volume 15, she published a total of twenty-eight book reviews, several of which would have been considered "controversial" in the Southern Miss of General McCain. A number of them, with such titles as *A Night of Violence: The Houston Riot of 1917*, *The Rising South: Southern Universities and the South*, and *Plantation Societies, Race Relations, and the South: The Regimentation of Populations*, were reviewed by liberal historian Neil R. McMillen, whose 1971 book—a judicious history of the White Citizens' Council movement—had brought him an unwanted meeting in Dr. McCain's office.[42] Another first-time reviewer, Thomas J. Richardson of the English department, would later serve as a *SoQ* associate editor from 1978 to 2004.[43]

Most importantly of all, Prenshaw dropped the journal's stated requirement that the *Southern Quarterly* publish only the work of Southern Miss faculty, shortening the journal's masthead to "A Scholarly Journal of Studies in the Humanities and Social Sciences." She then proceeded to publish the work of non-USM scholars, a number of whom hailed from colleges and universities measurably more distinguished than Southern Miss. Of the twenty-eight articles published in volume 15, only five were by USM faculty; contributors were from a mix of institutions that included the University of Michigan, St. Andrews College, Clemson, Brandeis, the University of Virginia, the University of Georgia, Baylor, and North Carolina State, as well as smaller southern schools such as Texas Woman's University, East Texas Baptist College, Southern Arkansas University, and Henderson State University.[44] Of the contributors to this first non-USM *Southern Quarterly* volume in 1976–1977, several would become widely recognized scholars in their respective fields: Henry J. Abraham (University of Virginia), Frank Annunziata (University of Michigan), Kathryn L. Seidel (North Carolina State), and Martha Swain (Texas Woman's University). The following year's volume continued this new trend, with contributors from Dartmouth, University of Miami, Baylor, University of Georgia, Notre Dame, University of Virginia, and Rice, as well as from smaller regional schools like King's College, Southwest Texas State, Louisiana State University–Shreveport, Berry College, Texas Tech, Murray State, Georgia State, University of Texas–Arlington, and Xavier University.

The topics covered in these first two non-USM volumes remained eclectic, with only about one-quarter of the articles on southern subjects. Prenshaw, however, was actively reforming the journal, including freeing it from administrative editorial meddling, establishing her editorial independence from the McCain-era old-guard, innovating the journal's coverage to include scholarly reviews of new cutting-edge books, and gathering in contributors from a wide range of institutions both within and outside the South. And in these transitional volumes (vols. 14–16) from 1975 to 1978 she doubled the percentage of articles by female scholars, compared to the McCain era, to nearly one in five published papers. And she began to publish in earnest essays on southern subjects, in particular essays on southern literature.[45]

## The *Southern Quarterly* and "Southern Studies"

After several years of reforming the journal, as if testing the waters in USM's new institutional political climate, in 1978 Peggy Whitman Prenshaw finally set the *Southern Quarterly* firmly on the path of "southern studies." No longer just a scholarly journal *for* "Southern" but rather now a scholarly journal *published by* USM, in 1978 the *SoQ* formally became a journal dedicated to studies of the region. It was now to be "a journal of the arts in the South." As such the meaning of the journal's title was turned on its head: unlike in 1962, from 1978 onward the title would be intended to allude to the journal's regional interests rather than to "the name of our school."

In the first issue of 1978, Prenshaw led with an "Editor's Note," the first in the journal's history. In this note, she announced the wholesale transformation of the *Southern Quarterly*:

> This issue marks the seventeenth year and a new venture for *The Southern Quarterly*. Beginning with this number, *SoQ* will concentrate on arts in the South. We think the new direction will give the journal a clearer identity and purpose, and we hope it will interest *SoQ* readers and attract new ones.
>
> We should like to invite essays, articles and book reviews on both contemporary and earlier music, art, architecture, popular and folk arts, film, theater, dance and literature. Special issues are being prepared on Elvis Presley and Walker Percy, and plans are being made for special issues on film and on architecture. We welcome inquiries and suggestions about these and other topics.
>
> With this issue readers will also notice a new cover design and a change from months to seasons to designate the numbers of the volume. We should like gratefully to acknowledge the service of Barney McKee, director of the University Press of Mississippi, in designing the cover and new layout. We should also like to thank Aubrey K. Lucas, President of the University of Southern Mississippi, and Charles W. Moorman, Vice President for Academic Affairs, for the University's continued support of *SoQ*. Finally, we should like to acknowledge the valuable past service of Glenn T. Harper, who for many years served as associate editor. This year Professor Harper will assume new administrative duties in the College of Liberal Arts.[46]

"A journal of the arts in the South." In effect Prenshaw refounded the *Southern Quarterly* with this first issue of volume 17 (Fall 1978). She professionalized the journal in conformity with general academic standards for scholarly journals, and contributed directly to the formation of regional "southern studies" with a focus on southern literature, literary criticism, and cultural studies, defining "the arts" broadly to eventually include everything from literature and history to the decorative arts and architecture to folklore and popular culture. Between 1978 and 1991 she took this journal from its parochial, eclectic beginnings to a learned journal of regional interests with a national audience. She took full editorial control, redesigned the cover, expanded the readership and scholarly subjects covered, introduced numerous innovations such as film/video reviews (from 1978), literary interviews (from 1981), an annual bibliography of southern art and architecture (from 1989), and art/photographic portfolios (from 1990). The *Southern Quarterly* became an up-and-coming journal for up-and-coming scholars.

To secure her editorial control, Prenshaw eliminated the editorial advisory board and ran the journal with three accomplished "advisory editors," all from the English Department (Jac L. Tharpe, Harry W. McCraw, and Thomas J. Richardson), and an "editorial assistant" who later was promoted to managing editor (Cheryl McAllister Saunders).[47] In 1980, Prenshaw replaced Professor McCraw with Noel Polk, a recently hired Faulkner scholar, also a native of Mississippi. In a remarkable feat of editorial longevity, Richardson served as advisory/associate editor for the rest of his career at USM through 2004, while Polk served as advisory/associate editor (1980–2000) and book review editor (1985–2004). Polk remained book review editor even after becoming the journal's editor in 2001. In accord with modern academic standards, the editors of this newly constituted "journal of the arts in the South" rarely published in their own journal, especially after the *SoQ*'s admittance to the prestigious Council of Editors of Learned Journals in 1986, even as they published widely throughout their careers. For example, after 1978 Prenshaw published just two essays in the journal during her editorship (1983, 1991) and a single book review (1981). Perhaps most notably of all, the most prolific of these scholars, Noel Polk, published but a single book review for the *SoQ* (1978) and never burdened the journal with his own work through a full quarter-century of editorial service.[48] The contrast with the old McCain-era *Southern Quarterly* could not have been greater.

As editor, Prenshaw aimed to produce a distinguished scholarly journal on the full gamut of "southern studies." She organized a wide range of special features and themed issues, by my count some twenty-five special issues between 1979 and 1991. Many were on southern writers, both contemporary and historical.[49] Staying true to the new focus on "the arts," between 1979 and 1989 she brought out numerous issues on decorative, performing, and fine arts.[50] As editor, Prenshaw also explored popular culture in the South, with such issues as Sense of Place: Mississippi (1979), Elvis: Images and Fancies (1979), The Small Town: Order and Image (1980), In Old New Orleans (1981), Country Music (1984), Black Church Ritual and Aesthetics (1985), and, upon leaving USM for a new endowed chair at Louisiana State University, a special double issue on The Texts of Southern Food (1992). The wide range of subjects covered and the emphasis on themed issues demonstrated both the breadth and the depth of the new southern studies, which the journal celebrated. By 1991 her role in fostering southern studies scholarship—as well as her own work on Elizabeth Spencer—was recognized in the title of her new position at LSU, where she was recruited as the inaugural Fred C. Frey Chair of Southern Studies.

Among her most important innovations as *SoQ* editor, however, was publishing literary interviews with notable southern writers. Professor Prenshaw recognized that thoughtful conversations with top-tier southern writers constituted a useful form of literary scholarship. They ranged from Erskine Caldwell, Eudora Welty, and Tennessee Williams, who were interviewed in the 1970s, to a veritable *Who's Who* of southern literature in the second half of the twentieth century. The interviews were conducted in a variety of contexts, which themselves are interesting. Many of the interviewers held their conversations in southern settings, sometimes at literary events, such as the contribution by Jere Real from a 1979 Tennessee Williams Festival in Lynchburg, Virginia, or Ashby Bland Crowder's interview with Reynolds Price during a visit to Hendrix College in Arkansas in 1988. Others were done in more intimate settings. Martha Van Noppen sat on Eudora Welty's sofa in her home in Jackson in 1978; Susan Ketchin joined Larry Brown for catfish at a country restaurant in Taylor, Mississippi, in 1991. The interviews are all fascinating. Not only do they reveal the personalities of these southern literary stars, but they represent a self-conscious community of writers. It is surprising how often they mention each other. Or rather, it is a testament to the quality of the journal in the 1980s and 1990s that many of the writers, when discussing their most important contemporaries, often reference other writers whose interviews were published in the *Southern Quarterly*. In all, Prenshaw published twenty-five such literary interviews between 1981 and 1991; her successors maintained this journal tradition, publishing forty-five more interviews in the following two decades.[51] After introducing literary interviews to the

*SoQ* in 1981, Professor Prenshaw continued with this publishing genre as the series editor for the University Press of Mississippi's highly regarded Literary Conversations book series. To date the press has published over a hundred titles in the series.

A key reason for the *Southern Quarterly*'s success in becoming a distinguished journal of "southern studies" was the consistent investment by USM in this scholarly journal and its editorial staff. In the first half of the 1980s the journal was able to sharpen the visual quality of its cover, using bright colors, and redesigning it in 1981 to incorporate the new *SoQ* logo and the journal's subtitle ("A Journal of the Arts in the South"), as well as upgrading the "editorial assistant" position, first to "business/production manager" (1981) and then to "managing editor" (1982) while paying enough of a stipend to keep the same person in the position—Cheryl McAllister Saunders.[52]

The mid 1980s saw a serious fiscal crisis in state funding, including for higher education in Mississippi, and USM from 1985 through 1988 wrestled with major financial cutbacks in state support. As the 1985 SACS report noted, "at a time when the institution seems poised for a giant step forward the financial resources available to the state are on the decline." In November of 1985 the governor imposed a $1.2 million mid-year cut on USM, followed by a proposed reduction of fully 21.5 percent in state funding for Mississippi's universities in 1986–1987, eventually resulting in the loss to USM of $3.4 million or over 9 percent of its annual budget.[53] The university responded with a laudably transparent faculty-based planning advisory council process, which labored through the 1987–1988 school year to find the necessary savings in the university's operations. Despite the usual controversies and "sometimes heated criticism," Dr. Lucas in the end took full responsibility and laid out a reorganization plan that worked, and which largely spared the College of Liberal Arts.[54]

For the *Southern Quarterly*, the mid 1980s were precisely when the journal hit its stride. In 1985, Dr. Prenshaw was appointed the new dean of the Honors College. Its roots went back to Liberal Arts's honors program in 1965, which was expanded university-wide in 1970. As the new dean, she "reorganized and revitalized" the Honors College in the 1985–1986 academic year while continuing as the *SoQ* editor and as a professor of English.[55] Also during this year, Prenshaw succeeded in having the *Southern Quarterly* join the Council of Editors of Learned Journals (CELJ). The CELJ serves to uphold the highest academic standards for scholarly journals. Its stated purpose is to address issues of editing learned journals including funding, peer review, plagiarism,

property rights, and copyediting, and generally sets standards for "the responsibilities, skills, and values required for editing scholarly journals."[56] In practical terms, CELJ membership guarantees that the journal engages in rigorous
peer review, the *sine qua non* of an academic learned journal. The Spring
1986 issue of the *Southern Quarterly* (vol. 24 no. 3) was the first to note, on its
colophon page, that it was a member journal of the CELJ. It has remained a
member ever since.

From the late 1970s through the early 1990s, Prenshaw's *SoQ* attracted a
new breed of younger scholars, many of whom published in the *Southern
Quarterly* relatively early in their careers and then went on to forge regional
and national scholarly reputations. These included William Bedford Clark
(1980), Thadious M. Davis (1981, 1983), Manning Marable (1985), Suzanne
Marrs (1985), Jerry W. Ward Jr. (1985, 1991), Suzanne Jones (1987, 1993), David
Evans (1988), and Don H. Doyle (1991). As well, the journal attracted contributions and commentaries from nationally known writers: Will D. Campbell
(1979), Willie Morris (1979), Doris Betts (1983), David Madden (1984), and
Margaret Walker Alexander (1991). Notable non-USM book reviewers—
all writing on the subjects of their scholarly specialties—included Robert
Hemenway (1982), Jerry W. Ward Jr. (1983 [twice]), William Bedford Clark
(1985), Dewey W. Grantham (1987, 1990), Patricia Galloway (1987, 1991), Alfred
E. Lemmon (1988), Bruce W. Chambers (1988), Susan V. Donaldson (1988,
1991), Kathryn Lee Seidel (1990), Barbara C. Ewell (1990), Michael Kreyling
(1990), Dawn Trouard (1991), Michel Fabre (1991), James H. Justus (1991), and
Camille Wells (1991).

Due to reliable financial and programmatic support from the USM administration (led by President Lucas) even in down-budget times, and editorial
confidence bred by respect for accomplishment and appreciation for scholarly
excellence, the journal flourished as a rigorous peer-reviewed, learned quarterly for southern studies. Averaging eight to nine essays per issue as well as
extensive book and film review sections, Prenshaw committed the journal
to covering the full range of subjects. The percentage of essays authored by
women doubled to nearly 40 percent, and there was a notable shift to publishing work on African American subjects (about 10 percent of the 440 papers published between 1978 and 1991). In concert with USM's institutional
ambitions, the *Southern Quarterly* was well on the way to becoming "distinguished." When the university by 1988 publicized itself as a "university for the
New South," it could be proud of sponsoring a learned journal that so clearly
mirrored USM's progressive institutional theme.

## A Mature Journal in Search of Itself

In the fall of 1991, the *Southern Quarterly* would celebrate the thirtieth anniversary of its founding. The timing was not particularly good. The university was in the middle of yet another round of state budget cutting (1990–1992), and USM was trying to figure out how to achieve $2.2 million in required cuts. Once again, however, President Lucas did not sugarcoat the severity of the financial situation, and once again the *Southern Quarterly* was spared.[57]

The thirtieth-anniversary issue included the surprise announcement that Peggy Whitman Prenshaw had retired as editor and had been recruited away to an endowed chair of southern studies at Louisiana State University.[58] The new editor, Stephen Flinn Young, was affiliated with the art history department and since the summer of 1989 had been working as the journal's managing editor. In his Editor's Note, he paid special tribute to Professor Prenshaw:

> Her forward-thinking leadership of the *Southern Quarterly*, her exemplary scholarship in southern literature and her enthusiasm for all intellectual pursuits will be sorely missed by the University of Southern Mississippi and by Mississippi, her home state.
>
> At this time of transition for the *Southern Quarterly*, Peggy Prenshaw's achievements with the quarterly that she transformed are worth special notice. With the fall 1974 issue of the *Southern Quarterly*, Peggy Whitman Prenshaw began her editorship of a journal devoted to publishing articles of general interest to scholars in the humanities. Four years later she changed this unspecialized journal into "a journal of the arts in the South."
>
> The move to create a scholarly journal for interdisciplinary study of southern culture was a prescient one, for within a few years centers for the study and appreciation of southern culture and artistic achievement had sprung up all across the region: the Center for the Study of Southern Culture at the University of Mississippi, the University of Southwest Louisiana's center for Acadian studies, Duke University's Center for Documentary Studies. *The Southern Quarterly*, as *The Encyclopedia of Southern Culture* recognized, helped to spark and to sustain new cultural scholarship.
>
> Special issues of the *Southern Quarterly* help tell this story of an awakening of intellectual interest in areas of southern culture which had been ignored—or perhaps worse, distorted by stereotypes—until then.

Young reminded the journal's readership of the many special features and themed issues during Prenshaw's editorship.

> When you add the numerous articles and interviews, review essays and commentaries covering the full range of "the arts in the South, defined broadly," one begins to grasp that throughout the creative life of southerners is a vast wealth, much wider and deeper than one journal can hope to encompass. But herein lies the enduring value of Prenshaw's achievement. She pointed the way. Fortunately for us, she will continue to serve *SoQ* as an editorial advisor.

Young also underscored newer initiatives such as the annual bibliography of the arts and architecture by Judith H. Bonner, a senior curator at the Historic New Orleans Collection, a private museum and research archive located in the French Quarter, which Prenshaw had begun in 1989, and the *SoQ*'s new art/photographic portfolio series—just launched in 1990—an expensive new venture for an academic quarterly at a cash-strapped state university.

> *SoQ* will continue to publish new work by southern photographers and artists in its portfolio series. We are justified in saying, then, that with our upcoming articles and interviews; reviews of books, films and exhibitions; as well as special issues devoted to topics as varied as Southern Cemetery Art and The Fiction of Cormac McCarthy, Peggy Prenshaw's vision of "a journal of the arts in the South" continues to serve well as a theme for *SoQ*'s future.

With the editorial continuity provided by the two associate editors, and continued financial support from USM (which now funded the editor's position separately from an academic appointment), the new editor was able to carry on. Over the following decade, Young maintained the same editorial staff—Noel Polk and Thomas J. Richardson as associate editors, with Polk as book review editor, and Lola Norris as managing editor—and instituted a three-person editorial advisory board of non-USM faculty.[59] Young continued the annual bibliography on architecture/decorative arts, while expanding the journal's publication of literary interviews and of art/photography portfolios; eventually he shifted the journal's core interests more toward cultural studies, with numerous special themed issues.

Throughout the 1990s, the *SoQ* as a journal was a relatively high-value publishing venue for southern studies, and particularly for studies of southern literature and cultural studies; for the vast majority of contributors, publishing in the *SoQ* brought prestige to them. For more established scholars, the *SoQ* clearly was a good journal to place their work, and they responded to opportunities to publish their work in the journal, to review books for the journal, and also to peer-review manuscripts. The journal attracted contributions from established national scholars on their principal subjects, such as Harriett Pollack on Eudora Welty (1990, 1996), Michel Fabre on Yusef Komunyakaa (1996), Joseph Millichap on Robert Penn Warren (1996), Kathryn Lee Seidel on Elizabeth Spencer (1997), Burton R. Pollin on Poe (1999), Philip C. Kolin on Tennessee Williams (1999); and from well-known southern writers including Cleanth Brooks (1993), Robert Penn Warren (1993), Ellen Douglas (1995), David Madden (1995), and Harry Crews (1998).

There were also many repeat contributors and repeat reviewers—clearly they wanted to contribute to *SoQ*, and no doubt it helped that USM's Noel Polk, who by the early 1990s was a nationally prominent Faulkner scholar, was the *SoQ* book review editor. Notable non-USM book reviewers—again, all reviewing books in their scholarly specialties—included Michael Kreyling (1992, 1999), James R. Justus (1991, 1998), Joe W. Trotter (1992), Susan V. Donaldson (1993 [twice], 1995, 2002), Alfred E. Lemmon (1993), Christopher C. DeSantis (1994, 1995, 1996, 1997, 1999), Suzanne Jones (1994), Barbara Ewell (1994, 1996, 1998), Robert W. Hamblin (1996, 2000), Patricia Galloway (1996), David Madden (1996), Ernest Suarez (1997), John Dittmer (1997), Marie Tyler McGraw (1998), Christopher Metress (1999, 2000, 2001), Richard H. King (2000), Brenda Murphy (2000), Randy J. Sparks (2002), and George Crandell (2003).

The *Southern Quarterly* was now a fully mature journal. As editor, however, Young kept tinkering with the journal's physical design and formatting. He twice redesigned the cover (1994, 1997), and introduced a total reorganization in 1994 of the journal's formatting and layout: larger size (8.5 x 11 inches), completely new cover design, and new interior title-sheet design. He also kept tinkering with his editorial advisory board, adding members, which by 1997 had expanded to ten members—none from USM, and three of whom were not university faculty.

After 1991, the *Southern Quarterly* expanded the number of essays that it published, averaging a full twelve to thirteen papers per issue (through

2004). This expansion in manuscript submissions and the number of published papers was impressive, especially since these were not flush times at USM and the journal had to generate its own revenue to pay for its increased printing costs. But even though the *SoQ* published 50 percent more essays in 1991–2004 (664 total) compared to the Prenshaw period (441 total), the editors maintained the journal's commitment to diversity of voice: nearly half of the contributors were female scholars, and about 10 percent of the essays addressed African American subjects. Gender, race, and class remained important analytical tools for southern studies scholars publishing in the *Southern Quarterly*.

After a decade as editor, Stephen Flinn Young suddenly resigned in 2000. As an unsigned "Editor's Note" at the back of the journal announced:

> We regret to announce that Stephen Flinn Young has resigned as editor of *The Southern Quarterly* in order to pursue other interests in his and Diana's new home in France. Stephen has been the driving force behind the *Quarterly* for about a decade now. Under his aggressive and imaginative editorship, SQ has expanded its readership and its coverage of All Things Southern. Indeed, he has for some time now, as the next couple of issues illustrate, been thinking more and more globally and redefining "southern" studies to include "regional" studies, thus broadening the number and kinds of worldwide contexts in which we should consider "southern" studies, while at the same time keeping *SQ*'s focus on concerns more traditionally southern and American.
>
> We wish Stephen and Diana well in their new home and their new lives.[60]

Oddly enough, the *Southern Quarterly* officially now had no editor. The two associate editors Noel Polk and Thomas J. Richardson produced a combined Fall/Winter issue (Vol. 39, nos. 1–2, 2000), and apparently sorted things out, no doubt with the help of Lola Norris who was now officially the *SoQ*'s managing editor. With the Spring 2001 issue (vol. 39, no.3), Noel Polk became editor (and remained book review editor), with Thomas Richardson continuing as associate editor, Lola Norris as managing editor, and Phillip Gentile as film and video review editor (as he had been since 1994). All seemed to be well.

## Crisis and Revival

A distinguished scholar of Faulkner, and the journal's long-serving co-associate editor and book review editor, Noel Polk knew that journal editors came and went. He also knew that the best editors could not, to politely paraphrase a famous Faulkner quip, "be at the beck and call of every damn customer with a two-cent stamp." When he became the *Southern Quarterly* editor, however, this thoughtful English professor of the "New South Mississippi,"[61] could not have imagined that USM was about to enter into a time of institutional crisis unseen since the "Exit 13" days of McCain's twilight years. Polk certainly would not have imagined that the *Southern Quarterly*, which he dearly loved, would become a casualty of this crisis and nearly get itself killed.

In 2001–2002 the journal was doing fine. Polk had updated the colophon page, and visually sharpened the *SoQ* front with high-gloss covers. The journal continued to attract contributions from its mix of established and junior scholars, as well as commentaries and other essays from prominent southern writers including Wendell Berry (2002), Fred Chappell (2002), Donald Harington (2002), and Lee Smith (2002), and literary critics such as Louis D. Rubin on southern literature (2002). It had a very healthy financial balance of accounts, and a pipeline of submissions under peer review. And then, all hell broke loose at the University of Southern Mississippi. Before it was over, Professor Polk had resigned his position at USM and as editor of the *Southern Quarterly*, and decamped to Mississippi State University where he was welcomed as editor of their CELJ-member journal, the venerable *Mississippi Quarterly*. Professor Richardson also left USM, for William Carey University, and Lola Norris chose to retire. The *Southern Quarterly* was to be abolished and its accounts liquidated. And why did all this happen? Because Noel Polk got on the wrong side of USM's new president, Shelby F. Thames, whose tempestuous presidency lasted from 2002 to 2007.[62]

In remembering those unhappy days, especially 2002 through 2004, I am reminded of William Faulkner's key lines from his 1950 Nobel Prize speech:

He [the writer] must teach himself that the basest of all things is to be afraid; and, teaching himself that, forget it forever leaving no room in his workshop for anything but the old verities and truths of the heart, the old universal truths lacking which any story is ephemeral and doomed—love and honor and pity and pride and compassion and sacrifice.

The long litany of unfortunate decisions that President Thames, who had raised into national prominence USM's polymer science program à la General McCain, made from April 2002 when he became USM's new president over the objections of the faculty (and at a time of, once again, major budget cuts in state funding), to March 2004 when Thames attempted to summarily fire two full professors—one a professor of sociology and the president of USM's newly revitalized AAUP chapter, and the other the nationally prominent Donne scholar, Gary Stringer, in English—simply could not be ignored. And Professor Polk took a lead in opposing Thames, especially in defense of his own colleague. It seemed, furthermore, that this was some kind of existential struggle between two worlds. On the one hand was the recrudescence of the Old Mississippi of the "closed society" in which nepotism, cronyism, and fear were back, in abundance. On the other was the "New South" Mississippi, an "open" society that made a university like USM so optimistic and important in a place like Mississippi, still so burdened by a dishonorable recent past.

Payback for Professor Polk's defense of academic freedom and his public opposition to the university's new president came swiftly, with severe budget cuts to the *Southern Quarterly* (2002–2003), institutional reorganization (2004), and finally, with professors Polk and Richardson and Ms. Norris all leaving USM in protest, a year-long publishing hiatus (2004–2005).

Though suspending publication usually is the death-knell of a learned journal, the *Southern Quarterly* did continue. With its management assigned to University Libraries, and the appointment of a new editor in 2005 with a mandate to revitalize the journal, we spent the next twenty-four issues rebuilding this interesting, distinctive, and distinguished journal of "the arts in the South."[63]

## A "Voice for Humane Learning"

Over the course of nearly fifty years, the *Southern Quarterly* has published a huge body of work.[64] Since 1978 much of it has been on southern studies. Though the journal has been a continual work in progress, and has to a remarkable degree mirrored the larger changes in the University of Southern Mississippi as I have tried to illustrate in this introduction, the *Southern Quarterly* remained over these decades a steady "voice for humane learning."

As part of the celebration of the journal's fiftieth anniversary, we have selected twenty-one representative essays and articles for this commemorative "best of" volume. The three we chose for the 1960s are examples of the best work published when the *Southern Quarterly* was a quarterly journal for "Southern" faculty. All three are about Mississippi, and given the time and place one may see hints of political conservatism in these works, especially in Skates and Hatcher, and of New Deal populism in Kelley. As to be expected, their scholarship reflects their times (the civil rights movement; Great Society federalism). They also seem, however, rather oddly relevant to today's political debates, issues, and controversies. Furthermore, these are not polemical essays, but are scholarly and measured and grounded in reasoned debate and often in irony, and thus are exemplars of the journal's original stated mission—though all are rather traditional political histories of leading historical figures, or of institutional histories. These essays (Kelley, Skates, and Hatcher) are examples of "usable histories" for a state which in the 1960s was riven by the violence of the extremist white backlash to the success of the civil rights movement and federal intervention, and by the continuing extreme poverty in the state.

Peggy Prenshaw's appointment in 1974 introduced serious literary criticism, represented by David C. Berry (1974) and his New Criticism study of the modern southern poet James Dickey's work. We also chose the historian Martha Swain's (1976) interesting account of Mississippi political history in the New Deal era, and the literary historian Kathryn L. Seidel's (1977) provocative essay on the "Southern Belle" in antebellum literature as examples of how the journal was beginning to attract ambitious new scholars, and in this case, female scholars on southern subjects. Willie Morris's (1979) essay shows how the *SoQ*, once it became "a journal of the arts in the South," began to tap into Mississippi's abundant literary talent, and besides, what Morris has to say is still very much worth listening to.

In the 1980s, the *SoQ* was an up-and-coming journal of southern studies, and these selections are examples. They are all serious work by younger scholars and suggest the range of subjects that the journal covered: from nineteenth-century literature to regional literary criticism to folk popular culture, and with Faulkner and W. E. B. Du Bois thrown in for good measure. Again, these relatively junior scholars went on to notably accomplished careers, and the *Southern Quarterly* was a welcoming venue for this new work. The *SoQ* had achieved a truly regional southern perspective, of which Mississippi was an important but no longer a predominant subject interest. The selections for the 1990s represent how the journal was becoming a place where established scholars were publishing on their major subjects, but also that the *SoQ* was still willing to take chances, as with the Margaret Walker Alexander (1991) address from the inaugural Natchez Literary Celebration.

For the 2000s, we chose these to represent the journal's commitment to not just "All Things Southern" but to a cosmopolitan approach to southern studies, specifically including the "global South," the African Diaspora and the Caribbean. I also note that we published the article by Randy J. Sparks (2006), a historian at Tulane University in New Orleans, on the heels of Hurricane Katrina and the death and destruction it wrought. Also, Robert L. Hall's (2007) study came to the *SoQ* as part of a publishing partnership we established with the Natchez Literary and Cinema Celebration (2006–2011), a partnership which I count as one of our greatest successes and which hopefully will continue in the future.

One may see in this select group of essays an editorial arc from an initial provincial interest in Mississippi (geographical, historical, and political) as a journal of "studies in the humanities and social sciences" (1962–1977) in which the South was essentially "white," to a redefinition of editorial interests under Peggy Whitman Prenshaw as "a journal of the arts in the South" (including everyday arts like the blues, as well as belles lettres). There was increasingly a focus on the South as a racialized region and on literary studies, with an evolving editorial style that became standardized around MLA-style in the mid-1980s, with intertextual notes for quotations, discursive endnotes, and a bibliography of works cited. In this collection we reproduce, with minor corrections, the various citation styles used in the original publications. Prenshaw's emphasis on more self-consciously cutting-edge essays continued through the 1990s and early 2000s. And finally there was a return to historical subjects after 2005, though without abandoning southern literature, cultural studies, and "the arts." Increasingly we sought to present the "many Souths" with transnational or cosmopolitan angles—the South as part of larger, Atlantic worlds—and the centrality of African American studies to Southern history.

Whether the *Southern Quarterly* will continue to exist should never be simply taken for granted. As with all intentional things, one must make choices. And, at this date, those choices for the journal's *longue duree* are still an open question. Or rather, the open question is whether Southern Miss today, which presents itself to the public as "a national university for the Gulf South region" will continue to invest in a scholarly learned journal like the *SoQ*. One can only hope that the answer is yes.

# Notes

1. J. L. A., "An Inaugural Editorial," *Southern Quarterly* 1.1 (1962): iii (emphasis in the original). Allen was on the faculty of the English Department, served as editor for just the first volume (1962–1963), and may have left USM shortly thereafter.
2. General McCain retired from the Mississippi National Guard in 1967. Chester M. Morgan, *Treasured Past, Golden Future: The Centennial History of The University of Southern Mississippi* (Jackson: University Press of Mississippi, 2010), 86; Monte Piliawsky, *Exit 13: Oppression and Racism in Academia* (Boston: South End Press, 1982), 12–13.
3. Quotes, Morgan, *Treasured Past, Golden Future*, 121. For an account of McCain's plagiarism in an article he published in the *Journal of Mississippi History* in 1967, see Piliawsky, *Exit 13*, 13–15, and for a complete study of the controversy, see Bradley G. Bond, "'Unmitigated Thievery': The Case against William David McCain," *Journal of Mississippi History* 72.2 (2010): 163–97.
4. The *Confederate Veteran* magazine was founded in 1893 as a principal voice for the Lost Cause mythology; the SCV was established in Richmond in 1896 and initially flourished, then rapidly declined in the early 1930s. In 1932 the organization suspended publication of the *Confederate Veteran*, and had just a few local chapters, with a total membership of only 1,000 members. See Heidi Bierich, "The Struggle for the Sons of Confederate Veterans: A Return to White Supremacy in the Early Twentieth-Century?" in Euan Hague, Heidi Bierich, and Edward H. Sebesta, eds., *Neo-Confederacy: A Critical Introduction* (Austin: University of Texas Press, 2008), 282–84. By the late 1980s, the SCV had 20,000 dues-paying members.
5. Ibid., 284. As Bierich notes, after 1953 the SCV "was led for nearly forty years by the openly segregationist McCain" (290).
6. Ibid., 284.
7. Ibid., 287.
8. Morgan, *Treasured Past, Golden Future*, 91.
9. Ibid., 122.
10. Ibid., 91, 97, 104. Some critics contended that by the early 1970s, McCain had turned his "good" local university into little more than a "degree factory": in fact a 1974 state commission found that USM offered the Ph.D. in 70 different subjects, the MA in 127 separate fields (twice the number as at Ole Miss or Mississippi State), and 263 different baccalaureate degrees (compared to the 57 BA degrees offered at Ole Miss); Piliawsky, *Exit 13*, 49.
11. Morgan, *Treasured Past, Golden Future*, 91–122.
12. The scandals included firing and demoting professors for their ostensibly nonacademic political activities (both liberal and conservative professors, ranging from the liberal English department chair W. D. Norwood Jr. [1969] to the arch-conservative historian William K. Scarborough [1968–1969]), to punishing faculty for dissenting from administration actions (in such departments as English, History,

Philosophy & Religion, Political Science [1970–1973]) including department chairs such as Treadwell Davis in history, and tenured faculty, to radically reorganizing USM's curriculum without any faculty input (1969–1970), to refusing students to organize a campus ACLU chapter (1970–1971)—after suing in federal court the Fifth Circuit Court of Appeals upheld the students' case (1971) and ordered USM to recognize the student group; to all sorts of other mal-administration and official chicanery. In 1974, a SACS accreditation committee visited USM, and in their preliminary report unsurprisingly noted the very low faculty morale on campus (the next ten-year re-accreditation review was scheduled for 1975). One faculty victim of USM's mal-administration of this era, Dr. Monte Piliawsky, an assistant professor of political science whose recent Ph.D. was from Tulane University, characterized his two years at USM (1970–1972) as "a twilight zone dominated by the Exit 13 syndrome, a place which fact and fiction, fantasy and reality all became hopelessly entangled . . . [where] academic freedom or freedom of expression for students and faculty is virtually unheard of"; Piliawsky, *Exit 13*, xv. "Exit 13" was the Southern Miss exit on Interstate 59, which has since been changed. For accounts of this unhappy period see Morgan, *Treasured Past, Golden Future*, 104, 118, 120, 122; Piliawsky, *Exit 13*, Part One.

13. For a history of the White Citizens' Council movement, see Neil McMillen, *The Citizens' Council: Organized Resistance to the Second Reconstruction, 1954–64* (Urbana: University of Illinois Press, 1971).

14. Bierich, "The Struggle for the Sons of Confederate Veterans," 285; Piliawsky, *Exit 13*, 16–17. The riot at Ole Miss on September 20, 1962, to keep Meredith from enrolling, resulted in 2 deaths, 30 wounded by gunfire, and 300 injured by flying rocks and bottles; the U.S. Attorney General Robert F. Kennedy federalized the Mississippi national guard and sent in 30,000 troops and 500 federal marshals to restore order on the University of Mississippi campus.

15. Morgan, *Treasured Past, Golden Future*, 88–91; Piliawsky, *Exit 13*, 21–27. After denying admission to another African American man (John Frazier) in 1964, McCain suddenly changed course, and in the fall of 1965, just two years after Kennard's death, Southern Miss admitted two African American female students, Gwendolyn Elaine Armstrong and Raylawni Branch; in 1966 USM recruited its first black student athlete, the basketball player Wilbert Jordan; and in 1969 awarded its first Ph.D. to an African American, Walter Washington, who became the longtime president of one of the state's two historically black public universities, Alcorn State University (1969–1994). In 1993, then-president Dr. Aubrey K. Lucas offered formal apologies for USM's actions against Kennard, and following the efforts of USM's African-American Student Organization to recognize Kennard on campus renamed a prominent historical building in the heart of campus after Kennard and Washington (Kennard-Washington Hall). Some fifteen years later, another round of student organizing, publicly supported by president emeritus Lucas and then-president Shelby F. Thames, resulted in the official reversal of Kennard's 1960 conviction by Forrest County Circuit Court Judge Robert Helfrich on May 17, 2006

(after Governor Haley Barbour denied a petition to posthumously pardon Kennard). Judge Helfrich declared the forty-six-year-old conviction "null and void." See Morgan, *Treasured Past, Golden Future*, 114–15, 121, 174–77, 282. Today (2011), African Americans comprise over 30 percent of Southern Miss's 17,000-plus students.

16. Some fifteen years earlier, in 1947, Mississippi State University had established a scholarly quarterly journal, the *Mississippi Quarterly*. Today (2011), the *Mississippi Quarterly* and the *Southern Quarterly* are two of the oldest continuing university journals of southern studies and are the only two university scholarly quarterlies in Mississippi that are members of the Council of Editors of Learned Journals.

17. In official usage today (2011), the university calls itself "The University of Southern Mississippi" [*sic*]. Colloquially it is still known as "Southern" or as "Southern Miss," though now even more frequently as "USM."

18. "Inaugural Editorial," iii. Since the 1980s, in conformity with standard usage, the journal's title generally is rendered without the definite article, that is, as the *Southern Quarterly* [*sic*]; hence the journal's logo, *SoQ*, which dates to the late 1970s.

19. [Allen], "Inaugural Editorial," iv.

20. Ibid., iii.

21. The inaugural editorial board was composed of Coldwell Daniel III (chairman), John N. Burrus, Thomas T. Chisholm, J. Treadwell Davis, Gilbert F. Hartwig, Arthell Kelley, Charles Moorman, Ray S. Musgrave, John F. Nau, Leon A. Wilber, and William D. McCain (President of the University).

22. Arthell Kelley was a geography professor and department chair for whom the current Geography Department building is named; Charles W. Moorman III (1925–1996), a professor of English at Southern Miss from 1954 to 1990 and author/editor of eleven books, served as dean of the graduate school (1966–1968) and then as the controversial vice-president for academic affairs (1968–1980), and is the namesake for USM's only term endowed chair in the humanities; Gilbert F. Hartwig, for whom the arena stage in the new Theatre and Dance Building (1999) is named; the historian J. Treadwell Davis, the department chair in the 1960s and namesake of a significant annual prize in the History Department.

23. Hatcher's article, "Some Mississippi Views of American Federalism, 1817–1900," 6.1 (1967): 117–41, is included in this commemorative volume of essays.

24. Harper served as assistant editor from 1966 to 1975, and then associate editor (1976–1978). He served as dean of the College of Liberal Arts for twenty years, retiring in 2003.

25. See the comprehensive Volume Index on the *Southern Quarterly* website, online at http://www.usm.edu/soq/volumeindex (Accessed 13 August 2011). Charles Moorman published eleven essays (several on England's Arthurian legend literature) between 1962 and 1978; Claude E. Fike, the long-serving dean of the College of Arts and Sciences (1961–1976), published four essays between 1965 and 1975; Harper contributed five essays on German political history between 1965 and 1975; even McCain published a specialist's piece, an archivist's bibliography on the Theodore Bilbo Papers in the Southern Miss special collections library (1965).

26. John D. W. Guice (1971, 1978) in history and his colleague Kenneth G. McCarty (1972), who later served as editor of the *Journal of Mississippi History*; Gary Stringer (1974, 1976) in English, later a nationally prominent John Donne scholar (John Donne *Variorum* project), and his colleague Philip C. Kolin (1974), who currently is the University Distinguished Professor of the Humanities in English and the newly appointed editor of the *Southern Quarterly* (2011).

27. Kelley's first publication in the journal, "Levee Building and the Settlement of the Yazoo Basin," 1.4 (1963): 285–308, is included in this commemorative volume of essays. The Southern Miss geography department was, by the mid 1980s, "the oldest continuous geography department" in the U.S.; Morgan, *Treasured Past, Golden Future*, 141.

28. Skates's essay, "From Enchantment to Disillusionment: A Southern Editor Views the New Deal," 5.4 (1967): 363–80, is included in this commemorative volume of essays.

29. Moorman (1962, 1963, 1965 [twice], 1967, 1969 [twice], 1969, 1972, 1974, 1975); Kay (1966, 1967 [twice], 1968, 1970, 1971, 1972 [twice], 1974).

30. Austin (1973, 1974), Cameron (1975), Lasater (1973, 1974 [thrice]), Lee (1973), Osborn et al. (1974), Prenshaw (1974), Tatalovich (1974), Witte (1974).

31. Claira S. Lopez, "James K. Vardaman and the Negro: The Foundation of Mississippi's Racial Policy," 3.2 (1965): 155–80; Robert L. Robinson, "Commodore Matthew C. Perry and the Protection of American Rights in West Africa," 5.1 (1966): 47–63.

32. Roger Pearson, "Ancestor Worship in Sub-Saharan Africa," 10.3 (1972): 223–44, which is a useful if "old-fashioned" study; Jesse O. McKee, "A Geographical Analysis of the Origin, Diffusion, and Spatial Distribution of the Black American in the United States," 12.3 (1974): 203–16, which is quite an ambitious topic for a thirteen-page paper.

33. Piliawsky, *Exit 13*, 55–56. In his last year at Southern Miss (1971–1972), Piliawsky wrote that "I was the administration's *bete noire* my second and last year at Southern . . . I had the distinction of being one of the very few USM professors ever to have an article rejected for publication by the *Southern Quarterly*" (112–13).

34. Prenshaw, "A Review of the Modern Language Association Survey of Teacher Evaluation Procedures," 12.2 (1974): 181–88.

35. "'Harmony with the Dead': James Dickey's Descent into the Underworld," 12.3 (1974): 233–44, which is included in this commemorative volume of essays.

36. In June of 1973, for example, Governor Waller had declared a statewide official observance of the tenth anniversary of Medgar Evers's assassination: Piliawsky, *Exit 13*, 171. For the 1974 state higher education commission, see ibid., 49. For the timing of McCain's announcement, see Morgan, *Treasured Past, Golden Future*, 120–21.

37. Morgan, *Treasured Past, Golden Future*, 122–23.

38. Ibid., 137.

39. To mark these changes, by the mid 1980s, Southern Miss was increasingly known as "USM": see examples of publicity materials in ibid., 144–53. For the new publicity logo and institutional theme in 1988, see 168.

40. He would leave the journal in 1978 to become the College of Liberal Art's associate dean, and then would be appointed dean of the College by President Lucas in 1983 (and serve in that capacity until 2003).

41. In his otherwise damning account, Piliawsky singles out Professor Scarborough as "a truly remarkable man; in fact, he is one of the genuine heroes of Exit 13. A Phi Beta Kappa graduate from the University of North Carolina, Scarborough holds a masters degree from Cornell and a Ph.D. in history from UNC. Among the several published books he has written is the definitive work on plantation management in the Old South. A tenured professor of history at USM, Scarborough consistently receives excellent ratings from the students in the faculty evaluation handbook": *Exit 13*, 81. For his description of Scarborough's travails in the last years of McCain's presidency and his refusal to buckle under, see 80–84. In May of 1969, Professor Scarborough in an interview with the *Student Printz*, the campus newspaper, explained: "The issue is not political. It's a question of how much control the administration should have over the activities of the faculty. They can get away with running the other ones off, by labeling them as left-wingers and communists. But I'm as conservative as anybody around, and I plan to stay": quoted in ibid., 81.

42. In 1990, Professor McMillen's major work, *Dark Journey: Black Mississippians in the Age of Jim Crow* (Urbana: University of Illinois Press, 1989), would win the Bancroft Prize, the most prestigious book prize for American historians.

43. The following year, volume 16 (1977–1978), Prenshaw would publish even more book reviews, thirty-six in all, several of which were contributed by the *SoQ*'s old-guard such as William H. Hatcher, Wallace G. Kay, and Charles Moorman. The times they were a-changing. McMillen again reviewed two titles that may well have been considered controversial at USM before 1975: *The Transformation of Southern Politics: Social Change and Political Consequences since 1945*, and *The Crisis of Conservative Virginia: The Byrd Organization and the Politics of Massive Resistance*. In another telling assignment, Prenshaw had gotten John Hebron Moore, the chair of history at Ole Miss, to review a new edited volume entitled *Perspectives and Irony in American Slavery: Essays by Carl N. Degler, Eugene D. Genovese, David Brion Davis, Stanley L. Engerman, William K. Scarborough, John W. Blassingame, Kenneth M. Stampp*, a collection of essays by some of the most influential new historians of slavery at the time, which pointedly included Professor Scarborough.

44. Two of these essays, one by Martha Swain of Texas Woman's University, "Pat Harrison and the Social Security Act of 1935," 15.1 (1976): 1–14; and the other by Kathryn L. Seidel of North Carolina State University, "The Southern Belle as an Antebellum Ideal," 15.4 (1977): 387–401, are included in this commemorative volume of essays.

45. Ironically, in the McCain era, there is a demonstrable lack of articles on southern literature in the *Southern Quarterly*. In contrast, in volumes 14–16, see the following essays on southern literary criticism: Carl R. Osthaus (1976); Daniel G. Ford (1977); Kathryn L. Seidel (1977); Patricia S. Box (1978); Marion Montgomery (1978); Edmund A. Napieralski (1977); Thomas J. Shlereth (1978); J. P. Telotte (1978); Molly S. Wieting (1978). Note that about half of these are by women scholars.

46. *Southern Quarterly* 17.1 (1978): [4]. Prenshaw had been planning these changes for perhaps a year, or at least since the fall of 1977. In the January 1978 issue (vol. 16, no. 2), for example, she included a typescript letter that was inserted for journal subscribers, in which she announced that the journal was going to shift its interests to "studies of the arts in the South" beginning with the fall issue (vol. 17, no. 1).

47. Tharpe, a Robert Frost specialist with an interest in southern literature, also taught in the USM Honors College, and then served as the *SoQ* Book Review editor (1980–1983); McCraw was a nineteenth-century American literature specialist; and Richardson was a specialist in southern literature. Saunders was the journal's editorial assistant (1978–1980), business/production manager (1980–1982), and managing editor (1982–1984).

48. Between 1971 and 1979 Tharpe had published a half-dozen articles/essays in the *SoQ* (1971, 1974, 1976, 1977 [twice], 1979) and also contributed three book reviews in 1978; in the 1980s he would contribute a book review (1980), a literary interview with Erskine Caldwell (1981)—which is included in the companion to this volume of *SoQ* essays, that is, Douglas B. Chambers, ed., *Personal Souths: Interviews from the Southern Quarterly* (Jackson: University Press of Mississippi, in press [2012])—and an essay in the special issue on Elvis Presley (1984). McCraw had published two articles in the early 1970s (1972, 1974), and contributed three book reviews in the post-McCain issues (1976, 1977, 1978). Richardson would publish one essay (1980), and only four book reviews (1976, 1978, 1982, 1991), while serving as an advisory (and later associate) editor.

   The CELJ is an allied professional association of the Modern Language Association. It dates to meetings of journal editors at the MLA since 1957, was established as a formal association in the early 1970s (as the "Conference of Editors of Learned Journals"), and changed its name in 1989 to the Council of Editors of Learned Journals. See "A Brief History," online at http://www.celj.org/book/export/html/39 (Accessed 15 August 2011).

49. These special issues and themed sections included Walker Percy (1980), George W. Cable (1980), Conrad Aiken (1982), a two-part series on Contemporary Southern Writers (1983), Stark Young (1986), Erskine Caldwell (1989), Caroline Gordon (1990), and Evelyn Scott (1990).

50. Including: Art and Feminism in the South (1979), The South and Film (1981), Art and Artists: From a Southern Point of View (1985), Southern Art and Artists (1986), Southern Women Playwrights (1987), Contemporary Theatre in the South (1987), The Arts in the South (1987), Clothing and Textiles in the Nineteenth-Century South (1988), and Visual Arts in the South (1989).

51. A selection of twenty of these literary interviews is being published as a companion volume to this one of *SoQ* essays: Chambers, ed., *Personal Souths* (in press [2012]). The interviews published while Prenshaw was editor were with the following: Harry Crews (1981, 1982); Erskine Caldwell (1981); Carlisle Floyd (1982); Eudora Welty (1982); Madison Jones (1983); Seven Contemporary Writers (1983); Lee Smith (1983, 1990); Peter Cooley (1985); David Madden (1987); Shirley Ann Grau

(1987); Jane Reid-Petty (1987); John O'Neal (1987); Reynolds Price (1988); Bobbie Ann Mason (1988); Tennessee Williams (1988); Beverly Lowry, Reynolds Price,
Elizabeth Spencer, and James Whitehead (1988) (panel discussion); Helen Caldwell
Cushman (1989); Virginia Caldwell (1989); Robert Amberg (1989); Judith McWillie
(1989); Bruce Childs (1990); James Seay (1991); Seven Fiction Writers (1991). Those
published after Prenshaw's editorship are: Clyde Edgerton (1991); Bobbie Ann Mason (1992); Will Campbell (1993); Lee Smith (1994 [thrice], 2009); Larry Brown
(1994); William Christenberry (1994); Gail Godwin (1994); Daphne Athas (1994);
Eve Shelnutt (1994); Nancy Lemann (1994); Tim McLaurin (1994); Herbert Singleton (1994); Dixon McDowell (1994) Josephine Humphreys (1994); Richard Marius
(1994, 2000, 2003); Mary Lee Settle (1995); Elizabeth Spencer (1995); David Madden (1995); Ellen Douglas (1995 [twice]); Lewis Nordan (1995, 2003); Doris Betts
(1996); Gurney Norman (1996); Chris Wiltz (1996); Minnie Bruce Pratt (1997);
James Conaway (1997); Jill McCorkle (1998); Carolyn Haines (1998); Harry Crews
(1998); William Styron (1999); David Bottoms (1999); John M. Barry (2001); Robert Morgan (2001); Ted Tally (2001); Donald Harington (2002); William Hoffman
(2002); Bishop Duncan Gray (2005); Ernest J. Gaines (2006); Del Shores (2009).

52. Saunders (who served from 1978 to 1984) was succeeded by Joycelyn Trigg (1984–
1989), Stephen Flinn Young (1989–1991) with Lola Norris as "editorial assistant"
(1989–2000) and then as "managing editor" (2000–2004), and finally Ann Branton
(2005–). For all intents and purposes, Lola Norris was the journal's managing editor from 1991 to 2004.

53. Quoted in Morgan, *Treasured Past, Golden Future*, 137.

54. Ibid., 137–41, quotation on 140.

55. Ibid., 140–41. Part of her responsibilities as Honors dean was also to direct the
newly expanded University Forum Lecture Series, funded with a sizable annual ap-
propriation (which in the 1990s was some $60,000) to bring in illustrious speakers
for a series of public lectures on campus; the lecture series had begun in the late
1970s as the Honors College Forum (still the colloquial name for the lecture series).
On the latter, see Morgan, *Treasured Past, Golden Future*, 130. The University Forum continues today (2011), though in much reduced form; I directed University
Forum for the 2009–2010 academic year, with a required four speakers per semes-
ter on a cumulative budget of $20,000 (about half provided directly by the Honors
College).

56. "A Brief History," online at http://www.celj.org/book/export/html/39 (Accessed 15
August 2011).

57. Morgan, *Treasured Past, Golden Future*, 170–74. In the end, in his February 1992
special faculty convocation, President Lucas explained that academic units would
take 28 percent of the direct budget cuts, and that indirect/nonacademic units
would take fully 72 percent of the cuts. One should note, in contrast, that in the
2009–2011 cycle of final budget cuts at USM, following the Great Recession, that
the current administration assigned about two-thirds of budget cutting to academic and only one-third to indirect/nonacademic units, and that the *Southern*

*Quarterly* had its operating budget cut by 65 percent, and also lost the administrative stipend paid to the editor.

58. S.F.Y. [Stephen Flinn Young], "Editor's Note," 30.1 (1991): 6. Maureen Ryan, a professor of English, was appointed the new dean of the Honors College.

59. They were Donald R. Mott (Butler University) who also was the film and video review editor (since 1988); Judith McWillie (University of Georgia); and Prenshaw (LSU).

60. Emphasis in the original. "Editor's Note," 39.1-2 (2000): 293.

61. See for example, the humorous and ironic New South–type memoir which this native of the erstwhile earnestly named Picayune, Mississippi, wrote of his upbringing: *Outside the Southern Myth* (Jackson: University Press of Mississippi, 1997).

62. For a judicious account of the many Thames controversies and scandals during his ill-fated presidency of USM, especially 2002–2004, see Morgan, *Treasured Past, Golden Future*, 241-57.

63. As editor, and with the help of the journal's editorial staff, most notably Ann Branton, the managing editor, we maintained membership in the CELJ; bolstered the journal's management with a full graduate assistantship (2006–2011), a redesigned website (with new digital volumes index), and staff subscriptions manager; shifted the journal's interests to historical studies while maintaining its traditional interests in literary criticism, cultural studies, and "the arts"; internationalized the journal (especially regarding the Caribbean), with a new seventeen-member editorial advisory board of distinguished scholars; maintained the annual architecture/decorative arts bibliography (begun in 1989); redesigned the front, with high-gloss covers, and featuring artwork of Mississippi artists; established a publishing partnership with the award-winning annual Natchez Literary and Cinema Celebration; produced a broad range of special issues: antebellum free blacks; Hurricane Katrina; Atlantic world; southern food; Louisiana/Haiti connections [sponsored by The Historic New Orleans Collection]; poetry in the South; southern speech; nineteenth-century African American literature; Emmett Till; Richard Wright centennial; the global South; Eudora Welty centennial; Robert Morgan; Afro-Atlantic spiritualism; southern humor; the South and the sublime; Tennessee Williams centennial.

The journal continued to attract major scholars on their main subjects, including William L. Andrews on nineteenth-century southern texts (2006), Ira Berlin on antebellum free blacks (2006), Cécile Vidal on French historiography of Atlantic studies (2006), Burton R. Pollin on Edgar Allan Poe (2006), Laurent Dubois on the Haitian Revolution (2007), Jessica Harris on southern foodways (2007), Gwendolyn Midlo Hall on Louisiana history (2007), Frances Smith Foster on nineteenth-century African American writers (2008), Donald Kartiganer on Faulkner (2008), W. Lawrence Hogue on Richard Wright (2009), John W. Lowe on southern literature (2009, 2011), Jerry W. Ward Jr. on Richard Wright (2009, 2011), Suzanne W. Jones on Ellen Douglas (2009), and Donald Cosentino on Afro-Atlantic cultural studies (2010). We also included publication of original poetry by nationally prominent southern poets, including James Applewhite (2007), Angela Ball (2007), Robert Morgan (2007, 2010), Carl Phillips (2008, 2011), Sonia Sanchez (2008), and Charles Wright (2007); and published thoughtful commentaries by public figures such as Senator Thad Cochran (R.-Miss.) on senatorial oratory (2008), the chefs Leah Chase (2007) and Robert St. John (2007), and the MacArthur Award-winning filmmaker Charles Burnett (2008).

As well, the *SoQ* was included in the American Historical Association list of journals, is under consideration for inclusion in JSTOR, and was twice nominated for the Mississippi Governor's Award for Excellence in the Arts (2011, 2012). The journal had a contributing staff of ten and a cumulative total budget of $70,000 under my editorship, about half of which was self-generated from revenue from subscriptions, royalties, reprint permissions, and journal exchanges, and is administered by the Office of the Provost with business management by University Libraries and editorial management by the College of Arts and Letters. By 2010, the *SoQ* was collected in nearly five hundred libraries worldwide.

In the 2010–2011 general fiscal crisis, amid shrinking resources at USM, the provost cut the *SoQ* managing budget by 65 percent (for 2011–2012), the editor's stipend was eliminated, and the graduate assistantship reduced, effectively defunding the journal at the university level on the eve of the *Southern Quarterly*'s fiftieth anniversary (2012–2013). I resigned as editor in August 2011, after completing volume 48, a special issue on the Tennessee Williams centenary, coedited with Philip C. Kolin.

64. By my count, through volume 48 (2010–2011) a total of 1,732 essays/articles, 836 book reviews (1974–2011), 70 literary interviews (1981–2011), 43 art/photographic portfolios (1990–2010), 22 annual art/architecture bibliographies (1989–2010), and 8 museum exhibition reviews (1989–1999).

PART I

# 1960s

# Levee Building and the Settlement of the Yazoo Basin

ARTHELL KELLEY

The Yazoo Basin as an area in Mississippi stands out in unique contrast to the remainder of the state. The rolling clay hills to the east give way to the level, deep alluvium of the Basin; the patchwork of crops of the yeoman farmers becomes seemingly endless cotton fields; the occasional farmhouse is supplanted by the numerous tenant shacks of the sharecroppers; the pine forest is replaced by a mixture of bottomland hardwoods; and the predominance of white population is replaced by a high percentage of Negro population. The agriculture of this region is characterized by high specialization in cotton production, by the dominance of the plantation system of farming, and by a high proportion of tenancy.

The Yazoo Basin derives its name from the Yazoo River which drains the entire Basin. It is referred to in numerous publications concerning various aspects of the area and by the Army Engineers as the Yazoo-Mississippi Delta and locally is known simply as the Delta. Physiographically, it is a basin, enclosed by the present meander belt of the Mississippi River and a crescent shaped line of bluffs, with all major drainage to the south, entering the Mississippi River through a single stream, the Yazoo.

*Mississippi opened for settlement.* When the present state of Mississippi was admitted in the union in 1817, the entire state north of 32 degrees north latitude, except Warren County, was Indian territory and not open to settlement. The first part of Mississippi territory opened to settlement, north of 32 degrees, was a section of what is today Monroe County in northeast Mississippi.[1] This segment of the Tombigbee River Valley is in the so-called black belt of Mississippi and Alabama and was quickly filled with cotton planters after its cession by the Chickasaws in 1816. The remainder of the state north of 32 degrees was opened to settlement as the result of three treaties with the Indians.

---

*Southern Quarterly* 1.4 (1963): 285–308.

The first, in 1820 at Doaks Stand, opened the west central part of the state and included the southern one-third of the Yazoo Basin. In 1830 the treaty of Dancing Rabbit opened all but the northeastern corner of the state, which was ceded by the Choctaws in the treaty of Pontotoc in 1832. This treaty resulted in the opening of all the land in the state to settlement and a rapid movement of settlers to the edge of the Basin, but there settlement stopped, or virtually stopped, until after the War between the States. Why did the Basin receive its greatest increase in population and in improved land some sixty years after the influx of settlers into the remainder of the state?

*Pre-Civil War period.* During the great land speculating period of 1832 to 1844, the north and central part of Mississippi was rapidly settled, much of it cleared and planted in cotton. During this period, however, the Yazoo Basin remained in the hands of the federal government and was offered in vain at $1.25 per acre. Few people were willing to tackle the dismal swamps of the river valley, which were swarming with mosquitoes and were subject to periodic overflow. Nevertheless, the cotton land fever of this period was responsible for a few settlers moving up or down the Mississippi River and settling along the river banks in what is today Washington and Bolivar counties. The first settlers are believed to have arrived in this area about 1828 and were men of English descent, emigrating from the older cotton states of Georgia, Alabama, Kentucky, South Carolina, Tennessee, and Louisiana. Only the more favorably situated river-front lands were settled between 1828 and 1848. The interior of the Yazoo Basin was an almost impassable swamp, cluttered with large trees and vines and growth of evergreen cane and bamboo through which no rider could pass, and only with difficulty could a man work his way through on foot.[2] This dense growth necessitated cutting of trails and roads with cane knives and axes before travel could be carried on. In spite of the hardships, a few scattered settlements had been made on the high banks of interior streams by 1840, but nothing like an organized agriculture existed for more than a few miles from the banks of the Mississippi. The river was practically the sole means of access to the new cotton plantations of the Basin. A few Indian traces could be followed through the swamps, but nothing worthy of the name *road* existed.

Settlement in the Yazoo Basin was indeed slow between 1837 and 1847. As speculation in land reached alarming proportions, President Andrew Jackson ordered that only gold and silver would be accepted in payment for government lands. When the collapse came, Mississippi alluvial lands were offered at twenty-five cents per acre, but there were few bidders.

By 1845 steamboat transportation on the Mississippi River had improved considerably, and it was clear that the Yazoo Basin with its rich, fresh soil was going to be developed as an area of cotton plantations. It was also realized that direct help from the state government and from Congress was badly needed if the full potentialities of the Basin as an agricultural domain were to be realized. The great flood of 1849 served to emphasize the need for flood control.[3]

The very early settlers in the Yazoo Basin were not unfamiliar with the necessity or the desirability of protecting their water-front properties with levees or dikes of earthwork. They had knowledge of the protection afforded New Orleans and many of the early plantations around the Natchez district by the construction of levees. The state had also shown interest in flood protection at an early date, the first legislation on levees, passed on February 18, 1819, authorizing the erection of a levee in Warren County.[4]

Fourteen years were to pass before the state legislature saw fit to introduce additional laws. From the earliest time of settlement along the Mississippi River until 1845, each planter had built and maintained his own levee, using the slaves on his plantation as a labor force.[5] As the lowlands of the Yazoo Basin were gradually settled and new county units organized, the state took increasing interest in land reclamation, and numerous acts were passed for the purpose of instructing the County Board of Police (now called Boards of Supervisors) in levee affairs. One of the great handicaps of the early levee system of the Yazoo Basin was the lack of continuity. Much of the land along the river was still in the hands of the government or was owned by absentee land owners. This left considerable gaps in the levee system because riparian land owners were held responsible for building the levees. To be effective at all, the levees had to be a continuing system.

The development of the levee system under the Board of Police, although inadequate because of too many districts and not enough central authority, was an improvement over the individual initiative system, but was still inadequate to build a continuous levee system. In an act by the state legislature in 1838, the Board of Police was authorized to divide the Yazoo Basin into five or more levee districts. For each district, five inspectors were to be appointed. These inspectors were to elect a president and would constitute the official levee board of that district. Each inspector was delegated to a portion of the levee in his district, but no inspector was to be charged with the supervision of levees or drains to a greater extent than ten miles from his home. The inspector was to make a survey of his portion of the district and make recommendations for the erection of levees or ditches wherever he deemed them necessary.[6] He had the power to call on three neighboring planters to assist him in determining the nature of the project pertaining to specifications, such as height and base of the levee, width and depth of drainage ditch, and beginning and termination points of the project. After ascertaining the work, the planter on whose land the construction was to take place was to be notified in writing, and the proprietor of the land was bound to execute the work within the time required by the Board of Police.[7]

Fines were imposed upon those inspectors who failed in their duty and also on landholders who neglected to construct the levees and drains required. When non-resident landholders could not be contacted by means of advertisement in newspapers, work on their property was to be let to the lowest bidder. This provision was necessary if any semblance of a continuous levee system was to be realized. "If high water threatened," Harrison points out, "the inspectors were empowered to order out the slaves of the delinquent planters and those of neighbors if necessary; provided that no slave was to work more than three miles from home."[8] Furthermore, when slaves were requisitioned for work on any levee or ditch, the owner of the slaves was to have from the owner of the levee or ditch where the work was done one dollar per day for each man working.

It is clear that during the early settlement of the Basin, the responsibility of building and maintaining levees and drain was placed squarely upon the river-front landholder. In 1844 a devastating flood covered the Yazoo Basin, destroying much of the levee system built by the planters. This flood served to illustrate that the riparian holders could not do the job unaided. Threats of fines or sale of property for failure to build proper levees and drains had failed to provide an adequate levee system for the Yazoo Basin.

After the recovery of the nation from the financial collapse of 1837, settlement in the Basin began to increase. A large influx began about 1846 and reached its peak in 1849 and 1850. The land records of almost every county in the Basin showed a tremendous increase in sales and transfer of land during this period. In Coahoma, Washington, and Bolivar counties, probably more than half the government land had been purchased by 1847.[9] The Yazoo Basin was moving into what some historians call its golden period of plantation economy between 1850 and 1861, and its populace was sure that the area would be developed into an agricultural domain if floods could be controlled. With the water-front landowner system of levee building and maintenance proving inadequate to assure safety from floods and with slaves considered too valuable to risk in malaria swamps and the heat of the summer sun, more and more requests were made for changes in the existing levee laws and for aid from the federal government to help in constructing an adequate levee system. After the flood of 1849, agricultural and commercial interests throughout the Basin pressed for federal aid. The Mississippi legislature as early as 1846 had requested of the federal government a grant of certain overflow lands for the purpose of levee building.

Beginning in 1850, the Mississippi legislature moved to strengthen the existing levee laws. The state authorized for trial in Issaquena County a new levee tax system which provided for a uniform acreage tax not to exceed ten cents per acre upon all lands lying on or within ten miles of the Mississippi River and a uniform tax not to exceed five cents per acre on all lands lying ten miles or more from the Mississippi. Later the same year the state offered to allow the counties of Bolivar, Washington, and Issaquena to assess and collect a levee tax on all state owned lands lying in those counties.[10]

Another improvement over the early levee laws was passed in 1850. This act authorized the levee commissioners for the several counties to hire suitable and qualified engineers to assist in the proper location and building of levees on the Mississippi.

Numerous conventions held during the late 1840s, especially those at Memphis and Chicago, in the interest of navigation and reclamation on the Mississippi River, plus many requests from the state legislatures of the lower Mississippi valley states, helped greatly in the passage of the second Swamp Land Act by the U.S. Congress. This act, passed on September 28, 1850, provided for the release to several states of all the unsold "swamp and overflowed" land within their borders belonging to the United States. As a result of this act the State of Mississippi received 3,290,285 acres of lowland, chiefly in the Yazoo Basin, the proceeds from the sale of which was to be used in flood control and drainage works.

In 1852 when the counties began to receive funds for levee building from the sale of the swamp lands, the state moved to place the levee program on a more businesslike basis. An act passed in 1854 by the state legislature ordered the Boards of Police to abolish the Board of Levee Commissioners and to put in their places a single Commissioner.[11] The new commissioners were to have much broader powers in carrying on levee work. Section 7 of this Act introduced a new method of obtaining levee labor. It instructed the Board of Police as follows:

... [draw] an imaginary line five miles east of the bank of the Mississippi River and to allot all slaves liable to road duty, within said limits, to work upon the levees of said county, within such districts as said board shall prescribe; each slave or slaves shall be liable to serve six days each year without compensation to the owners.[12]

All work days exceeding six were to be paid from the levee fund.

These new provisions brought many protests from the planters. They felt that no one individual should have such dictatorial powers. Also, the planters were not anxious to have their slaves working on the levee. They preferred to pay taxes and have the levee built by contractors. The value of slaves was going up, and planters were not anxious to have their slaves risk the danger of sickness or injury while building levees. Many protests reached the state legislature, and on March 8, 1856, the Reform Act of 1854 was repealed.[13]

Many planters and interested parties felt sure that the Yazoo Basin could be protected from floods, and a general desire for a consolidated county levee system under one board for the entire Basin was making itself felt. The general consensus was that an adequate levee system could be constructed to prevent flooding on the Basin since only one stream, the Yazoo, emptied into the Mississippi River in the area. The newspapers were filled with proposals for a general levee system, and the popular journals of the day also carried articles supporting various plans for protecting the whole Basin. Cotton lands became more valuable daily, and the price of slaves went up virtually every season. Because the suitability of the fertile alluvial soils for cotton was becoming appreciated, an era of prosperity, even wealth, seemed assured. Floods could not be allowed to threaten so golden a future. Slave-owning families from the older cotton states were anxious to acquire Yazoo Basin lands if they could be relatively free from flood danger. The Basin was becoming the frontier for the slave-operated plantation economy.[14]

In 1858, responding to public demand following the severe flood of that year, the state legislature ordered the county levee boards to begin liquidation of their business and to place all major levee work for the Yazoo Basin under one board responsible to the legislature.[15] The new levee board was to be composed of several duly elected county levee commissioners. They were to meet, elect a president of the board, and hire an engineer to survey and make recommendations for a continuous levee system for the Yazoo Basin. The new board was to secure its fund for levee and reclamation work from a uniform tax of ten cents per acre for five years on all overflow lands in the district. They were also authorized to issue scrip to obtain immediate working capital, but not to exceed five hundred thousand dollars or to extend the due date beyond 1863. Although running into several types of opposition, such as local interests, questions of the constitutionality of assessment laws, and high water, the work toward a continuous and sufficient levee system for the Yazoo Basin moved ahead at a rapid pace. The engineers, hired by the newly created board, made recommendations for the levees' improvement and also for the construction of new ones. Contracts were let, and during 1859 and 1860, work on the levees and drains was progressing at a rapid rate.

The cost of building and maintaining the levees was at last partly distributed to the inland land owners of the Basin, and not all the burden was placed on the riparian landholders. Levee work had proved costly, and the question of the cost of a continuous levee system for the Basin was raised many times during this period by both the state legislature and the taxpayers. Two great problems confronting the Levee Board were securing the right-of-way and dealing with the absentee landholder, who used every conceivable means to avoid paying his share of the cost of internal improvements. The river-front planters wanted to keep the levee as close to the river as possible; however, this practice resulted in the loss of expensive construction by cave-ins. In spite of the many difficulties, though, the Yazoo Basin was close to securing a greatly improved and partially continuous levee system when all progress was suddenly stopped by the War between the States.

With the war came the suspension of the reclamation work as well as acts to suspend the collection of taxes to support this work. In 1862 a flood hit the Yazoo Basin levees with full force and broke them in many places. In this flood, gauge heights at Cairo and below exceeded those of any other previously recorded flood except the flood of 1815.[16] Abandonment of the Basin began. Families left short of workers, either because of men off at war or slaves running off to federal camps, moved inland wherever high ground was available or to points farther removed. The river did not reach flood stage during 1863 and 1864, but much of the levee was destroyed or damaged by military operations since after the fall of Vicksburg and Union gunboats had free access to the river. Just as the war ended, the Yazoo Basin was swept by a flood which was remarkable for its duration. Whole sections of the largest works of the 1858 levee district were destroyed. Floodwaters covered the entire lowland and did not recede for months, destroying the few remaining livestock and making it impossible to get crops started. Hundreds of families left the Basin, many never to return.[17]

Who were these early settlers and what attracted them to this wilderness? The great majority were slave-holding planters from the older cotton states in search of new, fertile land. To clear land, build levees and drains, and risk crop destruction by floods took capital, and the yeoman farmer could not compete with the large planter and slave labor; therefore, the small farmer's entrance was delayed until the war had destroyed the plantation economy based upon forced labor. The slave-holding planters moved in by the river, which was the sole access to these new lands. Unlike new settlers in many pioneer areas, they did not suffer the trials and hardships common to pioneering. Sillers gives the following description:

> Comfortable quarters were provided for the slaves and comfortable homes for the masters and their families. The quarters for the slaves were made from hewn logs, "chinked" with clay or plaster, covered with boards, rived from cypress trees of the forest. They had plank floors and great open wood fireplaces which were especially prized by the occupants. These houses were built in double rows, giving the appearance of a village. The first homes of the planters were generally of the same material, with four rooms and a hall between, and with a gallery extending across the front. They were furnished with the handsome furniture brought from the home state of the planters. Steamboats and trading boats (floating stores) brought all the necessities and even luxuries to the very doors of the rich planters, who were able to live with ease and comfort, and to a degree in luxury, in the forest.[18]

With fields once cleared, abundant crops produced, and wealth accumulating, the planters' thoughts turned toward building homes worthy of their social standing. A few "ante-bellum" homes had been completed before the war, but the Basin settlement came too late to produce a social organization comparable to the older Natchez district. Most of the homes were constructed of native timber, sawed at first by hand, but later on some boards were sawed by power. Two- and three-story homes were common. The majority had galleries running around the entire house, both upstairs and down, and usually there was a large hall running the entire length of the house. A few houses were constructed with brick from local clay deposits.

By 1860, the five counties in the Yazoo Basin bordering on the Mississippi River had a total population of 65,649, of which 53,120 were Negroes and 12,529 were white. Those counties on the east, lying partly within the Basin and partly in the hill area, had a total population of 107,219, of which 70,097 were Negro and 37,122 were white. Sunflower County, occupying the geographic center of the Basin, had a population of 3,917 Negroes and 1,102 whites. Those counties lying wholly within the Basin had a population density of thirteen per square mile, and those partly in the Basin a density of twenty-nine per square mile. The ratio of Negro to white in the Basin counties was approximately five to one, while the ratio in the part-Basin counties was two to one, indicating a greater number of yeoman farmers in the hill area. The population in 1860 was strung out along the Mississippi River and the hill line, and a small number of settlers had pushed inland as far as the Sunflower River. Cotton acreage in the part-Basin counties was probably considerably greater than that in the Basin counties. The reported acreages were 325,000 and 164,000, respectively, with no report available for Washington and Sunflower counties, both Basin counties.

*Post-Civil War Settlement to 1900.* The Yazoo Basin at the termination of the war had almost reverted to a state of wilderness. Many of the homes had been burned and destroyed; the labor force was gone; cane and briars claimed the land, and there were no levees to protect against floods. Even those planters who returned were without work stock or capital, without which the production of a crop and the reclaiming of the land were impossible. Taxes were the only source of funds, and there was no money with which to pay taxes. The situation seemed bleak, and a new influx of settlement was twenty years away.

The first major task of the Basin population was to repair and rebuild the levee system destroyed by floods and war. This task had to be accomplished if much of the land already cleared was to be planted to crops. Even before the war actually ended, plans had been made to revive the 1858 levee districts. However, the Levee Commission was heavily in debt, and the prostrate planters were in no mood to be taxed at this time. Being taxed to pay off a debt created before the war did not receive serious attention from the planters. They were weary from paying taxes placed upon them by a reconstruction government. Even if they had been willing to pay this tax, it is doubtful whether many planters had money enough to do so. Total annual tax bills for Yazoo Basin lands were frequently well above the sale value of the land during the early post–Civil War period. Formal forfeitures to the Liquidating Levee Board and other levee boards and to the state took place in a wholesale way. In Sunflower County during 1870, a sale of tax-forfeitured land amounted to more than nine-tenths of the taxable land of the county.[19]

There was dissension, also, among the planters of the northern counties of the Basin concerning the formation of a Basin-wide levee program. They had never approved of the wide powers invested in the president of the 1858 Levee Commission. Because of much sentiment against a Basin-wide levee program, several of the leading planters of Bolivar, Washington, and Issaquena counties moved to form a levee district embracing these counties. Approval of the state legislature was sought, and the act approving the Board was passed in November 1865.[20]

The newly created Board was to secure its funds from a uniform tax of ten cents per acre per annum on all lands except those held in trust by the state and lands lying east of Sunflower River. In addition to the land tax, a production tax on cotton was authorized, amounting to one cent per pound per year on all cotton gathered in the counties of Bolivar, Washington, and Issaquena. Tunica and Coahoma counties were invited to join with the lower counties in the provision of this act. They chose not to do so. The act provided, however, that levees needed in Coahoma County to protect lands in Bolivar County could be built by the Board, and in case they were not built, lands in Bolivar County would not be subject to acreage or cotton taxes if they were flooded by waters coming from levee breaks in Coahoma County.[21]

Having declined in 1865 the opportunity to join with the Levee Board of the southern counties in the Basin to develop a general levee system, the upper Basin counties were left to their own desires. For seven years following the Civil War, no levee organization for the upper section was developed. Many of the large landowners felt that they could build private levees sufficient for their own protection and were opposed to a general levee system that might burden them with taxes. Land companies hoped to develop their land enough to attract settlers and then let the settlers build the costly levees.

By 1871 group action toward flood control in the upper Basin could no longer be denied, and a levee board was chartered in March 1871 by the state legislature. After five years of operation, however, the northern levee Board became hopelessly bankrupt and was abolished by the state legislature.[22]

While the Levee Commission of the lower Basin counties was making some headway toward repairing and rebuilding the levee system, the upper counties had accomplished little or nothing toward reclamation until after 1884. After the collapse of the Levee District Number 1 in 1876 (now the Yazoo-Mississippi Delta Levee District, with headquarters at Clarksdale, Mississippi), there was a succession of low water years that alleviated the immediate necessity of a levee system; at least the higher lands were not subject to injury during this period. However, the relatively safe period was short lived. The Yazoo Basin was flooded three years in succession: 1882, 1883, and 1884. After the 1884 flood, the levee spirit was rekindled in the northern counties of the Basin, and they were able to organize successfully a Levee Commission that rebuilt the existing levees of that time.

Although the threat of floods and the extreme poverty of the South retarded settlement in the alluvial lands following the Civil War, there were other factors equally important. One factor of great importance was the confusion of titles to the Yazoo Basin lands. As stated earlier, the 1858 Levee District was heavily in debt at the beginning of the war, and now in the postwar period these debts were even larger, with the accumulation of interest. Since the 1858 Board had been liquidated and a new Levee Board organized, the state organized in 1867 the Liquidating Levee Board to provide a method for the payment of these just debts, which amounted to over $1,500,000. In attempting to carry out the provisions of the Liquidating Levee Board Act, questions concerning the validity of the state and Levee District tax titles arose. Since practically every acre in the Yazoo Basin had been forfeited at one time or another to one or more of these levee boards, land titles throughout the Basin were involved in a series of land title cases. Harrison described the situation as follows:

> The system of State and levee board tax titles in Mississippi had reached such a state of conflict, because of the wholesale forfeitures of land for taxes following the Civil War, that it was necessary, if the Yazoo Basin was ever to be developed, to establish clear titles to the lowlands, so that transfers of property might again take place freely. The history of the Liquidating Levee Board and the events which followed its creation offer a fine example of how confusion of land titles may retard the economic development of an area and even of a state. During the twenty years (1865–1885) when levee and State tax titles were in conflict, there was very little agricultural or industrial development in the Yazoo Basin. With the perfection of these titles, improvements came rapidly.[23]

The state was anxious to settle the title question and get the lands again into taxpaying status in order to enter into a successful land-selling program because the economy of the Basin was falling into decay. The levee boards were without money or the means to obtain loans to repair the levees, which were gradually being washed away.[24] By 1877 some semblance of order was brought into the transfer of titles, and large land sales resulted. Among the largest was the transfer in the Yazoo Basin of some two million acres to the Louisville, New Orleans, and Texas Railroad Company in the fall of 1881. The railroad pushed its line to early completion and became an important influence in the development of the Basin.[25] Another large tract of some six hundred thousand acres was secured by the Delta and Pine Land Company in 1886. This Company engaged in an intensive land sale and settlement program which did much to stimulate agricultural development in the woodlands of the Yazoo Basin.[26]

During the 1870s, the Levee Board of the lower Basin pressed for federal aid for levee construction. Since settlement was slow and much of the taxable land was in the hands of the state, funds for needed work were extremely low. As a result of many pleas, the federal government established in 1879 the Mississippi River Commission, which gave the much needed aid in reclamation in the Yazoo Basin under the pretext of improving navigation. Federal funds were made available to the Levee Board to help repair the damage done by the 1882 flood and have been forthcoming annually since that date.

Considerable progress was made in reclamation during the latter 1880s. With the paralyzing influence of confused land titles removed, with railroads within the Basin expanding, and with federal funds aiding reclamation work, an era of prosperity seemed inevitable. Between 1881 and 1884, a railroad had been constructed down the axis of the Yazoo Basin from Memphis to Vicksburg. About 1890, this road passed into the possession of the Illinois Central Railroad Company, which was responsible for a great extension of the rail system in the Basin. By 1903, eight hundred and sixteen miles had been added to the system, and new lines were still going down. This extension of the railroads had a great influence on the lumber industries, which entered the Basin and grew enormously in the years between 1897 and 1903.[27]

With the great flood of 1897 came the cry for higher and better levees. New expenditures meant higher taxes and bonded debt, which a few years before would have brought protests, but not now. Land was selling freely and gaining in value. Drainage districts were being organized throughout the Basin. Many energetic land promoters came to the Basin between 1897 and 1910, and land values soon reflected the speculation which they started. Lumber companies began promotions to sell the cut-over areas to agricultural interests. The Yazoo Basin was on the threshold of a seemingly prosperous era of expansion and development. If bigger, stronger levees were needed to assure the future, few men would speak against them, even though they might require new debt and higher taxes.[28]

With many deterrents to settlement during the post–Civil War period removed or greatly reduced, by 1885 a migration of settlers toward the Yazoo Basin began that gained momentum with the years and lasted until the financial crash of 1929. The improved part of the Basin was along the river front and a few stream banks not very far into the interior. But expanded settlement brought on by railroad and lumber companies was in the poorly drained land between the streams. What was this country like beyond the river and what did these new settlers encounter? One new settler around Cleveland in Bolivar County had this to say:

> There was a small amount of cleared land then, and it was on the bayous, lakes, and rivers. The country was covered with blue cane fifteen to twenty feet high, and the land was rich as cream. Woodland was being sold by the Yazoo and Mississippi Valley railroad at five dollars per acre on long time terms, but it was expensive to clear and many people, both white and black, would quit after a year or two and sell for a small equity. I remember seeing one forty acres traded for a cow and another forty acres traded for a Winchester rifle. The only land and large plantations were on the Mississippi River front. . . .
>
> Land began having a value about 1895 and 1896, and people began clearing and going farther back from bayous and lakes, where land was not well drained. This increased one's open land but did not increase his bales of cotton in proportion to the cost of his crops. Then the people cleared more land, organized a drainage district, issued bonds, and have been catching the devil ever since, paying ninety-nine kinds of taxes. The insurance companies showed up about that time and took mortgages on the farm and everything on it, but the farmer's wife, and are now having as much trouble farming as any of the rest of us poor devils.[29]

The life of the pioneer settler in the interior Basin was not an easy one and was far different from that of the river-front planter in the pre–Civil War days. Many were lured into taking up acreage because of the rosy picture of rich land and fabulous cotton crops presented to them by the railroad and the land companies. In Sillers's book it is stated that "the mere physical work of keeping alive and clearing the woods challenged all the energies of both men and women." One early settler of Bolivar County is quoted as having said, "A good worker could cut one-fourth acre a day in the tall cane brakes."[30]

Evidently most of the settlers during this period were whites, at least those who went into the uncleared areas. This conclusion might be assumed from a remark made by this same east Bolivar County settler:

> There were few Negroes in this section when we arrived; therefore, we had white labor as farm hands. Dr. Meek brought in the first Negroes as farm workers, six families. A howl went up; the white settlers did not want them.[31]

However, this situation did not last long. As land was cleared, more labor was needed to plant and harvest crops. Cotton is a labor-consuming crop, and in the days before mechanization of cotton production, twenty to forty acres was considered a large enough unit for a family to handle. An early settler fortunate enough to succeed on the first forty or eighty acres purchased was eager to acquire more land to produce more cotton, get rich quick and retire. But unless a man had an exceptionally large family, his land accumulation would not have to exceed a quarter section before he was ready to rent improved land to tenant farmers. With the older plantations entering into contract with the freed Negroes for share cropping and with new settlers accumulating and clearing land, a great demand arose for tenant farmers. Since the Basin land would produce much more per acre than the hill lands, meaning more bales of cotton for the tenant's share of the crop, a strong migration of Negro farmers started toward the Yazoo Basin. In 1880, the counties of Washington and Bolivar, two old cotton-producing river-front counties, had Negro populations of 21,861 and 15,958, respectively. By 1900 these numbers had risen to 44,143 and 31,197, respectively.[32]

Negro population had increased in the Basin by 66 percent between 1860 and 1880, while during the same period the white population, though still a minority, had increased by 92 percent. The part-Basin counties still held the lead in total population. The Negro population in the part-Basin counties increased by 60 percent and the white by 69 percent. The counties of the Basin had a population density of twenty-one per square mile in 1880. During the same period, cotton acreage in the counties of the Basin increased 40 percent; in the part-Basin counties, 60 percent.

*Yazoo Basin settlement, 1900 to 1930.* The population increase in the Yazoo Basin after 1900 was sparked by several factors. Increased activity in levee building, aided by the federal government, assured the populace of increased flood protection. Expanded rail and road transportation made the interior of the Basin more accessible. Lumber and land companies put on a vigorous land selling campaign. The organization of drainage districts and the construction of drainage ditches placed into cultivation considerable land that had previously been too wet. The economics of cotton production was greatly improved over the latter part of the period up to 1900. The advent of the boll weevil in the older cotton-producing areas resulted in planters and farmers moving into the newly cleared area not yet infested with the insect.

Although a great campaign to reclaim the Basin from floods had been waged in the Yazoo Basin in terms of both labor and money since 1858, the existing levees had given way in every major flood and partially or wholly flooded the Basin. The question might arise why they are continued to be settled in the face of such odds. Answers are that the effort seemed to be worthwhile because of the land's natural advantage in cotton production and because of the fact that in most flood years the water came early in the spring and drained off rapidly enough for many to get in crops. Cotton could be planted in the mud by hand and germinated sufficiently enough to cultivate while the land dried. If this had not been the case, many planters would have been bankrupt.

As the levees became higher and Arkansas and Louisiana caught up with the Yazoo Basin in levee building, the flood waters rose higher. There seemed to be no end to the task of keeping out the Mississippi flood waters. The great flood of 1897 clearly demonstrated the need for greater heights in the existing levees, especially since the White and St. Francis rivers were being closed. Shortly after the damage created by the 1897 overflow was repaired, the Yazoo Basin was threatened again in 1903. The flood stage rose higher than ever, and although a vigorous campaign was fought with sandbag topping, the levee gave way in several places. After the 1903 flood, the levee Boards were plagued with a new threat to the levee program—caving banks. When the levee program started in the Yazoo Basin, it was only logical to place the levee atop the natural levee of the Mississippi River. This not only placed the embankment on the highest ground, but it left most of the best land behind the levee. Between 1865 and 1948 three hundred and seventy-four miles of levee had been abandoned; between 1882 and 1917, one hundred and eighty-seven miles were abandoned; from 1917 to 1928, eighteen miles were abandoned; from 1928 to 1948, changes made by the U.S. government placed outside the main line of levees about seventy-eight miles.[33] During the period from 1900 to 1930, the revetment program to retain the river was begun. There also arose during this period much debate on the feasibility of reclaiming the whole Basin, with reservoirs and spillways as part of the reclamation. However, nothing came out of the discussions at this time because the Levee Boards could not afford to do the work and the U.S. government had not as yet passed a flood control bill in favor of reclamation. Federal funds were spent on aids to navigation.

Although the Basin was threatened by high water in 1904, 1906, and 1907, no breaks occurred in the Yazoo Basin levees, and record volumes of water passed to the Gulf within the confines of the levees and hills.[34] The efforts to enlarge the levees after the 1903 flood seemed to be worthwhile. Freedom from flood waters was short lived, though, because in 1912 and again in 1913 flood crests rolled down the Mississippi River breaking through all previous high water marks. A gallant fight was put up to save the levees. A labor force of thousands turned out to top the levees with sand bags, both volunteer and paid labor, as well as many convicts from the state penitentiary at Parchman in Sunflower County. The upper district levees held, but several crevasses occurred between Rosedale, in Bolivar County, and the mouth of the Yazoo River. The great floods of 1912 and 1913 precipitated a crisis in the reclamation program. Unless federal aid on a greatly expanded scale could be made certain, attempts to reclaim the whole Basin would have to be given up and efforts concentrated on those parts which could be most easily protected.[35] As the result of a vigorous propaganda campaign in the interest of flood control, federal aid for actual flood control, not disguised as aid to navigation, seemed assured. With help thus in sight, the Levee Boards went forward as rapidly as funds would permit in repairing the damage done by the 1912 and 1913 floods. In 1914 the Mississippi Levee District, the southern Basin District, had a bonded debt of $2,150,000, which exceeded 10 percent of the assessed valuation of property in the District, a limit beyond which financial institutions were not anxious to lend money.[36]

In 1917, the federal government came to the aid of the Levee Board and for the first time fully started its levee building program as a measure designed for the control of floods. The Ransdell-Humphreys Act was specifically designed to relieve the Mississippi Valley of destructive floods by the building of higher and stronger levees and the placing of revetments where caving banks threatened the levees.[37] Under this act, the United States would pay two-thirds of the cost of flood control, and the local interests would be responsible for one-third. Local interests were also to furnish the right-of-way, unless the levee was to be moved a considerable distance back, in which case the United

States would pay the cost. Since the levee in the northern levee district did not break during the 1912 and 1913 flood, all federal funds were spent in the lower district. Although local interests in the northern district carried on improvement work during the 1917–1927 period, most of the funds were spent in the lower district.

Despite the danger of caving banks to the levees, there existed a feeling of security among the lay people behind the enlarged levee:

> The Yazoo Basin had been developing rapidly since 1900, despite the overflows of 1903, 1912, and 1913. More than 100 drainage organizations had been formed to take surface water from cotton lands. High prices of the World War I era brought with them an expansionist philosophy. Basin lands changed hands rapidly. Much northern capital flowed into the Basin. The impression prevailed that the levees would now hold against all floods. The standard grade and section set by the Commission had been reached. Many levee engineers began to look upon future work as largely of a maintenance character. It was widely thought that the levee contractors would have little work in the future and that many of the old companies would go out of business. The Mississippi River Commission joined in the optimism, and in 1926 predicted that the end of the flood control fight was at hand.[38]

Then came the spring of 1927. Heavy rains from January to April on already saturated soil in the upper Mississippi Valley brought heavy tributary floods to the Mississippi just as it was filled from heavy rains in the lower valley. Down the valley rolled the highest crest ever recorded on the Mississippi River. Harrison stated:

> The levees were designed to hold no such water as this. Despite an active high water campaign by the U.S. and local forces, crevasses began to occur as the flood passed down the river. Before it reached the Gulf, there were thirteen breaks in the levees of the lower Mississippi, and 23,000 square miles of alluvial valley were flooded. Every major Basin was affected. . . . Flood waters in 1927 entered the Yazoo Basin through a single crevasse on the 21st of April at Mound Landing in Bolivar County. This break quickly attained a width of over three thousand feet and reached a maximum discharge of 468,204 cubic feet per second. The lower Yazoo Basin was completely flooded, and an entire crop year was lost.[39]

Seven hundred thousand people were made homeless. People sought safety on levees, on roof tops, and in trees. A vast rescue fleet of small boats reported rescuing 330,000 people from house tops and trees. Property damages were estimated by several government organizations to exceed $300,000,000. Describing some consequences of this flood, Harrison said:

> The flood of 1927, and the great campaign for full Federal support for flood control which followed, truly established the Mississippi Valley levee and floodway program as a national project. Moved by the widespread suffering brought to the Mississippi Valley by the great 1927 overflow, hundreds of national organizations, as varied as the American Legion and the American Investment Bankers Association, strongly recommended full Federal responsibility for flood control. Even before the floodwater had receded it was virtually certain that strong Federal flood control act would be approved by Congress. One of the most extensive hearings ever held by a Congressional Committee was initiated soon after the rescue work was completed. Before the hearing and investigations of the Congress were completed hundreds of witnesses had been heard and five thousand pages of testimony recorded. Flood control for the Mississippi Valley had at last been firmly established as a national responsibility.[40]

As a result of these hearings, a bill was passed which provided for a comprehensive federal program of flood control, and thus came a program of spillways, cut-offs, and reservoirs. In 1928, a miniature replica of the entire Mississippi Valley and its tributaries was set up at Vicksburg, Mississippi, and later at Clinton, Mississippi, to aid in research on flood control. Flood waters can be traced down the valley, and heights can be calculated long before they reach critical points.

After the federal government took over the control of Mississippi River floods, water reached dangerous heights in 1929, 1937, and 1945. The levees, now greatly increased in height and often moved away from caving banks, held in every case. In 1937 a sizable section of the lower Yazoo Basin was flooded by backwater flowing up the Yazoo River. But the only serious threat came from sand boils, and an alert citizenry numbering hundreds brought these under control.

With every improvement in the federal flood-control works, the confidence of residents and property owners who live behind the levees has increased. And the economic development of the Yazoo Basin since the assumption of federal responsibility has unquestionably reflected this confidence.

# Notes

1.  Dunbar Rowland, *Encyclopedia of Mississippi* (1907), II, 181.
2.  Florence Warfield Sillers, compiler, *History of Bolivar County, Mississippi* (Jackson, Mississippi: Hederman Brothers, 1948), 5.
3.  Robert W. Harrison, "Levee Building in Mississippi before the Civil War," *Journal of Mississippi History*, XII (April 1950): 71.
4.  *Laws of Mississippi*, 1819, 78.
5.  Robert W. Harrison, *Levee Districts and Levee Building in Mississippi* (Washington, D.C.: Bureau of Agricultural Economics, U.S. Department of Agriculture, *et al.*, 1951), 1.
6.  *Laws of Mississippi*, 1838, 414.
7.  Ibid., 412.
8.  Harrison, "Levee Building," 65–66.
9.  Harrison, *Levee Districts*, 9.
10. *Laws of Mississippi*, 1850, 180–208.
11. *Laws of Mississippi*, 1854, 186.
12. Ibid., 188.
13. Harrison, *Levee Districts*, 12.
14. Ibid., 13.
15. *Laws of Mississippi*, 1858, 33.
16. Harrison, *Levee Districts*, 26.
17. Ibid., 27.
18. Sillers, op. cit., 8.
19. Harrison, *Levee District*, 43.
20. *Laws of Mississippi*, 1865, 51.
21. Harrison, *Levee Districts*, 28.
22. Ibid., 37–40.
23. Ibid., 41.
24. Ibid., 44.
25. Ibid., 51.
26. Ibid., 52.
27. Ibid., 155.
28. Ibid., 154.
29. Quoted in Sillers, op. cit., 170–71.
30. Ibid., 174.
31. Ibid.
32. U.S. Census, 1880 and 1900.
33. Harrison, *Levee Districts*, 198.
34. Ibid., 194.
35. Ibid., 217.
36. Ibid., 223.
37. Ibid., 226.
38. Ibid., 233.
39. Ibid., 234.
40. Ibid., 235.

# From Enchantment to Disillusionment

## A Southern Editor Views the New Deal[1]

JOHN RAY SKATES

In the winter of 1932–1933 the United States was being crushed under the enormous weight of economic inactivity that was the great depression. Thirteen million workers were unemployed, and the "Hoovervilles" which many of them inhabited dotted the landscape. As one writer observed, just before Franklin Delano Roosevelt's inauguration in 1933 it appeared that the American people were almost without hope.[2] President Roosevelt's answer to this chaotic situation was the New Deal, a gigantic accumulation of relief, recovery, and reform measures which remade America's economic face. What were Frederick Sullens's thoughts on that greatest exercise in positive government in American history?

Like other Southern conservatives Sullens was caught up in the enthusiasm and action of the first months of the New Deal, but, as FDR's program grew ever bigger, he seemed torn between his lifelong loyalty to the Democratic Party and his increasing mistrust of the leftist direction of the New Deal. Indeed, Sullens's views of Roosevelt's program followed an almost classic course for Southern conservatives in the 1930s, progressing from fervent support in 1933–1934, through suspicion and disenchantment in 1935–1936 to open hostility in the latter years of the decade. Sullens's gradual disenchantment with the New Deal gives added weight to one writer's assertion that the President could not hope to retain the support of Southern conservatives and at the same time allow his program to "remake the South."[3]

In the midst of the New Deal years, perhaps in despair or possibly to justify the social and economic revolution being wrought by the President, Sullens voiced the willingness of many Americans to forego old dogmas when he wrote the following:

*Southern Quarterly* 5.4 (1967): 363–80.

In the old days we assumed that certain things were natural and enduring; that the world would always have a place for an ambitious young man, that honest work and fidelity to duty would always reap a suitable reward, that the man who applied himself to his job intelligently and energetically would never need to worry about his future.

The depression, Sullens admitted, had swept away these old illusions, and it had proved that a man's economic fate was as dependent on external factors as on his own ambition and energy. This realization, he believed, was the "most damaging legacy of the depression."[4] Thus Sullens voiced one of the chief arguments for government action to combat the depression, and it was an amazing admission, for the New Deal was the very antithesis of Sullens's conservative temperament and his lifelong advocacy of limited government.

As the depression deepened in the last days of the Hoover administration, Sullens realized the need for potent government action to fight the economic breakdown. He called it startling that the leaders of government and business had offered no comprehensive plans to bring the country out of the worst depression in its history. "We ought to realize by this time that we cannot sit back and wait for things to right themselves," he warned. He also castigated the legislative bodies of the nation for inaction. "While the people stretch forth their hands and piteously cry for relief," he charged, "little men with little minds keep on debating." By mid-1933 Sullens feared a revolution in the United States. To forestall it, he warned, "Something must be done, and it must be done very soon, and it must be something drastic, far-reaching, bold, and determined." He advised critics of the New Deal that if they opposed the President's program, they must have constructive alternative proposals—and quickly. But strangely, as late as May 1933, Sullens wrote that Roosevelt did not want to interfere with the economy unless the business leaders of the nation showed no inclination to initiate national planning. If the leaders of private industry refused to cooperate, he observed, the President would step in with all his power.[5]

Indeed, the President had already stepped in boldly. In the first three months of his administration, the famous "Hundred Days," by one historian's accounting President Roosevelt "sent fifteen messages to Congress, guided fifteen major laws to enactment, delivered ten speeches, held press conferences and cabinet meetings twice a week, conducted talks with foreign heads of state, sponsored an international conference, made all major decisions in the domestic and foreign policy, and never displayed fright or panic and rarely even bad temper." It was an orgy of action unlike any other in American history, and Sullens was clearly delighted. "Foolish indeed is the person nowadays who cannot change his opinion overnight," he exclaimed, as the New Dealers rolled act after act through Congress.[6]

In the opening months of the New Deal Sullens appeared to have changed his deepest convictions. Among other things, he called for "vast bond issues for public works" and "minimum-wage and short week regulations." He was so enthusiastic that he offhandedly endorsed public power, a stand which a short time earlier would have been anathema to him. In speaking of a proposed power development at Muscle Shoals in northern Alabama, the ancestor of the Tennessee Valley Authority, Sullens proclaimed the project "socialistic—frankly and confessedly so," but, he asked, could the private power industry "which handed us Samuel Insull and busted us with bum bonds" say that the project was wrong? Indeed, could the leaders of an industrial system which had "dropped ten million [unemployed] people into our laps" criticize such demands as that of labor for a thirty-hour week?[7]

When opposition began to appear to some of the New Deal measures, Sullens quickly likened these critics to "rats, cowering in their corners. . . . baring their nasty teeth and threatening to bite." In the midst of the Hundred Days the *Daily News* dropped the syndicated articles of Dr. Glenn Frank from its columns because, in Sullens's words, Dr. Frank was a "chronic kicker, a constitutional objector, a confirmed destructionist." This meant, by Sullens's own admission, that Frank objected to the New Deal. A few days later a new column from the pen of Dr. Raymond Moley, a leading member of Roosevelt's "Brain Trust," appeared in Sullens's paper.[8]

Yet if Sullens's enthusiasm was unbounded during the first months of the New Deal, he was not altogether uncritical of the Roosevelt administration later in 1933 and 1934. Before 1933 was over he attacked that group of Presidential advisers known as the "Brain Trust." It did not take Sullens long to realize that this body of economic and political counselors, composed mostly of college professors, was a powerful force rapidly driving the President toward a liveliness and empiricism hitherto unknown in American government. This fact, plus the great personal popularity of President Roosevelt, caused Sullens to direct his early criticisms not at the President but at the members of the Brain Trust.[9]

Then too, in 1933 and 1934 FDR's early relief measures drew from Sullens an ambivalence that he would shortly manifest toward the whole New Deal.

Inevitably, the everpresent racial concern of Southerners helped to color Sullens's views on that subject. Although he was opposed to the dole because he believed that it encouraged idleness,[10] he was not sure what form the relief program should take. Before Roosevelt took office Sullens was even suspicious of relief loans furnished by the Reconstruction Finance Corporation, an agency he later came to admire as one of the few businesslike operations of the New Deal. He claimed that these loans encouraged people, particularly Negroes, to be idle and to live from the largesse of the Federal Government. He noted a short time later that some communities in Mississippi were troubled by people whom he terms "professional mendicants."[11]

Yet Sullens realized the necessity for relief. He explained to some of his complaining readers that the national government provided relief only because no other agency was capable of performing so great a task. It was harmful for the government to furnish support to so many of its citizens, he declared, but "It would be a great deal worse to have them all starving." So, he advised his readers, complaining did no good unless one offered alternative solutions.[12]

Although Sullens failed to form any firm opinions on the relief measures of the early New Deal, he did clearly support the early reform and revival measures. While voicing his strong support of the President's banking bill and stock exchange reforms, Sullens forecast the very principle on which the New Dealers based Roosevelt's first great recovery measure, the National Industrial Recovery Act. At the same time that he endorsed securities and banking reforms, Sullens called for a revision of the Sherman and Clayton Anti-Trust Acts. "Instead of being treated in the law as potential criminals," he said, "large business organizations should be recognized as socially useful instruments for the creation and distribution of wealth."[13] The first great recovery measure of the New Deal did just that.

Signed into law on June 16, 1933, the National Industrial Recovery Act exempted from the antitrust laws the new business groups that were formed under the act. With government approval, all the members of a particular industry cooperated in writing a code for that industry. This code regulated such things as wages and hours, work conditions, and competition, and provided punishment for violators of the code. The NIRA guaranteed to labor the right of collective bargaining. It was, as one writer put it, "a mighty attempt, organized by government to halt the decline through a massive experiment in national cooperation."[14]

Sullens admired this new act. He asserted that the "Roosevelt administration's industrial control bill . . . crumples up all our old theories about the proper relationship between government and private industry and tosses them in the wastebasket." He believed that the sponsors of the bill were attempting a quiet revolution to "readapt a complex industrialism in such a way that the essential features of both democracy and industrialism come through unimpaired." "Revolutionary?" Sullens asked. "To be sure; but isn't our whole system based on revolution?" He stated that "private ownership, private management, and private initiative" were traditional in the United States, but, he believed, under the NIRA the country could have "all these plus public control for the public good." When the Republican Chicago *Tribune* argued that the NIRA was the beginning of a fascist revolution in America, Sullens agreed that perhaps it was fascism and possibly Roosevelt was "some kind of Mussolini." But he replied that the country could not continue to sink deeper into the depression. Something must be done. When other economic powers failed to alleviate matters, the government had to step in. If the government succeeded, then nobody would care what kind of "ism" it used.[15]

From the outset Sullens was a vigorous supporter of the National Recovery Administration, the agency organized to administer the NIRA, and the *Daily News* proudly displayed the "Blue Eagle," the symbol of those businesses which were cooperating in the attack on economic lethargy. Throughout the last six months of 1933, the columns of the *News* were filled with editorials praising the NRA. Sullens looked on the act as having begun a new era in American economics. As he observed, it was clear that American industry had to be under "strict and intelligent control," or the American people would only be "gathering momentum for a new plunge into the ditch," and "one more plunge would just about finish the [industrial] machine and its riders as well."[16]

Nevertheless, Sullens quickly discovered a part of the NIRA with which he did not agree. Section 7A of the act guaranteed labor the right of collective bargaining, and even before the first year of the New Deal was over, Sullens accused organized labor of taking "an unfair advantage of the collective bargaining provision of the NIRA program." He claimed that although manufacturers had cooperated in raising wages, labor was about to undo this good work by demanding too much too soon. This was perhaps a natural reaction since Sullens was never an admirer of organized labor. Although he still supported the NIRA vigorously, Sullens realized by late 1933 that it might fail to defeat the depression, and he cheerfully predicted that if it failed, "The cards go back into the deck for another shuffle and a new deal."[17]

By the time the United States Supreme Court ruled on the NIRA, Sullens had already realized that the act was a failure, but by that time he had become somewhat distrustful of the course of Roosevelt's entire program. In May 1935, when the Supreme Court ruled unfavorably on the NIRA, Sullens wrote, evidently with a certain sense of relief, that the New Deal was "dead." His growing disenchantment was obvious a few days later when he declared, "The United States of America will never get back to a sound and enduring basis of prosperity if its people are regimented and unduly regulated."[18]

The agricultural counterpart of the National Industrial Recovery Act was the Agricultural Adjustment Act, passed by Congress in May 1933. This legislation was critically important to Sullens's overwhelmingly agricultural home state of Mississippi. Oddly, however, Sullens said less about the AAA than the NIRA, and what he did write was by no means consistent. In the days just after passage he was somewhat critical of the legislation, but this critical attitude shortly changed to one of support.

Under the Agricultural Adjustment Act, using a system of benefit payments, the Department of Agriculture hoped to increase farm commodity prices by limiting production. By the time the act became effective in May 1933, the crops for that year were already planted. Hence, as an emergency measure, the government ordered the plowing under of one-fourth of the cotton crop. Sullens opposed this. He said it was "a waste of time . . . for the Department of Agriculture to talk about 'cotton acreage retirement.'" Most of Mississippi's cotton acreage had been planted, he noted, and Mississippi's farmers were not going to destroy it. He claimed that "the effort of the federal government to curtail production by paying farmers to plow up acreage" was "no doubt well-meaning but sadly misguided." Sullens maintained that with cotton prices higher than in several years, farmers would be reluctant to plow up acreage, and if they agreed, they would plow under the worst land and cultivate the remainder more intensively. He concluded, "Plowing under cotton acreage comes mighty close to being the climax of absurdity."[19]

In late June 1933, Sullens's rather critical view of the AAA changed to an attitude of wait-and-see. It might work, he admitted, but then, it might not. By July 1933, he openly favored the act. In calling on the farmers of Mississippi to support the program, he warned, "Unless he [the farmer] co-operates with the government movement, he is hopelessly lost—and deserves to be." Sullens even sent a telegram to Mississippi's senior Senator Pat Harrison urging him to suggest to the President that unless Roosevelt put "the power of his personality" behind the program in Mississippi, it was likely to fail.[20]

Sullens's honeymoon with the New Deal was of such a glowing nature in the early months of the program that it even included advocacy of public power and the Tennessee Valley Authority, a program upon which Sullens later heaped unrestrained abuse. Since the end of the First World War a great government-built hydroelectric dam on the Tennessee River at Muscle Shoals, Alabama, had lain idle. Senator George W. Norris of Nebraska carried on a campaign throughout the Republican era of the 1920s to have that idle power source placed at the disposal of the people of the Tennessee valley through a federally sponsored public power project. In May 1933, Congress passed the Tennessee Valley Authority Act providing for government sale of power from the Muscle Shoals Dam and the building of other government-operated hydroelectric dams on the Tennessee River. Before he took office Roosevelt had hinted at such a project, and, then, Sullens had been receptive. "Government ownership means paternalism," he said, "but amid all the perplexing questions that confront the American people there are many things worse than paternalism."[21]

When the program became a reality, however, Sullens wasted no time in attacking it, and through the years of the TVA's development his criticism grew ever more strident. The Act was signed into law on May 18, 1933, and four days later, sounding suspiciously like a threatened power company stockholder, Sullens claimed that the threat of TVA public power was driving down the value of private power company stocks. To him the enactment was not an occasion for "wild-eyed enthusiasm," for, he warned, it would be many months before operations began, and even then public power was not likely to be much cheaper than that from private companies. Still later, after looking over the TVA's proposed rates, he concluded that it would be impossible for private power companies to compete, and he suggested that the government "acquire the property of power concerns" and permit the private concerns to "retire from the field."[22]

By the end of 1933 Sullens's opposition to the TVA and public power had hardened. He opposed the building of transmission lines into north Mississippi, saying that the farmers of the area could not afford electricity at any price. When the new power agency made preparations to buy property owned by private power companies in northeast Mississippi, Tennessee, and Alabama, Sullens dryly commented, "The impression is growing that the TVA is biting off more than it may be able to chew." When Dr. David Lilienthal, a director of the TVA, made a series of speeches which were critical of private power, Sullens immediately came to the defense of private ownership.[23]

Sullens opposed the TVA for many reasons, and he did not hesitate to state them vehemently and often. He claimed that the project was not worth the money it cost, that there was no market for its power, and that it would inevitably drive private power concerns out of business, thus injuring citizens who had invested their savings in the stocks of private companies. He maintained that public power was not as efficient as private power and that, though at first glance it appeared cheaper, it actually was more expensive because of the tax loss to the community.[24] Looking back on the program from a distance of several years, he called the "yardstick" principle, the provision by which the cost of TVA power served as a measuring device for all public utilities, "a myth and a hoax."[25] He observed that the TVA served only a small area of the country, while the project was subsidized by taxes from all the country's citizens. Moreover, the TVA had access to "cheap" government money, whereas private concerns had to borrow funds at market rates.[26] But Sullens stated his position most succinctly when he wrote that selling electricity was simply "not a government function."[27]

Through the remainder of 1934 and early 1935 Sullens returned repeatedly to attack the Tennessee Valley Authority. In fact, he carried on what could almost be called an editorial vendetta against the TVA. Calling it "the most serious mistake of the Roosevelt administration," he maintained that the entire project was a dangerous experiment which could soon collapse. He claimed that the program was a gigantic boondoggle, and he pointed out that the farmer-customers for TVA power could not afford electricity, much less the electrical appliances that it was supposed to make possible. He concluded that the "inefficiency, extravagance, and wastefulness of the TVA" would eventually form "one of the saddest chapters in American history." With a note of wishfulness he asserted that Roosevelt was "looking for an easy way out of the TVA power dilemma." Sullens's last hope was that the Tennessee Valley Authority Act would be voided by the United States Supreme Court, and he was greatly annoyed when the Court saw nothing unconstitutional in the act.[28]

As the New Deal passed on into 1934 and 1935 it became obvious that Sullens favored the lending agencies over what he would have called the "giveaway" agencies. He was especially complimentary toward the Home Owner's Loan Corporation, which was established to refinance mortgages

of homeowners who had suffered in the depression, and the Reconstruction
Finance Corporation, created by Herbert Hoover in 1932 in an effort to stimulate the economy and retained by Roosevelt as a part of the New Deal. The
efficient way in which these agencies operated clearly suited Sullens's idea
that governmental agencies should be solvent and businesslike. Although
he was sometimes critical of work relief projects like the Public Works
Administration and, after 1933, almost unwaveringly critical of direct relief,
he praised the RFC for not being a philanthropic institution, and for conduct-
ing its business on a sound basis. "Too bad," he lamented, "the same cannot be
said of other government agencies."[29]

Sullens's growing hostility to the entire New Deal by 1935 may be seen in
miniature in his opposition to unemployment insurance. He asserted that the
idea of compensation for the unemployed "emanated from the minds of a lot
of lousy loafers who don't want to work, who wouldn't work if the opportunity offered." "How long," he cried, "O lord, how long will it be until lawmakers
wake up to a realization of the fact that the tax burden is breaked on the backs
of industrious people who earn their living in the sweat of their faces and do
not owe a duty of any sort to the shiftless, thriftless idlers and incompetents."[30]

Thus, by the beginning of 1935 Sullens stood on the threshold of a retreat
from the New Deal. After the moderate economic revival of 1934–1935, he, like
so many middle class Americans, automatically began to revert to his long-
held conservative views of limited government and to view with suspicion the
increasing tempo of reform legislation which flowed from Washington.

Just before Congress convened in January 1935, Sullens loosed his bitter-
est blast at the New Deal up to that time. In a front-page editorial he warned
that the country faced a turning point in the year ahead. He listed all the
projects which demanded great sums of money, amounts unheard of a few
years before. He cautioned that Congress would shortly meet to "commence
the most gigantic attempt at treasury raiding in the history of nations." He
still refrained from a direct attack on Roosevelt, however, and he blamed this
unfortunate situation on the President's advisers. "Theorists and professors
constituting the Brain Trust," he wrote, "cling firmly to the idea that a nation
can spend its way out of depression and despair—something never before
done in human history." Angrily, he continued,

> From a sane and sober-minded point of view it is going to be a pitiable
> spectacle—powerful forces demanding the spending of more money, not
> knowing or caring a damn where it comes from, just so it offers opportuni-

ty to nearly everybody to live without working, or to have more abundant lives with a minimum of effort.

"The spending spree must stop," he cried. "Paying out good money to people for doing little or next to nothing isn't good business."[31]

By the middle of 1935 Sullens had doubts about almost every New Deal measure before Congress. He observed that there were questions as to the constitutionality of the Wagner Act, which he opposed, and social security, which he lukewarmly supported. Therefore, he advised, "Congress should adjourn for a few months and give the members a chance to get the fogs and mist out of their minds."[32]

In Sullens's mind the most serious problem arising out of the New Deal and the one most likely to wreck the entire program was the issue of government in business. He pointedly quoted the 1932 Democratic platform, which had favored "the removal of government from all fields of private enterprise," and he called on the President to live up to that pledge by removing federal authority from business and industry in all cases where it was possible.[33]

Time after time in 1935 Sullens returned to the theme "Get the federal government out of business." Calling it political, inefficient, destructive of morals, and dictatorial, he regarded governmental interference in private business as "one of the chief causes for the delayed recovery." He claimed that the effects of such a policy not only destroyed the businesses involved but created an atmosphere which filled the entire business world with uncertainty and fear. The American people, according to Sullens, wanted neither the "fantastic proposals of the extreme left" nor the "stand-pat chauvinism of the extreme right. What they need[ed] and crave[d]," he said, was "the traditional American system." But he failed to say what that was.[34]

Sullens was especially wary of the growing number of regulatory agencies which sprang up under the New Deal and which held, according to him, a death grip over American business. Not only were these agencies economically stifling, in his view, but they were beyond the pale of the Constitution. Consequently, when the Wheeler-Rayburn Bill (Public Utility Holding Company Act), which provided for federal regulation of some public utilities, was introduced, Sullens was furious. He feared the effect such a bill would have on the already shrunken market value of public utility stocks and bonds. He cried that the American people were "tired of rotten deals under the guise of the New Deal." He concluded by saying, "A man who won't fight for the money he has honestly earned, and invested in what he thought would yield him a modest return, is not very much of a man." Whether he was referring to himself he did not say. Still later he contended that the protection of utility companies from "governmental threats and unfair competition" would serve more successfully than anything else "to take men out of the bread lines and off the relief rolls." Such a course, he predicted, would bring "restored confidence, expanding credit, and restoration of faith"; it would "do more to restore real prosperity than can ever be accomplished by the government."[35]

Despite the rather bitter criticism that Sullens expressed during 1935, he was still a "good Democrat" who always backed the party at election time, and he was quick to respond to any Republican criticism of the New Deal. When former President Herbert Hoover called the New Deal a failure, Sullens hotly replied, "Perhaps the New Deal is not the handsome, happy, well-informed child we expected, but it is still infinitely better than any political abortion that would result from . . . the Republican party."[36]

Although his attacks on the New Deal became increasingly bitter in 1935–1936, Sullens continued to exempt FDR from his outbursts. He often hinted that all disagreeable portions of the President's program could be traced to Roosevelt's advisers. FDR, he noted, "would be a greater President if he possessed some of the coldbloodedness and keen discernment of Woodrow Wilson when dealing with his underlings." But he conceded that the President's mistakes were "errors of the head and not of the heart."[37] Perhaps Sullens was only getting in step for the Presidential election of 1936.

As a loyal Democrat Sullens naturally supported FDR in the campaign of 1936, though one could detect a certain lack of enthusiasm. In fact, before the first year of Roosevelt's second administration was over, Sullens was once again lambasting the New Deal. "Yes," he began, "we all voted cheerfully for the New Deal last November . . . but at that time we had no reason to believe that it would lead to so many surprise plays and absurdities under the guise of government." As more and more of his fellow Southerners became wary of the New Deal, Sullens detected a potential split developing within the Democratic Party. He observed that the Democratic Party was in a "damnably bad fix," and he warned that the party was in for "one helluva licking in 1940" unless the Democratic leaders returned to "sane principles of government."[38]

Sullens's renewed hostility stemmed from two measures before Congress in 1937 that he utterly opposed, the anti-lynching bill and the Fair Labor Standards Act. Most Southern leaders could hardly have viewed either proposal with more malevolence. The bill against lynching aimed at discouraging that bloody practice by imposing penalties on law enforcement authorities who allowed prisoners to fall into the hands of lynch mobs. The wages and hours law proposed a national minimum wage to be enforced by the federal government. Many Southerners viewed this as a Northern attempt to neutralize the Southern advantage of cheap industrial labor. The latter measure was supported by the President; the former was not. But Sullens made no such distinctions. "Mr. President," he explained, "your political nose will be out of joint . . . in Dixie just so long as you advocate that wage-hour bill and the anti-lynching measure." The South wanted neither measure, and the South, Sullens warned, was "still the stronghold of the true Democratic party." He not only warned of a possible party split over these measures, but he even foresaw the possibility of a third party movement in the South, a hint of rank heresy which would have been unthinkable to him a short time earlier. He viewed the anti-lynching bill as an effort by his party to attract Northern Negro voters, and, to Sullens, nothing could have been more inflammatory.[39]

For the wage-hour bill Sullens saw "utterly no excuse." He concluded that its passage would virtually "paralyze industry in the South and pour out a veritable cornucopia of industrial ills." But more important, he saw it as an effort by New England industrialists to discourage industry from moving South. When the United States Senate passed the bill, Sullens branded it "vicious" and "inexcusable" and predicted that it would mean the "death of the Democratic party." Noting that Mississippi's Senator Pat Harrison, one of his political favorites, had opposed the bill, Sullens concluded that Harrison, hitherto one of FDR's strongest supporters, had "parted company" with the President. The wage-hour law seemed to represent a turning point in Sullens' views of the New Deal. After its passage his criticism of the program was almost continuous. This was reflected in his comment that "thinking Mississippians . . . while still true to the cardinal principles of the Democratic party, are not willing to be led into the sort of communism that now seems to be running rampant in Washington."[40]

Perhaps the fight which drove Sullens over the brink, both in his criticism of the New Deal and in his increasing suspicion of the President, was the contest for the Senate majority leadership between Senator Pat Harrison of Mississippi and Senator Alben W. Barkley of Kentucky. In the mid-summer of 1937 Senate Majority Leader Joseph T. Robinson of Arkansas died. Harrison was the leading contender for the vacant post, but President Roosevelt threw his support to Barkley because of, as one authority asserts, Harrison's "ill-concealed conservatism." With the President's support Barkley was elected.[41] Although Sullens professed to harbor no ill will toward Roosevelt because of his support of Barkley, he nevertheless missed few opportunities to criticize the leadership of Senator Barkley, and it was only after this event that Sullens began to strike directly at Roosevelt himself. The fact that Harrison's defeat indeed rankled was shown when FDR offered a new tax program calling for an undistributed profits tax and a capital gains tax, both of which Sullens opposed. He gleefully noted that Harrison could now repay the President's betrayal by using his position as chairman of the Senate Finance Committee to block Roosevelt's tax program.[42]

Thus, in late 1937 and early 1938, Sullens no longer exempted Roosevelt from his criticisms. He called the President "over-ambitious" and accused him of "pig-headedness." As Roosevelt began to exhibit more antipathy toward "Big Business," Sullens claimed that the abuses attributed to business by the President existed "largely in his imagination." He berated Roosevelt for "castigating business and industry," and he pointed out that these two bulwarks of the economy were "more important than any President who ever held office." Finally, he accused the President of wrecking his second administration by refusing to listen to advice.[43]

In the late summer of 1937, just as the nation seemed on the highroad to recovery, the national economy again plummeted. This renewed recession was all the more bitter for being so unexpected. By that time Sullens had come full circle in his views of the New Deal. In 1932–1933 his answer for the nation's economic ills was retrenchment. That also was his solution for the recession of 1937–1938. Indeed, he believed that the sole cause of the new economic dip was the anti-business temper of the New Deal. According to him the nation's businessmen were holding back because

> Business and industry fear that the government cannot go on forever paying out more money than it takes in. Business and industry fear that we cannot spend our way back to prosperity. Business and industry fear that the . . . wage-hour bill means more economic paralysis. Business and industry fear that continued prodigious spending for relief . . . is undermining the morale of the people and making a nation of mendicants.

Sullens's cure was:

> Stop . . . all avoidable spending and balance the budget. Do not attempt further artificial stimulation of business. Keep government out of competition with private business. Protect the rights and property of United

States citizens. Drop, for the present at least, all promotion of legislation attempting to regulate, control or reform business.[44]

Thus Sullens's rejection of the New Deal and his philosophical break with its exponents was complete by 1938. Once more a thoroughgoing conservative, he had returned in 1938 from the unfamiliar, uncharted, and, for him, uncomfortable waters on which he had set out in 1933. It may have been that he realized that the depression, despite the relapse of 1937–1938, was running out. As the danger passed, he perhaps viewed the activism of the New Dealers as unnecessary. Certainly vigorous and enthusiastic government was foreign to his nature. Perhaps a clue to his real sentiments toward the New Deal may be found in an editorial which he wrote early in 1939. "The New Dealers have an idea when they say that America ought to be re-made and that they have set about the task of re-making it," he wrote. "It is not that so much against which we contend. Rather it is against the hurry and the panicky speediness with which they propose to do everything over and to bring us out at short length into a newly cast commonwealth."[45]

## Notes

1. Frederick Sullens served as editor and part owner of the Jackson, Mississippi, *Daily News* from 1907 to his death in 1957. A colorful journalist and lifelong Democrat who was intensely interested in politics, Sullens spoke out on most of the important issues in American history during the first half of the twentieth century, and he mirrored the Southern conservative viewpoint on most issues. Throughout his career the fiery editor was Mississippi's most widely read journalist. His views of the New Deal seem to reflect with almost textbook exactness the attitudes of most Southern conservative leaders.

2. William Leuchtenberg, *Franklin D. Roosevelt and the New Deal: 1932–1940* (New York: Harper & Row, 1963), 26–27.

3. Frank Freidel, *F.D.R. and the South* (Baton Rouge: Louisiana State University Press, 1965), 36.

4. Jackson *Daily News*, January 30, 1936.

5. Ibid., January 21, 22, May 11, 17, 1933.

6. Arthur M. Schlesinger, Jr., *The Age of Roosevelt: The Coming of the New Deal* (Boston: Houghton-Mifflin, 1958), 21; Jackson *Daily News*, September 17, 1933.

7. Jackson *Daily News*, April 14, 27, 1933.

8. Ibid., May 12, 21, October 20, 1933.

9. Ibid., August 10, 12, 1933.

10. Ibid., July 5, 1935.

11. Ibid., February 22, June 18, 1933.

12. Ibid., August 28, 1934.

13. Ibid., April 5, 1933.

14. Schlesinger, *Coming of the New Deal*, 94.

15. Jackson *Daily News*, May 27, June 13, July 1, 1933.

16. Ibid., July 16, September 14, 1933.

17. Ibid., November 9, 15, 1933.

18. Ibid., May 28, 30, 1935.

19. Ibid., May 23, June 16, 1933.

20. Ibid., June 28, July 8, 9, 1933.

21. Ibid., January 23, 1933.

22. Ibid., May 18, 22, June 20, September 18, 1933.

23. Ibid., December 26, 1933, January 6, May 9, 1934.

24. Ibid., June 6, December 19, 1934.

25. Ibid., January 11, 1938.

26. Ibid., August 22, 1954.

27. Ibid., June 10, 1934.

28. Ibid., October 22, November 17, 29, 1934, January 1, 1935, February 19, 1936.

29. Ibid., July 24, 1934, November 22, 1935.

30. Ibid., January 27, 1935.

31. Ibid., January 1, 13, 1935.

32. Ibid., July 11, 1935.

33. Ibid., August 14, October 1, 1934.

34. Ibid., January 6, 16, March 17, 1935.

35. Ibid., April 9, 10, November 30, 1935.

36. Ibid., March 25, 1935.

37. Ibid., January 28, June 23, 1935.

38. Ibid., August 2, September 1, 26, 1937.

39. Ibid., September 24, 1937, January 14, 19, 1938.

40. Ibid., July 25, 26, August 1, 1937.

41. Freidel, *F.D.R. and the South*, 52.

42. Jackson *Daily News*, December 2, 1937, April 8, 1938.

43. Ibid., November 13, 1937, January 4, 5, February 6, 1938.

44. Ibid., January 6, February 10, April 24, 1938.

45. Ibid., February 11, 1939.

# Some Mississippi Views of American Federalism, 1817–1900

WILLIAM H. HATCHER

It may well be that America's most singular contribution to the world of political theory and practice is the federal system. The *e pluribus unum* which is stamped on our coins symbolizes the national aspiration, if not always the practice, of "one out of many." It is notable that the American federal system has served as a model (not necessarily in every detail) for other decentralized political systems,[1] but these later federal systems have enjoyed the good fortune of having profited from Americans making most of the major mistakes in the process of developing a scheme that enjoys both the advantages of local self government and unity.[2] They, at least, have been able, perhaps as a result of our experience, to avoid the catastrophe of disunion and civil war, which resulted, in part, from the inability of Americans in the antebellum period to agree on an umpire for the federal system. One of the very few lessons learned from the Civil War, with regard to the nature of federalism, is that secession is not to be tolerated. The idea that the Constitution is a contract entered into by the states acting as sovereign entities is still abroad in the land.

Throughout the history of the United States, both before and after the Civil War, Americans have seldom agreed on the precise nature of the federalism they have created. The task of locating exactly the division between the powers of the national government on the one hand and the states on the other has been a difficult one at best and an impossible one at worst. And yet, if it has been difficult to locate with precision the dividing line between national and state authority, it has, to the contrary, been easy to locate the division of opinion on the subject. Beginning as early as the Constitutional Convention in 1787 and continuing throughout the history of the nation, the best minds (and less than the best) have been employed to discover the formula which

*Southern Quarterly* 6.1 (1967): 117–41.

will reveal the true nature of the federal scheme. Hamilton and Jefferson, Webster and Calhoun, and Lincoln and Davis are but a few of the earlier authorities who addressed themselves to this task of deciphering the code of federalism. Even those who seem at first glance to be in agreement because they have taken either the nationalist side or the states' rights side are usually in disagreement on particulars.

This article does not propose to examine all of the theories of federalism that have been advanced from 1787 to the present, as this is too much of a task for so short an article. Moreover, this has been done by authorities far more capable than this writer.[3] What is planned, instead, is a brief examination of the way some Mississippi political figures have viewed the federal system with the goal of ascertaining a phase of political thought—essentially constitutional thought—that has been present in the state from 1817 to the turn of the century. Before this can be done, however, a brief account of the national debates on the subject should be presented to supply a back-drop before which the Mississippi concepts of federalism may more clearly and more meaningfully be exhibited.

Discussions about the nature of the American federal system began in earnest at the Constitutional Convention.[4] That the Framers of the Constitution, however, failed to agree fully on the nature of federalism and thus failed to create a Constitution that clearly enunciates the precise nature of the American Union is evident from the fact that once the Constitution was ratified and put into force there immediately arose a division of opinion, not only among public figures generally, but also among the drafters of the document, as to the division of authority between the nation and the states. Also left unsettled by the Convention was the question of what agency was to decide when either the national or state authority over-stepped its constitutional bounds and prescribe the appropriate remedy for the infraction.[5] It was not until years later that the Supreme Court was generally seen to be that agent. Virginia, especially, in the early years of the republic, bitterly fought the contention that the Supreme Court was the final arbiter of federal-state power.

Bitter arguments over the nature of the federal system arise, of course, in periods of political crisis in the United States. The enactment of the Alien and Sedition Acts in 1798 by the Federalist-controlled Congress created the first notable crisis in which the nature of American federalism was brought into question, and resulted in a strong states' rights stand by Thomas Jefferson and James Madison. Jefferson in the Kentucky Resolutions of 1798 asserted that the states were the agents for determining when the federal "compact," from which the national government derives its authority, is violated and which measure should be taken to redress the wrong. He suggested "nullification" in the Kentucky Resolutions of 1799 as a legitimate response of the states to an unconstitutional enactment of Congress. Madison in the Virginia Resolutions of 1798 assumed also that the states are sovereign and that the Constitution is a "compact," and that the states can constitutionally "interpose" their authority to protect the people of the states. It is notable, however, that neither author suggested that citizens of a state were free to disobey the federal acts, unconstitutional though they may be.[6]

Even more noteworthy is the fact that the Kentucky and Virginia Resolutions did not, as was hoped by their authors, entice other state legislatures to pass similar resolutions. Indeed, those states that did respond condemned the states' rights position, arguing, among other things, that the federal courts, especially the Unites States Supreme Court, and not the states, were the appropriate agents to determine when Congress has exceeded its constitutional authority.

The same Federalist Party that objected so strenuously to the positions taken by Jefferson and Madison in the Kentucky and Virginia Resolutions reversed its field when, among other things, the Republican Party passed the Embargo Acts, and called up the state militias to serve in the War of 1812, a most unpopular war in New England. Late in 1814 on the invitation of the legislature of Massachusetts, Federalist delegates from northeastern states met at Hartford, Connecticut, and proclaimed that the states were the appropriate judges of when the Constitution has been violated and that the state may, indeed must, "interpose" its authority for the protection of the people of the state. Threats of secession, the ultimate weapon in the arsenal of states' rights, could be heard in the citadel of Federalism in these early years of the nineteenth century. In a few years, however, New England's sons would once again deny the legitimacy of such a states' rights position.

It was not only the South and New England that uttered states' rights sentiments in those early years. The state of Pennsylvania refused to abide by a decision of the Supreme Court of the United States ordering it to turn over certain prize monies from the Revolutionary War era to one Gideon Olmstead until the United States confronted the commonwealth with a force of some 2,000 men in *posse comitatus*. Indeed, Pennsylvania had threatened violence against the agents of the United States before she was forced to comply with the federal court order. This is the same Pennsylvania that condemned the Kentucky and Virginia Resolutions a few years before. To further demonstrate that consistency is not one of the virtues of Americans on questions of federalism, when the Pennsylvania legislature called for an amendment to the United States Constitution to create an impartial tribunal to settle disputes like this, the legislature of Virginia responded that the Constitution already provided for such a tribunal, the Supreme Court of the United States! Only a few years later this same Virginia legislature bitterly protested the exercise of this power when it affected her prerogatives.

In the famous *Cohens v. Virginia* case, decided by the Supreme Court of the United States in 1821, Chief Justice John Marshall affirmed the right of his Court to review decisions of state courts as prescribed by the Judiciary Act of 1789. Leading Virginians, however, including the very able Judge Spencer Roane, chief justice of Virginia's highest tribunal, disputed the right, asserting the Judiciary Act to be contrary to the Constitution of the United States. Marshall, as he had done in previous cases, denied that the states were totally sovereign, saying that for some purposes, at least, the United States is sovereign.

Although the states' rights position had at one time or another, prior to the Civil War, been taken by virtually all of the states of the Union, it became a virtual monopoly of the South from the late 1820s until the close of the Civil War. Becoming increasingly a minority in the nation's policy-making councils, the South with greater and greater determination adhered to the position that Jefferson had enunciated in 1798, and indeed, assumed a far more extreme position in time. The position of the South as the slavery issue became more heated grew so extreme that the nationalists in the South, represented largely by the Whig Party, were forced to change over to the states' rights position or remain silent.

Jefferson had merely mentioned nullification in 1799, but it was South Carolina, and not Kentucky, that first exercised this extreme states' right power. Although it was the upper South that championed the cause of states' rights in the late eighteenth century and in the early 1820s, it was the deep South that took up the cudgels in the late 1820s and early 1830s. Moreover, the South Carolinians carried the issue farther and reacted more radically than had their Virginia brethren a generation earlier. In fact, it is quite doubtful if Jefferson and Madison actually wanted the states to nullify the Alien and Sedition Acts or to take any physical or even legal action to "interpose" the states' authority; but South Carolina's ablest son, John C. Calhoun, and the state legislature called for nullification of the Tariff Acts of 1828 and 1832. A convention was called in the state and nullification accomplished in the latter year. Moreover, Calhoun formulated a theory of state secession which was to be implemented by his state in 1860.

The slavery controversy, of course, gave rise to the most vehement claims on the one hand for states' rights, including the right of secession, and on the other for national supremacy. By and large, however, no new theories on the nature of the federal system were offered after 1850. Interestingly enough, most of the arguments were quite logical and consistent, given the premise from which they were drawn. For example, the states' rights position, whatever the variations in detail, was based on the assumption (neither proved nor disproved, and probably impossible of either) that the Constitution was a compact among sovereign states and that the states (or the people of the states) retain sovereignty despite the substantial grant of powers to the national government. Moreover, the states, and not a national agency, were the appropriate judges of an infraction of the compact and were the proper instrument to propose and effect a remedy, whether it be interposition, nullification, or secession. Likewise, the nationalist argument, as expounded by Chief Justice John Marshall, Daniel Webster, or Associate Justice Joseph Story, makes sense if the basic premise is accepted. The nationalists asserted that the Constitution was not a compact entered into by the states, but was instead the creation of the American people as a whole. Because the national government, a creature of the Constitution, was not the creation of the sovereign states, its competency under the Constitution was not subject to the judgment of the states.

It is notable that following the Civil War and the defeat of Southern states' righters the victors did not successfully raise the banner of national sovereignty. Indeed, the tendency following the War was to continue with the concept of divided sovereignty, a concept as old as the Constitution itself. The doctrine of dual federalism,[7] a version of divided sovereignty, which was expressed by the Supreme Court of the United States in the Taney era (1835–1864) continued throughout the nineteenth century and well into the twentieth. The Supreme Court in *Texas v. White*,[8] for instance, referred to the federal system as an indestructible union of indestructible states. The doctrine of secession, the extreme position of antebellum states' righters, was, on the other hand, dropped. There was general agreement, however, that the

Supreme Court of the United States was the final arbiter of disputes over the nature of the federal system, something which the early states' rights advocates, of course, denied.

The doctrine of dual federalism served the new and powerful business interests which arose to preeminence following the Civil War. The states, being the first political entities that attempted to cope with the problems of a new industrial regime, were thwarted by a Supreme Court convinced of the efficacy of Social Darwinism. Relying on the Fourteenth Amendment, which was designed to protect the Negro, the Supreme Court sanctioned its use to protect big business. But when the Congress of the United States entered, of necessity, into the realm of economic regulation the doctrine of dual federalism was invoked frequently to deny such authority. Only with the great depression of the 1930s was this doctrine to expire. During this era (1865–1936) those who supported states' rights doctrines, then, were not necessarily nor wholly Southerners, but businessmen who realized that state regulation was to be preferred to national regulation—if regulation there must be. The doctrine of dual federalism is seen at its zenith in the controversial case, *Hammer v. Dagenhart* (1918), in which the Court concluded that Congress's power over interstate commerce was limited by the Tenth Amendment.[9] As the Democratic Party, by and large, became the party of change and reform, advocating greater and greater use of national political power to effect the change; and the Republican Party, by and large, became the party resisting change, one is confronted with the paradox: the party of Jefferson espousing a doctrine of national supremacy and the party of Lincoln (Lincoln had argued for an organic view of the American union) championing states' rights.

Drawing on its commercial powers, a Democratically controlled Congress had attempted to prohibit transportation into interstate commerce goods made by child labor, but the Supreme Court concluded that the statute invaded the reserved powers of the states. This doctrine of dual federalism is also found in such Supreme Court decisions as *A. L. A. Schecter Poultry Corporation v. Unites States*,[10] *Carter v. Carter Coal Company*,[11] and *United States v. Butler*.[12] The end of the doctrine, however, was in sight by 1936, for in the years following, the Supreme Court abandoned the idea that the powers reserved to the states place limitations on the powers delegated to Congress. Indeed, in 1941 the Supreme Court expressly rejected this states' rights doctrine.[13]

If the Supreme Court abandoned states' rights by the end of the 1930s the South, of course, had not, for with the rise of the movement to extend the rights of Negroes in education, transportation, housing, and voting, among other things, the South, particularly, revived the old arguments and asserted the old doctrines once again. Coupled with a substantial segment of the business community which finds states' rights a congenial doctrine to ward off (or make the attempt, at least) what they consider excessive congressional regulation of their affairs, states' rights is far from defunct. Once again, it is heard that the Constitution is a compact among the states and that the Supreme Court of the United States is not (or at least should not be) the final arbiter of national-state relations. To a remarkable extent it is a revival of the states' rights arguments of the antebellum period with one significant difference: no serious contention is made that a state has the right to secede.

Such, then, in brief compass is the outline of states' rights as it has appeared in the political literature of the United States. It is deeply engrained in the national character, and is probably inevitable in a nation of such geographic dimensions, diversity of interests, and vagueness of constitutional provisions pertaining to the division of powers between the nation and states and the relationships that are supposed to exist among the various parts of the federal system.

It is, of course, only when vital interests are threatened (or seem to be threatened) that the states' rights response is most protracted and intense. The Alien and Sedition Acts of 1798, the opposition of New England to Jefferson's Embargo and to "Mr. Madison's War," the resistance of Pennsylvania and Virginia to national judicial power, the tariff acts of 1828 and 1832, the slavery issues of the antebellum era, reform legislation of the twentieth century, especially the New Deal, and the race issues of the post–World War II years have all provoked a states' rights response. The relatively extended era of tranquility between the Civil War and the New Deal can be explained by the fact that the states' righters of the South were too busy engaged in the fundamental business of survival in the years immediately following the Civil War to contest too vigorously the relative nationalism of the victors. Moreover, the victors were not particularly eager to alter the federal system in any great measure,[14] particularly as it was in the interest of Northern business to retain a states' rights position on many issues. Also, from 1875 to 1945, the North left the Negro problem largely to the South. It is not surprising, therefore, that little is to be found of a states' rights character in the protest literature of the nation in the period 1865–1933.

Mississippi, of course, was a territory when the earliest theories of states' rights were introduced in the political literature of the United States, and therefore no reaction is to be found, or to be expected, to the Alien and Sedition Acts or to the struggle between the national government and New England in the administrations of Jefferson and Madison or to the contest between the federal judiciary and Virginia in Monroe's administration.

With no pretense that the following will constitute a comprehensive account of Mississippi's views on federalism, it will, nonetheless, present the views of a number of prominent Mississippi figures in the nineteenth century. Selection is based on the desire to get representative views in that era of the state's history, and, of course, on the availability of materials for the study.

One of the most interesting Mississippians in the early period of the state's history was Benjamin L. C. Wailes (1797–1861) who moved with his family to the state from his native Georgia in 1807. Settling at Washington, the territorial capital of Mississippi, Wailes early came to appreciate the importance of the national government, particularly the agencies of that government located there.[15] Probably typical of the intelligent and educated men of means of the state in its infancy, Wailes did not direct his attention to the society in which he lived. Something of a naturalist, he studied the flora and fauna of Mississippi, and like most of his neighbors did not engage in the early states' rights debates in the United States. This is because, as his biographer explains,

> The men of the region were not yet interested in studying their own social order, and lacking this interest they could not think of their own civilization as peculiar. Possibly the civilization of the region was too young to be self-conscious.[16]

It is hardly surprising, then, that Mississippians took little part in the early debates on states' rights, and gave that position little support even as late as 1832 when South Carolina nullified the tariff measures. Indeed, the official reaction of Mississippi was to oppose nullification at that time.[17] Moreover, Natchez became an area of strong Whig sentiment and was not, by and large, a producer of states' righters. Wailes, for example, remained a unionist throughout his life, even as late as 1860 when most Mississippians were secessionists. Being of the river county aristocracy Wailes did not succumb to the democratic fever of the interior of the state which by the 1820s had become thoroughly Jacksonian, that peculiar blend of states' rights and nationalism. It is illustrative that the capital of the state was removed from the whiggish river country in the west to the interior—and named Jackson.

Although Wailes came to be more and more conscious of the distinctiveness of Southern civilization, particularly from his frequent trips to the North, and he undoubtedly favored the South over the North, he had no general hostility for the latter region. He took, for example, great personal interest in the nation's capital, having what his biographer calls "an almost possessive attitude toward the capital of the United States."[18]

Wailes's opposition to secession is revealed in a July 1860 entry in his diary in which he criticizes a fellow Mississippian's attitude on the presidential election of 1860. His neighbor was, according to Wailes, a Breckenridge enthusiast, and "bitter against the North and utterly unreasonable and *frantic* in his denunciations: is for breaking up the Union and seems rather to desire the election of Lincoln to bring about that result."[19] Wailes refused to become a Democrat even after the Whig Party disappeared, a casualty of the sectional conflict. He regarded Democrats as being far too sectional in nature, but saw Republicans as being even more so; he thus remained a Whig long after that term had any real political significance. To the end of his life he refused to succumb to Southern nationalism, preferring, as mentioned above, to regard Washington, D.C., as his capital. This is explained, in part, by the fact that the Whig counties lost power to the interior of the state, leaving the Natchez area more or less politically impotent. The aristocrats of the Natchez area, largely powerless politically, tended to withdraw from politics altogether.

Another Whig who did not become a states' righter in antebellum Mississippi was the "Whig Orator of the Old South," Seargent S. Prentiss. A native of Maine, Prentiss came to Mississippi in 1827 after graduating from Bowdoin College. Settling at Natchez, the youth, barely nineteen years old, taught school for a while and then studied law in the office of Robert J. Walker, passing the bar examination in June 1829. In time he would become one of the most famous orators and lawyers (and one of the wealthiest) in the Old South.

A staunch and life-long Whig, Prentiss campaigned vigorously in the national presidential campaigns of 1840, 1844, and 1848 for the Whig candidates. In 1840, perhaps in part as a result, Mississippi voted Whig by almost 3,000 votes.[20] All of the river counties, the seat of the old aristocracy, gave the Whig candidate a majority, a phenomenon that continued, at least in the older river counties, in the elections of 1844 and 1848 also.[21]

A great admirer of Henry Clay, the all-but-perennial Whig candidate for President in the 1820s, 1830s, and 1840s, Prentiss campaigned in 1844 for that candidate in Mississippi, New Orleans, New York, Boston, Connecticut, Maine, and Pennsylvania. He criticized the Democrats for the destruction of the Bank of the United States, for bond repudiation in Mississippi, and spoke in favor of the protective tariff. On the latter issue he attempted to convince Mississippians that a protective policy would benefit the cotton planter and insure the continued prosperity of slave labor. He contended that a protective tariff was needed to guarantee continued demand for Southern cotton in New England mills. On the question of slavery he told his audiences that in the South, sensitive as he knew they were to abolitionist attacks from the North, that they need not worry unduly, for their peculiar institution was amply protected by the United States Constitution.[22]

Always a unionist, Prentiss in one of his many speeches in New Orleans, this one in 1845, said,

> We cannot do with less than the whole Union; to us it admits of no division. . . . Accursed, then, be the hand put forth to loosen the golden cords of Union; thrice accursed the traitorous lips, whether of Northern fanatic or Southern Demagogue, which shall propose its severance.[23]

Prentiss always drew large crowds at such events, and had many supporters, particularly among river county newspapers and fellow Whigs. One of the most brilliant orators of all time, he could hold an audience spellbound for two or even three hours. He died at the age of forty-two in July 1850, a victim of the increasingly bitter sectional controversy, debts, and overindulgence. His unionism, of course, would have been put to an even severer test had he lived another decade; and he may have followed Benjamin L. C. Wailes into political impotency if he had survived.

If Wailes and Prentiss represent the nationalist viewpoint in Mississippi in the antebellum period, John A. Quitman and Jefferson Davis represent the states' rights position. Of the two, the more extreme in his sentiments was the former, and indeed, probably the most ardent states' righter in antebellum Mississippi. Unlike Davis, who never held an elective office in the state, Quitman was twice governor of the state, state chancellor, and state legislator, in addition to being elected to Congress twice. Born in New York in 1799, he moved to Mississippi in 1821, settling at Natchez, and becoming in time a wealthy land and slave owner. A lawyer by profession, he was elected to the state legislature in 1827, and spent much of the rest of his life in public office. He died in July 1858, just two and one-half years prior to the secession of his adopted state, a goal which he had sought for Mississippi and the South for about a decade.

Quitman was a states' righter long before that position was popular in Mississippi. Expressing an anti-tariff sentiment in a letter to J. F. H. Claiborne, dated July 31, 1831, he said, "If Mr. Van Buren is a decided tariff and internal-improvement man, I have no notion of smoothing his road to the presidency by a compromising course of policy."[24] He favored nullification in 1832, and in the years following became progressively more states' rights oriented, "standing squarely," as he put it, "upon the doctrines of the Virginia and Kentucky resolutions of 1798–99."[25] Calling himself a "State-rights Democrat of the strictest school,"[26] he favored John C. Calhoun for President in 1832, and organized a "State Right association" in Adams County, presiding over its monthly meetings.[27] That these sentiments did not endear him to many Mississippians is a conclusion reached by his biographer who maintains that in this "he stood almost alone in Mississippi."[28]

In time, however, Quitman's states' rights posture became quite popular in the state. Returning home from the Mexican War, a hero and a Major General, he was elected governor in 1849, receiving 59 percent of the vote cast.[29] Undoubtedly acting in his favor was the Mississippi reaction to the Wilmot Proviso of 1846, for this strengthened the position of states' righters throughout the South. In his inaugural address Quitman emphasized his opposition to the abolitionists' attacks on the South and warned that their activities would cause "ultimate destruction of our domestic institutions, or the destruction of the Union."[30]

On Quitman's urging the Mississippi legislature sent delegates to the Nashville Convention, which met in 1850 and opposed Clay's compromise measures (California admitted to the Union as a free state, New Mexico organized as a territory without restriction on slavery, etc.) as well as congressional interference with slavery in the territories. Quitman opposed admitting California as a free state, favoring instead the extension of the Missouri Compromise line to the Pacific Ocean.[31] Also in that fateful year, 1850, Governor Quitman called a special session of the legislature before which he condemned the Compromise of 1850, and recommended secession unless the South's grievances were met. He even went so far as to suggest that committees of public safety, reminiscent of pre–Revolutionary War years, be established in each of the Southern states to map policy for future Southern action.

Mississippi may not have been ready as yet, however, for the extreme states' rights stand that Quitman took, for he withdrew from the race for governor in 1851 in the face of Union Party strength, and in his place the States Rights Democrats named Jefferson Davis, who lost by 999 votes.[32] In the early 1850s only South Carolina of the Southern states seemed to favor a program of secession, and for this and other reasons Quitman's position was undercut.

He was not long out of favor, however, for the Union Party weakened, and the former governor was elected to Congress in 1855. His views remained the same, for in Congress he expressed his states' rights views, blaming the North for the sectional controversy. To him, as was true of states' righters generally, the states are sovereign and not the American people in the mass, and certainly not the national government; indeed, he saw the national government as a mere agent of the states. Moreover, he argued in Congress that there was no middle ground between "concession or compromise"; and in his last House speech he was as unbending as ever, refusing to concede a point on the troublesome Kansas question. At this stage (1857) he preferred a showdown with the North, and though this would come shortly Quitman was not around to see it, for he died in 1858.

One Mississippian who did live to witness and participate in this "showdown" was Jefferson Davis, another states' righter, but not as uncompromising as Quitman. Born in Kentucky in 1808, Jefferson Davis settled in Warren County, Mississippi, in 1836, having spent only eight of his twenty-eight years in his adopted state to that time. Jefferson's father was a devout Jeffersonian, and during the nullification crisis of 1832 young Jefferson, a graduate of West Point and in the military service at the time, threatened to resign his commission rather than to take part in any move to enforce the tariff laws in South Carolina, as President Jackson threatened to do. Davis took this position despite the fact that he did not approve of nullification as a method of states' rights action.

After election to Congress in 1845, his first political office, Davis was appointed to the United States Senate in 1847, having returned from the Mexican War a hero. This was the Senate of Daniel Webster, Henry Clay, and John C. Calhoun, and in which Davis rose rapidly to prominence. The slavery issue— more specifically, the issue of the extension of the institution into the newly acquired territories—was a raging one in Congress in the late 1840s. Davis joined Calhoun and other Southerners in criticizing the spirit of the Wilmot Proviso which would deny legalizing slavery in the area taken from Mexico. His position was that the Constitution of the United States protected property everywhere in the United States, and as slaves were property, they could be taken into such areas, at least south of the Missouri Compromise line.[33] He argued in the Senate that the South needed more slave states to check the "sectional aggression of the North."[34] He had in mind, among other things, the Northern-supported tariff legislation.

Referring to the United States as a "Confederacy," Davis asserted, "My first allegiance is to the State of which I am a citizen, and to which my affection and association I am personally bound. . . ."[35] According to one of his most recent biographers, states' rights to Davis was something like a religion, and although this is probably true, it was not unusual in the 1850s, for both states' righters and nationalists were probably more emotional than rational on the issues of the day. Like many of his Southern brethren, Davis saw political liberty disappearing as the political power of the South declined in Washington. In answer to an attack on slavery by Senator Hale of Vermont, Davis asserted,

> We, sir, are parties to the Union only under the Constitution, and there is no power known in the world that could dictate to my little State a Union in which her rights were continually trampled upon by an unrestrained majority. . . .[36]

Davis's views on states' rights in this antebellum period were not identical with those of some of his Southern compatriots. He, for example, did not attend the Nashville Convention of 1850 at which a number of "fire eaters," such as Robert B. Rhett of South Carolina and William L. Yancey of Alabama, urged secession of the Southern states. Although he believed in the legitimacy of secession, and supported it when all else failed in 1860, he refused to place his stamp of approval on nullification of federal laws constitutionally adopted.[37]

Elected to the Senate for a six-year term in 1850, Davis resigned in a short time to run against Henry Stuart Foote for Governor of Mississippi and lost. He campaigned for Franklin Pierce in the Presidential campaign of 1852, and was rewarded with the post of Secretary of War, an office he filled with great distinction, and was returned to the Senate by the Mississippi Legislature in 1857. He was pleased with the Dred Scott decision of that year, and favored the acquisition of Cuba to bolster the slave power. Indeed, as was true of a number of Southern expansionists, he wanted the United States to include all the territory from the Canadian border to the Isthmus of Panama.

Davis in the United States Senate vigorously defended the position of the Southern states in the years immediately before secession and Civil War. During the debate over "Bleeding Kansas," for example, he asked Northern senators if any Southern senator had ever threatened the interests of the North, and commented, "We are on the defensive. How far are you going to push us? ..."[38] In a speech in Boston in 1858 he reminded the citizens of Massachusetts that theirs was a heritage of states' rights, saying,

> If I were selecting a place where the advocate of strict construction of the Constitution, the asserter of democratic state rights doctrine, should go for his text, I would send him into the collection of your Historical Association. ...[39]

In the heated politics of the presidential election of 1860, so fateful to the Union, Davis did not favor Stephen A. Douglas of Illinois because of the views of that champion of "popular sovereignty" on federal protection of slave property in the territories. He did not attend the convention of the Democratic Party which met at Charleston, but he did support Breckenridge, the choice of the Southern Democracy. However, he tried up to the end to avoid secession, even going so far as to ask Douglas, Bell, and Breckenridge to withdraw from the presidential race if a compromise candidate could be found. Bell and Breckenridge agreed but Douglas refused.

Davis's views on states' rights remained the same throughout the balance of his life, despite the fact that the failure of the Confederacy was due, in part, to the theory and practice of states' rights.[40] His view might be summed up in his own words spoken in the Senate just prior to secession: "... I love and venerate the Union of these States—but I love liberty and Mississippi more...."[41]

The most famous Mississippian whose public life spans the Civil War is Lucius Q. C. Lamar, for he held national office both before and after that conflict. Congressman, Senator, Cabinet member, and Associate Justice of the Supreme Court of the United States, he is undoubtedly one of Mississippi's most distinguished sons. Born in Georgia in September 1825, he moved to Mississippi in 1849 after graduating from Emory College. In 1850 he was admitted to the Mississippi Bar, and after serving for a short time as professor at the University of Mississippi, and after a brief sojourn in his native Georgia, he returned to Mississippi to stay in 1855. He was elected to Congress from Mississippi in 1857 and reelected in 1859. He participated in the slavery debates then going on rather heatedly in Washington, taking, quite naturally, the South's part, although he was not a "fire eater."[42]

Although in Congress he stated his position as, "I am no disunionist, *per se*,"[43] he walked out with the rest of the Mississippi delegation at the

Charleston Convention of the Democratic Party, was elected to the secession convention which met in Jackson in January 1861, and drafted Mississippi's ordinance of secession. He participated in the Civil War both as a Confederate diplomat and as an officer in a Mississippi regiment in Virginia. In 1864 he was appointed Judge Advocate of the military court in the Third Army Corps, and was at Appomattox when Lee surrendered.

Returning to Oxford, Mississippi, after the War, Lamar resumed his duties as a professor at the University, only to resign in 1869 when the institution became "radicalized." He did not return to public life for some time after the War, but when he did he was to advocate a policy of reunion and reconciliation with the North. In a speech at the University in 1866 he went so far as to pronounce states' rights as dead.[44] One of his biographers calls him the "first truly reconstructed statesman either North or South, to become the leading exponent of fraternalism between the sections."[45] Another biographer sums up his views on federalism at this stage of his career as follows: "To him it became clear as the sun that the one great want of the South was a great national aspiration nationally recognized."[46] He had his opportunity to express to a national audience this view, when on being elected to Congress in 1872 he delivered his celebrated eulogy on one of the South's greatest enemies, Senator Charles Sumner. From the eulogy the following expresses his postwar nationalism:

> Bound to each other by a common constitution, destined to live together under a common government, forming unitedly but a single member of the great family of nations, shall we not now at last endeavor to grow *toward* each other once more in heart, as we are already indissolubly linked to each other in fortunes?"[47]

Biographer Mayes assesses the eulogy rather optimistically as follows:

> The turning point of Mr. Lamar's political career was the Sumner eulogy. Indeed, that great speech is believed by his admirers and friends to have been the death blow to sectional animosity, and by consequence the turning point of our *post bellum* national history.[48]

Commenting on a portion of his career in the House of Representatives, Mayes says, "Mr. Lamar's whole course in the Forty-third Congress was concentrated on one thought: reunion and reconciliation."[49] Nonetheless, when he felt the vital interests of his state and section threatened he rose to the occasion; for example, when he successfully opposed the Force Bill in 1875.[50]

Lamar was elected by the Mississippi Legislature in 1876 to the United States Senate, the first ex-Confederate to be so elected, and he was reelected in 1882. Indicative of his independent spirit and concept of the role of the people's representative, he refused to be "instructed" by the Mississippi Legislature on the "Silver Bill" in the Senate. A staunch conservative on money matters, he was opposed to the "cheap money" bill and, despite the sentiment in Mississippi for the bill and the "instructions" of the legislature, he voted against it. This was prior to this reelection, and thus apparently did not alienate too many Mississippians. He was severely criticized by Jefferson Davis for violating his "instructions," and this hurt Lamar, for he had little but admiration for the ex-President of the Confederacy.

Lamar supported Cleveland for President in 1882, as did most all Mississippians, and was named Secretary of the Interior in 1883. Then when a vacancy occurred in the United States Supreme Court President Cleveland sent his name to the Senate for confirmation. Although there was considerable opposition to this appointment, the Senate by a vote of thirty-two to twenty-eight confirmed his appointment in January 1888. Lamar served with distinction on the Court until his death in 1893. Although he had had no previous judicial experience, Lamar was a lawyer, and had taught law at the University of Mississippi.

As is true in any period in American history, a number of cases came before the Supreme Court dealing with federal-state relations during Justice Lamar's tenure, and his general position was to support the claims of the states. For example, he seems not to have fallen victim to the doctrine of Social Darwinism which held, by and large, that any regulation, by states or the national government, of business affairs is contrary to "due process of law," a position a majority of the Court would take by about 1890. Indeed, Lamar dissented in the important case, *Chicago Milwaukee and St. Paul Railway Co. v. Minnesota* (1890)[51] in which the majority held that a Minnesota rate-fixing statute was violative of the due process clause of the Fourteenth Amendment. Lamar concurred with Justice Bradley's dissent which pointed out that the majority opinion practically reversed *Munn v. Illinois*,[52] a case decided in 1877 which upheld the right of states to regulate public utilities, including the right to fix maximum rates they could charge the public. Bradley pointed out that the regulation of railroad rates and other public utilities "is a legislative prerogative and not a judicial one."[53] Justice Lamar voted with the majority in *Budd v. New York* (1892),[54] which upheld the right of a state to set maximum prices to be charged by grain elevators. In *Kidd v. Pearson* (1888)[55] Lamar delivered the opinion of the Court upholding the right of a state to outlaw manufacture of intoxicants, despite its alleged violation of the commerce clause of the Constitution of the United States. This decision was used to buttress the Court's opinion in the famous sugar trust case[56] in 1895, a decision that can hardly be termed nationalistic. On the other hand, Lamar was not doctrinaire on the question of states' rights while he was on the bench, for in *Minnesota v. Barber*,[57] decided in 1890, he took a pro-commerce clause stance in the face of a state law discriminatory in nature.[58]

It was in the famous *Neagle* case of 1890 that Justice Lamar dissented vigorously, however, when the majority took a stand he felt to be quite outside the competence of the Court. This case, *In re Neagle*,[59] is one of the most interesting and dramatic ones in the history of the Supreme Court, and will require a bit of narrative before Lamar's dissent can be fully understood. The story (not the case) begins with the western migration of one Stephen J. Field from New England to California in 1849, where in 1857 he was appointed to that state's Supreme Court. The Chief Justice of the Supreme Court of California was one David S. Terry, a popular Californian who will figure prominently in the case years later. President Lincoln in 1863 appointed Field to the Supreme Court of the United States, and as was the practice in the nineteenth century, the justice would spend his summers assisting in holding various federal courts in his adopted state. One of the cases that came before him one summer in the late 1880s was *Sharon v. Hill*, involving a wealthy Nevadian and one Sarah Althea Hill, a Western damsel with an opportunistic nature. She alleged that she had in her possession a declaration of marriage signed by Sharon, and when their affair soured, she asked for a divorce and a share in Sharon's considerable holdings. Sharon sued in Field's court in San Francisco to have the paper surrendered and declared invalid on the grounds that it was forged. Field decided in Sharon's favor, but before the remedy could be effected Sharon died, and as executor his son asked the court to carry out the decree to surrender the forged document. Once again (in 1888) Justice Field decided in Sharon's favor, and in the meantime, Miss Hill had married David Terry, the former Chief Justice of the California Supreme Court. When the decision in the case was rendered Mrs. Terry made quite a scene, and when Justice Field directed the deputy United States Marshal (Neagle) to remove her from the court-room, her lawyer (Terry) drew a bowie knife and threatened anyone who touched his wife. Both Terry and his wife were jailed for six months for contempt of court.

Justice Field returned to Washington shortly thereafter to participate in the regular session of the United States Supreme Court, and soon official Washington got wind of rather serious threats the Terrys were making on the life of Justice Field should he ever return to California. Disturbed, the Attorney General of the United States appointed the deputy United States Marshal (Neagle) as Field's personal bodyguard while performing his circuit duties in California. Disregarding the advice of friends and colleagues that he postpone his return to California for a year (which would have been quite legal) Field returned to California the next summer. One day in a railway restaurant where Field and Neagle were dining the Terrys approached the Justice from the rear and Terry proceeded to assault Field with blows to the head. Neagle jumped to his feet and when Terry made a motion as if to go for his knife, the bodyguard shot and killed him. Mrs. Terry immediately tried to enlist a lynch mob to hang both Field and Neagle, but fortunately the sheriff saved both of them by arresting them and putting them in jail. Field was immediately released, but Neagle was held, charged with murder.

The question before the Supreme Court of the United States where the case was carried on appeal was the legitimacy of the writ of habeas corpus. The federal habeas corpus statute provided for the release of a person held in custody "for an act done or omitted in pursuance of a law of the United States."[60] Neagle's problem was that he could point to no specific "law of the United States." He was appointed Field's bodyguard by the Attorney General of the United States who had no specific constitutional or statutory authority to do so. All Neagle could do was to argue that the "law" was inferable from the Constitution of the United States, as he could cite no United States statute authorizing his appointment. The majority of the Supreme Court justices agreed with Neagle, for Justice Miller, speaking for the Court, said,

> In the view we take of the Constitution of the United States, any obligation fairly and properly inferrible [sic] from that instrument, or any duty of the marshal to be derived from the general scope of his duties under the laws of the United States, is a "law" within the meaning of this phrase.[61]

In his dissent, with which Chief Justice Fuller concurred, Lamar in a rather clear and carefully worded opinion denied that there is a "law" validating the issuance of the writ of habeas corpus, saying,

... we think that there was nothing whatever in fact of an official character in the transaction, whatever may have been the appellee's view of his alleged official duties and powers; and, therefore, we think that the courts of the United States have in the present state of our legislation no jurisdiction whatever in the premises, and that the appellee should have been remanded to the custody of the sheriff.[62]

Justice Lamar, of course was not saying in effect to Neagle that he was guilty of murder; he was merely stating that because Congress had passed no law authorizing the appointment of Neagle as Field's bodyguard, that Neagle was acting in no official capacity, and like any private citizen in a similar situation was amenable to the state laws. He felt that Neagle would receive a fair trial in California.[63]

It would be fairly easy to charge Justice Lamar with possessing a states' rights prejudice, and that this prejudice compelled him to decide against Neagle. This would be unfair, however, for Chief Justice Fuller agreed with him, and the Chief Justice was not a states' righter. Furthermore, Lamar agreed in his dissent that Congress did have the authority to pass a law providing for the protection of federal public officials. Moreover, Lamar's position on American federalism in 1890 was not that of Calhoun, and probably not even that of Lamar in 1861. It will be recalled that in 1866 he pronounced states' rights as dead. In all probability, Lamar in the postwar period had accepted neither the old doctrinaire position of states' rights nor the organic theory of the American Union that Lincoln and some postbellum writers espoused. His position seems to be somewhere between these two extremes, and a quote from his dissent in the Neagle case sounds very much like the position taken by most of the Framers of the Constitution:

[I do not question] the general proposition, that the federal government established by the Constitution is absolutely sovereign over every foot of soil, and over every person, within the national territory, within the sphere of action assigned to it; ... .[64]

This sounds very much like divided sovereignty rather than state sovereignty, which usually accompanied the doctrinaire view of states' rights.

Thus, Mississippi closed out the nineteenth century with a rich heritage of theories of federalism, ranging from the nationalism of Wailes and Prentiss to the states' rights of Quitman and Davis. Lamar seems to occupy a position somewhere between nationalism and states' rights; or to put it more realistically, Lamar was a states' righter—albeit more cautious than the extremist Quitman—before the War, and became, because of his desire to effect reunion and reconciliation, a mild nationalist after the War. In his most significant statement on the subject in the postbellum era, Lamar, now an Associate Justice of the Supreme Court of the United States, did not propound a doctrine of state sovereignty, as had been done by the antebellum states' rights advocates, but took his stand on "divided sovereignty." Thus, Lamar, more successfully than Davis, made the transition from antebellum states' rights to a postwar position that was probably more in the mainstream of American thinking in the last decades of the nineteenth century—neither a position of extreme nationalism nor a position of extreme states' rights.

## Notes

1. Canada, perhaps, is the outstanding example. It is true, however, that Canadian federation, accomplished just one hundred years ago this year, was initially modeled more along the lines of Hamiltonian federalism than Jeffersonian.
2. K. C. Wheare in his *Federal Government* (New York, 1964), 4–5, defines the American federal system as one in which there exists the principle of the "general and the regional governments being co-ordinate and independent in their respective spheres."
3. The latest and best is Walter H. Bennett's *American Theories of Federalism* (University, Alabama, 1964) on which I have relied for much of the material in the initial pages of this article.
4. A most interesting account of the confusion that surrounds the use of the term "federal" is Martin Diamond's "What the Framers Meant by Federalism," in Robert A. Goldwin (ed.), *A Nation of States* (Chicago, 1961), 24–41.
5. It is interesting, in view of the trend toward a more centralized federal system throughout most of our history, that the author of Federalist no. 45 feared state usurpation of national powers more than he feared national usurpation of state powers.
6. Bennett, *Federalism*, 93.
7. The term, "dual federalism," has been employed by the late Professor Edward S. Corwin as an appropriate label for the theory that the reserved powers of the states limit the delegated powers of Congress.
8. 7 Wall. 700 (1869).
9. 247 U.S. 251.
10. 295 U.S. 495 (1935).
11. 298 U.S. 238 (1936).

12. 297 U.S. 1 (1936).

13. *United States v. Darby Lumber Co.*, 312 U.S. 100: 123–24.

14. I have in mind here particularly a number of United States Supreme Court decisions, such as the *Civil Rights Cases*, 109 U.S. 3 (1883) and the *Slaughterhouse Cases*, 16 Wall. 36 (1873), among others, in which the Court stopped short of interpreting the Fourteenth Amendment as substantially altering the existing federalism.

15. Charles S. Sydnor, *A Gentleman of the Old Natchez Region, Benjamin L. C. Wailes* (Durham, NC, 1938), 43.

16. Ibid., 131.

17. Charles S. Sydnor, *The Development of Southern Sectionalism, 1819–1848* (Baton Rouge, 1948), 219.

18. Sydnor, *Wailes*, 284.

19. Ibid., 285.

20. Dallas C. Dickey, *Seargent S. Prentiss: Whig Orator of the Old South* (Baton Rouge, 1946), 195.

21. Arthur C. Cole, *The Whig Party in the South* (Washington, 1913), maps in the appendix.

22. Dickey, *Prentiss*, 261–62.

23. Quoted in ibid., 297.

24. J. F. H. Claiborne, *Life and Correspondence of John A. Quitman* (New York, 1860), I, 108.

25. John E. Gonzales, "John Anthony Quitman in the United States House of Representatives, 1855–1858," *Southern Quarterly* 4 (April 1966): 282.

26. Ibid., 277.

27. Claiborne, *Quitman*, I, 111.

28. Ibid., II, 277.

29. James H. McLendon, "John A Quitman, Fire-Eating Governor," *Journal of Mississippi History*, 15 (April 1953): 75.

30. Ibid., 80.

31. Ibid., 82.

32. Ibid., 88.

33. Hudson Strode, *Jefferson Davis, American Patriot, 1808–1861* (New York, 1955), 198.

34. Ibid., 215.

35. Ibid., 309.

36. Ibid., 217–18.

37. Ibid., 230.

38. Ibid., 300.

39. Ibid., 311.

40. See, for example, Robert McElroy, *Jefferson Davis: The Unreal and the Real* (New York and London, 1937), 675. On states' rights and the Confederacy, see Frank L. Owsley, *State Rights in the Confederacy* (Chicago, 1925).

41. Strode, *Davis*, 332–33.

42. Edward Mayes, *Lucius Q. C. Lamar: His Life, Times and Speeches* (Nashville, 1896), 80.

43. Ibid., 81.

44. Ibid., 157.

45. Wirt Armstead Cate, *Lucius Q. C. Lamar: Secession and Reunion* (Chapel Hill, 1935), vii.

46. Mayes, *Lamar*, 168.

47. Ibid., 187.

48. Ibid., 181.

49. Ibid., 229.

50. Ibid.,

51. 134 U.S. 418.

52. 94 U.S. 113.

53. 134 U.S. 418: 461.

54. 143 U.S. 517.

55. 128 U.S. 1.

56. *United States v. E. C. Knight Co.*, 156 U.S. 1 (1895).

57. 136 U.S. 313.

58. The Minnesota statute outlawed the sale of any meat not passed by Minnesota inspectors within twenty-four hours after being slaughtered, an obvious burden on interstate commerce.

59. 135 U.S. 1 (1890).

60. 135 U.S. 1.

61. 135 U.S. 1.

62. 135 U.S. 1.

63. This may or may not have been so, in view of the general excitement caused by the shooting, the popularity of the Terrys, and the nature of raw frontier justice.

64. 135 U.S. 1: 77.

PART II

# 1970s

# "Harmony with the Dead"

## James Dickey's Descent into the Underworld

DAVID C. BERRY

Rilke, in a sonnet to Orpheus, writes:

Does he belong here? No, out of both
realms his wide nature grew.
More knowing would he bend the willows' branches
who has experienced the willows' roots.[1]

Speaking of this poem, Walter A. Strauss says that "this is the doctrine of the double realm, life and death. Orpheus, as a result both of his descent and his dismemberment, is perfectly at home in both realms and unites them . . . His being-here and being-beyond are coextensive because the thread joining them has been restored. Everything now becomes explicable under the category of 'der klarste Bezug'—the clearest connections."[2]

Rilke, speaking further of this unity of life and death, says that "death is that *side of life* which is turned away from us and not illuminated by us: we must make the effort to muster the greatest consciousness of our being which is at home in *both of these un-differentiated domains nourished inexhaustibly by both* . . . Life's true form extends through *both* domains, the blood of the greatest circulation courses through both: *there is neither a Here nor a Beyond, but only the great unity*."[3]

James Dickey connects the world of the dead and the world of the living, but to say that he realizes a unity in them, each sharing an undifferentiated domain inexhaustibly nourished by the other, puts it too strongly. The category of "der klarste Bezug" is closer, for Dickey connects both worlds, and in doing so is usually renewed, nourished.

*Southern Quarterly* 12.3 (1974): 233–44.

"The decisive factor in appraising the nature of the modern Orphic," Strauss tells us, "is not so much in the magical mission of the poet, but in the account and interpretation of his experience as reflected in his poetry—the nature of his Orphic journey, that quest for a dark but 'pure' center. These journeys are made more poignant by the fact that the poets, in their own descent into Hades are directly conscious of their 'ancestor' and model, Orpheus."[4] Such is true in the case of Dickey, as a poem from his first collection, *Into the Stone*, indicates:

### Orpheus Before Hades

The leaf, down from the branch
Swirling, unfastened, falls;
Halfway from there to the ground
Is hypnotized, and stays.
No leaf is as still as that.
The earth-colored forest sways
*Whose leaf is the center of waiting.*

A great gray cloud lets fall
Its leaves, like the eyelids of fossils,
To a great stone skin on the ground.
I stand, in the frozen field,
In tow-sacks and burlap arrayed.
My breath disappears overhead
*And white is the center of waiting.*

The spring comes out of the ground.
A wood shades into the air.
Each bough is as light as a fern.
All of life comes in on a breath.
My eyes turn green with the silence
Of the thing that shall move from the hillside
*Where love is the center of waiting.*

My tongue is of cloth, and I sing,
As she would be singing, like water,
In a land where the cricket is flaking,

Yet chins, on the copper grassblade.
The sunlight is thinking of woman,
And black is the world, in its body,
*When flesh is the center of waiting.*

God add one string to my lyre,
That the snowflake and leaf-bud shall mingle
As the sun within moonlight is shining,
That the hillside be opened in heartbreak,
And the woman walk down, and be risen
From the place that she changes, each season,
*Her death, at the center of waiting.*

Orpheus in this poem serves as the Janus-face between the living and the dead, being at the center of both worlds, as the refrain of each stanza insists. Nature, in the poem, responds to Orpheus's impending descent by sharing with him the interface: a falling leaf is hypnotized at a point halfway in its plunge from the branch to the ground; snow is *"the center of waiting"* between the "great gray cloud" and "the great stone skin on the ground"; spring and flesh likewise are centers of waiting. Such a pattern follows the cycle of the seasons, in the order of fall, winter, spring, and summer. Orpheus is the center of this cycle, poised at the edge of time and eternity; he asks to be able to mingle "the snowflake and leaf-bud," to mix life and death. Laurence Lieberman is right in stating that connect is the central word in Dickey's *Falling*, as it has been up to that volume.[5] This opinion certainly holds in "Orpheus Before Hades," in which Orpheus is an archetypal symbol of man's desire for union of spirit with spirit.

Crunk points out that Dickey's imagination "seems to flower when he moves among the dead."[6] This "flowering" is found in two different relationships: the dead of Dickey's family, and the dead of World War II. When Dickey descends into the underworld, it is usually to connect with somebody.

The renewal aspect of communion with the dead is evident in one of Dickey's early poems, "The Sprinter's Mother."[7] While the poet is sprinting, his mother seems to rise over the threshold:

The strings of his teeth ache with her voice
Opening for him: the turn leans: she is rising
To touch the flowers: at his shoulder, a body, Half, a tinge . . .

Her cries are shyly balanced,
As if taken back to blood.
And, panting, blowing, he understands
How it is all proved, by childishness,
As she turns
Slowly into his face, not as a heelprint,
But as a held look he lets his breath
Gather to sustain, *and the world*
*Flowed together in a new way, trembles,*
*Comes back at him*, touches at his hair.[8]

"Poem" (*Into the Stone*), dealing with the continuity between Dickey's dead uncle and Dickey's son, describes the death of the uncle:

There were powerful strides in his sighing.
He rose. His body made a centaur of the bed.
With him, four-square,
Death stood on wooden legs. He swayed about in its form.
He looked for a way out of dying
Like a myth and a beast, conjoined.

In this poem the uncle is the Orphic figure at the interface of life and death; he is between the continuous time of myth and the ephemeral time of mortality, both united in one man. Here is Dickey's description of the uncle's death:

His last long breath, drawn up
All the way from the legs of the bed,
Like Apollo blew on my mind.
I felt the sun turn mortal in the air.
He fell from his fabulous mount.

Then Dickey becomes the connection between life and death, between the dead uncle and Dickey's son:

Thirty years, more slowly than cancer,
You fall from there, Uncle.
Upon my growing son,
Unfolding your face in his features.

In such a way the living and the dead share one space.

The thread of continuity is even more evident in "The String" (*Into the Stone*). Again Dickey is the agent connecting both worlds:

> It seems to me that the passing on of the technique of making tricks with string, from the dead through the living brother, who is now a father, to *his* boy, says something about the passing on of whatever one is privileged to pass on through the generations. And the fact that it's a string seemed to me to be indicative of something important and mysterious that passes between the generations, a kind of thread of continuity.
>
> So I wrote the poem and used the refrain, "Dead before I was born," as a death bell tolling . . . But the obsessive fact in the protagonist's mind is that he had a brother who died before he was born, and his way of communicating with his dead brother is to show string tricks to his own son.[9]

The poem itself is written in language as straightforward as this comment upon it, yet only in the poem does one feel the poignancy—without sentimentality—of the tricks, and this poignancy is best seen in a stanza in which Dickey employs two massive physical structures and an ancient philosopher to carry the weight of temporality that anyone in this world has to be aware of.

> The gaze of genius comes back.
> The rose-window of Chartres is in it,
> And Diogenes' lines upon sand,
> And the sun through the Brooklyn Bridge,
> And, caught in a web, the regard
> Of a skeletal, blood-sharing child
> *Dead before I was born.*

Like the brilliance of the window, the lines upon the sand, and the sun through the bridge, the "communication" is only momentary; but in being able to be passed on, it becomes a ritual, an act forever available, yet one never present except through ceremony.

Also found in *Into the Stone*, "The Underground Stream" is a poem in which Dickey tries to exorcize his memory of the dead brother. Dickey, in this case, tries to break the thread of continuity, which he so strongly feels. Lying near a well, he imagines his brother:

> The tall cadaver, who
> Either grew or did not grow,
> But smiled, with the smile of singing,
> Or a smile of incredible longing
> To rise through a circle of stone,
> Gazing up at a sky, alone
> Visible, at the top of a well,
> And seeking for years to deliver
> His mouth from the endless river
> Of my oil-on-the-water smile,
> And claim his own grave face
> That mine might live in its place.

Ironically, the dead brother has the smiling face, Dickey the grave one (*grave* as the face of one buried, *grave* as a description for solemnity); Dickey would have the roles reversed, himself with the smiling face, the dead brother with the grave. One reason Dickey had the *grave* face is that he suspected that the only reason he had been born was to replace this brother, Eugene, who at six years of age died of spinal meningitis.[10]

But *Drowning with Others* reflects the fact that Dickey was unsuccessful in breaking this continuity with the dead brother. In "In the Tree House at Night" the dead brother's spirit is felt so strongly that Dickey's sense of identification is threatened:

> I stir
> Within another's life. Whose life?
> Who is dead? Whose presence is living?
> When may I fall strangely to earth,
> Who am nailed to this branch by a spirit?
> Can two bodies make up a third?

The two bodies Dickey is referring to are his and that of his brother Tom; the spirit is Eugene, though Dickey does not make these identifications in the poem, where his question is "Who am I?" Once more this sharing of life with the dead provides an Orphic or energizing, nourishing effect:

> as my dead brother smiles
> And touches the tree at the root;

A shudder of joy runs up
The trunk; the needles tingle;
One bird uncontrollably cries.

In "Armor" (*Drowning with Others*) the reason Dickey dons the armored suit is because

There is no way of standing alone
More, or no way of being
More with the bound, shining dead.

And Dickey's reason for joining the dead is to look for the being he thinks that he was "in a life before life"—in the life of the brother Dickey feels he was born to replace. Having assumed his dead brother's *being*, he then hangs the armor in a glade and enters his "own life," where a "night nearer death" he breathes through his sides "like an insect," his closed hand lying like the dead. Again, as in "The Underground Stream," Dickey seeks to exorcize this brother's spirit in order to escape fulfilling his brother's role. He leaves the armor in the glade so that he "might be naked on earth"—have his own life. The problem he then confronts is that of wondering who he shall be when he dies. Such is the result of moving between two supposedly mutually exclusive worlds, the living and the dead. After this poem there are no others in which Dickey deals with the consummation of oneness he and his dead brother attained.

Considering now Dickey's connection with the war dead, he "contacts" his forefathers as a result of going underground in "Hunting Civil War Relics at Nimblewill Creek" (*Drowning with Others*). While his brother Tom moves the detector over the terrain, Dickey says that he feels underfoot

The dead regroup,
The burst metals all in place,
The battle lines be drawn
Anew to include us
In Nimblewill,
And I carry the shovel and pick
More as if they were
Bright weapons.

Dickey notices his brother Tom, who smiles

> as if
> He rose from the dead within
> Green Nimblewill
> And stood in his grandson's shape.

And what follows is that energizing, what Rilke calls nourishing, response:

> No shot from the buried war
> Shall kill me now ...

And he falls to his knees to work the pick,

> To go underground
> Still singing ...
> Without a sound,
> Like a man who renounces war,
> Or one who shall lift up the past,
> Not breathing "Father,"
> At Nimblewill,
> But saying, "Fathers! Fathers!"

Descent, contact with the inaccessible, celebration: the three Orphic themes are united in this poem.

In "The Island" (*Drowning with Others*) Dickey appears in the role of Rilke's Orpheus:

> A light come from my head
> Showed how to give birth to the dead
> That they might *nourish* me.[11]

Between Dickey and the dead soldiers there is an exchange:

> Each wooden body, I took
> In my arms, and singingly shook
> With its being, which stood for my own
> More and more, as I laid it down.

More than empathy is expressed, for there is a movement toward a fuller identity or fuller consciousness:

At the grave's crude, dazzling verge
My true self strained to emerge
From all they could not save
And did not know they could give.

After covering and currying the graves, Dickey says that "a painless joy" came
to him and that he

Kicked off his old fatigues,
Saluted the graves by their rank,
Paraded, lamented, and sank
Into the intelligent light,
And danced, unimagined and free.

As in "Hunting Civil War Relics at Nimblewill Creek," the themes of descent,
contact, and celebration are again united.

"A View of Fujiyama after the War" (*Drowning with Others*) is also life-
enhancing. The scene is deceptively peaceful:

It could be a country where no one
Ever has died but of love.

But we find that Dickey is there awaiting "someone to come from the dead
/ Other side of the war to this place." He waits, wondering if the dead man
should pass by if such a one could

know that to live at the heart
Of his saved, shaken life, is to stand
Overcome by the enemy's peace.

Not overcome by violence, which toppled the island in World War II, but
overcome by the peacefulness which has come to the island—at the interface
of violence and peace—Dickey pauses at the threshold of life and death as if
both were in adjacent rooms, separated only by a swinging door.

In "Horses and Prisoners" (*Helmets*) Dickey again fulfills the role of Rilke's
Orpheus, the role, according to Rilke, being that of

one of the staying messengers
who still holds far into the doors of the dead
bowls with fruits worthy of praise.[12]

"Horses and Prisoners" portrays harmony with the dead, renewal, and joy:

> my mind like a fence on fire,
> Went around those unknown men:
> Those who tore from the red, light bones
> The intensified meat of hunger
> And then lay down open-eyed
> In a raw, straining dream of new life.
> Joy entered the truth and flowed over
> As the wind rose out of the grass
>
> Leaping with red and white flowers:
> Joy in the bone-strewn infield
> Where clouds of barbed wire contained
> Men who ran in a vision of greenness,
> Sustained by the death of beasts,
> On the tips of the sensitive grass blades,
> Each footstep putting forth petals,
> Their bones light and strong as the wind.

The last two lines further reveal Dickey's relationship to Rilke's Orpheus:

> the dead . . . who invigorate the earth.
> What do we know of their share in this?
> It has long been their way to marrow the loam
> through and through with their free marrow.
>
> Are *they* the masters, who sleep with the roots,
> and grant to us out of their overflow
> this hybrid thing made of dumb strength and kisses?[13]

The petals in Dickey's poem, on flowers sprung up where the prisoners stepped before they died, incites Dickey's empathy not only with the prisoners but with their horses as well, for he felt his "long thighbones yearn / To leap with the trained, racing dead." To go down for Dickey is to go up; thus, we are not surprised to hear him say, as a result of this transformation, that

> When death moves close
> In the night, I think I can kill it.

He has been strengthened, which is what Rilke claimed was the effect of accepting both sides of life: the living and the dead.

Orpheus only sought contact with Eurydice. He did not wish to take her place, to share her consciousness. "Drinking from a Helmet" (*Helmets*) offers a variation of this theme, for in this poem consciousness is shared with the dead.

> On even the first day of death
> The dead cannot rise up,
> But their last thought hovers somewhere
> For whoever finds it.

Dickey finds this thought when he puts on the dead man's helmet, and again there is a sense of renewal, of defiance to death:

> In the brown half-life of my beard
> The hair stood up
> Like the awed hair lifting the back
> Of a dog that has eaten a swan.
> Now light like this
> Staring into my face
> Was the first thing around me at birth.
> Be *no more killed*, it said.[14]

And we hear Dickey say:

> Warmed water ran over my face.
> My last thought changed, and I knew
> I inherited one of the dead.

The thought he inherited was that of

> two boys facing each other,
> Quietly talking,
> Looking in at the gigantic redwoods,
>
> The smaller one curled catercornered
> In the handlebar basket.

Dickey says that he will return to the surviving brother and will inform him of what has transpired; from the dead to the living, Dickey is again the agent of continuity.

There are two war poems, however, in which Dickey is unable to descend into the realm of the dead. In "The Driver" (*Helmets*) Dickey tries to assume the consciousness of the soldier who once drove a now rusted and sunken halftrack. Dickey descends

> Ten feet under water . . .
> Getting used to the burning stare
> Of the wide-eyed dead after battle.

But having noted that he is alive beneath that "lyrical skin that lies / Between death and life, trembling always," he finds it impossible to be that dead driver, even though he has descended to his position:

> "I become pure spirit," I tried
> To say, in a bright smoke of bubbles,
> But I was becoming no more
> Than haunted.

Failing to become "spirit," he rises to the surface

> Very nearly too late, where another
> Leapt and could not break into
> His breath.

The other war poem in which Dickey is unable to make contact with the dead is "The Firebombing" (*Buckdancer's Choice*). In this poem Dickey has no feeling for those whom he killed in the war:

> My hat should crawl on my head
> In streetcars, thinking of it,
> The fat on my body should pale.

But he is without feeling, lacking even shame, able only to recall the aesthetic aspect of the killing. And it is not the killing for which he seeks absolution, but

this detachment,
The honored aesthetic evil,
The greatest sense of power in one's life,
That must be shed in bars, or by whatever
Means, by starvation
Visions in well-stocked pantries.

His failure is one of imagination, being

unable
To get down there or see
What really happened.

Again he is unable to descend:

It is that I can imagine
At the threshold nothing
With its ears crackling off
Like powdery leaves,
Nothing with children of ashes, nothing not
Amiable, gentle, well-meaning.

It is only for his own that Dickey can truly descend, for the members of his family and for his fellow soldiers; he cannot enter the realm of the deceased enemy.

When he descends into the realm of his dead family it is usually for the sake of continuity, as in "Poem" and "The String," though in this regard we see him descend in "The Underground Stream" and in "Armor" to break this thread of continuity. Though he rises nourished from such an encounter, it is not expressed with the intensity of the celebration we see in the war poems, where the descent is employed to renew his life and to salute death. Except in "Drinking from a Helmet" the theme of continuity is not as important as that of descending into the underworld and encountering those who dwell there. In the war poems exploration is enough. In encountering the dead Dickey seems to realize life most intensely. The way up, as Heraclitus tells us, is the way down; or as the Biblical paradox puts it: to find your *life* you must lose it: an Orphic configuration, which Dickey follows.

## Notes

1. Rainer Maria Rilke, *Sonnets to Orpheus*, trans. M. D. Herter (New York: Norton, 1942), 27.

2. Walter A. Strauss, *Descent and Return* (Cambridge: Harvard University Press, 1971), 186.

3. Strauss, 167, citing Rainer Maria Rilke, *Briefe II: 1914–1926*, trans. Walter A. Strauss (Wiesbaden: Insel-Verlag, 1950), 480–81.

4. Strauss, 10.

5. Laurence Lieberman, review of *Poems 1957–1967*, by James Dickey, *Hudson Review* 20 (August 1967): 514.

6. Crunk, review of *Drowning with Others*, by James Dickey, *The Sixties* 7 (Winter 1964): 42.

7. James Dickey, "The Sprinter's Mother," *Shenandoah* 6 (Spring 1955): 17–18.

8. (Italics mine).

9. James Dickey, *Self-Interviews* (New York: Dell, 1970), 89.

10. Ibid.

11. (Italics mine).

12. Rilke, *Sonnets to Orpheus*, 29.

13. Ibid., 43.

14. (Italics mine).

# Pat Harrison and the Social Security Act of 1935

MARTHA SWAIN

A s the chairman of the Senate Committee on Finance during the New Deal, Mississippi's Byron Patton (Pat) Harrison was the "shepherd" of many of the key measures of the decade. His work in securing the passage of the social security bill is particularly interesting because he drew upon the administrative talents and actuarial knowledge of a number of individuals including two natives of his home state, Murray W. Latimer and Leonard Calhoun. Moreover, an account of the adoption of this far-reaching piece of legislation is an excellent vehicle for demonstrating the managerial ability of a senator who spent a decade in promoting legislation that was always the work of his colleagues.

In June 1934, as the Seventy-third Congress approached adjournment, it heard a presidential message calling for action from the next Congress on a comprehensive program to further "the security of the citizen and his family through social insurance." Before that June had ended, Franklin D. Roosevelt created the Committee on Economic Security and directed it to study problems relating particularly to unemployment and old age and to draft recommendations for legislation. On January 17, 1935, Roosevelt submitted to Congress the work of the committee accompanied by a message endorsing its recommendations for old age annuities, unemployment insurance, and grants for maternity and children's services. He called for immediate legislative action. Given the honor of sponsoring the bill were Representative David J. Lewis of Maryland and Senator Robert Wagner of New York, the authors of an unemployment insurance bill that had died in the previous Congress. While there was some thought that the social security bill, as it came to be called, should be referred to a special committee, congressional leaders insisted that the measure should go to the Ways and Means Committee; in the Senate there was no opposition to its going to the Finance Committee.[1]

*Southern Quarterly* 15.1 (1976): 1–14.

Senator Harrison had expressed confidence in October of 1934 that an unemployment insurance bill would be passed by the next session of Congress. As events would prove, he was amenable as well to the additional protection against economic insecurity included in the administrative proposal. Apparently, he was not impressed by conservative criticism that the bill infringed upon traditional concepts of self-help and rugged individualism, nor was he susceptible to home-grown fears, later articulated by his friend Frederick Sullens, the editor of the *Jackson Daily News*, that "able-bodied Negroes [would] sit around in idleness on front galleries, supporting all their kinfolks on pensions, while cotton and corn crops are crying for workers to get them out of the grass."[2]

Harrison asserted immediately after Roosevelt's congressional message that economic security legislation "will be expedited as the President has asked." On the next day he held an extended conference with Edward F. McCrady, the Assistant Secretary of Labor, to set up machinery for Finance Committee hearings scheduled to begin on January 22 simultaneously with the Ways and Means Committee hearings.[3] The rare procedure of concurrent hearings was taken at the request of the administration in order to hasten passage of the bill. North Carolina's Robert L. ("Muley") Doughton, the chairman of the House committee, in a pique of jealousy over Harrison's initiative set his own committee's hearings to begin a day earlier in order, as columnist Raymond Clapper put it, "to win the toss for the kickoff."[4] While Edwin E. White, executive director of the Committee for Economic Security, schooled the representatives on the proposals, Senator Wagner appeared before the senators. He was followed by Secretary of Labor Frances Perkins and a battalion of social workers, actuarial experts, and labor economists who had worked in an advisory capacity in drafting the bill. Actually, it was not until February 20 that the Senate committee completed its public hearings.

The dialogue in the Senate hearings revealed that certain senators were reluctant to see an intrusion by the federal government into the social arenas that the bill encompassed. Clearly, Senator Harrison had his work cut out for him if he were to bring an unfettered social security program out of his committee. He was authorized to ascertain the reactions of forty-eight governors to the warnings of Virginia's Harry Flood Byrd, who claimed that federal funds would not be distributed for old age assistance and unemployment insurance without abhorrent federal regulations. But there was little question that the forty-four state legislatures scheduled to meet in 1935 stood ready to pass correlative state legislation. According to the *New York Times*, thirty-three governors had been mandated through their elections to support the President.[5]

Probably the best known witness to appear before the Finance Committee was the widely publicized Dr. Francis E. Townsend, whose own plan to end the poverty of the over-sixty age group consisted of monthly payments of $200 to be spent within thirty days. The monumental cost of such a steady rain of checks, estimated at twenty billion dollars, was to be met by a universal 2 percent sales tax on all transactions. On February 16 he faced a semicircle of hostile senators. The Mississippi senator refused to shake hands with Townsend for the benefit of photographers, angrily stating, "I don't want to advertise the Townsend plan." A week later Harrison, who knew of the widespread support enjoyed by the doctor, telephoned Secretary of the Treasury Henry Morgenthau and asked that a Treasury Department expert appear before the Finance Committee on the "'Old Man' Townsend stuff" and "just cut it to pieces." Morgenthau, who told Miss Perkins that his department was "not crazy about going up there on it," concluded that he would have to comply with Harrison's request; "He's a very difficult man to refuse because he's always been so friendly." Morgenthau realized that for use among constituency fans of the popular physician, Harrison and his committee wanted the weight of the Treasury Department thrown against the Townsend scheme. "You can send somebody who can demolish it in ten minutes," Miss Perkins told Morgenthau. Consequently the secretary sent a Treasury spokesman to the committee hearings.[6]

Sensing that the administration controlled the House committee, opponents of the bill concentrated their fire upon the Senate committee in the belief that the real testing was there. The senators, however, held other committee memberships that competed for their limited time to spend in hearings; thus by the time the parade of hostile witnesses came before the committee few members were present to hear their testimony. Absenteeism ran high and only Harrison sat through all of the hearings.[7]

Few representatives of employers appeared before the Finance Committee partly because business did not yet understand the bill. One of the most influential of the businessmen who did appear was Marion B. Folsom, assistant treasurer of Eastman Kodak Company and a member of the advisory committee that had assisted in drafting the bill. His favorable testimony was highly influential because he was able to make himself understood, a talent which few of the government witnesses possessed. After Folsom's testimony Harrison invited him into his private office and explained that the committee members were busy on several other bills and that he himself has little time to study the social security program. "We've had these actuaries; we've had Miss Perkins; we've had Senator Wagner—this, that and the other," the chairman explained, and "either we're dumb or they can't express themselves. We don't know what the hell they're talking about." Since Folsom was the first person who could "talk a language" the committee could understand, Harrison asked for his recommendations on amendments and scribbled them down on his personal copy of the bill. The senator later wanted Folsom to attend the executive sessions in an advisory capacity but decided it was best not to bring in outsiders. Frequent reference to his opinions, however, reflected Folsom's great influence on the legislative revision of the social security bill.[8]

Although the Finance Committee hearings ended in late February 1935, it was May before the committee went into executive session to consider amendments. Meanwhile, on April 5 the Ways and Means Committee reported out its version of the social security bill, and House debate ensued two weeks later. Unfamiliar with the complicated provisions of the bill, the representatives engaged in desultory debate and "talked chiefly to be on record as endorsing old age pensions."[9] Of the Mississippians in the House, Wall Doxey (Holly Springs), Dan McGehee (Meadville), John E. Rankin (Tupelo), and William Whittington (Greenwood) said nothing. Aubert C. Dunn of Meridian spoke only to offer a resolution endorsing old age pensions submitted by the Meridian Share-the-Wealth chapter. On the floor the administration bill weathered a storm of almost fifty amendments, including two proposed by Mississippians, both of which were shouted down. Sensitive to the state's financial limitations, William Colmer of Pascagoula had proposed that four-fifths of the $15 monthly payments for old age assistance be paid by the federal government, and Aaron Lane Ford of Ackerman proposed that $14.85 be paid from the Treasury with only $.15 contributed by a state. On April 19, in a striking administration victory, the House passed the social security bill by a vote of 372 to 33.[10]

Edwin Witte, characterized by one of the drafters of the bill as a "walking encyclopedia on welfare and social insurance matters,"[11] worked closely with Harrison in the executive sessions of the Finance Committee which ran for two weeks beginning on May 7. It was here that serious obstacles to the administration plan were to be anticipated, for several of the committeemen were known to be among the most conservative members of the Senate. To Harrison's "exceptionally able" management of the committee, Witte largely attributes the eventual discharge of a favorable report.[12]

To counteract the effect of the May 6 Supreme Court invalidation of the Railroad Retirement Act, Harrison had Justice Department representatives appear before his group to distinguish between the pension program of the doomed act and the fledgling social security bill. The chairman delayed the vote on the compulsory old age insurance title until after a speech by Witte; then when Harrison called for an immediate vote, every senator considered doubtful voted in the affirmative. When the Mississippian was uncertain how the vote would run on some motions, he postponed taking a count until later meetings; on the most controversial items he put off a vote until he was confident of passage. On the crucial last day, when a number of key votes were taken, Harrison held Michigan Senator James Couzens's proxy in his pocket and managed to win over the support of three senators whose votes had been in the doubtful column. In short, according to Witte, "with a less adroit chairman, the social security bill would probably have emerged from the Senate committee in a very unsatisfactory form, if indeed a favorable report could have been secured." Arthur Altmeyer, a member of the Committee on Economic Security and later a member and chairman of the Social Security Board, credits the Mississippi senator for "great skill and loyalty" in his conduct of the hearings and executive sessions.[13]

Another member of the inner group that worked with the Committee on Economic Security has added to Witte's account of Harrison's chairmanship. Dr. Joseph P. Harris recalls that Harrison was "a wonderful chairman" who was able to translate issues into a language which the committee could understand. Whenever the committee fell into a wrangle over a technical problem, Harrison would interject a "without objection, it will be so ordered," and proceed to the next item. The "railroad" technique worked because Harrison knew just when he had a majority support and could expedite the proceedings by cutting off diversionary discussion.[14]

The Finance Committee made important changes in its overhaul of the House bill. It eliminated the requirement that state old age pensions provide a "reasonable subsistence compatible with decency and health," a stipulation particularly obnoxious to those senators who saw within it the possibility of federal dictation of payments to racial minorities. In particular deference to Senator Byrd, the phrase was stricken. The Committee, in order to reduce ultimate costs, also insisted that recipients of old age insurance be required to cease work, and it authorized the sale of voluntary annuity insurance to those persons not covered by compulsory old age provisions, a plan which had been eliminated by the House. The voluntary annuity program was heatedly opposed by Augustine Lonergan, whose state of Connecticut was the home of many private insurance companies. (Harrison cast the deciding vote that restored the voluntary annuities but later acquiesced in their removal by Senate floor action.) The senators also lodged the Social Security Board in the Department of Labor although it had been designated an independent agency by the Ways and Means Committee. The senators were no more kindly disposed toward turning the administration of social security over to Miss Perkins than was the House, but the president urged its placement in the Department of Labor. As Witte put it, Harrison "felt rather edgewise" toward the woman secretary. In addition, the Finance Committee added a new title which called for annual allotments to states for aid to the permanently blind.[15]

Federal grants for maternal and child health services had created a furor within the American Medical Association and it adopted resolutions opposing the services and condemning government health insurance, a social service that had been dismissed by the Committee on Economic Security as unfeasible. Although Harrison's basic conservatism led to a common conclusion among his contemporaries that he personally opposed social security legislation, his own actions belie the charge. At one point his commitment to a program of economic security appeared to be so genuine that he attempted to include a catastrophic illness provision within the social security bill. He gained no support because the committee feared that such expanded services would be too expensive.[16]

Finally, on May 17, the committee reported out the social security bill without a recorded vote, but other legislation proceeded it on the Senate calendar. As was the case when the administration bills were under his wing, Harrison made national radio broadcasts, speaking first on "Old Age Pensions" and on the second night on "Unemployment Insurance." For the latter subject he spent a week arming himself with supportive evidence that social security was not unconstitutional. His particular emphasis in both statements to the public was that the programs were not emergency measures but rather enduring reforms which looked far into the future.[17]

It took five days for Harrison to get the social security bill through the Senate—a considerable length of time compared to most of the bills he handled. In the opening speech on June 14 he attempted to sidetrack opponents by anticipating criticisms before they could be offered. He asserted that the bill sought to alleviate the hazards of economic insecurity by encouraging state action, that the Justice Department had deemed the program constitutional, and that no private pension plan was as favorable as the pension program of the Wagner-Lewis bill.

Wagner and Finance Committee members Robert M. La Follette (Wisconsin), Alben Barkley (Kentucky), and Edward Costigan (Colorado) formed the "back-up team" for Harrison, but the persuasive comments of none of the five senators silenced Huey P. Long, who gave notice that he intended to lower the pension age from sixty-five to sixty and enlarge the benefits through his share-the-wealth tax plan. After an unusually cocky speech by the Louisiana "Kingfish," Arizona's Henry Fountain Ashurst, by all accounts the oratorical champion of the Senate, reduced Long to silence on June 15 and a Democratic crackdown on Long began. Harrison won an agreement to limit debate which thus thwarted any filibuster plans, and Long's five-billion-dollar wealth-sharing plan was defeated without a roll call on June 17.[18]

Bennett Clark, a formidable member of the Finance Committee from Missouri, sought an amendment to exempt industries with private pension plans from participating in the old age insurance program. When his proposal came up for debate on June 18, Harrison moved to defeat it. Although he initially favored Clark's idea, he found upon closer inspection that "there is more to it than might appear." The risk was too great, Harrison argued, that the Clark amendment would result in the discharge of older men and widespread company practices of taking out government insurance for older workers and private insurance for younger employees. Harrison also feared that the amendment would affect the constitutionality of the whole measure.[19]

Clark claimed that Harrison had relied solely upon the advice of Murray Latimer, a native Mississippian who had become a prominent actuary and chairman of the Railroad Retirement Board. According to Clark, Latimer opposed the amendment for the same reason that it was said that Charles Sumner did not believe in the Bible—"He didn't write it." The Missourian was annoyed, too, because Harrison had arranged for Leonard Calhoun, a Mississippian who had become the majority expert of the Finance Committee on social security; Thomas H. Eliot of Massachusetts, who had drafted the original bill; and Edwin Witte to sit near him on the floor of the Senate to offer information when technical questions arose. Again Wagner and La Follette offered supportive arguments for Harrison's position, but the Senate on June 19 adopted the Clark amendment by a vote of 51 to 35 shortly before the entire bill passed by a vote of 76 to 6.[20]

The designation of Utah's William H. King and Georgia's Walter F. George as conference committee colleagues of Harrison alarmed advocates of the bill, for the two were opposed to the old age insurance title. Frances Perkins was especially concerned because the Senate conferees were known to be wavering toward concessions to the House in its adamant stand that the Social Security Board be made an independent agency. The Clark amendment was the greatest bone of contention between the two houses, however, and when the conferees returned the bill to both houses for a test vote on the amendment, the House refused to accept it.

Doughton, one of the strongest opponents of the Clark amendment, agreed with the head of the American Federation of Labor William Green that any exemption of private company participation would fatally cripple the social insurance program. Green was greatly exercised that private pension plans were used as a "club" over workers to tie them to jobs and maintain low wages and long hours. Harrison agreed with Doughton, but the senator was committed to work for the Clark amendment as a product of the majority of his committee. He told the Senate that the conference committee met more than a dozen times and that the Senate conferees were altogether unable to win over Doughton's group to Clark's protection of private pension plans. On other than one amendment, the two houses were in agreement on the conference report, which included the removal of the Social Security Board from Miss Perkins' department.[21]

In the end, when the Senate conferees yielded to the House managers, Clark himself admitted that the senators had put forth a "devoted" and "single-minded" effort for his proposal. He was confident that the joint special committee appointed to study the question of private pension plans would arrive at an independent solution. In the final days before adjournment, August 8 and 9, the House and Senate adopted the conference report, neither house resorting to a roll call. On August 14 President Roosevelt signed the bill into law before a group of more than thirty people who had worked to secure its passage. When Harrison returned to the Senate floor after the rites, he told his colleagues: "This will prove one of the most beneficial pieces of legislation enacted by this administration. I am happy to have had a part."[22]

Participants in the 1930s and the latter-day historians agree that, while the Social Security Act was one of the "most revolutionary pieces of social legislation ever enacted by Congress" (the words of participant-historian Wilbur J. Cohen), the measure has major shortcomings.[23]

The first title, providing for matching federal funds for grants-in-aid up to $15 a month for old age assistance to needy persons over sixty-five years of age, basically permitted the dollar amount of the monthly payments to be determined by the states. Stripped of stipulations for "reasonable health and decency," the bill resulted in widely divergent and inadequate support. By September 1938, the old age assistance recipient in Mississippi received a monthly sum of $6.37; in California the amount was $32.39. The controversial and almost defeated Title II provided that those employees who were to be covered by the old age "retirement" insurance (and nearly one-half of the workers of the 1930s were not) must make compulsory contributions from their pay envelopes; on a matching basis employers were to be taxed on their payrolls. Both provisions by nature were deflationary. William E. Leuchtenburg states that the regressive taxes and the accumulated reserve of funds thus drawn from workers and employers "did untold economic mischief."[24] The recessions of 1937–1938, which came right at the time that the first deductions were made, would be laid partially to social security taxation. Furthermore, in the third significant program instituted by the act, the basic responsibility for unemployment insurance was relegated to the states, resulting in unequal and inadequate payments in the absence of national standards.

Yet, when viewed from the perspective of the Senate Finance Committee room and the Senate chamber, the social security program, with its inherent weaknesses of limited coverage, stingy benefits, state standard-setting, and regressive taxation, was as much as could be gotten in 1935. Neither the legislative nor the executive leadership was as naive or purposely negligent as the present-day critics may imply. Morgenthau and his aides knew that the taxes would divert income from consumption to savings, but the Treasury Department was committed to keeping a firm hand on the budget. Morgenthau's devotion was excelled only by conservative senators who would have killed a more expensive program. Roosevelt viewed the payroll contributions as a matter of political necessity. "With those taxes in there, no damn politician can ever scrap my social security program," he told Miss Perkins.[25]

Pat Harrison, along with other southern congressmen, knew that some states could contribute little toward assistance for the needy and temporarily unemployed, but he told the Senate that his committee had concluded that "in its present financial condition the Federal Government is going as far as it can go."[26] When he returned to Mississippi in the summer of 1935, he found that Governor Martin S. (Mike) Conner blamed him for the fact that the social security law called for state funding, compelling the governor to call the legislature into special session to consider appropriations. Conner had urged the Mississippi congressional delegation in January to recognize relief to the aged as a national problem to be met entirely through federal wealth taxes. To his constituents the senator again declared that Congress would have never approved a plan by which the federal government assumed the full financial burden.[27]

A few contemporaries of Harrison, who were bitterly disappointed by the limitations of the Social Security Act and who would have had a vastly enlarged federally financed social insurance program, tended to scoff at Harrison's efforts. One of them in particular, Abraham Epstein, a specialist in the social insurance field, characterized both Harrison and Doughton as conservatives who "found the entire subject unfamiliar, irksome, and its aims altogether contrary to their previous convictions." Such critics were unfair to Harrison. Thomas Eliot, who more than anyone else authored the bill, agreed that the Mississippi senator was not warmly committed to social welfare but he sensed that Harrison, as a loyal administration senator, was committed to producing the most feasible and respectable bill possible. Reminiscing two decades later about the passage of the social security bill, Eliot remembered the Mississippian as a "keen, industrious, and determined" chairman with whom he and Leonard Calhoun spent several summer evenings on Harrison's front porch instructing the conscientious senator on "every detail of every section" of the complicated and difficult bill.[28]

Harrison defended the Social Security Act of 1935 and said of it, "I know of no legislation since I have been in Congress, in whose passage I have taken a part, of which I am prouder of my part than this social security legislation."[29] Still he was aware of the wide range of criticism leveled at the act, and as early as 1936 he anticipated that certain weaknesses would be rectified, as indeed they were in 1939 when he directed a more liberal social security program through the Senate.

## Notes

1. *Congressional Record*, 73 Cong., 2nd Sess., 10769-71 (8 June 1934); Arthur J. Altmeyer, *The Formative Years of Social Security* (Madison: University of Wisconsin Press, 1962), 80. Frances Perkins remembered that Roosevelt once said that the measure was to be a Harrison-Doughton bill and curiously remarks that years later, "the President erroneously referred to the Social Security Act as the 'Wagner-Lewis bill.'" *The Roosevelt I Knew* (New York: Harper & Row, 1946), 296.
2. *New York Times*, 30 October 1934: 37; *Jackson* (Miss.) *Daily News*, 20 June 1935: 6.
3. *New York Times*, 18 January 1935: 1; 19 January 1935: 1.
4. *Washington Post*, 23 January 1935: 2.

5. *New York Times*, 1 February 1935: 28; 4 February 1935: 2.

6. *Washington Post*, 17 February 1935: 7; *Jackson Daily News*, 17 February 1935: 1; Henry Morgenthau Diary (Franklin D. Roosevelt Library, Hyde Park), Book 3, 412–19.

7. Witte, *Development of the Social Security Act*, 90–91.

8. Marion B. Folsom Memoir, Columbia Oral History Collection (COHC), 390–32; Witte, *Development of the Social Security Act*, 89. Folsom, who later became the Secretary of Health, Education, and Welfare, was a Georgia friend of Senator George. His Georgia origins pleased Harrison.

9. Abraham Epstein, *Insecurity: A Challenge to America*, 2nd rev. ed. (New York: Agathon, 1938), 744.

10. *Cong. Record*, 74 Cong., 1st Sess., 5027 (23 March 1935); 5970 (18 April 1935); *New York Times*, 19 April 1935: 1.

11. Thomas H. Eliot, "The Social Security Bill: 25 Years After," *Atlantic Monthly* (August 1960): 74.

12. Witte, *Development of the Social Security Act*, 95. Witte personally told his young assistant Wilbur J. Cohen that without Harrison's help the old age annuities (i.e., what is commonly called "social security") would not have been approved by the committee. Cohen to Felton M. Johnston, 18 April 1972, copy in possession of the author.

13. Witte, 103; Altmeyer, *Formative Years*, 30. See also the COHC memoir of J. Douglas Brown, 52–53.

14. Joseph P. Harris Memoir, COHC, 30.

15. Paul H. Douglas, *Social Security in the United States: An Analysis and Appraisal of the Federal Social Security Act* (New York: Greenwood, 1936), 110–12; Altmeyer, 40–41; Witte, 102.

    Harrison's coolness toward Miss Perkins stemmed in part from his initial treatment in her office when he went on her second day in office in 1933 to pay a courtesy call. The front office secretary took his name and then told him that when it was convenient she would notify Miss Perkins of his presence. After a twenty-minute wait, and still unannounced, he asked the secretary to tell the new Cabinet member of his call "when you get around to it." Then he left. Shocked when she learned of her secretary's treatment of the chairman of the Finance Committee, Miss Perkins asked Frank Blane to smooth things over with the senator. Harrison was only partially mollified. He told Blane that he understood Miss Perkins had not been responsible for her secretary's action, but he added, "You go back and tell Miss Perkins . . . I forgive her. You don't have to tell her this, but you could add that I ain't agoin to love her." Maurine Mulliner Memoir, COHC, 44–45. Blane was a native Virginian who had become director of the American Public Welfare Association.

16. Altmeyer, 33; Robert J. Myers Memoir, COHC, 92–93. Harrison's concern for public health was due to the influence of Dr. Felix J. Underwood, the state health officer of Mississippi, who had testified on behalf of the health care provisions of the bill before the Finance Committee. Dr. Underwood pointed out that Congress had pro-

tected cattle from screwworm, sheep from scabies, and hogs from cholera; hence "the citizen himself and his family certainly should have equal protection." *Hearings before the Finance Committee on the Economic Security Act*, 74 Cong., 1st Sess., 415.

17. *Washington Post*, 18 May 1935: 1; 31 May 1935: 4.

18. *Cong. Record*, 74 Cong., 1st Sess., 9267-173, 9283-94 (14 June 1935), 9367 (15 June 1935).

19. Ibid., 9521 (18 June 1935).

20. Ibid., 9631 (19 June 1935). Calhoun, 1921 graduate of Millsaps College, was a former law professor of the University of Virginia who did legislative liaison work for Harrison. According to Dr. Bernice Bernstein, another of Witte's assistants, Calhoun possessed a "sharp mind" and an effective approach. Pleading, "I'm a poor country boy [and] I don't know what this is really all about" in a southern drawl enabled him to find out how certain individuals actually stood on various issues. The information he garnered was relayed to Harrison who used it to determine appropriate strategies useful in getting around objections to legislative proposals. Bernstein Memoir, COHC, 95–96. Calhoun later became the Assistant General Counsel of the Social Security Board.

   Latimer graduated from Mississippi College in 1918 and was serving as a counsel with the Department of Labor in 1933–1935. He was the Chairman of the Railroad Retirement Board from 1934–1946.

21. Frances Perkins to Marvin McIntyre, 21 June 1935, Roosevelt Papers, Roosevelt Library, Hyde Park, Official File 121-A; Green to Doughton, 15 June 1935; Doughton to Green, 26 June 1935, Doughton Papers, University of North Carolina Library, Folders 493, 494; *Cong. Record*, 74 Cong., 1st Sess., 11309 (17 July, 1935).

22. *Cong. Record*, 74 Cong., 1st Sess., 12793 (9 August 1935); 13078 (14 August 1935).

23. Wilbure J. Cohen, "From Dream to Reality," *LithOpinion* (Amalgamated Lithographers of America), Fall 1970: 73; Paul K. Conkin, *The New Deal* (New York: Crowell, 1967), 60–62; Barton J. Bernstein, ed., *Towards a New Past: Dissenting Essays in American History* (New York: Pantheon, 1968), 274; Arthur Schlesinger, *The Coming of the New Deal* (Boston: Houghton-Mifflin, 1958), 313–14.

24. William F. E. Leuchtenberg, *Franklin D. Roosevelt and the New Deal, 1932–1940* (New York: Harper & Row, 1963), 132–33.

25. John M. Blum, *From the Morgenthau Diaries*, Vol. I; *Years of Crisis, 1928–1938* (Boston: Houghton Mifflin, 1959), 300. Roosevelt is quoted by Leuchtenburg, 133.

26. *Cong. Record*, 74 Cong., 1st Sess., 9440 (17 June 1935).

27. *Jackson Daily News*, 17 January 1935: 1; 28 September 1935: 1.

28. Epstein, *Insecurity*, 743; Eliot, "The Social Security Bill," 75.

29. *Jackson Daily News*, 28 September 1935: 1.

# The Southern Belle as an Antebellum Ideal

KATHRYN L. SEIDEL

When Margaret Mitchell tells the reader that "Scarlett O'Hara was not beautiful," but that "men seldom realized it when caught by her charm,"[1] she is continuing a long tradition in the physical description and personality of the Southern belle. A hundred years earlier in 1832, John Pendleton Kennedy described Bel Tracy, heroine of *Swallow Barn*, as "headlong and thoughtless, with quick impulses, that gave her the charm of agreeable expression, although her features are irregular, and would not stand a critical examination. Her skin is not altogether clear; her mouth is large, and her eyes of a dark gray hue."[2] Physically, Bel is a girl with whom any feminine reader can identify; she is not a born beauty but a beauty by virtue of her passionate and vigorous personality. The implied message of hope for even the unattractive reader is crucial, since the reading audience from 1820 to 1850 increasingly were women with leisure time for reading, and with interests in reading about the situation of women like themselves whose sphere was essentially the home and whose lives were occupied by love, marriage, and children.[3]

In fact, the literary portraits of the Southern belle in antebellum novels reflect several concerns and ideals of the social and literary milieu in which these novels were written. Bel Tracy, the first significant Southern belle in American fiction, has most of the attributes that are popularly associated with the belle figure. She is the daughter of a landed Virginia family who live in a great plantation home. She is motherless, young, and exuberant; she is a talented horsewoman and skilled in music. Proud of her aristocratic heritage, she has one flaw, "a vein of romance in her composition"; she desires not so much a man as a "gallant cavalier" of the kind who appears in the novels of Sir Walter Scott.[4] Sheltered by her father, she has no mother to instruct her as to what actually to expect from life. She is finally rescued from her fantasies by a stalwart lad, and the novel ends with their marriage.

---

*Southern Quarterly* 15.4 (1977): 387–401.

The milieu which produced such literary Southern belles as Bel Tracy developed from a number of social and literary factors, including Southerners' notions of the superiority of their way of life, the actualities of plantation life, and the literary convention of the sentimental novel, which gave rise to a new subgenre, the plantation novel. Southerners came to be, in their moral ideals, Victorians who reacted strongly against the corruption of their society. The Industrial Revolution appeared to have wrought more harm than good; materialism, greed, poverty, and prostitution seemed to be undermining human morality. The Victorian counter to the corruption of the materialistic, industrialized world was the home. During the first half of the nineteenth century in both England and the United States, the home was elevated to the status of a sacred refuge from the corrupt world; the home became the temple of civilization's most cherished values and virtues.[5] As Walter E. Houghton contends in *The Victorian Frame of Mind*, a woman's place was that of guardian of this sanctuary; her influence was meant to correct the sins of "Revolution, prostitution and Atheism."[6] The horror of the fallen woman, whether prostitute or unfaithful wife, that one sees in Victorian fiction and nonfiction results in part from a horror of the corruption in society that the fallen woman represented. As Houghton points out, pure, spiritual love was consequently "exalted as a corrective for two of the marriage evils of the time: prostitution and a marriage system dominated by the commercial spirit."[7]

The Victorian tendency to idealize home and its guardian, woman, was abetted in the southern United States by Southerners' belief that their civilization was superior to that of the North. Upperclass Southern landowners believed themselves to be descendants of English aristocracy, particularly the Cavaliers of the seventeenth century.[8] That the plantation owner and his family ruled legitimately was supported by "noble blood." That his sons and daughters were by analogy princes and princesses in their dominions was fitting.[9]

The psychological frame of mind of Southern men also contributed to the portrait of the belle in this period. After the exhilaration of the Revolutionary period, a sense of social decline seemed to afflict the South. Jeffersonian democracy flourished, rather than the more aristocratic notions of Hamilton which many Southerners would have preferred. William R. Taylor explains in *Cavalier and Yankee* that Southerners "grasped for symbols of stability in order to stem their feelings of drift and uncertainty and to quiet their uneasiness about the inequities within Southern society."[10] One such symbol was medieval feudalism which transformed Southern men from simply country squires into gallant knights. The immense popularity of Scott's novels is quite logical in this context. Another symbol of order was the home, which Southerners felt must be guarded against the chaotic and immoral forces of industrialization and of democratic change. The anxiety of the Southern gentlemen thus paralleled that of the Victorian in England, with the added incentive of an "aristocratic lineage" propelling him to the worship of the home.

The Southern belle as an ideal satisfied Victorian morality and the Southerners' need to find in home a persistent standard of order and decency. Southerners' notions of their aristocratic origins assured that the belle would be protected from reality, championed, and wooed in a manner befitting a princess. In addition, plantation life was well suited to the idealization of woman because of her necessary isolation from the "world." The young girl had few tasks other than to ride, be obedient, learn to sew, and perhaps learn to read and write. Unlike her brothers who attended prep schools and college, a girl was to stay home until such time as a suitable, that is lucrative, marriage was arranged for her. If she were pretty and charming and thus could participate in the process of husband-getting, so much the better. Because of the demands of plantation life, however, the career of the carefree belle was short-lived after marriage. Suddenly a girl was expected to become a chaste matron, an overseer of the plantation, a nurse, and a mother.

Plantation life in the South engendered an entire subgenre of the novel which embodies many of the values of Southern life and in which the first literary Southern belles appear. These novels resemble the popular domestic novels of the day in that they concern the lives of young women whose goal is marriage and of wives whose interests are the home and children. But the plantation novel is more complex than the sentimental novel. First, as William R. Taylor and Francis P. Gaines contend, these novels are not simply literary reflections of the actual plantation economy. They were written because of a "defensive attitude" among Southerners whose social and economic order was under attack by the democratic and industrial North.[11] The planter wishes "to appear aloof from money-making, and the plantation was to be represented as something other than a setting for human and economic exploitation."[12] Thus the plantation was often represented as an ideal oasis of civilization in a corrupt world. If the maiden-belle in these novels seems to us a bit sweet, it is because she is represented as the ideal daughter of this way of life. Plantation novels also depict the matron-wife she becomes as retiring and self-sacrificing, more common in the fiction than in reality. That the Southern belle is often motherless in the novels suggests not only the significance of the father to the belle, but the lackluster role of the married woman after a flamboyant career as a belle.

Borrowing the heroine from the sentimental, domestic novel, the plantation novel depicted the belle as a pure maiden with no purity-threatening force from without. Instead, plantation novels asserted that a girl's own nature was to be curbed because feminine assertiveness could be dangerous. Replacing the seducer in novels such as *Clarissa* and *Pamela* as the representative of evil are often the father and the brother. Without the presence of a mother, the heroine is entirely dependent on her male relatives, particularly her father, who is often austere and authoritative. Bel Tracy, for example, has a stern father and a philandering brother, whose influence on her is considered dangerous to her character. Her father's influence demands repression of her liveliness and obedience to his authority. Thus Bel is meek and lively at once, her purity threatened more by her loose-living brother than an outsider. Mild as these incestuous themes are, they are covertly present in Southern fiction from the 1830s to the 1850s.

The position of woman as an ideal in the plantation novel was also a response to the infant movement for women's rights, much in the journals of the time. The "new woman" of the movement was altogether condemned by most of the authors of plantation novels; women were offered the compensation, or rather, the "higher offices" of home and hearth. The domestic pedestal was supposed to offer the highest possible achievement and satisfactions, preferable certainly to jobs, votes, and other alternatives championed by the woman's movement. Bel in *Swallow Barn*, for example, is educated at home, and Kennedy is quick to censure parents who would consider educating their daughters in schools located in the impure world.

The psychology of a Bel Tracy can perhaps be ascertained only in an indirect way, for her drives, needs, and instincts were not directly treated in fiction. The nonfiction of the day, however, provided the antebellum period with a psychology of the feminine ideal. The remarks of Thomas R. Dew in four issues of the *Southern Literary Messenger* are fairly representative of the prevailing opinion of the "passionate" components of a feminine ideal like Bel Tracy. "On the Characteristic Differences between the Sexes and on the Position and Influence of Woman in Society" (1835) offers the view that woman and man are physically different, such that "her inferior strength and sedentary habits confine her within the domestic circle."[13] She is therefore forced to rely upon her man as her "shield." Her means of winning this protection is not by changing property laws, by logic, or by education; it is by "those qualities which delight and fascinate—which are calculated to win over to her side the proud lord of creation, and to make him a humble suppliant at her shrine. Grace, modesty, and loveliness are the charms which constitute her power." Dew is suggesting that woman be a Circe, a temptress, the archetype of the Dark Lady. Her power is the power of sex, which curiously is to be housed in a personality which is meek, modest, and chaste.

Dew is thus calling for woman to be deceptive and repressed, to deny her sexuality except to use it to snare men into marriage. He continues, "She cannot give utterance to her passions and emotions like a man. . . . She is thus frequently required to suppress the most violent feelings; to put a curb on her most ardent desires, and at the same time to wear the face of contentment and ease" (498). Dew's use of the vocabulary the modern reader has come to associate with the defense mechanisms of the ego which Sigmund Freud described, particularly Dew's recognition of the belle's suppression and repression, suggests that this woman was urged to deny her sexual feelings, in fact, to present the façade of passion without feeling it. If the Victorian male is a hypocrite, as Houghton argues, so is the Victorian woman. Dew presents the coquette as the epitome of this system, citing the "wonderful control which the coquette ultimately acquires over her feelings. The general opinion is, that coquettes are cold and feelingless . . . that all their demonstrations of emotion are the result of hypocrisy. This may sometimes be the case, but not always. Persons of this description, may even have intense feelings; but from constantly restraining and curbing them . . . they acquire perfect mastery over them" (499). Dew does not explain, however, how a woman is to avoid repressing positive feelings such as warmth and affection. Dew acknowledges that vanity and hypocrisy frequently characterized coquettes, but he does not explain how one can avoid these vices.

Dew continues that a woman who possesses these personality traits before marriage is the glory of hearth and home after the marriage. His imagery for marriage suggests an Edenic scene created by a married Eve who before marriage seemed more a Lilith: "Such a companion makes the home of her husband a paradise on earth, and the thought of him and his happiness, soon interweaves and intertwines itself with all her little schemes and projects, with all her desires and ambition, and her house becomes the true scene of domestic happiness and of the domestic virtues" (501). Woman cannot expect to excel in any walk of life but the domestic. Woman's inferior intellect, Dew contends, as shown by her lack of achievement in the arts, will ever prevent her from leaving the home. Doubtless Sarah J. Hale, Caroline Lee Hentz, and

Harriet Beecher Stowe, the popular women writers after 1835, the date of these remarks, were challenged by such assertions which were by no means Dew's alone.

Perhaps the most subtly influential of these writers on the image of the literary belle is Sarah Josepha Hale, essayist, novelist, and editor for forty years of *Godey's Lady's Book*, the magazine which became the arbiter of decorum for three generations of Americans from 1828 to 1877. Throughout her magazine articles and fictional works Hale continuously champions a more abundant and better education for women as a counter to the cultural tendency of woman who is "still endeavoring to heighten and set off her personal attractions by dress and accomplishments, that she may thus secure the constant devotion of some gallant knight."[14] Because Hale agrees that vanity is woman's worst fault, she proposes education as a corrective to the shallow emphasis on feminine beauty of her time: "It is the bane of beautiful women to trust in their beauty; yet while they are continually receiving homage for their charms, how difficult it is to convince them it will not always be thus! Nothing ... except the most watchful discretion and ... education ... can prevent such a female from becoming vain."[15] She also believes that it is woman's duty to correct male obsession with wealth. In her novel *Northwood* (1829), the narrator states, "The inordinate thirst for riches is the besetting sin of Americans; situations, institutions, education, all combine to foster it" (146). To save men from their obsession with wealth by providing corrective moral and cultural influences on their husbands and children, women, Hale argues, would have to be educated.

Hale's fiction is devoted to the sad consequences for a woman of faulty education. In particular, she often treats the topic of the belle whose feeble education has developed only her narcissistic opinion of herself as a lovely bauble, whose attempts to fill up a mind left blank are comprised of fantasies of gallant and mysterious gentlemen. Beautiful though these girls are, their characters are lacking; they do not prefer "good health, good habits, and good morals" in a husband. Lydia Romelee in *Northwood* rejects a worthy suitor to wed a rich but dissolute plantation owner, whom she has known for only three weeks. Her fickleness is attributed more to "an injudicious education than to her heart" (19). The marriage is an unhappy one. Lydia is ostracized as a foreigner by Charlestonian society, whose women think her nose is too long, her forehead too low, her complexion painted, and her manners "rustic if not dowdyish." The men, however, think she is an "angel," but the narrator makes it clear that Lydia needs the comfort of women friends more than the admiration of men. Her husband is a tyrant who allows her no life of her own: "He thought . . . his wife's happiness must consist in studying and contributing to his. . . . Her wishes had, beneath the paternal roof, been laws to all who approached her; and the transition from a goddess receiving adoration to an obedient wife, was a falling off . . . she had never anticipated" (31–32). Hale is careful to show that the fault is not of Southern or Northern temperament, but of a wife whose vanity blurred her judgment and whose education had not prepared her to reform the intemperance of her husband.

Caroline Lee Hentz creates heroines who combine the virtues Hale extols with the beauty and liveliness in the belle that Kennedy prefers. The heroine of *Linda: The Young Pilot of the Belle Creole, A Tale of Southern Life* (1850) is "the most spoiled, petted, warm-hearted, impulsive, generous little tyrant that ever ruled over a Southern plantation."[16] Like so many Southern belles, she is motherless and has a close relationship with her father. But when he remarries, the stepmother's cruel treatment of Linda resembles that of the evil stepmothers in such fairy tales as "Cinderella" or "Hansel and Gretel." Linda's consolation is education, so that when she matures into a lovely, ringleted belle, Linda has been sobered by suffering and education, unlike the sheltered Bel Tracy.

Her troubles continue, however, for her stepmother wishes Linda to marry her stepbrother Robert. Linda is horrified by what she considers to be a "wicked," incestuous match with a man she has always regarded as a brother. Hentz makes it clear that the stepmother's evil stems from materialism: "Robert is rich, and you have a large fortune. We wish to unite them. An all-sufficient reason, and one which . . . outweighs every other" (104). To the stepmother, money as a reason for marriage overrides even incest taboos and lack of love. It is this attitude that Hale and Hentz denounce vehemently: that women are chattel, bought and sold by parents in the guise of marriage. Linda's firm morality eventually reforms Robert, and the novel ends with the death of Linda's father, an event which releases Linda so that she can marry the man she loves.

The influence of the seduction novel is strong in this novel. Robert is a typical swarthy, black-eyed villain who seeks to commit incest with his sister (at least this is the pious Linda's interpretation). The incest taboo is a theme of such seduction novels as Susanna Rowson's popular sequel to *Charlotte Temple* (1791), *Lucy Temple* (1828). The Freudian implications of the incest theme in the American novel (a brother can be a substitute for the father) have been explained as the failure of the authors to deal with adult heterosexuality.[17] Hentz, however, confronts this theme directly, recognizing that Linda must overcome her attachment to her father, reject her brother, and not fear the experience of adult love. Thus Linda must defend her virtue in the face of incest, assert the value of love over money, reform her would-be seducers, resolve her close ties to her father, and marry the good man she loves. This is quite a task for the heroine, but ideal woman that she is, Linda is able to triumph.

The heroine of Hentz's *Eoline; or Magnolia Vale* (1852), is Eoline Glenmore, a motherless girl who longs to remain with her father on his plantation and desires no activity other than to sing with her lovely voice, like the eolian lyre whose name is so like her own. She has no "wish to be a belle."[18] Nevertheless, her modesty and self-reliance are matched by her loveliness: "Her complexion had the fairness of the magnolia blended with the blush of the rose. Her hair, of a pale golden brown, reminded one of the ripples of a sunlit lake by its soft wave . . . Her eyes, blue, soft, and intense as the noonday sun in June, had a kind of beseeching loving expression—an expression that appealed for sympathy, protection, love" (22). Considering this saccharine description, it is remarkable that Eoline also has the courage to refuse her father's wish that she marry the neighbor's son to join their estates. To reject this materialistic marriage, she breaks with her father completely, is disinherited, and accepts a life of poverty as a music teacher in the town of Magnolia Vale.

Eoline reveals that she is as passionate as she is courageous. She prefers a man who is Byronesque: "I am wicked, because I feel as if I could really admire a man more, who is capable of some great crime nobly repented of, if he have correspondingly greatness of character, than one amicably weak and constitutionally timid" (161). One of her suitors turns out to be secretly married; Eoline, like a mediating angel, reconciles him with his wife. Finally, she falls in love with a man who fulfills her requirements—and he happily is the same neighbor's son whom she had earlier rejected. She marries for love; on her wedding day she appears "fair as the magnolia of the South, and blushing as its rose" (251).

The image of the belle in these novels is one of a beautiful, intelligent, yet modest woman with impeccable morality. Her mother is dead and she is quite close to her father, although the closeness can be in relationship of rebellion, and she seeks a gallant but gentle authoritarian like her father to marry for love not for money. That he and she usually have money is meant to appear incidental. In only one novel published before the Civil War does one find a portrait of a belle who is not admirable, Harriet Beecher Stowe's *Uncle Tom's Cabin or Life Among the Lowly* (1852).

The novel itself is an inverted plantation novel; instead of the usual pattern of life among the aristocracy, Stowe presents "Life Among the Lowly." Instead of a benevolent white plantation owner, the reader meets three progressively worse owners: Mr. Shelby whose financial difficulties force him to sell his black friends; Augustine St. Clare whose artistic, careless, and indolent temperament produces a man of thought, not action; and Simon Legree, a nouveau riche opportunist from the North, whose cruel and licentious treatment of the female slaves represents the nadir of the Southern plantation owner.

As ethical beings, the women fare better. Evangeline St. Clare, or Little Eva, is the young virgin who inspires two of the men in the novel: her father and Uncle Tom himself. She is the typical belle: "The shape of her head and the turn of her neck and bust was peculiarly noble, and the long golden-brown hair that floated like a cloud around it, the deep spiritual gravity of her violet blue eyes, shaded by heavy fringes of golden brown."[19] She is so lovely, in fact, that her father fears she may grow up to become a coquette like her mother was. Her temperament is spontaneous and affectionate, and with no one is she more demonstrative than her father. They hold hands, play games of "pelting each other with roses." Eva attempts both to convince her father that slavery is wicked and also to correct his tendency towards dissipation; owning slaves has "caused" a weakening of his character. When Eva dies, one wonders what might have become of her attachment to her father and her friendship with Uncle Tom had she lived into adolescence. But she is spared the complications of adolescence and dies the pure virgin, an embodiment of anti-slavery sentiments and Christian virtue.

If Simon Legree is the villain of the novel, then Marie St. Clare is his female counterpart. Like so many of the belles before her, Marie is a motherless only child who is spoiled by her father and servants alike. That she has slaves to wait on her, Stowe implies, is responsible for the failure of her marriage. Since she expects others to give her love and attention, she believes that she never has to do anything in return. Thus she cannot be her husband's moral guide; instead, her vanity and selfishness leave her barren of love, morality, and inspiration. St. Clare marries her because she is "the reigning belle of the season" and thus "he became the husband of a fine figure, a pair of bright eyes, and a hundred thousand dollars ... and none of these items were precisely the ones to minister to a mind diseased" (218).

The failure of a Southern belle to be the moral ideal that Hale, Stowe, and Hentz espouse is a direct result of a petted, narcissistic childhood, Stowe asserts. Never developing anything other than her beautiful façade, Marie cares only for attention and for her wardrobe; she insists upon going to church in order to show off her clothes. Marie cannot adjust to marriage, for when St. Clare discontinues the "gallantries" of courtship, Marie pouts and cries, no longer receiving the attention she craves. Later, when Eva is born, Marie regards her daughter with suspicion and jealousy, since this rival now claims her husband's attention. Bored, with no inner resources to provide her with strength, in a few years "the blooming young belle changes into a faded, sickly woman, whose time was divided among a variety of fanciful diseases" (220–21). Hypochondria and hysterical outbursts for attention replace coquetry as her characteristic behavior.

Marie is a case study in defense mechanisms. To preserve her image of herself as a misunderstood and sickly woman, she denies she is selfish, and projects her worst qualities onto the black slaves about her, calling them selfish ingrates. Believing them "selfish" and "over-indulged" allows Marie to rationalize her cruel behavior. Stowe is intent on showing that Marie's ideas of humane treatment of her slaves are parallel to the rationalizations of many Southerners for retaining the institution; Marie calmly explains that one slave was "never whipped more than once or twice." Marie tells the Northern visitor, a common character in plantation novels, here Cousin Ophelia, "You don't know what a provoking, stupid, careless, unreasonable, childish, ungrateful set of wretches they are" (237). Yet Stowe carefully shows it is Marie who is all these things; even as a housekeeper she is "indolent, childish, unsystematic" (278). Such domestic failure would horrify Mrs. Hentz and Sarah Hale, for whom the orderly home is a second Eden. As her ultimate villainy, Marie orders the pretty young quadroon Rose to be taken to the local whipping house where, Marie knows, Rose will be sexually abused as well as tortured. Marie's jealousy of Rose's youth and beauty is the spiteful envy of a fading belle; it also parallels her envy of her daughter whose youth and beauty is captivating the hearts of the men on the plantation, white and black. Her paranoid reaction when the Northerner, Ophelia, opposes her, "Everybody goes against me," reminds one of Southern defensiveness under Northern criticism.

Thus Eva is the inspiration Hale and Hentz call for in women. But Marie St. Clare, with her narcissistic vanity and selfishness, is cruel and defensive, embodying the worst offenses of the South. Stowe is careful to appeal to her female audience's preference for the sentimental novel by presenting them with the poignancy of a mother wishing to remain with her child, and a wife with her husband. The audience might be shocked by Simon Legree's sadistic licentiousness, but they would be appalled to see families split apart. Finally, to see a white woman order one slave sold and another used sexually was to witness the degradation of the ideal that white women were supposed to represent.

The outcry was heard from citizens, clergy, politicians, essayists, and writers of fiction. Just as one irate reader sent Harriet Beecher Stowe the severed ear of an unfortunate black slave, so did the Southern apologists issue books in retaliation. Several responses appeared in 1852, the year of the publication of *Uncle Tom's Cabin*, following the serialization of the novel which had appeared the previous year. Caroline Lee Hentz's *Marcus Warland* portrayed the benevolence of the system and the virtues of the Southerners involved. Another of her novels, *The Northern Planter's Bride* (1854), didactically combined reasons for retaining slavery with a pleasant story. Sarah Hale's *Northwood* was revised and reissued; it now extolled marriage between individuals of the North and South as a solution to the political rift between the two sections. William Gilmore Simms, whose earlier books *The Partisan* (1835) and *Katharine Walton* (1851) had asserted Southern life and women as ideals, continued to do so in *The Golden Christmas: Chronicle of St. John's Berkely* (1852), as if in answer to Stowe's charges.

Perhaps more understandable in the context of *Uncle Tom's Cabin* is Almira Lincoln Phelps's "Southern Housekeepers" in *Women of the South* (1861), in which young ladies are exhorted "to know what labor is, that you can feel sympathy for the slaves."[20] Phelps says the highest office of woman is "to arrange and control in the little empire of the home . . . to minister to your parents . . . even though it call for the sacrifice of your own enjoyments. This picture may be far different from the one of your own fancy, where gay parties with all the excitements of a life of pleasure occupy the foreground" (189). Phelps acknowledges the detrimental effects of belledom in her essay, "Belles," in which she asks the young girl to observe that "those who, like the butterfly, flit from flower to flower, selfishly seeking pleasure and amusement, are wholly indifferent as to the effects of their heartless attention upon the future happiness of those whom they may choose to flatter" (193). Such comments typify the remarks of many writers whose essays and novels after the publication of *Uncle Tom's Cabin* reiterated the value of education, the dangers of vanity to the Belle, and the rewards of home life. Stowe's life had severely challenged the antebellum ideal for woman, and in response essayists and novelists vigorously defended the old ideal of Southern women. Even Stowe, by presenting the villainous Marie St. Clare, obliquely reinforced the ideal by suggesting that the best Southern women should be opposite in temperament and behavior from Marie.

Thus writers of the antebellum period were actually united in their concept of the belle. She was to be an inspirer to men: early in the century she was portrayed as a force against materialism, especially the marriage for money; later she was to be a force against the lucrative institution of slavery. She was to hold court from a domestic altar, a setting which would remove her from the corrupt world. She was to be educated, however, so that her seclusion in the home would not make her a naive victim of worldly men. And she was to be charming but virtuous, lovely but modest, for vanity could interfere with her first duty: to inspire men.

Finally, the Southernness of the belle provided authors with a perfect vehicle with which to portray the feminine ideal of their age. Southerners believed not only in the Victorian's ideal of woman but also in the Southern woman as the epitome of their refined and "noble" civilization. Thus the Southern belle in literature before the Civil War was portrayed as an untouched Eve in a domestic garden, or a goddess on a pedestal, unsullied by money, experience, and vanity. As Stowe discovered, to criticize this flower of civilization was to attack the South itself.

## Notes

1.  Margaret Mitchell, *Gone With the Wind* (New York: Macmillan, 1936), 7.
2.  John Pendleton Kennedy, *Swallow Barn or A Sojourn in the Old Dominion* (Philadelphia: Carey & Lea, 1832), 78.
3.  Helen Waite Papashvily, *All the Happy Endings, A Study of the Domestic Novel in America, The Women Who Wrote It, The Women Who Read It, in the Nineteenth Century* (New York: Harper & Bros., 1956).
4.  Kennedy, 109.
5.  Walter E. Houghton, *The Victorian Frame of Mind 1830–1870* (New Haven: Yale University Press, 1957), 341–92.
6.  Ibid., 252.
7.  Ibid., 385.
8.  The actual facts of the matter were forgotten. Frederick Law Olmstead, writing in 1861, points out that for all the cordiality and hospitality of the "old families" of the plantations, their names were not those of Cavaliers but "tinkers and tailors, poacher and pickpocket, indentured servants bound for Virginia." *The Cotton Kingdoms: A Traveller's Observations on Cotton and Slavery in the American Slave State* (New York: Mason, 1861), II, 335.
9.  Of the authors studied, only Kennedy is aware that Bel's patrician snobbery is pretentious at best, based on an illusion, not on verifiable reality. Bel herself is unaware

of the fantasy in which she lives and seeks to have her gentlemen conform to her image of them as knights. They respond both by sheltering her from the fact that she and they are not aristocrats and by using the ruses of medieval courtly love, thus reinforcing her fantasy. Ned's "love disease" resembles that of Troilus himself; his behavior is wild, melancholy and erratic, his hair grows too long, his clothing is unbrushed. See Kennedy, 192.

10. William R. Taylor, *Cavalier and Yankee: The Old South and American National Character* (New York: George Braziller, 1961), 146.

11. Gaines, *The Southern Plantation: A Study in the Development and the Accuracy of a Tradition* (New York: Columbia University Press, 1924), 19.

12. Taylor, 147.

13. *Southern Literary Messenger*, I (May 1835), 495.

14. Sarah Josepha Hale, *Sketches of American Character* (Boston: Freeman Hunt, 1831), 104.

15. Hale, *Northwood: A Tale of New England* (Boston: Bowles and Dearborn, 1829), 104.

16. *A Tale of Southern Life* (Philadelphia: A. Hart, 1850), 8.

17. See "Preface," Leslie A. Fiedler, *Love and Death in the American Novel* (New York: Criterion, 1960), 12.

18. Caroline Lee Hentz, *Eoline; or Magnolia Vale* (Philadelphia: T. B. Peterson, 1852), 204.

19. Harriet Beecher Stowe, *Uncle Tom's Cabin or Life Among the Lowly*, in *The Annotated Uncle Tom's Cabin*, ed. Philip Van Doren Stein (1852; rpt. New York: Paul S. Erickson, 1964), 209.

20. In *Women of the South Distinguished in Literature*, ed. Mary Forrest (New York: Derby and Jackson, 1861), 189.

# A Sense of Place and the Americanization of Mississippi

WILLIE MORRIS

When I was running *Harper's Magazine*, an irascible friend from New Orleans who had been living in New York City for a long time used to come to the bar on Madison Avenue and 34th Street where we'd congregate with our writers after work. One afternoon there were a couple of people there from Mississippi, and we were talking about change in our native state. After listening to a little of this, my friend from New Orleans launched into a tirade: "You fellows are writers, and you have the gall to say you want to change Mississippi? You must be insane. Here you are from a place that's produced the best damned writers in America . . . and the most haunting landscape in all the United States . . . and a spoken word that would make a drunk Irishman envious . . . and miscegenation that's the envy of Brazil . . . and a sense of the histrionic that would pale the Old Testament . . . and a past so contorted that it embarrasses the people of Scarsdale . . . and you say you want to *change* Mississippi?" He finished with an exultant flourish: "Why if I were you, I'd put up big green signs at every point of entry into Mississippi which said, 'Posted. No Trespassing.'"

I will admit something in the brooding Celtic side of me responded to my friend's wild injunction. I described something of this scene in a book I once wrote, and I received two dozen letters from Mississippi people saying my friend was absolutely right. Three of the correspondents said they would put up the signs themselves. I am a writer, and everyone I ever knew from Mississippi who has used the written word knows in his deepest heart that Mississippi is different, that there is something almost indefinable in our chemistry which makes us so, that there is a resonance in the very word *Mississippi* which demands the attention of the spirit, that, black and white, we are obsessed with the slow mournful passing of the seasons and the stories we

*Southern Quarterly* 17.3–4 (1979): 3–13.

tell on each other and the things our people were and did, the peculiar quality of our humor and the opposition of our good-mannered civility and our rebelliousness, and the dark shadows of our past that, in combination, makes us unique among our contemporary Americans. I see this every time I'm in the company of Mississippians in Northern places. When Mississippians meet by chance far away, is it not something to behold? The swapping of tales about family and places, the talk of mutual friends down here—and we always know someone in common in Itta Bena or Tchula or Osyka—the stories about football or fishing or some long vanished preacher—are signs of an extraordinary mutuality. I have met black Mississippians in the North who were much more similar to me in background and preferences than the Yankee Wasps I worked with every day. If I were forced to distill, to isolate from all this, some common denominator to our curious distinctiveness, I would say it had to do with an *awareness of community*, a profound feeling for communal origins. When William Faulkner said in the opening paragraph of his essay "Mississippi" that "Mississippi begins in the lobby of a Memphis, Tennessee hotel and extends south to the Gulf of Mexico," we knew in our hearts the heroically strange kingdom which lay in between.

Yet this, of course, is only part of the broader question before us, for the Deep South, and I think especially in Mississippi, the American twentieth century arrived much later, and with infinitely more frenzy and destructiveness, than it did in other sections of the United States. There are reasons for this that would fill volumes of history, and indeed have. As the century progressed, Faulkner himself spent more time on the Snopeses than on the Compsons. In Mississippi, as in much of the lower South, the old warring impulses to be both Southern and American have created their own special tension, and I think no more so than today, when the communal heritage of our native land is threatened by that relentless urge to mobility and homogeneity which I fear is the hallmark of the greater society.

Mississippi, as God help us we all know, has often given itself to extremes, and through the years two of the greatest ones have been the desire, on the one hand, to dwell forever with all the myths and trimmings of a vanished culture which may never have truly existed in the first place, certainly not the way we wished it to, and the frantic compulsion, on the other, to reforge ourselves as an appendage of the capitalistic, go-getting entrepreneurial North. The quest of the Yankee dollar, in the pejorative meaning, has never been far from the better angels of our nature.

Between these two extremes there have been complex lights and shadings, and considerable ambivalence and suffering. And until quite recently one constant has been the Northern view of the South—and especially of Mississippi as the most Southern of the South—as a kind of crucible of the national guilt, a playing ground for the nation's oscillating guilts about itself. It was not too many years ago that D. W. Brogan, who was a British historian but who might just as well have been speaking for much of the Northern sentiment, called Mississippi, for instance, "the most savage and backward of all the forty-eight American commonwealths."

Yet one of the many ironies of our history is that even in dire moments we Mississippians considered ourselves intensely American. All through our early history Mississippians were warriors for nationalistic causes, for continental expansion, for laying to rest the specter of European domination. Even the rhetoric of secession was couched in language that was deeply Americanistic—the constitutional ideals of the founders. Throughout the 1850s my great great uncle Henry S. Foote, United States senator and then governor of Mississippi, spoke—as did others—of the "good old Union, sage fruit of our immortal ancestors." In his first inaugural Lincoln was wise in appealing to "the mystic chord of memory" which might hold the Union together, those chords were strong in Mississippi, but the sound of a distant drummer prevailed, to what staggering costs. L. Q. C. Lamar, a Mississippian, was instrumental in bringing North and South together again after the bloodiest war mankind had ever known. In two world wars Mississippians were noted for their devotion to the flag. In Yazoo City as a boy I played taps over the graves of many Mississippi boys of both races brought home from Korea. The Americanization of Mississippi began before Mississippi was even admitted to the Union. And on election night in 1976, it was the electoral votes of Mississippi which swung the balance to the first Southern President of the United States in well over one hundred years. Given our complicated, disparate, ethnic American society, I believe the United States has a reservoir of good will and understanding among ourselves and a tradition of making our system work—the most monumental of our failures being the Civil War—that is unmatched by any other nation in the world. And Mississippi both partakes of this rare human achievement and contributes to it. Few Mississippians can better testify to the importance of being both Mississippian and American than my friend Turner Catledge, who brought to his direction of the greatest newspaper in the world, the *New York Times*, his love for both.

For black Mississippians the urge toward being American was at once more complex and more straightforward. Never have there been more splendid Americans than the black Mississippians who through the decades had the courage to demand justice and equality under the American ideals they shared. The oldest and most incorrigible of all hyphenate-Americans, C. Vann Woodward wrote in his *Burden of Southern History*, were the white Southerners and their ancient contemporaries, the Southern blacks. America, the finer instincts of it, are in the very soul of Mississippi, and always have been, and that is something not to be forgotten, nor taken lightly.

Now we are witnessing, I think, three peculiar transformations in our life which have surfaced so recently—in a generation or perhaps even less—that although as Mississippians and Americans we may pay lip service to their presence, we may not yet be wholly aware of their long-range consequences.

One is the patent fact that the North, or the non-South, has become heir to many of the problems of a society such as Mississippi. The exodus of black Southerners to the great cities of the East and the North surely constitutes the largest and most dramatic migration of a people in the history of the human race. The triumph of Allis-Chalmers in rural Mississippi and elsewhere in the South has become more and more complete. Brother Will Campbell, God bless him, driving through the Mississippi Delta one recent afternoon with our mutual friend, the writer Marshall Frady, looked out into a cotton field and claimed he saw a tractor going up and down the furrows all by itself, without a driver. And as time went on, as the blacks arrived in the North, they found their traditional advocates, the white Northern liberals, were leaving for Westchester County. The tormenting social problems of school integration, inadequate living conditions, and all the rest which the North might have prepared itself for—it certainly preached to Mississippi about them long enough—seemed to rise full born there in the acute urban context. The collapse of civil order in one Northern city after another, continuing now in the mayhem of the streets, is no cause for rejoicing among Mississippians; it should be a source of the deepest human sorrow.

Second, in these years we are seeing a Mississippi that is catching up to the older social ideals and values of the more pristine America. Nowhere, of course, has this been more evident in Mississippi than in the massive integration of the public schools. This has brought dislocations, and up to a point a drift to private academies, and we have a long, long way to go. Yet, who twenty years ago would have foreseen the day to day manifestations of this vast social change? Who, in 1961 when Meredith was admitted to Ole Miss, would have predicted it? The emerging biracialism of Mississippi can be seen everywhere—in the newspapers, television, parent-teacher meetings, in a courtesy and politeness between the races in public places. Perhaps it takes someone who does not live here year round to feel this true sense of change—and to me all this is less a result of the Americanization of Mississippi, although the federal presence certainly was the catalyst to the process, as Mississippi itself responding to its own genuine heritage: whites and black living together.

I was watching an Ole Miss-Alabama football game on national television not too long ago with some Northern friends in New York. There were Confederate flags everywhere. The Ole Miss band broke into "Dixie" about once every five minutes. Meanwhile, down on the field, the Ole Miss and Alabama cheerleaders were black and white, so were the bands—and so, of course were the football teams. An Ole Miss halfback, a black from Meridian, scored on a long touchdown run. Black and white Ole Miss players embraced each other and exchanged the soul slap. The Confederate flags waved in the stands. The band played an energetic "Dixie" for the twentieth time. One of my Northern friends watching the game said: "*What the hell's going on down there?*"

Ben Williams, the first black to play football for the Yazoo Indians, was also among the first blacks to play for Ole Miss. In his senior year at Ole Miss, Ben Williams—now with the Buffalo Bills—a black boy from Yazoo County—was elected Colonel Rebel.

"What the hell's going on," indeed? Certainly not perfection—nothing in the human race in Mississippi or elsewhere is perfect—but dramatic moments are revealing of more subtle, and perhaps more everlasting realities.

My third point is that we are also seeing a Mississippi that threatens to be severely damaged—one hopes not inundated—by the rampant commercialism which the Europeans of the 1950s called with much hostility "Americanization," and which may very well be more than we ever bargained for.

Not long ago a Northern literary critic called me "the youngest of the established Deep Southern writers who lived in the South of pre-suburbia." That is quite an intoxicating phrase. True or not, I can assure you that when I was growing up, the closest thing Yazoo City had to suburbia was the hamlet called Little Yazoo, which consisted of a general store which never had anything you ever needed, a bootlegger in the back of a dilapidated garage, a Negro undertaker who was the richest man in town, and a precarious unpainted establishment with a sign in front saying: "Roaches, minnows, worms, and hot dogs."

All this was before the television culture, before the neighborhood shopping centers and supermarkets and the new federal expressway swooping down out of Jackson through the lush green hills of kudzu toward my beloved Yazoo. My growing up then was the Mississippi many of us know and remember. That was back when the only device protecting Republicans, as the saying went, was the game laws. It was a lazy town, stretched out on its hills and its flat places in a summer sun, lethargic and dreamy. People sat out on the front porch in wisteria nights with the grass wet in dew. We were forever playing tricks on everybody. And it seemed we were always listening to older people telling stories, their voices blending into the nights, about the Great Flood of '27, or about the owner of the funeral parlor who walked down main street and killed one of the newspaper editors with a pistol, then came back to his funeral parlor and lay down in a coffin and shot himself in the head. Always these stories being told! About the eccentricities of certain ancient ladies of a generation before, about the big funeral of 1929 of a military hero from an old family and how the monoplanes flew over the grave and dropped flowers, about love affairs never consummated and rivalries which sometimes never ended in bloodshed, about old gentlemen in starched high collars and tobacco stains on their whiskers. We were so isolated then. Time seemed to stand still for us when we wished it to, although I think we wanted it to move on, to hurry up toward something—young fools that we were.

The beauty of the Mississippi land engulfed us—the smell of it in springtime, the katydids in the trees, the dark wetness of the shadows. The black people were everywhere, moving up and down the streets, the sounds of their music and laughter wafting over from the next block—the town would have been ghostly and bereft without them. On one of these nights a big passenger plane mistook the few lights of the dirt airport for Jackson, circled Yazoo and finally came to a skidding halt in the mud. Everyone who heard the motors drove out to the airport before the plane landed, and a representative of the chamber of commerce put up a stepladder and said to each frightened passenger climbing down, "Welcome to Yazoo." In those days the presence of inevitable death was everywhere, the eternal passing of generations, and people talked of those who had died years before. In the cemetery under its elms and oaks and magnolias I would touch with my hand the burial stones I know to this day by heart:

My husband with thee departed all my hopes.
Asleep in Jesus, Blessed Thought.
God's finger touched him, and he slept.
Remembered in life, lamented in death.

And I remembered the political barbecues in the park or in some dusty clearing in the woods, the politicians sweating in the sun and blaming everything on the black people, the patent medicine posters on the sides of barns and stores, the vast flat countryside drowsing in the heat of July.

I recall Jackson in those years as if time has stood still for me, visiting my grandparents on North Jefferson Street across from the Jitney-Jungle—the long walks at twilight through the forests of crepe myrtles, the old ladies on the galleries exchanging pleasantries, "Come in and have some ice-tea, you heah?" Then on to look for foreign stamps on the letters in the trashbin at the state capitol. Jackson was a sleepy state capital town then, with broad boulevards of houses faintly ruined, and over it all an atmosphere of containment.

Now all my own people are dead. My grandparents and great aunts and uncles lie in the crumbled old section of the cemetery in Raymond, only a few yards from a rusty wrought-iron fence enclosing fifty unidentified Confederate dead. When my mother died last year, I had to close down the house where I grew up in Yazoo and put it up for sale—the trial of finding family things in the back corners of closets: a program for my mother's piano recital in 1916, a faded photograph of my father in a baseball uniform in front of the Standard Oil Building on State Street in Jackson in 1922, another of my great grandmother holding a parasol in 1885, yellowed clippings from high school. The moment came that I stood alone in the empty house. Did I know then how it would grow to haunt my dreams and nightmares? In the gloom of it that day I strained to hear my mother's music on the piano again, my father's footsteps on the porch, the echoes of boys playing basketball in the backyard, the barks and whines of Toby, Sam, Jimbo, Duke, and Old Skip. When I left the house, I locked the door and did not look behind me.

These are *Mississippi* things I describe. They are common, are they not, to all of us.

Now Jackson from Highway 55 looms before one like a city devastated by some alien intrusion. It all seemed to have happened so quickly: the parking lots, motels, franchise stores, pizza parlors, all those accoutrements out at the edge of the great American schizophrenia, a whole beautiful terrain wiped out and vanished. The view could have been Cleveland, Ohio. And down in those older sections whole neighborhoods likewise seemed to have disap-peared—North State Street a thoroughfare for barter and commerce, of one duplex after another, and chrome and asphalt and concrete where venerable landmarks had been. My grandparents' house torn down for a parking lot for a shopping center. A solitary magnolia stands in a plot of grass near where the house had been. Not long ago I found my name in the bark of the tree, carved there by me when I was ten years old.

Surely all this, too, is common to us. Mississippians drive every day from suburbias to work through urban sprawls identical to any Eastern or Midwestern city. My neighbor on Long Island, Craig Claiborne of Indianola, whose writings in the New York Times and elsewhere have made him the country's foremost writer on food, was telling me just the other day that even the Mississippi recipes he is getting nowadays have a certain national uniformity. "Yankee recipes from Mississippi?" I asked my friend Craig. "No, but kind of Yankee-ized," Craig said. A new air of acquisitiveness envelops the whole South. At a recent conference Dean Faulkner Wells, the niece of William Faulkner, told me the sidewalks were gradually being demolished in Oxford and that at the new McDonald's near the Ole Miss campus the propri-etors had put up a photograph of Mr. Faulkner near a poster advertising the quarter-pound cheese burger. What would Major de Spain think of that—or Uncle Isaac McCaslin?

Robert Penn Warren was speaking of his native southern Kentucky when he said in an interview: "I began to look for a place down there, but suddenly I saw it was a different world. The people aren't the same people. Oh, more prosperous and all that, but not the kind I had known—with a certain per-sonal worth. So we are stuck with a new world. With certain virtues I'd be the first to grant, but perhaps some fatal defects." A bit extreme, perhaps, but most of us must have had similar thoughts of late.

Benjamin Forkner and Patrick Samway may have been speaking of Mississippi just as of the South as a whole when they wrote in the introduc-tion to Stories of the Modern South: "Certainly the post–World War II South offers little to allay the fears of the 1920s and the '30s. The New South of commerce, speculation, and industrial growth has become a permanent real-ity. Of course no one would argue that the rapid development of the South and of Mississippi in the twentieth century has been without its advantages. Southern universities have prospered. And many of the negative legacies of the past, the oppressive poverty, the vicious sharecropping system, the rural isolation and illiteracy, are gradually disappearing. But the necessary changes

have brought their modern plagues, and no Southerner, no matter how enthusiastic he may be about progress and the new wealth, would deny that the
face of the land has lost something of its old character."

My feeling for Mississippi as a physical place today is like a montage: old
men in front of a country cafe in Belzoni, watching big cars speed by; the
ghastly descent on the main road to Vicksburg with the rootless franchise
stores, and so close to that haunted battlefield where thousands of boys died;
a whitewashed Negro church out in the red hills with Negro children climbing a tree beside it; the bar of a Holiday Inn in Jackson at midnight, country
people in town for the day juxtaposed with executives from Chicago, all getting drunk to the strains of Willie Nelson; land ripped raw from some new
development near Port Gibson within sight of the Presbyterian hand on the
church pointing to the Lord; the eternal quiet of a crossroads hamlet in the
Delta where time has not moved.

In a class of young writers here at the university yesterday a student asked
me whether in the face of all these changes Mississippi can retain those qualities of the spirit that have made it unique. I told him I did not know. I went on
to suggest to the young student, however, that the preservation of those qualities must derive, in the future of Mississippi, from those old impulses of the
imagination which have made the literature of Mississippi the most powerful
in twentieth-century America. It is no accident, I said, that Mississippi produced Faulkner, the greatest of all American novelists, and perhaps the greatest of all novelists, and Eudora Welty, and Walker Percy, and Shelby Foote, and
the distinguished others. I must add that I, as a younger writer, am proud to
be part of this remarkable heritage.

These impulses of the imagination that gave us our literature were an expression of many things:

—the act of speech, of stories handed down, where a distinctive language—which still exists in Mississippi—vivid, concrete, sly, dramatic, is
deeply honored

—the language of music, the rich evocation of real, sensual things, which
also remains strong and vital here

—the love of a place—where individual human beings, relationships, family histories, the link with generations gone, not only mattered, but but-
tressed the everyday life

—the ineluctable perception of a common past: a past of guilt and tragedy and suffering, but also of courage and nobility and caring

—and at the very base of all this was that rarest and most indispensable sustenance for literature: and that is memory.

The young people of Mississippi must learn to remember who they are, and where they come from. They must be encouraged to remember; there is a message to be carried.

At the Delta Arts Festival in Greenwood last spring, a member of the Chamber of Commerce asked me: "What can we do to improve Mississippi's image?" I replied that we let the people of the Bronx, or Boston, or Detroit worry about Mississippi's image as much as they desired—but that Mississippians should concern themselves with their image among one another.

This conference in itself is an undying memento that Mississippi's sense of place is still cherished.

On looking over these notes this morning I found myself curiously disappointed in them. There was so much to be said on a subject I feel to be at the soul not just of Mississippi, but of the America of which it is a part. But after a while, I decided the hope for belonging, for belief in a people's better nature, for steadfastness against all that is hollow or crass or rootless or destructive, is as old as mankind itself and cannot be encompassed in some formula, or credo, or statement, or rationale. Wherever we live, we Americans who call ourselves Mississippians will find a way to remember.

PART III

*1980s*

# Cable's The Grandissimes

## A Literary Pioneer Confronts the Southern Tradition

ALFRED BENDIXEN

There was a well-established Southern literary tradition when George W. Cable's *The Grandissimes* appeared in 1880, but it was a tradition devoted to stifling any criticism of the South. One could find something resembling an honest account of life in the works of the Southwestern humorists, but these works were generally regarded as subliterary. The plantation myth that formed the core of what was regarded as "serious" Southern writing tended to ignore or gloss over the realities of slavery. The owners of plantations appeared as gracious and benevolent masters devoted to the welfare of their happy darkies. Southern fiction was more likely to show a slave refusing the offer of freedom and asserting his enjoyment of servitude than to present slave families divided on the auction block. In these books, Northern visitors were more likely to be converted to Southern ways of life than to call for change. As Louis D. Rubin Jr. has shown, the defensiveness that marked nineteenth-century Southern writing induced even writers of talent to sacrifice artistic truth to the purposes of propaganda.[1]

The plantation myth had its origin in such antebellum works as John Pendleton Kennedy's *Swallow Barn* (1832, revised 1851) and Caroline Lee Hentz's *The Planter's Northern Wife* (1854), but Southern propaganda had its greatest success in the period after the Civil War. By 1880, the efforts of the Northern radicals to impose racial equality on the South had clearly failed. Northerners were more concerned with healing the old wounds left by the war than with seeing that the freed slaves received fair treatment. Carpetbaggers and scalawags provoked more disdain than former confederates. Soon, Thomas Nelson Page's "Marse Chan" would make even former abolitionists weep, and Albion Tourgée, whose novel, *A Fool's Errand* (1876), offered the most effective attack on Southern racism since Stowe's *Uncle Tom's*

*Southern Quarterly* 18.4 (1980): 23–33.

*Cabin*, would lament that American writing had become "not only Southern in type, but distinctly Confederate in sympathy."[2]

Confronted with rapid change and the haste of industrialized life, late nineteenth-century readers eagerly retreated into the pastoral world offered by Southern writing, a world that ignored the realities of the present and romanticized the past. These readers were charmed by the discovery that life had once been graceful and leisurely; for them, the phrase, "the burden of the past," would have had little meaning. What history seemed to teach was that the past had been simpler and easier, that men had been nobler and kinder. Literature was an escape from time, and history was reduced to nostalgia.

But George W. Cable was no escapist. His stories in *Old Creole Days* placed a romantic haze over New Orleans, but he knew that beauty, charm, and grace could mask indolence, hypocrisy, and deceit. He faced the realities of racial injustice and refused to blink. As a reformer, Cable was out of step with the South and most of the nation. The result was the eventual loss of his literary reputation. Reviewers in the 1880s favorably compared him to the finest authors in America and Europe, but when he died in 1925, he was virtually forgotten. Although he seems to have had little direct influence on the major writers of the Southern Renaissance, with whom he is now often compared, critics are justified in praising him as the first modern Southern writer. One of Cable's most astute critics, Louis D. Rubin Jr., has written:

> In an important sense, *The Grandissimes* may be said to be the first "modern" Southern novel. For if the modern Southern novel has been characterized by its uncompromising attempt to deal honestly with the complexity of Southern racial experience, then *The Grandissimes* was the first important work of fiction written by a Southerner in which that intention is manifested. In this respect, Cable opened up the path along which Ellen Glasgow, William Faulkner, Thomas Wolfe, Robert Penn Warren, Eudora Welty, William Styron, and others would follow.[3]

The modern spirit of *The Grandissimes* goes far beyond Cable's willingness to treat the issue of race or to expose the violence and injustice that characterized the worst aspects of Southern life. If Cable seems modern, it is largely because he approached the South with the critical detachment of a Faulkner instead of with the nostalgia of a Page. Like the great Southern writers of the twentieth century, he had a rich sense of history and knew that the present always had to face the problems of the past. Moreover, like them, he was consciously a literary experimenter who recognized that the old forms of fiction were inadequate and that the complexities of Southern life required a new and complex kind of writing.

Unfortunately, Cable's achievement does not match that of the best Southern writers in our century. In spite of its dramatic force and imaginative power, *The Grandissimes* is too often marred by lapses into prose that is sentimental, preachy, and sometimes even clumsy. Nevertheless, Cable was a true literary pioneer who tried to explore and enlarge the possibilities of fiction. Those who have attempted to classify *The Grandissimes* have generally spoken of it as a mixture of poetic melodrama and social realism, but it has been called everything from an historical romance to a comedy of manners.[4] There seems to be some agreement that H. H. Boyesen was right in predicting that the book would "be the kind of novel which the Germans call 'Kulturroman,' a novel in which the struggling forces of opposing civilizations crystalize [*sic*] & in which they find their enduring monument."[5] Scholars have been less likely to note Boyesen's feeling that Cable had enough material for "a dozen novels, all tolerably unhackneyed."[6] Cable himself recognized the ambitiousness of his project: "I have grasped at so much. It is the wild, virgin soil that I have to break up; a field never plowed before. The Creole character, the Creole society, the philosophy of these things, Creole errors and defects & how to mend them, all clamoring to be treated by a tyro in a love story."[7]

In 1894, Cable described his attempt to introduce "personalities new to the world of fiction" into "the very old and familiar" story of "a feud between two families."[8] Yet he was interested in doing much more than simply telling a story. In a letter to Boyesen, he proclaimed "that the great problem of a novel should be something beyond and above the mere puzzle of the plot, something great and thought-compelling, that teaches without telling, that brings to view without pointing, that guides without leading and allures without fatiguing, through the dimness and shadow and uncertainty of a new path out at last upon the illimitable savannahs of God's sweet, green, nourishing truth."[9]

In spite of the overwrought prose, the metaphor of the new path seems to me the most revealing of Cable's comments on his own art. Like the modern Southern writers, Cable realized that to tell the truth he had to take risks. Although the modern reader may feel that Cable offers too much telling, pointing, and leading, *The Grandissimes* certainly demands more from the reader than most novels of the period. Cable may interject an occasional ironic comment, but he delays presenting critical information and places the reader into "an atmosphere of hints, allusions, faint unspoken admissions, ill-concealed antipathies, unfinished speeches, mistaken identities and whisperings of hidden strife."[10] The metaphor of the journey through "dimness and shadow" is particularly appropriate since it seems to allude to the second chapter of the book which describes the Frowenfeld family's journey to New Orleans. Expecting a paradise, the family finds instead: "A land hung in mourning, darkened by gigantic cypresses, submerged; a land of reptiles, silence, shadow, decay" (9). They discover a world that quickly kills those who fail to become acclimated. The family's journey is also the reader's journey into the novel, into a strange fictional world that had never been adequately described before; it is a journey that confounds and contradicts pleasant expectations, a journey that challenges the reader as much as it does Frowenfeld.

The goal of the journey is a better and truer understanding of the South, which, as Cable knew, meant an understanding of history. Cable was the first Southern writer fully to understand how the past shaped the present; history could help him explain "why Louisiana has grown up so out of joint" (26). More important, however, he knew how to use the past to define the present, to create a work that "contained as plain a protest against the times in which it was written as against the earlier times in which its scenes were set."[11] The action of the novel covers a period of one year, beginning in September 1803, but the characters tell stories dating back to the first settlers. In September 1803, New Orleans was still under the nominal control of the Spanish, although an agreement to transfer the colony to France had been concluded, and rumors of Napoleon's intent to sell his newly gained possession to the United States were already circulating. French control lasted only from November 30 to December 20, when the Americans took command. Thus, the citizens of New Orleans were compelled to change their national allegiance rapidly.

This moment in history provided Cable with an ideal means of examining the issues of Reconstruction. In both periods, proud aristocrats, who were used to depending on slave labor, were forced to accept their membership in a nation that claimed to value freedom and democracy. In both cases, the transition involved the imposition of a military governor with broad powers. Land titles were in doubt, and the direction of political and economic change was unclear. Tension was increased by the influx of new settlers who hoped to take advantage of the situation. Although faced with the need to accept change in their forms of government and ways of life, the Creoles, like the ex-Confederates, were more likely to cling to the customs of the past. Those willing to cooperate with the new government were widely regarded as traitors. Eventually, the Creoles grudgingly accepted their place in the union, declaring they would make their wants known to the central government in Washington—just as Reconstruction Southerners did. However, although white Southerners were ultimately reconciled to the new ways of life, in both cases the issue of racial justice remained unresolved, and blacks continued to be the victims of oppression. Cable's fidelity to historical truth thus demanded a complex plot involving many conflicts, some of which had to remain unresolved. Rejecting the plantation myth's simplistic glorification of the simple and uncomplicated past, *The Grandissimes* insists that all moments of history both past and present, are difficult and demanding.

As his history, *The Creoles of Louisiana*, demonstrates, Cable believed firmly in progress. Denying the myth of decline in that work, he urged the Creoles to gain a "pride of ascent," a pride in the ways in which nineteenth-century man is better than his ancestors.[12] Like Frowenfeld, Cable wanted the South "to follow the course of modern thought" (143). While the plantation myth affirmed nostalgia and the values of a simple, leisurely life, Cable believed in the gospel of work. Although he was too critical an observer of the New South to accept Henry W. Grady's views, Cable was more likely to praise a hardworking storekeeper than an idle planter. In *The Grandissimes*, the Creoles who best survive the effects of change do so because they can adapt to new economic conditions and overcome their disdain for commerce and "hard and patient labor" (141). It is not surprising that in his later life, Cable became a good friend of Andrew Carnegie.

In Cable's novel, as in many of Faulkner's works, a character's foolish admiration for the past is subject to the author's more critical examination, an examination that often undercuts the character's pride in his ancestry. Agricola Fusilier may take delight in his descent from Lufki-Humma, the Indian princess, but Cable shows us a young girl, unloved by her savage father, who becomes the pawn of the manipulating Listening Crane until she runs off with the first white men she sees and becomes the prize in a game of dice. The first settlers may have had a vast amount of courage, but as Cable shows in this novel and in *The Creoles of Louisiana*, they often lacked humanity. One of the lessons of the past is the need to adapt to change. Fusilier, who glorifies the past instead of learning from it, is ironically much like Listening Crane, an old and foolish man who cannot accept the destruction of his ambitions and dreams.

History in *The Grandissimes* is not to be worshiped but confronted and rectified; the past presents more burdens than blessings. Honoré Grandissime must assume responsibility for his father's actions and for his family's past mistakes. He courageously restores the plantation to Aurora and Clotilde and attempts to give his partially black half-brother the recognition his family would deny. Yet, as the Bras-Coupé story shows, the past is not so easily overcome. The powerful story ends with the mutilated slave feeling the touch of a baby and removing his curse from the land. The story, the most commented on and praised section of the novel, seems to be one in which forgiveness replaces vengeance. Although such a theme indicates Cable's ultimate hope, the book clearly shows that the curse has not been fully lifted. Palmyre still thirsts for revenge, and the compulsion to tell and retell the story shows that Bras-Coupé still haunts the imagination of both blacks and whites in the novel, just as the sins of the past continue to haunt the present.

*The Grandissimes* is structured around a series of conflicts, not all of which are satisfactorily resolved. Conflicts exist between families (the Grandissimes and the De Grapions), between members of the same family (Honoré and Agricola, Agricola and Sylvestre), between races (Honoré and Honoré f.m.c., Agricola and Palmyre), and between nationalities (the Creoles and the Americans). Into this world of struggle appears Joseph Frowenfeld, the well-meaning, studious, and naive intruder who attempts to assume the role of mediator and finds himself involved in conflicts of his own. On a thematic level, these conflicts become rich—between democracy and aristocracy, the old and the new, the North and the South, American and European values, justice and racism, pride and love, vengeance and forgiveness, innocence and experience, and the list could go on.

As one chapter title indicates, the most difficult conflicts of all are the "Wars within the Breast" (129). Most of the characters are forced to struggle with contradictory feelings, to question long-held attitudes and beliefs, to redefine themselves and their relationships with others. They emerge from this process of questioning and self-examination either changed or destroyed. Honoré must decide whether loyalty to family tradition or to moral conviction is to guide him. Although he succeeds in making the right decision, Honoré f.m.c. and the black characters are not able to redefine themselves in terms of the new society that is created. When the f.m.c. asserts "Ah ham nod a slev," Frowenfeld responds: "Are you certain of that?" (195). One of the questions Cable is concerned with is: what does it mean to be free? And he knew that the Emancipation Proclamation was not a sufficient answer, for, as Frowenfeld says, "there is a slavery that no legislation can abolish,—the slavery of caste. That, like all the slaveries on earth, is a double bondage. And what a bondage it is which compels a community, in order to preserve its established tyrannies, to walk behind the rest of the intelligent world!" (143). Neither whites nor blacks could be fully free until the issues of racism and caste had been confronted and overcome.

*The Grandissimes* is a book filled with questions. Frowenfeld spends much of his time seeking the answer to questions. Some of the chapter titles underscore the novel's concern with asking basic questions: "And Who Is My Neighbor?" (14) and "Fo' Wad You Cryne?" (212). Sometimes, however, the questions are implicit. When Frowenfeld asserts that he is an American, Agricola replies: "You are not. You were merely born in America" (86). The question Cable is raising is one that has preoccupied many of our writers: "what does it mean to be an American?" Cable knew that the Civil War had not answered that question. He knew that the South would not really be the principles of freedom and equality.

The presentation of conflicts and questions gains an allusive richness through the symbolic patterns, established by the names of the characters. On the most obvious level, names like Brahmin Mandarin de Grandissime suggest a family pride based on antiquated and foreign systems of caste. As the head of the family, Honoré must redefine the term "honor" so that it stands for moral principles and not family pride. The feud between the families is underscored by military allusions: a Fusilier is a soldier armed with a flintlock musket and De Grapion suggests "grape," a word referring to a kind of ammunition. However, Aurora and Clotilde now have the surname, Nancanou, which suggests "unknown," and is therefore appropriate for two characters who create an aura of mystery.

The names often point to the racial conflicts. Dr. Keene's observations on race are anything but keen, as his debate with Clemence establishes. Clemence, of course, meets with no clemency. Bras-Coupé's name explicitly points to the maiming effects of slavery, but the name may have been partially inspired by Cable's knowledge of an unsuccessful slave revolt at Pointe Coupée in 1795, which would be close to the time of Bras-Coupé's arrival in Louisiana.[13] The meaning of Palmyre would have been familiar to nineteenth-century readers who would have known the Syrian city's history either from Gibbon's *Decline and Fall of the Roman Empire*, or William Ware's bestseller, *Zenobia or the Fall of Palmyra* (1837), or one of the travel books of the time. Under the leadership of the Queen Zenobia, Palmyra attempted an unsuccessful revolt against Aurelian and the Roman Empire. Palmyre is therefore an appropriate name for a woman engaged in futile rebellion against more powerful forces.

Cable seems to have selected the name, Joseph Frowenfeld, with care. He knew the Bible extremely well and certainly knew of the old testament Joseph, the "dreamer" who is sent into a strange land and prospers until he is falsely accused of an illicit sexual involvement (See Gen. 37, 39–41). The evidence against Joseph is a garment that is left behind when he hastily flees, which corresponds to the hat Frowenfeld leaves. Although all the details do not match, this would not be the first time that a writer used the name Joseph to refer to his naive hero, as the reader of Fielding's *Joseph Andrews* knows. The most important parallel is that Joseph's salvation stems from his ability to be of service to the Egyptians as an interpreter of dreams, just as Frowenfeld becomes the interpreter of the Creoles' dreams. Given the German origin, the name Frowenfeld suggests *woman's field* (*frau* and *feld*). Such an interpretation finds support in the passage in which Palmyre is soothed by "his womanly touch, his commanding gentleness, his easy despatch" (135). As the representative of spiritual and moral forces working for peace and civilization, Frowenfeld clearly possesses qualities that the nineteenth century thought of as belonging to the woman's field of endeavor.

Cable's failure to give life to Joseph Frowenfeld is probably the single greatest weakness in the novel. Several critics have reminded us that Frowenfeld is not simply Cable's spokesman but a naive young man who must learn to cope with a complex world.[14] Cable rejects the plantation myth's belief that any Northerner who actually saw the South would be converted to its customs, but he also shows that Northern principles cannot easily convert the South. The problem is not that Frowenfeld is too simple a character, but that Cable is trying to do too much with him. His "large philosophy" sounds ridiculous "in a little parlor" (203). Although, as Clotilde suggests, Frowenfeld is innocent of everything (213), he possesses "that frankness and ardent zeal for truth which had enlisted the early friendship of Doctor Keene, amused and attracted Honoré Grandissime, won the confidence of the f.m.c., and tamed the fiery distrust and enmity of Palmyre" (141). The novel is based not only on his attempt to understand Creole society, but on the ways the Creoles understand and misunderstand him. In fact, the Creoles treat him as though he possesses some kind of magical power. Agricola seems to believe that Frowenfeld will vindicate the Creole cause. Honoré f.m.c. and Palmyre each unsuccessfully turns to him for love potions, and Aurora goes to him for basil which will bring money into her house.

Frowenfeld's interaction with the Creoles is too complex to fit into any simple scheme. In spite of his virtues, he has to depend on the aid of others, and even with their help, he is only partially successful. He spurs Honoré to action, and Honoré teaches him to temper his zeal with caution. The growth of these two characters is paralleled by that of Raoul Innerarity, who begins as a dilettante and a bumbler but becomes a businessman, husband, and peace-maker. The novel presents the growth of these characters, and the marriages between Honoré and Aurora and between Frowenfeld and Clotilde suggest both the reconciliation of the feuding families and of the North and the South. Nevertheless, there is much that remains unresolved.

With Raoul's help, Frowenfeld can stop Agricola's duel with Sylvestre, but Agricola, although softened, does not abandon his old prejudices; he provokes his own death at the hands of the f.m.c., and dies like an old Confederate, con-fused and uncertain, but proclaiming his loyalties to his sovereign state. None of the characters can prevent the horrible and violent death of Clemence. Frowenfeld and Honoré find love, but Dr. Keene, Palmyre, and the f.m.c. do not. Frowenfeld can help heal the bullet wound in Palmyre's breast, but not the wounds in her heart. Frowenfeld and Honoré can prevent the f.m.c.'s first attempt to drown himself, but not his second one.

At one point, Frowenfeld says that "the truth only is incredible" (208). But it was the truth of history to which Cable remained faithful. Cable under-stood how much Reconstruction had resolved and how much it had failed to resolve. The reconciliation of the North and the South had been achieved, but the attempt to reconcile the races ended, as Newton Arvin points out, in "failure and tragedy."[15] The name, *Grandissime Brothers,* turns out to be merely a linguistic victory, as the Emancipation Proclamation was. Instead of becom-ing truly free, the f.m.c. and Palmyre are forced to flee into exile and remain unredeemed by love. The issues raised in *The Grandissimes* were not resolved in 1803–1804 or in 1880; they have not yet been resolved today. Perhaps it is not accidental that the novel ends with an ironic chapter, entitled "No!" (336).

Cable went on to devote many years of his life to saying "no" to racism and the lies of the plantation myth. In doing so, he became, as H. H. Boyesen pre-dicted, the "founder of a new school" of Southern writing, writing committed to a complex probing of the moral issues of both the past and the present.[16]

## Notes

1. See *The Writer in the South* (Athens: University of Georgia Press, 1972) and Ru-bin's essay, "Southern Local Color and the Black Man," *Southern Review* 6 (Autumn 1970): 1011–30. For a discussion of black figures in antebellum American literature

and of the plantation myth, see Jean Fagin Yellin, *The Intricate Knot* (New York: New York University Press, 1972).

2. "The South as a Field for Fiction," *Forum* 6 (1886): 405. For a fuller account of post-bellum fiction, see Jay Martin, *Harvests of Change* (Englewood Cliffs, NJ: Prentice-Hall, 1967).

3. *George W. Cable: The Life and Times of a Southern Heretic* (New York: Pegasus, 1969), 78. All biographical information on Cable in this essay comes from Arlin Turner, *George W. Cable: A Biography* (Durham, NC: Duke University Press, 1956).

4. The most perceptive comments on Cable's writings may be found in the works by Rubin, Martin, and Turner cited earlier and in Newton Arvin, Introduction, *The Grandissimes* (New York: Hill and Wang, 1957), v–xi; Richard Chase, *The American Novel and Its Tradition* (Garden City, NY: Doubleday, 1957), 167–76; Richard Bozman Eaton, "George W. Cable and the Historical Romance," *Southern Literary Journal* 8 (Fall 1975): 82–94; John Cleman, "The Art of Local Color in George W. Cable's *The Grandissimes*," *American Literature* 47 (November 1975): 396–410; and Robert O. Stephens, "Cable's *The Grandissimes* and the Comedy of Manners," *American Literature* 51 (January 1980): 507–19.

5. Quoted in Arlin Turner, "A Novelist Discovers a Novelist: The Correspondence of H. H. Boyesen and George W. Cable," *Western Humanities Review* 5 (Autumn 1951): 346–47.

6. "A Novelist Discovers a Novelist," 347.

7. Quoted in Philip Butcher, "Cable to Boyesen on *The Grandissimes*," *American Literature* 40 (November 1968): 393.

8. "After-Thoughts of a Story-Teller," *North American Review* 158 (January 1894): 17.

9. "A Novelist Discovers a Novelist," 358.

10. *The Grandissimes* (New York: Hill and Wang, 1957), 96. All further quotations from *The Grandissimes* are from this edition and will be cited parenthetically in my text.

11. Excerpt from Cable's diary quoted in Arvin, viii.

12. *The Creoles of Louisiana* (New York: Charles Scribner's Sons, 1889), 51.

13. *The Creoles of Louisiana*, 125.

14. See Stephens' article and Donald Ringe, "The 'Double Center': Character and Meaning in Cable's Early Novels," *Studies in the Novel* 5 (Spring 1973): 52–62.

15. Arvin, xi.

16. "A Novelist Discovers a Novelist," 368.

# Southern Writers

## Notes Toward a Definition of Terms

THADIOUS M. DAVIS

Because Southern literature has consistently been identified as a distinct area of American literary studies, in a way that New England or Midwestern literature has not, I believed that I would have no difficulty in preparing a project on Southern women writers. I discovered, however, that the opening statement presented an unanticipated problem. Who or what is a Southern woman writer? Should the emphasis be placed on Southern or on woman? Or equally on both? I decided, somewhat arbitrarily, that equal emphasis on the two terms made sense. Yet there was still difficult territory ahead. "Woman" seemed obvious enough, but "Southern" was another matter.

Should a writer be classified as "Southern" if she were born in the South, lived in the South, or wrote in or about the South? All of these possibilities seemed relevant, but in thinking about inclusions I needed to sharpen my classifications. Clearly, even without a working definition, I had no intention of claiming a Willa Cather for the South, despite her birth on a Virginia farm and the first ten years of her life there. Lillian Hellman, born in New Orleans, was definitely in, though at least half of her work was not. What should be done about Sonia Sanchez, born in Alabama, but more New York than Southern, or Nikki Giovanni, who was born in Ohio, but reared by Southern parents and grandparents and educated in Tennessee? Could Edith Kelley possibly belong on the basis of her novel *Weeds*? What should become of a writer born in the South, but never using "Southern" materials? What if she happened to have been born in another region, lived in the South for some period and wrote about the South? The novelist Daphne Athas, born in Gloucester, Massachusetts, and a New Englander until her thirteenth year, came to mind because she has been a North Carolina resident for thirty years, though the locals still call her a "Yankee."

*Southern Quarterly* 19.2 (1981): 10–16.

These are the kinds of questions that unfolded like images in Alice's mirror, but with the force of Sherman's March to the Sea. Because the problems appeared most acute with post-Southern Renascence authors, I turned to the past, to that sense of history that Southerners allegedly possess, for tentative solutions.

The characteristics of Southern writers from the end of the Civil War to the Renascence that have been identified by such critics as C. Hugh Holman and Louis D. Rubin Jr. are a sense of place, a preoccupation with the past, a sense of family and community, and a desire for the concrete. There is nothing in this list, however, that specifically distinguishes the *Southern* writer from any other writer who establishes a base in a particular community or tradition. Other critics have added characteristics to the list—a tragic sense, a recognition of failure and defeat, and an acceptance of paradox but these too remain generalities applicable to many different groups of writers. In "The View from the Regency-Hyatt," Holman clarifies the distinctive characteristics of Southern authors as being "the presence of the Negro and the shame of his enslavement and second-class citizenship; the historical experience of military defeat, military occupation, and reconstruction; and a predominately agricultural economy."[1] Holman provides a more precise description; nevertheless, he does so in terms primarily related to the region as a place, not to the differentiation of the writers. Rubin and Robert Jacobs have defended the use of such general characteristics by concluding "that the characteristics we have described as typical of Southern writers are by no means exclusively or peculiarly so. . . . Not the exclusive existence of any of these characteristics in modern Southern fiction and poetry, but the collective presence of all of them together typifies the work of the writers. . . . Granted . . . the variety in the constellation that is modern Southern literature, still, we keep returning again and again to common themes, common attitudes, common preoccupations."[2]

Despite the soundness of their conclusions, Rubin and Jacobs mainly take into account the works of white, primarily male, writers of the Renascence, Faulkner, Cabell, Warren, Wolfe, the Fugitives-Agrarians (Laura Riding excluded). Ellen Glasgow and Eudora Welty are usually considered major writers, but receive less attention than male authors in the formulation of theories. Flannery O'Connor and Katherine Ann Porter, both too talented to be ignored, do not conveniently fit into the pattern established by the accepted list of characteristics. And the majority of modern black Southern writers, including Richard Wright, bear little relationship to the characteristics.

Essentially then, Rubin and Jacobs described their "typical" works, and reason from these to "typical" characteristics of Southern writers. Their method is heavily dependent upon subject matter manifested in the literature.

A new reference work, *Southern Writers: A Biographical Dictionary*, edited by Robert Bain, Joseph Flora, and Louis Rubin, provided little help. Not only did the editors not define Southern writers, but they also included questionable entries, such as Chester Himes, Jessie Redmon Fauset, and Elizabeth Hardwick, without a word of justification. They had excluded more obvious choices, Rita Mae Brown and Alice Walker. These editors and Southernist critics fail to mention that it is increasingly more difficult to identify *Southern writers* by the method of attending to their subject matter.

One reason for the difficulty is that the South today is different from the "Souths" of the past. Granted, the changing South or "New South" has been a phenomenon for the last fifty years. As Walker Percy observes in "Southern Comfort" (*Harper's*, January 1979), "the suspicion arises that nothing is really changing, or that if it is, the change may be real and even good but also somehow dispiriting, having to do with the Americanization of the South and such boring items as Economic Progress with a Southern Accent, New Orleans, City of Contrasts (the Vieux Carré in all its charm depicted against a backdrop of the Superdome and the Hyatt)." Percy's observation is an intelligent assessment.

As a physical place and a background for writing, the South is changing, losing its cohesiveness—slowly in the Mississippi Delta region or in the backwoods of the Piedmont, rapidly along the "progressive" East Coast from Virginia to Florida and along the Gulf Coast all the way up to Dallas. Faulkner would have trouble recognizing New Orleans and Memphis—front and back doors of Oxford, Mississippi—but not too much trouble with Oxford itself because, like most of the small towns in the South, Oxford has little impetus for drastic change. It is important though that the writers today, an Ellen Douglas in Mississippi or Shirley Ann Grau in Louisiana, may have difficulty tapping their resources of old, or they may be quite comfortable with the Sun Belt McDonalds and Atlanta condominiums, as Kelly Cherry and Lee Smith are. The raw materials for the writers in or of the South are no longer homogenous. How, then, can *Southern writer* be defined?

After examining a long list of writers who are or have been considered *Southern*, from Caroline Gordon, Elizabeth Spencer, and Margaret Walker Alexander to Doris Betts, Sylvia Wilkinson, and Alice Walker, I isolated several attributes that point toward a definition.

First, place of birth in itself is not a major factor in determining a Southern writer. Southerners, like the rest of the nation, have grown more mobile in the past twenty years. However, writers either born in the South or descended from Southerners tend to retain ties with the region. Apparently, the nucleus of a Southerner's extended family generally remains in the same area of native soil, be it rural or urban, and that nucleus causes a significant involvement with Southern life and thought. Ernest Gaines, for instance, was born (1933) into a plantation community in Louisiana, but has lived in California since the 1940s. Over the years, he has returned to the region of his birth because family members remain there and he retains connections with them. Gaines's best known work, *The Autobiography of Miss Jane Pittman*, is in fact based upon the life of his aunt Augusteen Jefferson, with whom he spent much of his early boyhood. The relationship between Gaines and Miss Augusteen leads to a second observation in defining Southern writers.

More important than place of birth is the place central to the individual writer's formative years. By place, I mean the exterior reality with its nexus of relationships that shapes the writer's individual sense of landscape or cityscape, or people and society. If a writer's imagination responds to or reacts against the social processes, economic conditions, kinship configurations, and communical stratification of a specified area of the South more strikingly than to any other place, then that writer is a Southern writer. The imagination may be shaped, at least partly, by what is most prominent in objective social reality or by what is absent from it. The regions and places of the South can exercise a strong hold over the formative imaginations of so many distinct personalities precisely because its social processes have been more exaggerated than those in other areas of the country, and an awareness of those processes are instilled in the young by the older generations, who apparently enjoy a greater degree of intergenerational intimacy and contact than in other regions.

The writer, then, whose imagination is nurtured by the South becomes a Southern writer. He or she has, as Faulkner remarked, "figuratively speaking, taken the artist in him in one hand and his milieu in the other and thrust the one into the other like a clawing and spitting cat into a croker sack." The result can be a Faulkner, born white in a closed, traditional world that viewed increasing industrialization and disintegration of rural patterns as threats to the old values, to the integrity of the individual, family, clan, and community. His imagination formed in response to the specific world of northern Mississippi, and his writing reflects a desire for continuity and stability. The result can also be a Richard Wright, born black in a caste-defined world that attempted to keep blacks in subjugation by law or custom. His imagination reacted against the Mississippi and Arkansas societies of prejudice, racial violence, and segregation codes. The response in his writing is a desire for change and assertion.

Wright and Faulkner are only two prominent examples; there are numerous others: Daphne Athas, whose imagination was fed by small town North Carolina from the moment of her arrival at thirteen and whose *Entering Ephesus* effectively portrays the way in which the region took hold of her imaginative processes; or Harriet Arnow, who left Kentucky after her graduation from college but whose creative energies have consistently tapped the wellspring of the Kentucky mountains, the place of her formative experiences. Every imaginative life may be an exchange, but the point is that the *Southern writer* chooses to be, perhaps cannot avoid being, nourished creatively and imaginatively by the South.

My third observation towards a definition of Southern writers has to do with an attitude toward self and by extension toward fictional characters. The Southern writer sees himself or herself as being *different*. There was a time in the 1920s and 1930s when writers connected with the South by heritage or inclination could be regarded as Southern partly because of their struggle to achieve a deserved place in the American literary establishment, not so much for themselves as individual artists, but for the region as a whole. H. L. Mencken's "Sahara of the Bozart" struck a deep cord and helped foster a unity of purpose, a purpose informed by an acute awareness that their region was different from the rest of the nation. Thus, despite modernity and industrialism, the South between the world wars was still wrestling with the problems Holman stresses in his list of characteristics—the experience of slavery, defeat in the Civil War, dependence upon an agricultural economy. Now, the differences are more oblique. The South may physically resemble the rest of the country, but psychologically it continues to labor under a sense of difference. The writers today are not united in their vision of the South or in their conception of the role of Southern writing. Nevertheless, they do seem convinced of their difference; whether factual or not, that difference sets them apart, makes them distinct.

The "terrible burden" of being a Southern writer, which Faulkner recognized, remains so—though more often than not contemporary writers infuse it with a comic spirit. Its seems quite appropriate that Walker Percy's "moviegoer" and Doris Betts's "ugliest pilgrim" remind us of O'Connor's people; neither the sense of the past nor a tragic sense isolates these individuals, but their conviction of their "difference" does. This subjective vision of self as different pervades the writing, and in the final analysis forces the objective observer to agree than Anne Tyler or a Heather Ross Miller, no less than a Sherwood Bonner or a Harper Lee, is different.

A shared characteristic among these three attributes is the attention to place, not so much as subject matter as a conditioning factor that affects the writer's own personal vision and aesthetic sensibility. My primary focus for definition, then, is on the artistic process of the writer, not on the exterior reality forming the objective plane of his or her South. It is, after all, a subjective region of the imagination entered into in creative writing; and while that writing contains specific details, based in the external world, so that the reader will have familiar bearings, it also transforms all into an internal world imagined, projected, and shared by the artist.

My notes toward a definition of "Southern writers" certainly are incomplete. I am still refining my conceptions and my use of the term, but, at the very least, I feel more confident about my rejection of Sanchez as a Southern writer and my inclusion of Athas.

## Notes

1. *The Roots of Southern Writing* (Athens: University of Georgia Press, 1972), 107.
2. *South: Modern Southern Literature and Its Cultural Setting*, ed. Louis D. Rubin Jr. and Robert D. Jacobs (Garden City, NY: Doubleday Dolphin Books, 1961), 13.

# "Tough Times"

## Downhome Blues Recordings as Folk History

JOHN SOLOMON OTTO AND AUGUSTUS M. BURNS

Phonograph record companies viewed the advent of the radio as a medium of mass entertainment with considerable concern. In the early 1920s when the radio began to attract sizable audiences, record companies intensified their efforts to discover new groups of potential record purchasers. They quickly found an untapped market which previously had been ignored: black Americans. Advertising their black-oriented releases as "race records," the companies began releasing recordings by gospel performers, jazz artists, and blues singers. From 1920 to 1924, the earliest blues recordings featured women vocalists, who sang vaudeville blues penned by professional composers. These artists were accompanied by jazz bands and pianos.[1] After 1924 the companies expanded their offerings to black audiences. They started recording "downhome" blues sung by male and female musicians who usually accompanied themselves on the guitar or piano. These downhome blues musicians usually composed their own songs by drawing from a body of traditional formulaic verses, or by commenting on widely shared experiences in black life.[2] Downhome blues were thus commercialized folksongs, sung in a traditional style. They expressed the values of the folk—in this case working-class blacks with a rural background.[3]

The record companies have transcribed literally thousands of downhome blues from 1924 down to the present. These recordings represent a massive body of oral evidence about black folklife.[4] Downhome blues musicians sang about the concerns of working-class blacks, relatively few of whom left any written records, or even oral testimonies about their lives. Downhome blues recordings are thus a potential new source for writing the history of poor black Americans—a group often dismissed as "inarticulate" by scholars who rely on written sources.[5] Originally issued on fragile 78 rpm shellac discs,

*Southern Quarterly* 21.3 (1983): 27–43.

hundreds of these recordings have now been reissued on long-playing micro-groove albums which are readily available to anyone interested in American Studies.

Although most downhome blues deal with romantic themes and mistreat-ing lovers, the rich spectrum of black folklore and history can now be found in downhome blues recordings. There are, for example, snatches of the fa-miliar animal tales of black folklore, which have been interpreted as coded comments on race relations:

> Black cat said to the white cat,
> let's go across town and clown.
> Black cat said to the white cat,
> I believe I'll go across town and clown,
> Lord, the white cat told him,
> you better set your black self down.[6]

There are ballads about folk heroes such as "Stackolee":

> I remember one September, on one Friday night.
> Stackolee and Billy Lyons had a great fight.[7]

Maxims and proverbs are well-represented in downhome blues:

> Ashes to ashes, dust to dust.
> Show me a yellow woman that a man can trust.[8]

Even riddles can be found:

> Now it's belly to belly, skin to skin.
> Two things rubbing and nothing going in.[9]

There are versions of the "dozens," a form of verbal dueling:

> Yonder go your mama, goin' out across the field.
> Runnin' and shakin' like an automobile.

> I hollered at your mama, and I told her to wait.
> She slipped away from me like a Cadillac-Eight.[10]

There are jokes, often commenting on social relations, such as this reference to skin color differences among Afro-Americans:

Now, a yellow gal rides in an automobile
a brown skin gal rides the same.
A black gal is carried in an old hay wagon,
she's gettin' by just the same.[11]

There are anecdotes such as this fictional encounter with a skunk:

I caught a pretty little animal, it was striped black and white (2x)
What it done to me, it spoiled me the rest of my life.

I thought it was a squirrel, I took him into my camp (2x)
When I put him down, all my clothes was damp.

I never smelled a smell, that smelled so doggone bad (2x)
It was the worst old smell, baby, the harder I rubbed.

It was a doggone polecat, and he [sure] ain't no friend of mine (2x)
He's as pretty as a wax doll, but he ain't worth a doggone dime.[12]

One can also find "toasts" (folk narrative poems) such as this bowdlerized version of the "Freaks' Ball" or "Bulldaggers' Hall":

Tell Double Crossing Ed.
Tell Abyssinia Ned.
Tell old Pistol Pete.
Everybody gonna meet.

Tonight we need no rest.
We really gonna throw a mess.
We gonna break out all the windows.
We gonna kick down all the doors.
We gonna pitch a Wang-Dang-Doodle,
all night long, all night long.[13]

There are "boasts" or tall tales:

I got an ax-handle pistol on a graveyard frame,
that shoots tombstone bullets wearing balls and chain.
I'm drinking TNT, I'm smoking dynamite,
I hope some screwball will start a fight.
Cause I'm ready, ready as anybody can be.
I'm ready for you, I hope you ready for me.[14]

There are numerous references to sorcery and folk medicine:

Now, run here conjure man,
and your brother mojo Sam.
I want to tell you voodoing daddies,
she's going back to Birmingham.

I want goofer dust, sprinkled all
around my baby's door.
Maybe next time she won't try to leave me,
she won't try to leave me no more.[15]

There are satirical comments on folk religion which have their homologues in
the ubiquitous preacher tales of black folklore:

Yes, I'm gonna get me religion, and
I'm gonna join the Baptist Church.
Yes I'm gonna get me religion, I
say I'm gonna join the Baptist Church.
You know, I want to be a Baptist Preacher,
so I won't have to work.[16]

There are blues about mistreatment which have their counterparts in the protest tales of black folklore:

Ain't but the one thing, see what I done wrong (2x)
Moved my family down on Tom Moore's farm.

Go to work in the morning, stops at one o'clock (2x)
Hold back dinner time, but sure can't hold back dark.

Standing on the levee, with his spurs in his horse's flank (2x)
Whip in his hand, watching the boys from bank to bank.[17]

And finally, there are many downhome blues about topical problems in
black life: farming, migration to the cities, crowded urban life, factory work,
the World Wars, and unemployment. These topical blues, sung by musicians
who served as the spokespeople for working class blacks, are valuable commentaries on issues that touched the black community. Therefore, topical
blues may be regarded as folk historical sources, which reflect black perceptions and evaluations of historical events and processes that have usually been
reported from the viewpoint of outside observers.[18]

The Great Depression, for example, produced dozens of recordings which
comment on the economic hardships visited upon blacks. Subsequent to the
Depression, each postwar recession likewise yielded blues music which discussed the economic difficulty attendant to blacks. In the recording studios
blues singers were subjected to few constraints in their presentation of material. Their records were headed for consumption by black America, in cities
and rural areas where they would not become a part of the mass entertainment network of white America. Consequently, they commented openly on
economic troubles and government economic policies. Topical blues were often a reflection of the singer's personal experience, which could include losing
a job or being fired, going on relief, or working on a government project. At
times, the artist would sing about the experiences of friends, kinfolk, or fellow
workers.[19] These songs provide insight into black experience and attitudes,
and when combined with more standard historical sources enable a research-
er to explore black working-class perceptions of the Great Depression, the
New Deal, and the various postwar recessions.

The stock market crash in 1929 is of course the traditional point of departure which marks the onset of the Great Depression. Within a few months of
the crash, working-class blacks had felt the first tremors from the contraction.
They responded in part by reducing their record purchases. So severe was
their withdrawal from record buying that the "race record" market began to
disappear. Some record companies collapsed, while others attempted to survive through merger. Nearly all slashed their record prices.[20] In another effort
to reduce costs, the companies recorded fewer artists, turning to performers whose lyrical inventiveness enabled them to appeal to the fickle blues-
buying public. Thus, as Paul Oliver reports, the blues of the Depression era

was "sometimes less rich musically than it had been hitherto, but the content of the verses, which mattered greatly to those who bought the discs, was of more immediate social relevance than at any previous time."[21] Moreover, the blues of the 1930s reflected urban rather than rural concerns as the record companies focused on their urban audience since it was a cheaper audience to reach. They abandoned the expensive field recording caravans which had once toured the rural South searching for new blues talent.[22]

By 1931, blues singers had recorded a number of "hard times" blues. Perhaps the most powerful in the genre was Nehemiah James's "Hard Time Killin' Floor Blues" (1931):

Hard time here 'n everywhere you go.
Times is harder than ever been before.

And the people are drifting from door to door.
Can't find no heaven, I don't care where they go. . . .

Let me tell you people, just before I go.
These hard times will kill you just dry along so. . . .

When you hear me singing my true lonesome song.
These hard times can last up so very long. . . .
If I ever get off this killing floor,
I'll never get down this low no more. . . .

If you thought you had money, you'd better be sure,
Cause these hard times will drive you from door to door. . . .[23]

In the black neighborhoods unemployment "appeared earlier, was of greater intensity and lasted longer . . . than elsewhere in the community." Many black workers experienced discriminatory layoffs as whites sought jobs formerly reserved for blacks.[24] With no payroll coming in, unemployed urban blacks faced eviction and destitution:

The times are getting tighter,
getting tighter every day (2x)
But the rent man comes as usual,
when he knows that we can't pay.

I stood him off so long,
until I'm afraid to facing him now (2x)
Because I know when I do facing him,
there's going to be a row.

[Now] my coal bin is empty,
not a lump these can you find (2x)
I would buy coal by the bushel,
if I only had a dime.

Just a lonely alley where
my baby used to find some wood (2x)
But now she can't find a splinter,
no one in that neighborhood.

[Now] the times is so tight,
they keep you walking up and down the street (2x)
With all these debts a coming in,
not a one of them can we meet.[25]

Rather than passively accepting hard times, one bluesman condemned black Republicans who voted for Herbert Hoover in 1928:

Just before the election,
you's talking how you was going to vote (2x)
And after election was over,
your head down like a billy goat.[26]

Hoover's effort to deal with the Depression-induced destitution relied on local relief agencies and private charities, and many of those in need received inadequate assistance or were missed altogether. Upon his election in 1933, Franklin Roosevelt expanded federal responsibility for relief, hoping to provide a more comprehensive relief system. The Federal Emergency Relief Administration (F.E.R.A.) began to supply grants to state and local relief agencies. By October 1933, 18 percent of all blacks were on the relief rolls.[27] Skeptical of the administration of such government largesse, unemployed blacks lined up at the relief offices, hoping for fair treatment but fearing discrimination:

[Now]. I'm, going down to the relief,
I want a order today (2x)
If I don't get some groceries, my
baby'll run away.

[Now] Uncle Sam is helping millions
seems like he'd help poor me (2x)
Now, I'm going down there tomorrow morning,
and ask for sympathy.[28]

Roosevelt's F.E.R.A., of course, did not have as its objective the elimina-
tion of unemployment. Subsequently, the Roosevelt administration planned
to initiate federally sponsored work relief to supplant the F.E.R.A., which had
a legislative life of only two years.[29] But the ending of the F.E.R.A. gave some
blacks a feeling of disquietude. Sang one bluesman:

Now, Everybody's crying: "Let's Have a New Deal."
Relief station is closing down,
I know just how you feel. . . .

Now, I woke up this morning, doggone my soul,
My flour barrel was empty,
I swear I didn't have no coal. . . .

Now, you go to your [case] worker,
And put in your complaint,

Eight times out of ten,
You know they'll say I cain't. . . .
They don't wanna give you no dough,
Won't hardly pay your rent,
And it ain't costing them one doggoned cent. . . .

Refrain: Everybody's crying: "Let's Have a New Deal,"
'Cause I've got to make a living,
If I have to rob and steal.[30]

To many blacks the most important work relief agency for minorities was the Public Works Administration (P.W.A.), which assumed control of major construction projects, low-rent housing programs, and slum clearance. Harold Ickes, director of the agency, insisted that blacks be well represented on P.W.A. payrolls. In addition, P.W.A. projects included schools, hospitals, and housing tracts for blacks.[31] Understandably, the P.W.A. was lauded in blues recordings:

Lord, Mister President, listen to what
I'm going to say (2x)
You can take away all of the alphabet,
but please leave the P.W.A.

Now, You're in Mr. President,
and I hope you're there to stay (2x)
But whatever changes you make,
please keep the P.W.A.

P.W.A. is the best old friend I ever seen (2x)
Since the job ain't hard, and the boss ain't mean.

I went to the poll and voted,
and I know I voted the right way (2x)
Now I'm praying to you Mr. President,
please keep the P.W.A.[32]

Federally sponsored slum clearance projects, however, did not always receive black acclaim. Tearing down low cost housing, however dilapidated, did not always mean that the destroyed housing would be replaced. One result of such housing policy, therefore, was overcrowding in some of the black neighborhoods where slum clearance occurred. Ironically, many of the people ousted by federal slum clearance found themselves ineligible for the new housing projects. In other cases, displaced renters could not afford the cost of the new housing when it became available. Urban blacks thus crowded into the remaining slums as landlords subdivided multi-room apartments into one-room "Kitchenettes."[33] Long before the appearance in 1964 of Martin Anderson's path-breaking *The Federal Bulldozer*, bluesmen had noted the consequences of slum clearance. As one artist sang:

Everybody's working in this town,
and this worries me night and day (2x)

Yes, that mean working crew that works for the W.P.A.
Well, well, the landlord came this mornin',
and he knocked on my door.

He asked me if I was going to pay my rent no more.
He said: "You have to move if you can't pay."
And then he turned, and he walked slowly away.

So I have to try, find me some other place to stay.
That house-wrecking crew's comin' from the W.P.A.

Well, well, I went to the relief station,
and I didn't have a cent.
They said: "[sit still?] where you staying,
and you don't have to pay no rent."

So when I got back home,
they was tacking a notice to my door.
This house is condemned, and
you can't live here no more.

So a notion struck me, I'd better be on my way.
They're gonna tear my house down, ooh,
that crew from the W.P.A.[34]

By 1936, the Works Progress Administration (W.P.A.) had supplanted the P.W.A. as the major work relief agency. Drawing 90 percent of its workers from the relief rolls, the W.P.A. initiated a seemingly endless number of small works projects. And although black percentages on the W.P.A. rolls exceeded the black percentage of the general population, racial discrimination pervaded the administration. Black wages generally lagged behind wages paid to whites for comparable work, blacks were hired primarily in unskilled wage categories, and few blacks could be found in administrative and supervisory positions. Nor did W.P.A. work always provide workers with sufficient income to procure the necessities of life. Many turned to local relief agencies in order to make ends meet.[35]

I was working on the project,
begging the relief for shoes (2x)
Because the rock and concrete . . .
given my feet the blues.

Working on the project with holes in all my clothes (2x)
Trying to make a dime . . .
To keep the rent man from putting me outdoors.

I am working on the project
trying to make both ends meet (2x)
But the payday is so long . . . until
the grocery man won't let me eat. . . .

Working on the project with pay-day
three or four weeks away (2x)
Now you can't make ends meet . . .
when you can't. . . . Get no pay.[36]

The Federal Emergency Relief Administration ended in 1935. The Civil Works Administration, the other major federal relief program in the very early New Deal, had ended in 1934. Consequently, general relief again became the province of local government, although the federal government did distribute commodities to local relief agencies. Since blacks had higher unemployment rates and lower wages than whites, they were disproportionately represented on general relief rolls. In every city, black people lined up at warehouses and welfare stores to receive surplus food and clothing.[37]

Now, me and my baby we talked last night,
and we talked for nearly an hour.
She wants me to go down to the welfare store,
and get a sack of that welfare flour. . . .

Now, you need to get you some real white man,
you know, to sign your little note.
They give you a pair of them keen-toed shoes
and one of those pinch-backed soldier coats. . . .

President Roosevelt said them welfare people,
they going to treat everybody right.

Says they give you a can of them beans
and a can or two of them old tripe.

But I told her no, baby, and I sure
don't want to go.
I say I'll do anything in the world for you
but I don't want to go down to that welfare store.[38]

"Welfare Store Blues" (1940) was a crushing indictment of the local discrimination which hampered federal attempts to aid poor blacks, but it was
also one of the last "hard times" blues. As the United States recovered from
the desperation of the mid-thirties, the public temper moderated. Military
armament added to the economic recovery, and blacks shared in the war-
time economic boom. Prosperity did not altogether erase the specter of the
Depression, however, nor did it cause blacks to forget the ambivalent quality
of the New Deal relief programs:

Yes, this is an awful thing [yes] to
hear a black man say (2x)
Yes, you know, I done throwed my shovel away,
because I don't have to work on that W.P. and A.[39]

At the end of the war, economic conversions—including the return to the
job market of millions of veterans—meant the end of war industry jobs in
which many blacks had been employed:

Refrain: Hard Times, hard times here with me now (2x)
If they don't get no better,
I believe I'll leave this town.
Said, you know, the company and
the union men began to meet
[Poor?] production . . . we'll give you
four days a week.

I left home this morning, you know
right early soon.
I bet my best friend girl, she'd [just?]
meet me in the afternoon.

Well, the men began to talk,
for they want to raise on the hours.
This is a bad time, we laying them
off by the thousands.[40]

The three economic recessions of the Eisenhower Presidency signaled to
many blacks another post–World War II economic distress. During Ike's first
year in office, a declining stock market, a fall in orders for durable goods,
excessive inventories and a drop in military spending initiated a economic
downturn.[41] As unemployment escalated among blacks one bluesman harkened back to the Great Depression:

Me and my baby were talking
and what she said was true.
She said: "It seems like times is getting tough,
like they was in '32.

You don't have no job, our bills are past due,
So now tell me baby, what we gonna do?"

Refrain: Tough times, tough times, is here once more.
Now if you don't have no money, people,
you can't live happy no more.

I had a good job, working many
long hours a week.
They had a big layoff, and they got poor me.
I'm broke and disgusted—in misery,
Can't find a part-time job, nothing
in my house to eat.

I went down to the grocery store,
said I'll get a little food on time.
The man said: "Wait a minute, see
how do we stand,
I'm sorry to tell you, but you're too
far behind."[42]

By March 1954, unemployment stood at 6 percent; among blacks it was 10. Inspired by the story of two club patrons who had just been laid off, guitarist J. B. Hutto composed a blues that looked back to the hard times of 1929 and the flush times of 1944:[43]

> I went to work this morning,
> was all set to start.
> My boss walked up and told me,
> "Son, [raised?] my hours,
> Things are so slow, don't think
> we need you anymore."
> He told me, "Things are so slow,
> don't think we need you anymore."
>
> I had to tell my wife, she didn't fuss.
> Finance took the car, we'll have to ride the bus.
> Things are so slow, don't think they'll
> be right anymore.
> I told her, "Things are so slow,
> don't think they'll be right anymore."
>
> I had a dream last night,
> I was standing in a great long line.
> A line like they had boys, in 1929.
> Things are so slow, don't think I can make it anymore.
> I said, "Things are so slow,
> don't think I can make it anymore."
>
> In 1944, everything was going along strong.
> I say it's ten years later, boys, and
> everything's going wrong. . . .[44]

Bluesmen also found parallels between the Republican administration of 1931 and the Republican administration of 1954:

> Well, do you remember, baby 19 and 31.
> That's when the Depression, baby, yes, begun.
> Refrain: Yes, darling, yes, you know what I'm talking about.

Well, the Democrats put you on your feet, baby,
you have the nerve to vote them out.[45]

Black voters, of course, were of two minds about the Eisenhower
Administration. While many would agree with the bluesmen who found
the Republicans lacking, Eisenhower scored more heavily with black voters than any Republican presidential candidate who had run since the Great
Depression.[46] Congressman Adam Clayton Powell, a prominent figure in
black politics, had in fact openly supported Eisenhower in 1952 and had urged
other blacks to do likewise. But the sluggish economy of the 1950s proved an
effective antidote to Powell's prescription for many blacks. Blues composer
J. B. Lenoir brought out his controversial "Eisenhower Blues" in 1954. It was
banned shortly after its release:[47]

Hey, everybody I'm talking to you.
I been telling you jivers, this
is the natural truth.
Refrain: mm-mm-mm, I've got those Eisenhower Blues.
Thinking about me and you, what on
earth are we gonna do.

My money's gone, my fun is gone.
The way things look, how can I be here long.

Taking all my money to pay the tax.
I'm only giving you people the natural facts.
I'm only telling you people my belief.
Because I am heading straight for relief.

Ain't got a dime, ain't even got a cent.
I don't even have no money to pay my rent.
My baby needs some clothes, she needs some shoes.
People I don't know what I'm gonna do.

All in all, 1954 was a banner year for downhome blues sales. Within a few
years, however, the appeal of downhome blues had slackened considerably.
Rhythm-and-blues and rock-and-roll supplanted the more traditional musical styles. In addition, topical blues seems to have diminished in its appeal as

black Americans substituted political action for political commentary. One paradox of the civil rights movement of the fifties and sixties is that the political action of civil rights was abetted considerably by the Eisenhower appointment of Earl Warren to be Chief Justice of the United States Supreme Court, even as bluesmen were making known their dissatisfaction with the Eisenhower economic policies.

The recession in 1958 failed to attract the attention of blues artists. B. B. King did record a tongue-in-cheek "Recession Blues," but it was never issued:

> Since this recession, I'm losing my baby,
> because the times are getting so hard (2x)
> Yes, I have to stop running around,
> and you know it's breaking my heart.
>
> Yes, I can't afford liquor, [people]
> all I can buy is beer and wine (2x)
> Well, I get my baby what she wants,
> and she stays cross all the time.
>
> Yes, please, please somebody
> please go up to Washington for me (2x)
> Yes, think about us out here
> help to get me out of this misery.[48]

Yes, vestiges of the past do linger. In 1974, at the height of another recession, a Mississippi-born bluesman recorded "My Mind's Going Back to 1929":

> Say, my mind's going back to 19 and 29 (2x)
> Say, I lose my job, and I didn't have one more dime.
>
> I got a job in the country, with a pair
> of them old long-eared mules (2x)
> You know they changed my name,
> and called me that old pine fool.
>
> Every Saturday evening, I'd put on
> my new clothes and leave home (2x)
> You know, I'd go and have a little fun,
> drinking corn whiskey all night long.[49]

In summary, downhome blues recordings thus not only entertained, they also defined social situations and offered ways of coping with them. Topical blues may therefore be viewed broadly as history—"a cycle of journeys in search of fair treatment and better times."[50] By recording topical blues about depressions and recessions, blues musicians not only mirrored black experiences, but they also influenced the attitudes and actions of black Americans.

# Notes

1. Giles Oakley, *The Devil's Music: A History of the Blues* (New York: Harcourt, Brace and Jovanovich, 1976), 92–96; Jeff Todd Titon, *Early Downhome Blues: A Musical and Cultural Analysis* (Urbana: University of Illinois Pres, 1977), xiii–xvii, 64–65.
   In the black English dialect, the term "downhome" does not refer to a geographic region but rather to a way of life—black rural culture and its partial extension to the cities. Jeff Todd Titon, "Thematic Pattern in Downhome Blues Lyrics," *Journal of American Folklore* 90 (1977): 318.

2. William Ferris, "Blues Roots and Development," *The Black Perspective in Music* 2 (1974): 124; David Evans, "Techniques of Blues Composition among Black Folk-singers," *Journal of American Folklore* 87 (1974): 240–49; William Ferris, *Blues from the Delta* (New York: Anchor Press, 1978), 57–75.
   Blues songs usually have a twelve-bar structure, three-line verses with an AAB rhyme scheme, and tonic, subdominant, and dominant cord progression patterns. Peter Guralnick, *Feel Like Going Home: Portraits in Blues and Rock 'N Roll* (New York: E. P. Dutton, 1971), 22, 24.

3. John Greenway, *American Folksongs of Protest* (Philadelphia: University of Pennsylvania Press, 1953), 8; Titon, *Early Downhome Blues*, 210–24.

4. For discographies of downhome blues recordings, see John Godrich and Robert Dixon, *Blues and Gospel Records 1902–1942* (London: Storyville Publications, 1969). Discographical information for blues recordings cited in this article is taken from above.

5. See Lawrence W. Levine, *Black Culture and Black Consciousness: Afro-American Folk Thought from Slavery to Freedom* (New York: Oxford University Press, 1977), xi–xii, 217–39.

6. Willie Lane, "Black Cat Rag." Reissued on "Black Cat Trail," Mamlish S-3800. For interpretations and collections of black animal tales, see Levine, *Black Culture*, 102–21; Langston Hughes and Arna Bontemps, eds., *The Book of Negro Folklore* (New York: Dodd Mead, 1958), 1–30; Richard M. Dorson, *American Negro Folktales* (Greenwich, Conn.: Fawcett, 1967), 66–123; J. Mason Brewer, *American Negro Folklore* (Chicago: Quadrangle Books, 1968), 3–19.

7. Furry Lewis, "Billy Lyons and Stack O'Lee." Reissued on "Ten Years in Memphis 1927–37," Yazoo L-1002. For references to "Stagolee (Stackerlee)" as well as other

black folk figures, see G. Malcolm Laws Jr., *Native American Balladry* (Philadelphia: American Folklore Society, 1964), 89–91, 253–54; Hughes and Bontemps, eds., *Negro Folklore*, 359–61; Brewer, *American Negro Folklore*, 313–25.

8. Stick Horse Hammond, "Truck 'em Down." Reissued on "Packin' Up My Blues: Blues of the Deep South 1950–1961," Muskadine 102. For a study of black proverbs and aphorisms, see J. Mason Brewer, "Old Time Negro Proverbs," *Publications of the Texas Folklore Society* 11 (1933): 101–5; Brewer, *American Negro Folklore*, 313–25.

9. Arkansas Johnny Todd, "Keep 'em Down." Reissued on "Blues from the Deep South," Kent KST 9004. Riddles are touched upon in Brewer, *American Negro Folklore*, 349–52.

10. Speckled Red, "Dirty Dozens." Reissued on "AC/DC Blues," Stash ST-106. The "dozens" are discussed in Roger D. Abrahams, "Playing the Dozens," *Journal of American Folklore* 75 (1962): 209–20; Paul Oliver, *Aspects of the Blues Tradition* (New York: Oak Publications, 1968), 235–46.

11. The Delta Boys, "Black Gal Swing." Reissued on "Country Blues Classics: Vol. 3," Blues Classics 7. See J. S. Otto and A. M. Burns, "The Use of Race and Hillbilly Recordings as Sources for Historical Research: The Problem of Color Hierarchy Among Afro-Americans in the Early Twentieth Century," *Journal of American Folklore* 85 (1972): 344–55.

12. Barbecue Bob, "Black Skunk Blues." Reissued on "Chocolate to the Bone," Mamlish S-3808. For collections of black jokes and anecdotes, see Roger D. Abrahams, *Deep Down in the Jungle: Negro Narrative Folklore from the Streets of Philadelphia* (Chicago: Aldine, 1970), 210–51.

13. Howlin' Wolf, "Wang Dang Doodle." Reissued on "Howlin' Wolf," Chess 1469. For discussions of "toasts," see Abrahams, *Deep Down in the Jungle*, 97–172; Bruce Jackson, *"Get Your Ass in the Water and Swim Like Me": Narrative Poetry from the Black Oral Tradition* (Cambridge, MA: Harvard University Press, 1974), passim. For unexpurgated texts of "Freaks' Ball" toast variants see Jackson, 148–50.

14. Muddy Waters, "I'm Ready." Reissued on "Muddy Waters: Sail On," Chess 1539. See Mimi Clar Melnick, "I Can Peep Through Muddy Waters and Spy Dry Land: Boasts in the Blues," in D. K. Wilgus, ed., *Folklore International* (Hartboro, Penn: Folklore Associates, 1967), 139–49.

15. Big Lucky, "Goofer Dust." Reissued on "River Town Blues," Hi Records SHL 32063. There is an extensive literature on black herbalism and conjuring, see Newbell Niles Puckett, *Folk Beliefs of the Southern Negro* (Chapel Hill: University of North Carolina Press, 1926); Zora Neale Hurston, *Mules and Men* (Philadelphia: J. B. Lippincott, 1935), Part II; Mimi Clar, "Folk Belief and Custom in the Blues," *Western Folklore* 19 (1960): 173–90; Harry Hyatt, *Hoodoo-Conjuration-Witchcraft-Rootwork* (Washington, D.C.: American University Bookstore, 1970), 2 vols. For a detailed treatment of hoodoo themes in the blues, see Paul Oliver, *Blues Fell this Morning: The Meaning of the Blues* (New York: Horizon Press, 1960), 138–44.

16. Son House, "Preachin' Blues." Issued on "The Legendary Son House," Columbia CS 9217. For collections of tales and jokes concerning black folk religion, see Hughes

and Bontemps, eds., *Negro Folklore*, 139–62; Brewer, *American Negro Folklore*, 107–18; Abrahams, *Deep Down in the Jungle*, 195–210.

17. Billy Bizor, "Tom Moore's Farm." Issued on "Texas Blues: Vol. 2," Arhoolie F 1017. For protest tales, see Dorson, *American Negro Folktales*, 300–320; Brewer, *American Negro Folklore*, 82–104.

18. See Paul Oliver, *The Meaning of the Blues* (New York: Collier Books, 1960), passim; Paul Oliver, *The Story of the Blues* (Radnor, Penn: Chilton Book Co., 1969), 103–4; Charles Hudson, "Folk, History and Ethnohistory," *Ethnohistory* 13 (1966): 53–54; Richard M. Dorson, "History of the Elite and the History of the Folk," in Richard Dorson, ed., *Folklore: Selected Essays* (Bloomington: Indiana University Press, 1972), 239–42, 257.

19. Titon, *Early Downhome Blues*, 43–44; Oliver, *Story of the Blues*, 106.

20. Robert Dixon and John Godrich, *Recording the Blues* (London: Studio Vista, 1970), 64–77.

21. Oliver, *Story of the Blues*, 103–6.

22. Oliver, *Meaning of the Blues*, 27; Michael Stewart and Don Kent, Notes to "Hard Times Blues: St. Louis 1933–40," Mamlish 53806.

23. Skip James, "Hard Time Killin' Floor Blues," Parmount 13065 (Grafton, Wisconsin, 1931). Reissued on "The Mississippi Blues 1927–1940," OJL-5.

24. Robert Clifton Weaver, *The Negro Ghetto* (New York: Harcourt Brace, 1948), 54; Raymond Wolters, *Negroes and the Great Depression: The Problem of Economic Recovery* (Westport, Conn.: Negro Universities Press, 1970), 113–14.

25. Charles Jordan, "Tough Times Blues," Vocalion 1568 (Chicago, 1930). Reissued on "Hard Times Blues," Mamlish 53806 mistitled as "Tight Times Blues."

26. Barbecue Bob, "We Sure Got Hard Times Now," Columbia 14558-D (Atlanta, 1930). Reissued on "Hard Times," Rounder 4007.

27. Searle Charles, *Minister of Relief: Harry Hopkins and the Depression* (Syracuse: Syracuse University Press, 1963), 15, 18, 21, 27.

28. Blind Darby, "Meat and Bread Blues (Relief Blues)," Vocalion 02988 (Chicago, 1935). Reissued on "Savannah Syncopators," CBS 52799.

29. Richard Sterner, *The Negro's Share: A Study of Income, Consumption, Housing, and Public Assistance* (New York: Harper & Bros., 1943), 218; Charles, *Minister of Relief*, 101.

30. Carl Martin, "Let's Have a New Deal," Decca 7114 (Chicago, 1935). Reissued on "Country Blues Classics: Vol. 4," Blues Classics 14.

31. Wolters, *Negroes and the Great Depression*, 197–200.

32. Jimmie Gordon, "Don't Take Away My P.W.A.," Decca 7230 (Chicago, 1936). Lyrics transcribed in Oliver, *Meaning of the Blues*, 60.

33. Sterner, *The Negro's Share*, 323; Weaver, *The Negro Ghetto*, 67–68.

34. Casey Bill Weldon, "W.P.A. Blues," Vocalion 03186 (Chicago, 1937). Reissued on "Country Blues Classics: Vol. 3," Blues Classics 7.

35. Charles, *Minister of Relief*, 120, 145–46; Sterner, *The Negro's Share*, 249, 251–52.

36. Peetie Wheatstraw, "Working on the Project," Decca 7311 (Chicago, 1937). Reissued on "Kokomo Arnold / Peetie Wheatstraw," Blues Classics 4.

37. Sterner, *The Negro's Share*, 218, 287, 292.

38. Sonny Boy Williamson, "Welfare Store Blues," Bluebird B8610 (Chicago, 1940). Reissued on "Sonny Boy Williamson," Blues Classics 3. This is one of the many variants of Walter Roland's "Red Cross Blues," Banner 32822 (New York, 1933).

39. Lightnin' Hopkins, "Candy Kitchen," RPM 378 (Houston, 1940s). Reissued on "Lightnin' Hopkins," Kent KST 9008.

40. Sunnyland Slim and his Sunnyland Boys, "Hard Times," Tempo Tone 1001 (Chicago, 1948). Reissued on "Chicago Slickers 1948–1953," Nighthawk 102, but attributed to Floyd Jones.

41. Robert J. Donovan, *Eisenhower: The Inside Story* (New York: Harper and Bros., 1956), 165, 209, 212; Robert L. Branyan and Lawrence H. Larsen, *The Eisenhower Administration, 1953–1961: A Documentary History* (New York: Random House, 1971), Vol. I, 249–50.

42. John Brim, "Tough Times," Parrot 799 (Chicago, 1953). Reissued on "Elmore James / John Brim; Whose Muddy Shoes," Chess 1537.

43. Donovan, *Eisenhower*, 215; Mike Rowe, *Chicago Breakdown* (London: Eddison Press, 1973), 122–23.

44. J. B. Hutto, "Things Are So Slow," Chance 1165 (Chicago, 1954). Reissued on "Chicago Blues: The Early 1950s," Blues Classics 8.

45. Bobo Jenkins, "Democrat Blues," Chess 1565 (Detroit, 1954). Reissued on "Country Blues Classics: Vol. 2," Blues Classics 6.

46. Branyan and Larsen, *Eisenhower Administration*, 250–56; Leadbitter and Slaven, *Blues Records*, 191.

47. J. B. Lenoir, "Eisenhower Blues," Parrot 802 (Chicago, 1954). Reissued on " J. B. Lenoir," Chess 2 ACMB-208.

48. B. B. King, "Recession Blues." Previously unissued (Chicago, 1958). Issued on "Blues Is Killing Me," Juke Joint Records 1501. The recession of 1958 is discussed in Almo Richardson, *The Presidency of Dwight D. Eisenhower* (Lawrence: Regents Press of Kansas, 1979), 134.

49. K. C. Douglas, "My Mind's Going Back to 1929," "K. C. Douglas: The Country Boy," Arhoolie 1073.

50. See Titon, "Thematic Patterns in Downhome Blues Lyrics," 317, 329.

# The Black Faith of W. E. B. Du Bois

## Sociocultural and Political Dimensions of Black Religion

MANNING MARABLE

W. E. B. Du Bois—founder of the National Association for the Advancement of Colored People and editor of its journal, the *Crisis*, sociologist, civil rights leader, and "Father of Pan-Africanism"—is seldom viewed as a Christian. His biographers note that he frequently attacked all Christian denominations for their support of racial segregation. In published articles Du Bois described himself as an "agnostic" and questioned the "immortality" of man ("Immortality" 18).[1] As a college student and in later life, he affirmed that "work, systematic and tireless," was his only true faith (*Autobiography* 124). In December 1940 he announced that he worshiped "Truth and Truth only . . . I will face each sunrise with one prayer: There is no God but Love and Work is his Prophet" ("Crow Flies"). At the end of his career Du Bois declared, "I believe in communism," renouncing American "free enterprise [as] leading the world in disaster" (*Autobiography* 57), and died in exile in Ghana. This image of Du Bois reveals only one aspect of his multifaceted character. For also throughout his life he wrote extensively on the black church. His earliest published essays focus on black religious life in his native town, Great Barrington, Massachusetts;[2] one of his final articles, written in 1962, was an introduction to a photographic study of "Store Front Churches" in Buffalo, New York's ghetto. In the intervening years he wrote several hundred articles on religion, the black church, and the social and political function of religious institutions. Du Bois was simultaneously an agnostic and an Anglican, a staunch critic of religious dogma and a passionate convert to the black version of Christianity. His belief in his people was expressed in his own black faith for the world.

Du Bois's religious sensibility was formed early in life. His grandfather, Alexander Du Bois, was senior warden of the black Episcopal Parish of St. Luke, founded by the black residents of New Haven, Connecticut, in 1847

---

*Southern Quarterly* 23.3 (1985): 15–33.

(*Dusk* 107–8; *Autobiography* 67). His mother, Mary Burghardt, was deeply religious and frequently but softly chastised her high-spirited son to attend church services regularly and "never go into a liquor saloon or even near it" (*Autobiography* 81).³ Life in Great Barrington, Massachusetts, during the Gilded Age was largely defined by the church and its strict moral code. Du Bois and his mother attended two churches: a small Negro Methodist Zion Church, formed by a small colony of "'contrabands,' freed Negroes from the South," and Great Barrington's Congregational Church, which was patronized by the leading merchants, farmers, and "professional men" of the community (*Autobiography* 83, 88).⁴ Even as a teenager, Du Bois noticed the class divisions within his small community that were manifested in the existence of various denominations. The local Catholic church "was perched across the river beyond the mills, and thither the [Irish] girl servants trudged faithfully early mornings to mass. This and other traits of the Irish became the basis of jokes and ridicule in town. . . ." Colored people, by contrast, despite their lower-class status, were cordially welcomed in white middle-class congregations. The Episcopal church catered to "older families and the more well-to-do," and most of Du Bois's extended family in the region belonged to this congregation. In the northern section of the town near the mill was an unpretentious, "small white wooden Methodist church," attended by "the less well-known inhabitants of Great Barrington" (*Autobiography* 82, 89–90).

Du Bois graduated from high school in June 1884 and his mother died several months later. His subsequent academic career would have been in doubt had it not been for the timely intervention of three leading citizens: the Reverend Mr. Scudder, the pastor of the Congregational church; Edward Van Lennep, superintendent of the Congregational church's Sunday school and principal of a local private school; and the Reverend C. C. Painter, a retired Federal Indian Agent and former pastor of several Congregational churches in Connecticut. The church in Great Barrington and Painter's churches agreed to donate one hundred dollars annually for Du Bois's college education. The black youth desired to attend Harvard, but Painter insisted that "the reconstructed South . . . was the place for me to be educated." Over the objections of "my family and colored friends," Du Bois was sent to Fisk University in Nashville in September 1885 (*Autobiography* 103, 105; *Dusk* 22; *Correspondence* 5).

Painter's decision to send Du Bois to the South fundamentally shaped the young man's life. Growing up in New England, Du Bois had known little racial prejudice, and his contacts with other blacks were few and brief. In Nashville, a world of color was revealed, and the young Puritan was sorely out of place at first. "I was thrilled to be for the first time among so many people of my own color . . . Never before had I seen young men so self-assured and who gave themselves such airs, and colored men at that; and above all for the first time I saw beautiful girls" (*Autobiography* 107). Years of sexual repression and Calvinist training put him at odds with his contemporaries, who had "loose sexual morals." Years later Du Bois admitted frankly, "I actually did not know the physical differences between men and women. At first my fellows jeered in disbelief and then became sorry and made many offers to guide my abysmal ignorance. This built for me inexcusable and startling tempta-tions" (*Autobiography* 280). Regarded as a "liar" or "freak" when he asserted his virginity, he sought familiar refuge in the arms of the church. Dutifully attending church services, revivals, and morning prayers at the beginning of each school day, Du Bois tried desperately to find inner tranquility. Writing to the Reverend Scudder in February 1886, the young college freshman ob-served that he had "united with the Church and hope that the prayers of my Sunday-School may guide me in the path of Christian duty." Du Bois faith-fully continued to correspond with members of the Great Barrington Sunday School class until at least 1892 (*Correspondence* 5, 18–19). But in Nashville, he encountered controversy in his faith from "fundamentalist" quarters. One of Du Bois's classmates, "Pop" Miller, brought him before the congregation and accused him of "a particularly heinous form of sin," public dancing. Du Bois protested in vain that he had "never attended public dance halls" and had only engaged in the "innocent pastime . . . at the homes of colored friends in the city." Fisk University teachers supported Miller, warning the young sinner "that my dancing might well be quite innocent, but . . . my example might lead others astray." Du Bois deeply resented their intervention, and much later concluded that this little tempest "lead to my eventual refusal to join a religious organization." But for the moment, he still "never questioned [his] religious upbringing. Its theory had presented no particular difficulties: God ruled the world, Christ loved it, and men did right, or tried to; otherwise they were rightly punished" (*Autobiography* 110–1, 127).

Another aspect of the black social and religious experience became a part of Du Bois's development in the summers of 1886 and 1887. In east Tennessee he obtained a minor position as a rural schoolteacher at twenty-eight dollars per month. At last he encountered "the real seat of slavery . . . I touched intimately the lives of the commonest of mankind—people who ranged from barefoot dwellers on dirt floors with patched rags for clothes, to

rough hard-working farmers, with plain, clean plenty" (*Autobiography* 114).
His school house was nothing but a log hut with no door, "a massive rickety
fireplace" and little furniture. "I was haunted by a New England vision of neat
little desks and chairs, but alas the reality was rough plank benches without
backs, and at times without legs," Du Bois noted. "They had the one virtue of
making naps dangerous, possibly fatal, for the floor was not to be trusted"
(*Autobiography* 115–16). Among his class of nearly thirty youths, many older
than himself, was "a thin, homely girl of twenty, Josie"—later to be described
as an unforgettable figure in *The Souls of Black Folk* (64).[5]

The crucible of southern black life and labor was opened to Du Bois. Here
he found warmth and unpretentious friendship he had not thought possible.
Frequently after classes were finished he visited the families of his pupils: sitting on the porch eating fresh peaches with Josie and her talkative mother;
visiting Doc Burke's farm, helping himself to fried chicken, wheat biscuits,
string beans, and plump berries. Here he also discovered the mystery of sex,
as Du Bois slept with an "unhappy wife who was my landlady." Time for these
folk seemingly stood still. To be sure, life "was dull and humdrum," Du Bois
wrote in his last *Autobiography*, "I have called my community a world, and so
its isolation made it. There was among us but a half-awakened common consciousness, sprung from common joy and grief, at burial, birth or wedding;
from common hardship in poverty, poor land and low wages; and, above all,
from the sight of the Veil that hung between us and Opportunity" (118–20,
280).

But the essence of black life was to be found on Sunday mornings, as
the dawn broke above the rural countryside. In the center of Alexandria,
Tennessee's colored district were "the twin temples of the hamlet, the
Methodist and the Hard-Shell Baptist churches." In these unadorned wooden
halls the black rural folk made "the weekly sacrifice with frenzied priests at
the altar of the 'old time religion.'" It was here that the families of his students
sang in "soft melody and mighty cadences" the black spirituals of slavery. At
first Du Bois was baffled by this experience. "We in Berkshire . . . were very
quiet and subdued, and I know not what would have happened those clear
Sabbath mornings had someone punctuated the sermon with a scream, or
interrupted the long prayer with a loud Amen!" Sensitive about his strict
background, and yet alienated from the Congregational church in Nashville,
Du Bois was "determined to know something of the Negro in the country
districts." Their deep expressions of spirituality were utterly new to him. As a

budding scholar, and more importantly as a black man, he was determined to understand their religion, and to integrate it into his own embryonic world-view (*Autobiography* 114, 119–20).

The basic anatomy of the black religious experience was expressed in three factors: "the Preacher, the Music, and the Frenzy." The black minister, Du Bois later suggested, "is the most unique personality developed by the Negro on American soil." The black minister during slavery emerged as a powerful force in community life. "He early appeared on the plantation and found his function as the healer of the sick, the interpreter of the Unknown, the comforter of the sorrowing, the supernatural avenger of wrong, and the one who rudely but picturesquely expressed the longing, disappointment, and resentment of a stolen and oppressed people." Thus the social dynamics which produced white clergy and religious institutions differed radically from the organic evolution of the black church and its preachers. The transition from traditional African social systems to the plantation South was nothing less than "a terrific social revolution, and yet some traces were retained of the former group life, and the chief remaining institution was the Priest or Medicineman." This charismatic representative of the *nommo* or essence of his people, a synthesis of "bard, physician, judge, and priest," became within the American South "the Negro preacher." During Reconstruction and after, other basic characteristics were added to his social profile; he was at once "a leader, a politician, and orator, a 'boss,' and intriguer, and idealist. . . . The combination of a certain adroitness with deep-seated earnestness, of tact with consummate ability, gave him his preeminence," Du Bois noted, "and helps him maintain it" (*Souls* 141–42).

The music of black faith "is that plaintive rhythmic melody," Du Bois wrote in *The Souls of Black Folk*, "which, despite caricature and defilement, still remains the most original and beautiful expression of human life and longing yet born on American soil." Even as a small boy "these songs have stirred me strangely," Du Bois reflected. "They came out of the South unknown to me, one by one, and yet at once I knew them as of me and of mine." The spirituals and the "Sorrow Songs" revealed the anguish and hope of a people in bondage, a mass of illiterate slaves whose spiritual strivings brought together an aspiration of secular emancipation and religious freedom. In such songs, "the slave spoke to the world" in an Aesopian language, partially "veiled and half articulate." "Steal away to Jesus" could mean different things to the masters and the slaves. There was the "cradle-song of death which all men know—'Swing low, sweet chariot . . .'"; and songs which revealed the full glory of the end of life's oppression—"'My Lord, what a morning! when the stars begin to fall'. . . ." In the Carolina swamplands, the slaves sang:

> Michael, haul the boat ashore,
> Then you'll hear the horn they blow,
> Then you'll hear the trumpet sound,
> Trumpet sound the world around,
> Trumpet sound for rich and poor,
> Trumpet sound for Jubilee,
> Trumpet sound for you and me.

The spirituals were simultaneously sorrowful and yet filled with hope, or as Du Bois expressed it, "a faith in the ultimate justice of things. The minor cadences of despair change often to triumph and calm confidence." In the face of oppression, the music provides a "faith in life"; it offers "sometimes assurance of boundless justice in some far world beyond." The transition to Jim Crow and lynching was the secular political reality which created the living aesthetic space for such songs to continue to capture "the tragic soul-life" of black people. They express the hope "that sometime, somewhere, men will judge men by their souls and not by their skins" (141–42, 187–91).

The "Frenzy or 'Shouting,' when the Spirit of the Lord passed by, and, seizing the devotee, made him mad with supernatural joy, was the last essential of Negro religion," Du Bois wrote, adding for emphasis, "and one the more devoutly believed in than all the rest." The shout was at once a purgation of the believers' anxieties, fears, and doubts created under slavery and segregation; it was a catharsis, the expression of transcendence, a cry of faith and hope, a physical and collective explosion which was necessary for a people wedged in the permanent vise of social anxiety and frustration. "It varied in expression from the silent rapt countenance or low murmur and moan to the mad abandon of physical fervor—the stamping, shrieking and laughing, the vision and trance." The common rapture was expressed by man, but was not of man: the frenzy, for the black Christian, was "the visible manifestation of God." Without this catharsis, Du Bois wrote, blacks believed that "there could be no true communion with the Invisible" (*Souls* 143).

The soul-searing experiences in the Tennessee countryside placed Du Bois increasingly at odds with established Christian theology, and with himself. When assigned a text on Christian logic at Fisk, it now "affronted my

logic. It was to my mind, then and since, a cheap piece of special pleading."
University president Erastus Cravath secured a scholarship for Du Bois's
postgraduate work at Hartford Theological Seminary. But Du Bois would
not accept it. "I believed too little in Christian dogma to become a minister.
I was not without faith: I never stole material or spiritual things; I not only
never lied, but blurted out my conception of truth on the most untoward
occasions; I drank no alcohol and knew nothing of women, physically or
psychically, to the incredulous amusement of my more experienced fellows" (*Autobiography* 124, 127). His graduate training at Harvard University,
under the direction of William James and George Santayana, pushed the
black scholar far from "the sterilities of scholastic philosophy to realistic
pragmatism" (*Autobiography* 133). While in Boston, however, he pursued his
relationship with the black church. On Thanksgiving night, 1891, Du Bois
organized and participated in the Aristophanes play, "The Birds," at the
black community's Charles Street Church. Nevertheless, he expressed blunt
criticisms of the black church in an 1891 paper prepared for the National
Colored League of Boston: "A religion that won't stand the application of
reason and common sense is not fit for an intelligent dog." But his hostility
toward the white Christian church was far more profound. In his diary, Du
Bois attacked the Anglo-Saxon's "high Episcopal Nicene creed" as a rationale
for white supremacy. Musing on the Biblical image of "Ethiopia [stretching]
forth her hands to God," the young Harvard man fumed: "the spectacle [of]
the venerable colored dame in this rather unbalanced position in regard
to the Anglo-Saxon god has become somewhat nauseating to the average
young Negro of today." For the white West, with the possible exception of
the "self-forgetful Quakers," God was dead, Du Bois decided (Broderick
18–19, 23).

If racial oppression and segregation had compromised and destroyed the
reality of God among most American whites, Du Bois thought, then he would
refuse to participate in the charade. In his first teaching post at Wilberforce
University, a small black Methodist institution, he "wandered casually" into a
local black prayer gathering. "Suddenly and without warning, a student leader
of the meeting announced that 'Professor Du Bois will lead us in prayer.' I
simply answered, 'No, he won't.' and as a result nearly lost my new job." An
outraged president forced Du Bois before the School's governing board of
bishops, and "it took a great deal of explaining" to convince its members "why
a professor at Wilberforce should not be able at all times and sundry to address God in extemporaneous prayer. I was saved only by the fact that my

coming to Wilberforce had been widely advertised and I was willing to do endless work . . ." (*Autobiography* 186). He quickly acquired the reputation as a troublemaker, cynic, and "agnostic" by refusing "to attend the annual 'revivals' of religion which interrupted school work every year at Christmas time." In May 1896 he threatened the college treasurer in order to receive back payment for his salary (*Autobiography* 187–88). Such irreverent behavior did not go unnoticed beyond Wilberforce. After a fifteen-month stint at the University of Pennsylvania, where he compiled the first major sociological survey of Afro-American urban life, *The Philadelphia Negro*, Du Bois applied for a position at Atlanta University. The college's president, Horace Bumstead, was by nature and political training a cautious man. Several trustees and prominent friends of Atlanta University expressed "objections and misgivings" to him when learning of Du Bois's possible appointment. Bumstead later wrote that "Atlanta University has always had a pronounced religious, though undenominational life," and that its teachers were expected "to help to maintain it." But on that point, such assurances "were not very easy to get" from Du Bois. When asked of his religious affiliation, he curtly replied, "'none to speak of.'" But though reluctant to speak of his religion or to say what he would do at Atlanta, and despite grave "objections and misgivings," he was permitted to join the faculty (qtd. in *Autobiography* 109–10).

Yet the spiritual commitment Du Bois held for his people, which deepened and enlarged his analytic critique of the total society, could not be expressed as a complete rejection of black Christianity. Repeatedly his sociological research focused on the centrality of religion within black life, not only in *The Philadelphia Negro*, but also in his 1897 study of black life in Farmville, Virginia, completed for the U.S. Department of Labor, and in his 1898 study of Atlanta, Georgia (*Some Efforts*). The black "First Baptist" Church in Farmville is described by Du Bois in intimate detail as "a roomy brick edifice seating five hundred or more persons, tastefully finished in Georgia pine, with a carpet, a small organ, and stained-glass windows":

> Underneath is a large assembly room with benches. This building is the central club-house of a community of a thousand or more Negroes. Various organizations meet here,—the church proper, the Sunday-school, two or three insurance societies, women's societies, secret societies, and mass meetings of various kinds. Entertainments, suppers, and lectures are held beside the five or six regular weekly religious services. Considerable sums of money are collected and expended here, employment is found for the

idle, strangers are introduced, news is disseminated and charity distributed. At the same time this social, intellectual, and economic centre is a
religious centre of great power. Depravity, Sin, Redemption, Heaven, Hell,
and Damnation are preached with much fervor, and revivals take place every year after the crops are laid by; and few indeed of the community have
the hardihood to withstand conversion. Back of this more formal religion,
the Church often stands as a real conserver of morals, a strengthener of
family life, and the final authority on what is Good and Right. (*Souls* 144)

Du Bois-the-agnostic confronted the vibrant reality of black spiritual and social life, and could not stand apart from it. As a Pan-Africanist and as a sociologist, he came to political terms with the black church in these words: "the
Negro church of to-day is the social centre of Negro life in the United States,
and the most characteristic expression of African character" (*Souls* 144). The
uneven and contradictory synthesis of his religious doubts and faith was expressed, at last, in his famous theory of "double consciousness." If the Negro
was at once "an American, a Negro; two souls, two thoughts, two unreconciled
strivings; two warring ideals in one dark body" (qtd. in Meier 190), then his
soul for the white world would be expressed in agnosticism, or at best, only in
the most critical and formal guise. The soul of Du Bois confronting the black
world had no choice except to embrace black Christianity.

As a mature scholar and leader of the NAACP, Du Bois maintained his
contradictory position on religion. Before the white world, he made few concessions. Reverting to the denomination of his paternal grandfather, he was
nominally an Episcopalian for a time (*Correspondence* 131). But inside the
color line, he gave poetic expression to his love of God in his "Credo," first
printed in October 1904:

I believe in God, who made of one blood all nations that on the earth
do dwell. I believe that all men, black and brown and white, are brothers. . . . knowing that men may be brothers in Christ even though they
be not brothers-in-law. . . . I believe in the Devil and his angels, who
wantonly work to narrow the opportunity of struggling human beings
especially if they be black; who spit in the faces of the fallen, strike them
that cannot strike again, believe the worst and work to prove it, hating
the image which their Maker stamped on a brother's soul. I believe in
the Prince of Peace. I believe that War is Murder. . . . Finally, I believe in
Patience—patience with the weakness of the Weak and the strength of

the Strong, the prejudice of the Ignorant and the ignorance of the Blind; patience with the tardy triumph of Joy and the mad chastening of Sorrow;—patience with God!

If the Christian ideal retained its meaning, the Christian church as a whole had not. White Christianity, "together with the wisest and richest of the people in the United States, defended [slavery] for 250 years," he declared in 1927 (*Crisis* 34: 168). Now white Christians supported institutional racism, lynchings, and political disfranchisement of blacks. Regretfully, "I have little faith that Christianity can settle the race problem, but I have an abiding faith in men" (Preface). In a biting editorial, "The Negro and the Church," published in the NAACP journal *Crisis* in October 1913, Du Bois denounced Christian "hypocrisy" and charged that the church ruthlessly denied "power" to blacks. "The Negro problem is the test of the church" (also *Christian Century*).

A brief review of Du Bois's published writings indicates both a revulsion of the church and a curious attentiveness about its activities and internal debates, especially regarding the Afro-American. In private correspondence with the Reverend Samuel H. Bishop, general agent of the American Church Institute for Negroes, and in a published essay in June 1907, he criticized the Episcopal church for its "hypocrisy." Despite his nominal membership, "I have particular affection for the Church," Du Bois informed Bishop. "I think its record on the Negro problem has been shameful. . . . So far as the Negro problem is concerned the southern branch of the church is a moral dead weight and the northern branch of the Church never has had the moral courage to stand against it." The Episcopalian leadership was woefully "behind other churches in recognizing human manhood and Christian equality" ("Christianity"). In August 1920 in *Crisis*, he heartily congratulated the Methodist Episcopal Church for elevating two black men, Robert E. Jones and Matthew W. Clair, to the posts of Bishop after "a fight of 25 years," adding, "There are still white Christians in Zion" ("Opinion"; "Nine New"). But when the same northern Methodists attempted to merge with the southern Methodists, breaking off relations with the all-black African Methodist Episcopal (AME) church, the *Crisis* editor was filled with scorn. Unity between white Methodists was taking place at the sacrifice of racial equality, he declared. Somewhat sarcastically, he inquired if northern white Methodists still had "the present address of Jesus of Nazareth?" ("Methodists"; *Crisis* 29:7).

Du Bois plotted the erratic racial progress of the Baptist World Alliance and praised the organization for holding an interracial convention in segregated Atlanta in 1939 (*Phylon*). Du Bois's disputes with the Catholic church symbolize his strained relations with others. In 1924 the Knights of Columbus published his book, *The Gift of Black Folk*; Du Bois praised "Catholic priests and sisters teaching the colored South . . . for their unselfish work"; he "admired much" of the church's "mighty history." But in March 1925 in his private correspondence with Joseph B. Glenn, Du Bois charged that "the Catholic Church in America stands for color separation and discrimination to a degree equaled by no other church in America, and that is saying a very great deal." In hundreds of years, it had "ordained less than a half dozen black Catholic priests either because they have sent us poor teachers or because American Catholics do not want to work beside black priests and sisters or because they think Negroes have neither brains nor morals. . . ." Catholic parochial schools rarely accepted black applicants, and "the Catholic University in Washington invites them elsewhere. . . ." In short, the "'nigger' haters clothed in its Episcopal robes" were promoting racism every degree as vicious as "the Ku Klux Klan" (*Correspondence* 308–11). The Catholic and Protestant churches failed generally on the race issue, Du Bois perceived, because they had forgotten the living meaning of the teachings of "Jesus, the Jew." The ordeal of the Christ who perished for all humanity was obscured by the coarse blinders of race hatred ("The Church").

The black American church, in contrast, served a fundamentally different function: it was the organizational and spiritual center of black life and as such touched every minute aspect of the segregated community's endeavors. It was a race-conscious organization—it could hardly have been otherwise during the Jim Crow era—yet its strength served to preserve and to defend the basic humanity of Afro-American people, and its true vision of itself was one without color or class barriers. Even as a senior at Fisk University, Du Bois recognized that being a Christian meant that "we should not forget the practical side" of Christianity; that is, good works which uplifted the most oppressed groups of society (*Fisk Herald*). A decade later, speaking before a Fisk University graduate audience, he merged the ideals of black faith with the political struggle to transform the material conditions of Afro-Americans. "The German works for Germany, the Englishman serves England, and it is the duty of the Negro to serve his blood and lineage, and so working, each for each, and all for each, we realize the goal of each for all." As for the collective expression of all blacks, the church and its clergy were crucial in this process of self-achievement. Afro-American ministers must and "will transform the mysticism of Negro religion into the righteousness of Christianity." Only by "cherish[ing] unwavering faith in the blood of your fathers," could this spiritually moved mass of back humanity achieve political freedom ("Careers"). In late 1900, Du Bois contributed a brief essay on "The Religion of the Negro" to the Boston publication *New World*, which expanded upon these themes. "The Negro church antedates the Negro home," he noted, an historical fact which created "the expression of the inner ethical life of a people in a sense seldom true elsewhere." The church is a haven in a heartless world, as blacks search for meaning in a segregated and politically oppressive society. "Conscious of his impotence, and pessimistic," the Negro "often becomes bitter and vindictive; and his religion, instead of a worship, is a complaint and a curse, a wail rather than a hope, a sneer rather than a faith." And at these moments, "one type of Negro stands almost ready to curse God and die. . . ." Yet he finds salvation within the Veil, and a spiritual deliverance from earthly suffering. Silently as ever broods "the deep religious feeling of the real Negro heart, the stirring, unguided might of powerful human souls who have lost the guiding star of the past and seek in the great night a new religious ideal. Some day the Awakening will come," Du Bois predicted, "when the pent-up vigor of ten million souls shall sweep irresistibly toward the Goal, out of the valley of the Shadow of Death . . . [toward] Liberty, Justice, and Right . . ." (614–25).

His faith in the historic goals of black religion did not exempt specific denominations from Du Bois's criticism. The black church found "greatness" only as it linked the spiritual strivings of the masses with a social commitment to challenge Jim Crow laws, political disfranchisement, and all forms of bigotry and economic deprivation (*Crisis* 38: 207). In his edited volume, *The Negro Church*, published in 1903 as part of the Atlanta University Social Studies series, and in subsequent periodical articles, Du Bois carefully scrutinized the progress of the black church. He reminded more conservative black clergy that black religion demanded uncompromising political protest, in the antebellum tradition of slave preacher and rebel Nat Turner. Occasionally in *Crisis* he commended the work of young black ministers who had come "forward to preserve and rescue the good that is in the Negro Church" (12: 18). In his organizational work, he cooperated with many black ministers who shared his politically liberal views. In the Niagara Movement, formed by Du Bois and the radical journalist William Monroe Trotter in 1905 to oppose the accommodationist program of Booker T. Washington, black religious leaders were especially prominent: Reverdy C. Ransom of Boston; J. Milton Waldron of Jacksonville, Florida; Byron Gunner of Newport; George Freeman Bragg of Baltimore; and Sutton E. Griggs of Nashville. The vast majority of black clergy "enunciated a gradualist philosophy of self-help, racial solidarity, and economic progress," thus clearly aligning themselves with Washington's "Tuskegee Machine." But gradually, many northern-based bishops and black religious leaders began to reflect Du Bois's militant political beliefs. Waldron had been a past supporter of the Tuskegee philosophy while located in Jacksonville; after relocating to Washington, D.C., he rapidly fell into Du Bois's faction and became local president of the NAACP (Meier 180, 218–21). One of Du Bois's closest associates was African Methodist Episcopal Zion (AMEZ) Church Bishop Alexander Walters, the presiding chairman of the first Pan-African Conference held in London in 1900, in which Du Bois served as secretary. Bishop Walters, a founder of the militant National Negro American Political League in June 1908, and the nation's leading black Democrat, frequently advised Du Bois—and sometimes with disastrous consequences (Meier 186–87).[6] Du Bois was particularly harsh with the AME Church. In January 1929, he criticized it for failing to provide sufficient financial support for the South African missionary work led by his former Wilberforce student, Charlotte Manye ("Postscript"). Repeatedly he denounced the many "fakers" and "frauds" among the AME Church's leadership (*Crisis* 39: 234–35; "Crow Flies"; "Winds").

What was the cultural purpose of the black church beyond its necessary engagement in political life on behalf of Afro-Americans? Du Bois constantly returned to the central themes provided by his experience in eastern Tennessee, and, later, his sociological research conducted in Philadelphia, Farmville, Virginia, and Atlanta. The church was the cradle for the Afro-American gift of song, that rare element of Negro culture which had been constantly nourished. In 1903 Du Bois published a short *Bibliography of Negro Folk Songs* as a means to encourage scholarly research into Afro-American popular and spiritual music. He praised the musical "labors" of John Wesley Work and his wife Alice Work, music professors at Fisk University who had "resurrect[ed]" and made "eternal the Negro spiritual" (*Crisis* 32: 32–34; 34: 167). In *Crisis* he applauded black musical directors in both segregated public schools and the churches for instructing a young generation of black pupils in the spirituals (*Crisis* 12: 18). This did not mean that Du Bois did not appreciate other more popular forms of black music. He noted with grudging approval the development of "Ragtime" melodies and in an early issue of *Crisis* congratulated popular black composer J. Rosamond Johnson for the creation of "a new and distinct school of Negro music" (*Crisis* 3: 190). In 1925, at the height of the Harlem Renaissance, Du Bois penned a brief essay, "The Black

Man Brings His Gifts," which praised the work of William Christopher Handy, the "father of the blues."[7] But his polished New England upbringing seldom failed to assert itself: Du Bois always held a special affection for those among his race who mastered European classical music.[8] Du Bois was a friend of the great black concert tenor Roland Hayes and frequently attended his performances (*Correspondence* 328–29). In March 1918 he was the first to bring to national attention a gifted, new "baritone soloist," a nineteen-year-old Rutgers University student named Paul Robeson, in this regard (*Crisis* 15: 229–31). The songs of black religious praise were the basis for the Negro's special ability in all music. In response to one *New York Times* critic who urged blacks to croon only "old-time" plantation melodies, Du Bois tartly declared, "It is to be trusted that our leaders in music, holding on to the beautiful heritage of the past, will not on that account, either be coerced or frightened from taking all music for their province and showing the world how to sing" ("Our Music").

But the greatest gift of black faith went to the heart of the Christian tradition: its radical reinterpretation of Christ as an historical and spiritual figure for early twentieth-century American society. As a socialist, Du Bois condemned not merely the profit-motive of monopoly capital and its exploitation of labor but also found its espousal of Christian rhetoric empty of social content. In a December 1913 *Crisis* editorial, for example, he again blasted the racism of the Episcopal church, declaring that any acceptance of bigotry was an abrogation of the teachings of the Son of God. "The church of John Pierpont Morgan [is] not the church of Jesus Christ," he concluded. For the special Christmas issue of the *Crisis* in December 1925, Jesus returns to earth and is immediately disillusioned with the gross spectacle of wealth and public avarice which is held in his name. Defiantly he speaks from the heights of the Woolworth Building in Manhattan to condemn the northern mob—"and the people were dumbfounded" ("Sermon on Tower"). In *Darkwater: Voices from Within the Veil*, Jesus returns to earth in Waco, Texas, and teaches white racists to "love" oppressed blacks. When an escaped black convict is unjustly burned alive, a voice comes to him "out of the winds of the night, saying: 'This day thou shalt be with me in Paradise!'" (123–33). During the Great Depression, Du Bois suggested that Christmas should be abolished, since "Jesus Christ is not usually invited to his birthday celebration" ("Crow Flies"). The living legacy of Christ, Du Bois suggested, could be realized only in a rededication to his historic example as a spiritual rebel against established dogma and prejudice of the social order. In December 1909, Du Bois declared that white abolitionist John Brown was a nineteenth-century martyr in the true tradition of Jesus Christ ("John Brown"). Christ was undoubtedly "the greatest of religious rebels," he wrote in 1928 (*Crisis* 35: 203–4). Later in his political life, as Du Bois moved closer to Marxism-Leninism, he viewed Christ in a more radical context. In February 1948, he suggested that the opponents of South African *apartheid* were truly Christians in the great tradition of Christ himself ("Pan-Africa"). The revolutionary heroes in the emancipation of the world's colored and exploited masses were Mohandas K. Gandhi, V. I. Lenin, and Jesus: their principles could promote an international "fight for freedom" and economic justice ("Shall We Fight"). The political purposes of the black church merged with the figure of Jesus to create a secular "freedom fighter" in the battle to uproot racism and capitalism. In the consciousness of the oppressed, in "the Second Coming," Jesus would be born black.[9]

Du Bois was ideologically consistent in politics. As his literary executor Herbert Aptheker writes, "All his life Du Bois was a radical prophet. He tore the Veil; at the same time, he had a particular perspective from which he saw this country and world, past, present, and future . . ." (249, 260–61). Before the sterile walls of segregation, he denounced intolerance; and in the Jim Crowed houses of prayer, he defied hypocrisy. Yet his "paradoxical behavior" in religion is no paradox at all.[10] Du Bois saw himself as a legitimate child of the Renaissance and Western culture, but the "Veil" of race permitted him to question the ethical directions of the hegemonic social order. For him, the stoic figure of Saint Francis of Assisi could be transformed into a radical who sought "to satisfy the world's great wants" ("St. Francis"). White Christianity had failed only because it did not comprehend its inherently radical commitment to serve humanity. Black Christianity, in contrast, had fulfilled that mission for Afro-Americans and served as an example for the larger world. Thus Du Bois the "prophet" or "religious radical," could find peace within this faith. His God was the God of black liberation:

> I am the smoke king,
> I am black . . .
> Up I'm curling from the sod,
> I am whirling home to God.
> I am the smoke king.
> I am black. . . .
> I am darkening with song,
> I am heartening to wrong;
> I will be black as blackness can,

The blacker the mantle the mightier the man,
My purpl'ing midnights no day dawn may ban.
I am carving God in night,
I am painting Hell in white.
I am the smoke king,
I am black.
    ("Song of Smoke")


## Notes

1. Despite the title of the book which includes his essay (*We Believe in Immortality*), Du Bois observed, "My thought on personal immortality is easily explained. I do not know."
2. Articles under the headings "Great Barrington News" and "From the Berkshire Hills" in the New York *Globe*, 29 September 1883, 29 December 1883, and 22 November 1884.
3. Writing at the age of ninety, Du Bois added: "I never did, and indeed, so strong was the expression of her wishes that never in my life since have I felt at ease drinking in a bar. . . . When the Murphy crusade for total abstinence swept the valley, I as a boy was one of the first to don the blue ribbon. I kept the pledge until I went as a student to Germany" (*Autobiography* 81–82).
4. For a time, Du Bois and his mother lived "next to the horsesheds of the Congregational church." Du Bois's family was Episcopalian, but he and his mother joined the church, becoming its only "colored communicants."
5. "My journey was done, and behind me lay hill and dale and Life and Death. How shall man measure Progress there where the dark-faced Josie lies? How many heartfuls of sorrow shall balance a bushel of wheat? . . . And all this life and love and strife and failure,—is it the twilight of nightfall or the flush of some faint-dawning day?" (*Souls* 64).
6. In 1912 Walters was president of the Colored National Democratic League, which campaigned actively for Woodrow Wilson. Walters solicited a statement from the Democratic presidential nominee which pledged his commitment to blacks' civil rights. On the basis of this letter, which Walters later published in his autobiography, Du Bois tendered his resignation from the Socialist Party and publicly supported Wilson. Once elected, Wilson issued a strict segregationist policy throughout the federal government and repudiated his promises to the small black electorate (Walters 126; *Correspondence* 211–13; *Autobiography* 264).
7. Handy was quite pleased with Du Bois's comments and on 7 April 1925 forwarded an autographed copy of his collection, *Blues: An Anthology*, to the black leader. Handy noted, "The service you are rendering our Race in particular and the American people in general . . . is incalculable" (*Correspondence* 313).

8. At Fisk University, Du Bois became a member of the Mozart Society. Even late in life he affirmed, "It did great things for my education" (*Autobiography* 123).
9. Du Bois occasionally suggested in his writings that Christ should appear again, but only as a Negro ("Crow Flies").
10. August Meier and other historians view the contradictory strands of Du Bois's public career as "an ambivalence that is perhaps the central motif in his ideological biography." The duality they describe is fundamental to the political, social, and psychological behavior of most blacks who live and work in an institutionally racist society. Du Bois's theoretical achievement is his dialectical unity of opposites, the ability to create sound political programs on the quicksand of racist violence and segregation (190).

## Works Cited

Aptheker, Herbert. "The Historian." *W. E. B. Du Bois: A Profile.* Ed. Rayford W. Logan. New York: Hill and Wang, 1971, 249–73.

Broderick, Francis L. *W. E. B. Du Bois: Negro Leader in a Time of Crisis.* Stanford: Stanford University Press, 1959.

Du Bois, W. E. B. "As the Crow Flies." *Amsterdam News,* October 24, 1941.

———. *The Autobiography of W.E.B. Du Bois: A Soliloquy on Viewing My Life from the Last Decade of Its First Century.* New York: International, 1969.

———. *A Bibliography of Negro Folk Songs.* Atlanta: Atlanta University Press, 1903.

———. "The Black Man Brings His Gifts." *Survey Graphics* 53 (March 1, 1925): 655–57.

———. "Careers Open to College-Bred Negroes." *Two Addresses Delivered by Alumni of Fisk University, in Connection with the Anniversary Exercises of Their Alma Mater.* Pamphlet. June, 1898. Nashville: Fisk University, 1898, 1–14.

———. "The Church." *Crisis* 11 (April 1916): 302.

———. "Christianity." *Horizon* 1 (June 1907): 3–10.

———. "A Chronicle of Race Relations, 1939." *Phylon* 1 (1940): 90–97.

———. *The Correspondence of W. E. B. Du Bois: Volume I, Selections, 1877-1934.* Ed. Herbert Aptheker. Amherst: University of Massachusetts Press, 1973.

———. "Credo." *Independence* 57 (October 6, 1904): 787. Reprinted in *Darkwater,* 3–4.

———. *Darkwater: Voices from Within the Veil.* 1920. New York: AMS, 1969, 123–33.

———. *Dusk of Dawn: An Essay Toward an Autobiography of a Race Concept.* New York: Schoken, 1968.

———. "Editorial." *Fisk Herald* 5 (January 1888): 8.

———. "Editorials." *Crisis* 7 (December 1913): 80–81.

———. "Editorials." *Crisis* 12 (May 1916): 28–32.

———. "Immortality." *We Believe in Immortality.* Ed. Sydney Strong. New York: Coward-McCann, 1929, 18.

———. Introduction. "Store Front Churches." By Milton Rogovin. *Aperture* 10.2 (1962): 64, 68, 77, 84.

———. "John Brown and Christmas." *Crisis* 5 (December 1909): 1–3.

———. "John Work: Martyr and Singer." *Crisis* 32 (May 1926): 32–34.

———. "Men of the Month." *Crisis* 3 (March 1912): 190.

———. "Men of the Month." *Crisis* 12 (May 1916): 18.

———. "Men of the Month." *Crisis* 15 (March 1918): 229–31.

———. "The Methodists." *Crisis* 12 (July 1916): 137.

———. "The Negro and the Church." *Crisis* 6 (October 1913): 291.

———., ed. *The Negro Church: Report on a Social Study made under the direction of Atlanta University: together with the Proceedings of the Eighth Conference for the Study of Negro Problems, held at Atlanta University, May 26, 1903.* Atlanta: Atlanta University Press, 1903.

———. *The Negroes of Farmville, Virginia: A Social Study.* Washington, D.C.: Government Printing Office, January 1898.

———. "The Nine New Bishops." *Crisis* 20 (August 1920): 182.

———. "Opinion." *Crisis* 20 (August 1920): 165–66.

———. "Opinion." *Crisis* 29 (November 1924); 7.

———. "Our Music." *Crisis* 40 (July 1933): 165.

———. "Pan-Africa." *People's Voice.* [New York] (February 7, 1948).

———. "Postscript." *Crisis* 38 (June 1931): 207.

———. "Postscript." *Crisis* 34 (July 1927): 167–68.

———. "Postscript." *Crisis* 35 (June 1928): 203–4.

———. "Postscript." *Crisis* 36 (January 1929): 21–22.

———. "Postscript." *Crisis* 39 (July 1939): 234–35.

———. Preface. *The Negro, The Hope or the Despair of Christianity.* By Reverdy C. Ransom. Boston: Ruth Hill, 1935.

———. "The Religion of the Negro." *New World* 9 (December 1900): 614–25. Reprinted as "Of the Faith of the Fathers" in *The Souls of Black Folk*, 140–51.

———. "The Sermon on the Tower." *Crisis* 31 (December 1925): 59.

———. "Shall We Fight for Freedom?" *Chicago Defender*, April 13, 1946.

———., ed. *Some Efforts of American Negroes For Their Own Social Betterment Report of an Investigation under the direction of Atlanta University: together with the Proceedings of the Third Conference for the Study of the Negro Problems, held at Atlanta University, May 25–26, 1898.* Atlanta: Atlanta University Press, 1898.

———. "The Song of the Smoke." *Horizon* 1 (February 1907): 4–6.

———. *The Souls of Black Folk: Essays and Sketches.* 1903. Greenwich: Fawcett, 1961.

———. "St. Francis of Assisi." *Voice of the Negro* 3 (October 1906): 419–26.

———. "Will the Church Remove the Color Line?" *Christian Century* 48 (December 9, 1931): 1554–56.

———. "The Winds of Time." *Chicago Defender*, January 4, 1947.

Meier, August. *Negro Thought in America, 1880–1915: Racial Ideologies in the Age of Booker T. Washington.* Ann Arbor: University of Michigan Press, 1963.

Walters, Alexander. *My Life and Work.* New York: Fleming H. Revell, 1917.

# Subverting History

## Women, Narrative, and Patriarchy in *Absalom, Absalom!*

SUSAN V. DONALDSON

William Faulkner's portrayal of women has attracted heated debate ever since Maxwell Geismar charged the Mississippi writer with misogyny more than forty years ago.[1] Albert Guerard, for one, has observed that Faulkner's reputed hostility to women presents special problems precisely because "it is unrepressed and even undisguised" (109). Even critics predisposed to defend Faulkner's characterization of women, like Cleanth Brooks, unwittingly find themselves resorting to a paternalistic vocabulary of "active" men and "fostering and sustaining women," as John Duvall pointed out in a fine article a few years ago (qtd. 44). Indeed, from Duvall's perspective, such readers rely on terms and precepts inherited from a good many of Faulkner's male narrators—a disturbing reminder indeed for readers concerned with characterization of women in the Yoknapatawpha saga (45).

Nowhere would Faulkner's own paternalism and unease with women appear to be more embedded in his fiction than in the history of Thomas Sutpen as it is told and retold in *Absalom, Absalom!* From the very beginning of Rosa Coldfield's narrative, it would seem, Sutpen's intent is clear, to establish a plantation dynasty in Mississippi, the very nature of which is interchangeable with patriarchy, the passing of power and property from father to son. In this history, as it is made by Sutpen and constructed by the novel's four narrators, women appear to serve only as the means of perpetuating that dynasty—as mothers, wives, and sisters—figures standing in the shadows and margins of the narrative.

What happens, though, if we consciously resist the stories told by and about Thomas Sutpen, if we direct our attention not to Sutpen, the center of those stories, but to their margins and shadows? In short, what happens

*Southern Quarterly* 26.4 (1988): 19–32.

if we read as feminist readers and refuse to accept the making of history in *Absalom, Absalom!* as inevitable or "natural"? I would argue that such a "resistance to codification," in Judith Fetterley's words, reveals a very different novel, one that, like Penelope, unravels as quickly as it weaves a tapestry of words, history, and paternalistic myths (viii). We might discover, in fact, not one but two stories, one about the making of historical narrative and patriarchy and one about their unmaking.

Such a reading requires a self-conscious determination to resist the various entanglements offered by a text as compelling as *Absalom, Absalom!* and by earlier readings as well. Students of reading and gender, like Elizabeth Flynn, Patrocinio Schweickart, Elizabeth Meese, and Jonathan Culler, suggest that such resistance essentially involves "reading the text as it was not meant to be read, in fact, reading it against itself" (Schweickart 50). As Schweickart observes, one must "identify the choices proffered by the text and, equally important, what the text precludes—namely, the possibility of reading as a woman *without* putting one's self in the position of the other, of reading so as to affirm womanhood as another, equally valid, paradigm of human existence" (50). And by focusing on what the text and its interpreters preclude as well as include, we can uncover what we might call the "otherness" of storytelling and story-making, as Elizabeth Meese might suggest: all those aspects of the text that have been repressed in earlier readings to accommodate interpretive conventions required by cultural priorities (xi).

In the case of *Absalom, Absalom!* interpretive conventions have led us to focus our energy as readers on the hypnotic story of Thomas Sutpen.[2] His determination to wrest a plantation and an aristocratic dynasty from the wilderness of North Mississippi also attracts the full attention of the text's narrators—Rosa Coldfield, Mr. Compson, Quentin Compson, and Shreve McCannon. For them and for students of the South as well, Sutpen's story seems to evoke the tragic dimensions of the region's history, in which property, race, family, and hubris are inextricably intertwined.

But by listening to those "garrulous outraged baffled ghosts" (5) who populate the novel and who endlessly recite Sutpen's story, we neglect those characters in *Absalom, Absalom!* who retreat to the silent regions of the novel—Sutpen's second wife Ellen, who takes to her bed and slowly withers away; Judith, Sutpen's daughter, who puzzles the narrators with her impenetrable calm and silence; Sutpen's mysterious and elusive first wife, who may or may not be pondering revenge; and Clytie, Sutpen's mulatto daughter, who eventually burns down the House of Sutpen.

These are characters who seem to live in the breaks and empty spaces of the narrative, who threaten to disrupt and even destroy the continuities of history woven by the narrators. As such, they form their own narrative of sorts, a muted story underlying Sutpen's dominant history (to borrow Elaine Showalter's terms), a muted story, moreover, of gaps, disruptions, discontinuities, and even precipitous endings. If the story told by the four main narrators, then, suggests the making of history, this muted story hints at its unmaking.

This is not to say, however, that the story of Thomas Sutpen's rise and fall does not compel considerable attention. By the lights of the Compson family, Sutpen might be a vulgar, ill-bred man masquerading as an aristocrat, but he is still vital enough to attract the storytelling efforts of three generations of Compsons, from Sutpen's only friend General Compson to Quentin Compson huddled with his roommate Shreve in a cold Harvard dormitory. And even Rosa Coldfield, who considers herself Sutpen's sworn enemy and who pronounces him a demon "*not articulated in this world*" (214), insists that her brother-in-law's story must be told so that, as Quentin Compson, her reluctant audience, wryly thinks, people will "*know at last why God let us lose the War: that only through the blood of our men and the tears of our women could He stay this demon and efface his name and lineage from the earth*" (8).

Above all, what attracts the attention of these four narrators is the need to place Sutpen's story in some sort of understandable sequence. For they are all concerned with the making of history, with devising explanations for the curious and the uncertain and with imposing coherence on separate events by seeking cause-and-effect relationships establishing connections. There are, after all, a good many connections that need to be established to understand the fragmented pictures of Thomas Sutpen's story handed down by the community—his abrupt appearance in Jefferson, the way he makes his money to buy and design Sutpen's Hundred, his decision to marry Ellen Coldfield, the friendship between Charles Bon and Henry Sutpen, Thomas Sutpen's mysterious trip to New Orleans, Judith Sutpen's broken engagement, Henry Sutpen's murder of Bon, Sutpen's courtship of Rosa, and Judith's decision to raise Charles Bon's son. As Mr. Compson reminds us, "we have a few old mouth-to-mouth tales; we exhume from old trunks and boxes and drawers letters without salutation or signature, in which men and women who once lived and breathed are now merely initials or nicknames out of some now incomprehensible affection which sound to us like Sanskrit or Chocktaw . . ." (124).

Hence the need to establish sequence and plot in those old mouth-to-mouth tales becomes all the more pressing, especially in regard to the puzzling decline and fall of the Sutpen family's history. For Rosa the explanation lies with her definition of Sutpen as a demon unarticulated in this world whom only civil war can eventually destroy. For Compson the answers lie with the impassioned friendship of Henry and Charles Bon and the octoroon mistress that Henry discovers. For Shreve and Quentin the plot goes back even further, to Thomas Sutpen's first marriage and its legacy of miscegenation and the possibility of incest.

However different the conclusions reached by the storytellers are, their concerns and their very language remain remarkably the same. They are determined to impose order and sequence on the story of Thomas Sutpen, to bridge the breaks between the pieces they have inherited, and the effort to find connections is underscored by the hypotactic style eventually appropriating the stories of each and every one of the narrators. The length and complexity of their very sentences, as one subordinate clause inevitably follows another, reflect both their determination to make connections and the storytelling antecedents uniting them. Not without reason, then, do Quentin and Shreve make frequent mention of the stories' underlying similarities. "*Yes, we are both Father,*" Quentin thinks. "*Or maybe Father and I are both Shreve, maybe it took Father and me both to make Shreve or Shreve and me both to make Father or maybe Thomas Sutpen to make all of us*" (326–27).

This last remark is particularly revealing because it suggests just how dependent all these storytellers, with the possible exception of Rosa Coldfield, are on the fragmented stories that Thomas Sutpen tells General Compson on two occasions: once during Sutpen's chase of the runaway French architect brought in to help build the plantation manor and once during the Civil War when Sutpen tries to puzzle out where his grand design has gone wrong. For like the storytellers who follow him, Sutpen deliberately seeks out causes, effects, and connections. "'You see, I had a design in my mind,'" he says, reflecting on his daughter's shattered engagement, his son's disappearance, and the imminent loss of his great wealth. "'Whether it was a good or a bad design is beside the point; the question is, Where did I make the mistake in it, what did I do or misdo in it, whom or what injure by it to the extent which this would indicate'" (329). And it is this same casting about for reasons and causes that distinguishes the storytellers who later reconstruct his life and the story of his family.

Indeed, in a manner of speaking the novel's narrators are all heirs to Sutpen's own storytelling and design-making. By accepting that legacy and by passing stories of the ambitious planter to the next storyteller, they reenact the line of succession that Sutpen himself yearns to establish—the passing of grand design from father to son. The fragments of old tales and the compelling urge to establish continuity are handed down from General Compson to Mr. Compson, who in turn bequeaths the tales to Quentin, who finally passes the stories on to Shreve, just as Rosa Coldfield, herself an heir of sorts, passes on the legacy of storytelling to Quentin and tells him that "maybe some day you will remember this and write about it" (6). Successors to Thomas Sutpen as storyteller, they are themselves fathers of their own tales to be passed on to storytelling sons.

In this respect, feminist critics like Teresa de Lauretis might recognize the narratives Faulkner's storytellers weave and re-weave as essentially oedipal, stories of fathers and sons leaving little room for sisters, wives, or daughters except as adjuncts to that central bond between father and son. Essentially, de Lauretis builds her definition of oedipal narrative on Roland Barthes's characterization of "the pleasure of the text" as "a staging of the (absent, hidden or hypostatized) father" (10). Even more emphatically than Barthes, though, de Lauretis argues that narrative in general as defined in Western culture constitutes patriarchy and is constitutive thereby. The very movement of narrative, by her lights, "specifies and even produces the masculine position as that of mythical subject, and the feminine position as mythical obstacle or, simply, the space in which that movement occurs" (143). Hence in storytelling patterns established by "major" female tales of ancient heroes like Oedipus and Perseus, even characters like Medusa and the Sphinx, survive "inscribed in hero narratives, in someone else's story, not their own" (109).

It is, in fact, as figures in someone else's story, marginal characters at best, that women exist in tales told by Sutpen to General Compson and in the stories to follow. As the planter himself bluntly remarks, they are simply "incremental to the design which I had in mind" (300). Sutpen's great design of establishing a plantation—and implicitly, a patriarchy—that can be passed down his male line offers no other possible place for women than that of making the continuity of his plantation dynasty possible. They are adjuncts to the tale but not tellers or even voices in their own right. Thinking back on the story that Sutpen passes on to General Compson, Mr. Compson notes briefly, "So it was no tale about women, and certainly not about love" (310). If there is any room at all for women in the few stories that Sutpen himself tells, it is in the corners and shadows of the narrative. Even in his tale of the slave uprising on Haiti, the girl who becomes his first wife is only "a shadow that almost emerged for a moment and then faded again but not completely away" (308).

Women are relegated to the same dim corners and shadows in all those stories following Sutpen's tale. All the women in Sutpen's family, from his first wife to Clytie, are regarded by the narrators, even Rosa, as mere adjuncts to Sutpen's design, helpless pawns who readily succumb to Sutpen's manipulations, ambitions, and bombast. In a novel about talking and about a driven man whose very shoulders are described as "forensic" and "oratorical," the Sutpen women are remarkably silent and remote (344). Even when narrative attention focuses on them, as in stories of Judith's adolescence and courtship, Ellen, Judith, Clytie, and Sutpen's mysterious first wife slip into the more distant regions of the tale. In adolescence, for instance, Judith is so inaccessible that she seems to be beyond even the reach of her grandfather Coldfield's voice. From the perspective of Mr. Compson, unwittingly repeating Sutpen's narrative strategy of expelling women to the margin, Judith appears to move in a "complete detachment and imperviousness to actuality almost like physical deafness" (84). Similarly remote is Ellen, who has been "corrupted," according to Mr. Compson, by Sutpen's ambition to manufacture at Sutpen's Hundred a ready-made aristocratic family and dynasty (86). Acquiescing to Sutpen's design, she escapes, Mr. Compson asserts, into "a world of pure illusion in which, safe from any harm, she moved, lived, from attitude to attitude against her background of chatelaine to the largest, wife to the wealthiest, mother of the most fortunate" (83). From this perspective, stamped by Sutpen's own design and narrative, women do *appear* to lead lives "not only divorced from, but irrevocably excommunicated from, all reality" (240). They are indeed divorced from the reality deliberately woven by storytelling and the making of history in *Absalom, Absalom!* Ellen herself suggests something of that retreat from history when she takes to her bed on the eve of the Civil War.

If there is any role in history for the novel's women, it would seem to be the one suggested by Rosa Coldfield, the only woman in the dominant story who is permitted a voice. For even Rosa, who is described as "*the chief disciple and advocate of that cult of demon-harrying of which ... [Sutpen] was the chief object,*" accepts the role as servant to the making of Thomas Sutpen's history (347). Although she considers herself the town's poet laureate fiercely guarding the heroism of the past, she is ultimately no less an adjunct to Thomas Sutpen's design than Ellen is. Her very voice serves not so much her own purposes and desires as those of Sutpen's looming ghost, "as if it were the voice which he haunted where a more fortunate one would have had a house" (4). And like the other women in the making of this history, even her voice retreats to the margins of the narrative. We are told that her voice "would not cease, it would just vanish" as it gave life and breath to the shadow of Thomas Sutpen (4). Indeed, Rosa herself seems to vanish as the making of Sutpen's story attracts the storytelling efforts of Mr. Compson, Quentin, and Shreve. Once she refuses Sutpen's pragmatic proposition that she bear a son before the two commit themselves to marriage, Rosa no longer has any place in the narrative. She is eventually reduced to a reference in Mr. Compson's letter about her funeral, herself an adjunct to Mr. Compson's own storytelling design.[3]

Such retreats into the margin, though, whether by Rosa's voice or by Ellen in the last two years of her life, suggest the possibility of severing the connections and disrupting the history so carefully constructed by the narrators in the dominant story. Like Ellen, who retreats to a darkened room in "baffled incomprehension" (97), these withdrawals remind us of the breaks, inconsistencies, and absences that the narrators seek to repair in order to establish order, sequence, and connections, in short, to make history (see Brooks 286). They remind us that these connections are tentative, speculative, and ultimately uncertain, comparable to General Compson's definition of language as "that meagre and fragile thread . . . by which the little surface corners and edges of men's secret and solitary lives may be joined for an instant now and then before sinking back into the darkness" (313).

They also repeatedly remind us of the uneasiness of narrators confronted with the difficult task of imposing order on the separate fragments of Sutpen's life. Too many times the narrators must recount events that seem to take place, in Rosa's words, "without rhyme or reason or shadow of excuse" (17). Too many times they must confront the breaks in the plots they reconstruct—their lack of knowledge about Sutpen's interview with Henry on the Christmas Eve before the war, Sutpen's trip to New Orleans, Bon's feelings for Judith, the years Henry and Bon spent during the war, and Henry's reasons for murdering Bon at the very gates of the Sutpen manor. "It's just incredible," Mr. Compson admits. "It just does not explain. Or perhaps that's it: they don't explain and we are not supposed to know" (124).

Hence the narrators frequently reveal fears that such breaks will bring their storytelling efforts to an abrupt and precipitous end. They are forever telling each other to wait so that they can carefully establish narrative sequence and even forestall hasty conclusions. As Quentin tells Shreve, Sutpen's first story told to General Compson is so hastily narrated and abrupt that the general is forced to cry, "'Wait wait for God's sake wait' about like you are until he finally did stop and back up and start over again with at least some regard for cause and effect even if none for logical sequence and continuity" (308). It is a plea that is echoed time and time again by both Quentin and Shreve in particular whenever the narrative they fabricate between them threatens to come to a rapid conclusion—in speculation about Sutpen's final meeting with Henry in a Confederate camp, in reconstructions of Wash Jones's murder of Sutpen, in the fictions they weave of Charles Bon's motives. We even hear this plea for prolonging the narrative in the cries for extra time uttered by Bon and Henry as imagined by Shreve and Quentin in the last section. Like their narrators, Henry and Charles are apparently trying to stave off the final confrontation. As such, characters and narrators suggest that Peter Brooks's definition of the motives propelling narrative is all too apt. Narrative desire, he notes in *Reading for the Plot*, "is the wish for the end, for fulfillment, but fulfillment must be delayed so that we can understand it in relation to origin and to desire itself" (111).

It is this desire, I would suggest, that the muted story of *Absalom, Absalom!* threatens to thwart. This second story seems all the more subversive because it follows none of the narrative patterns of sequence, order, and cause and effect characterizing the dominant story. Indeed, it is not even properly told. If it exists at all, it is in the margins, breaks, contradictions, and silences inhabited by the women who supposedly serve as tools in Thomas Sutpen's design and implicitly in the telling of history. And as a story that is *not* told, it undermines the plots and connections so carefully constructed by the dominant narrators and even threatens to bring their plots to an abrupt end altogether.

Indeed, instead of offering answers, solutions, and connections, as the dominant story does, this untold story simply poses questions, and, more often than not, the silent women in Thomas Sutpen's story who retreat to the far regions of the narrative serve as emblems of those questions, empty spaces that can never quite be filled by the endless words that weave Sutpen's tale. They are women who all give pause to the carefully constructed narratives of history. Judith's very existence, for instance, seems to slow down the fevered calculations of the Bons' lawyer conjured up by Quentin and Shreve. As the two young men themselves speculate, "you could maybe even have seen the question mark after it and the other words even: *daughter? daughter? daughter?* trailing off not because thinking trailed off, but on the contrary thinking stopped right still then ..." (376). Like Judith, in fact, Ellen, Clytie, and Sutpen's first wife all seem to fall "into the space where the *daughter? daughter? daughter?* never had quite showed" (385–86).

It is in that space that we are reminded of the tenuous connections required by the making of history and patriarchy. Early in Mr. Compson's story,
for instance, we are told that Ellen retreats to her room in "bewildered and
uncomprehending amazement" after Henry's mysterious interview with his
father and his abrupt disappearance from Sutpen's Hundred (103). And even
though Mr. Compson seeks an explanation for that disappearance in the existence of Charles Bon's octoroon mistress, the tentative nature of that conclusion is made clear by the repeated coupling of Ellen's baffled retreat with
Henry's furious departure from Sutpen's domain. Even more resistant to explanation are Judith and Clytie, whose elusiveness defeats the best storytelling
efforts of both Mr. Compson and Rosa Coldfield. For both narrators, Judith
and Clytie resist the categories that fit so easily into the narrative of patriarchal history making—dutiful daughter, eager betrothed, faithful servant, obedient retainer. Rather, they are women whose most characteristic traits are
their contradictions. To Mr. Compson Judith is "absolutely impenetrable, absolutely serene: no mourning, not even grief" (157). So elusive is she that she
seems to subvert the very order of narrative sequence, for Mr. Compson tells
us that she is a "*daughter doomed to spinsterhood who had chosen spinsterhood
already before there was anyone named Charles Bon since the aunt who came
to succor her in bereavement and sorrow found neither but instead that calm
absolutely impenetrable face*" (228). Similarly, Clytie is anything but a mere
servant, especially to Rosa Coldfield, to whom the black woman is "*perverse
inscrutable and paradox: free, yet incapable of freedom who had never once
called herself a slave ...*" (195).

More to the point, the sudden entry of these women into the narratives
of the dominant story often undermines the best efforts of the narrators
to establish sequence and continuity. In the early part of Compson's story,
for instance, Judith serves primarily as "the blank shape, the empty vessel"
in which Charles Bon and Henry seek each other and themselves (148). But
when Compson recounts the episode in which Judith bestows Charles Bon's
letter upon General Compson's wife—the first time, incidentally, that Judith
moves to the narrative center—the storytelling abruptly breaks, and we as
readers are returned to the year 1909 and the Compson porch, where Quentin
and his father are talking. Similarly disruptive is Clytie in Rosa's second round
of storytelling. It is Clytie who stands between Rosa and Judith on the stairs
of Sutpen's Hundred the day Charles Bon is killed, and it is her presence,
described by Rosa as "*that furious yet absolutely rocklike and immobile an-
tagonism*," which stops Rosa in her headlong rush up the stairs and even shifts

her narrative back to the days of the courtship of Judith and Charles Bon (170). And as if Clytie's interruption were not enough, Judith appears at the stairs and utters a single word, "Clytie," the sound of which once again shifts Rosa's story back into the past to that early summer of wisteria, "when she silently dogs Judith's and Bon's footsteps." Even that brief recovery of memory is checked by Judith's second response on the stairs, "*Yes, Rosa?*"—a question that returns Rosa to the moment on the stairs and, as she observes herself, enters "*calmly into the midstride of my running*" (186).

Equally striking are the unexpected breaks preceded by brief mention of that elusive first wife in the stories told by Sutpen of his early days on the Haitian plantation. For as Quentin tells Shreve, Sutpen's story, told to General Compson during the hunt for the escaped French architect, suddenly stops with the young entrepreneur's engagement to the daughter of his Haitian employer. It is at this stage of the narrative, Quentin says, that Sutpen "stopped talking, telling it" (318). It would be thirty years before Sutpen would pick up the narrative thread and continue the telling of the story to General Compson. And when the latter finally relates his decision to put aside his wife, not just Sutpen's story is broken off. Quentin's narration is interrupted as well; we return to the scene of storytelling at Harvard in 1909. The story that Quentin and Shreve then tell together jumps ahead twenty-eight years.

Indeed, both that first wife and Clytie threaten to bring these stories—and, implicitly, the making of history—to a precipitous end. It is "the old Sabine," after all, who is pictured by Quentin and Shreve as brooding on vengeance and Sutpen's eventual downfall (378). According to the history they construct, she may—or may not—be plotting the meeting of Sutpen and Charles Bon that promises to reveal the secrets of Sutpen's past and to destroy his dynasty—in short, to bring his history to an abrupt halt by cutting through delays, hesitations, and pleas for time to prolong history's making. So subversive is her presence (or nonpresence, as the case may be) that we cannot even be certain she actually exists. As the third-person narrator of *Absalom, Absalom!* notes, she and her calculating lawyer are fabrications created by Quentin and Shreve, "people who perhaps had never existed at all anywhere, who, shadows, were shadows not of flesh and blood which had lived and died but shadows in turn of what were . . . shades too" (379). Indeed, the "old Sabine" is one of the most conspicuous empty spaces in the narrative, a character whose very name occupies no place in the round of stories. Only in the third-person narrator's "Genealogy" is her name given as "Eulalia Bon" (475). If she lives at all, it is in the shifting frontier between history and its making, and as such, the shadow she casts upon Sutpen's story reminds us of its fictionality, of the arbitrary connections and order it seeks to make.

Most subversive of all, though, is Clytie, who brings an end to the history of the House of Sutpen by setting fire to the manor. She does so in part to keep the dying Henry Sutpen, now sequestered in the house, from being arrested for the long-ago murder of Charles Bon, but her action also succeeds in preventing Henry from telling and retelling the story of the Sutpens. For it is a story that seems to beg to be told and retold as suggested in that hypnotic encounter between Henry and Quentin the night that Rosa and Quentin travel to Sutpen's Hundred. Thinking back on the night, Quentin fears that "waking or sleeping it was the same and would be the same forever as long as he lived" (464). Again and again he hears himself ask Henry who he is, how long he has been there, and why he has returned home, and repeatedly the troubled young man hears Henry's answers. Clytie's action, though, brings an end to the telling and retelling of stories and the making of history, as Rosa, one of those makers of history, recognizes as she desperately fights off the men pulling her out of the burning house.

Not for nothing, then, does Mr. Compson early on suggest that perhaps Clytie's name should really be Cassandra, "to designate the presiding augur of . . . [Sutpen's] disaster" (74). One of the most silent characters in the text as a whole, her very presence serves to contradict the "forensic" and "oratorical" swaggering upon which Thomas Sutpen relies to define himself and his patriarchal design. She is, in fact, nearly the opposite of her progenitor Raby in "Evangeline," a short story predating the writing of *Absalom, Absalom!* and offering an early version of the Sutpen saga.[4] Unlike Raby, who tells the story of Judith, Charles Bon, and Henry Sutpen to an irreverent first-person narrator, Clytie has no words to offer to the making of Sutpen's story. She is, rather, one of the contradictions and anomalies inadvertently left over by Sutpen's patriarchal design and by the making of history. Ultimately, she is, like the other Sutpen women, the empty space providing not just the tools for making patriarchy and narrative but also the breaks, discontinuities, and precipitous endings bringing that effort to a close.

Therefore, we would do well to remember that what is *not* told in a story like Thomas Sutpen's may be as important as what *is* told. For if, as de Lauretis suggests, an oedipal or patriarchal narrative conceives of the subject and movement of the tale as masculine and of the space and setting as feminine, the space may hold just as much portent for the movement of the masculine subject. By paying attention to those empty spaces, breaks and margins in

*Absalom, Absalom!* and by resisting earlier characterizations of the text as a story primarily about Sutpen and his narrators, we discover a narrative that unravels almost as quickly as it is woven and history that is unmade nearly as soon as it is made. We also discover that those women characters who have been the subject of so much anguished commentary may indeed be more subversive than they appear through the eyes of earlier critics. For what we learn in the end from such a double reading, one that concentrates both on what is told and *not* told, is not just the seductions of patriarchy but its limits and weaknesses as well.

## Notes

1. A summary of the conference paper on which this article is based appeared as "Subverting History: Women and Narrative in *Absalom, Absalom!*" in *Commemorating the Past: Celebrations and Retrospection*, Southeastern American Studies Conference Proceedings 1987, ed. Don Harkness (Tampa, FL: American Studies Press, 1987), 37–40. I should also note here my thanks to Professor Noel Polk of the University of Southern Mississippi and Professor Walter Wenska of the College of William and Mary, both of whom took time out to read and comment on an earlier version of the essay.
2. See, for example, the essays in *William Faulkner's Absalom, Absalom! A Critical Casebook* (Muhlenfield, ed.). A notable exception in this respect is Deborah L. Clarke's fine article, "Familiar and Fantastic: Women in *Absalom, Absalom!*"
3. I am indebted to Professor Wenska for this insight.
4. For background on the writing of "Evangeline" and *Absalom, Absalom!* in general, see Muhlenfeld (xi–xxxix) and Joseph Blotner's note on "Evangeline" in Faulkner's *Uncollected Stories* (709).

## Works Cited

Barthes, Roland. *The Pleasure of the Text*. Trans Richard Miller. New York: Hill and Wang, 1975.

Brooks, Peter. *Reading for the Plot: Desire and Intention in Narrative*. New York: Vintage, 1985.

Clarke, Deborah L. "Familiar and Fantastic: Women in *Absalom, Absalom!*" *Faulkner Journal* 2 (1986): 62–72.

Culler, Jonathan. *On Deconstruction: Theory and Criticism after Structuralism*. Ithaca, NY: Cornell University Press, 1982.

de Lauretis, Teresa. *Alice Doesn't: Feminism, Semiotics, Cinema*. Bloomington: Indiana University Press, 1984.

Duvall, John N. "Faulkner's Critics and Women: The Voice of the Community." *Faulkner and Women: Faulkner and Yoknapatawpha, 1985.* Ed. Doreen Fowler and Ann J. Abadie. Jackson: University Press of Mississippi, 1986.

Faulkner, William. *Absalom, Absalom!* Corrected text. New York: Vintage, 1987.

——. *Uncollected Stories.* Ed. Joseph Blotner. New York: Vintage, 1981.

Fetterley, Judith. *The Resisting Reader: A Feminist Approach to American Fiction.* Bloomington: Indiana University Press, 1978.

Flynn, Elizabeth A., and Patricinio P. Schweickart, eds. *Gender and Reading: Essays on Readers, Texts, and Contexts.* Baltimore: Johns Hopkins University Press, 1986.

Geismar, Maxwell. *Writers in Crisis: The American Novel between Two Wars.* Boston: Houghton Mifflin, 1942.

Guerard, Albert J. *The Triumph of the Novel: Dickens, Dostoevsky, Faulkner.* New York: Oxford University Press, 1976.

Meese, Elizabeth. *Crossing the Double-Cross: The Practice of Feminist Criticism.* Chapel Hill: University of North Carolina Press, 1986.

Muhlenfeld, Elisabeth, ed. *William Faulkner's* Absalom, Absalom! *A Critical Casebook.* New York: Garland, 1984.

Schweickart, Patrocinio P. "Reading Ourselves: Toward a Feminist Theory of Reading." Flynn and Schweickart 31–62.

Showalter, Elaine. "Feminist Criticism in the Wilderness." *The New Feminist Criticism: Essays on Women, Literature, and Theory.* Ed. Elaine Showalter. New York: Pantheon, 1985, 243–70.

PART IV

*1990S*

# On Welty's Use of Allusion

## Expectations and Their Revision in "The Wide Net," *The Robber Bridegroom*, and "At The Landing"

HARRIET POLLACK

When Eudora Welty argues that Isak Dinesen's tales all had their "start in other tales—for a tale must have its 'start,' as a good bread must" and that those starts were most frequently from "fables . . . fairy tales, stories from the Bible and the Arabian Nights and Ancient Greece and Rome" (*Eye of the Story* 262), she applies a principle she had undoubtedly learned in her bedroom studio, at work. For Welty's own habit of telling "twice-told tales" is distinctive. Welty's fictions are built on allusions to well-known stories and story patterns—and on literary, more than autobiographical, memory. She has freely appropriated legend, history, fairy tale, folklore, myth, ballad, and poetry. She also has reworked southern gothic, romantic, and pastoral formulas. Critics sometimes think of her as a genial southern storyteller who knows numberless time-honored tales as well as how to combine them in curious amalgamation. Scholarly readers with the classics on their minds have sometimes paid more attention to Welty's sources than to her uses of them.[1] Source hunting in itself, however, is not an adequate critical response to Welty's allusions. What needs to be attended instead is the relationship of her sources to her new text: that is, the work performed when two or more narratives are simultaneously brought to a reader's mind. Could we not, then, see her as technical innovator, experimenting with readers' expectations through her use of allusion and, simultaneously, her mixing of genres?

The first step is to map out the process characteristically initiated by Welty's allusions and then examine the specific uses she makes of that process in three allusive fictions: "The Wide Net," *The Robber Bridegroom* and its story double, "At The Landing." Welty's fiction often evokes three types of allusion: (1) allusion that recollects a secondary literary genre and so mixes the genre

*Southern Quarterly* 29.1 (1990): 5–30.

of Welty's story—suggesting to a reader conflicting expectations (conflicting reading strategies) that interact: (2) allusion in its conventional sense—allusion to specific literary referents—which in Welty's case is often complicated as she calls up not one, but several, literary memories, again guiding her reader to shape conflicting expectations and to bring these into interaction; (3) interallusiveness among Welty's own fictions as another type of literary memory which her fiction evokes.

Welty's allusions, like all authors' allusions, bring together at least two texts or story patterns in readers' minds. Knowledge of the text-at-hand is modified by knowledge of a text evoked. This process has been analyzed into four discrete actions by Ziva Ben Porat: (1) recognizing the marker as closely related to—or from—a reference text; (2) identifying the evoked text, if it was not immediately recognized; (3) modifying the initial meaning of the marker to suit the next text; and (4) calling up the evoked text as a whole to form intertextual patterning. I would add a fifth process to Porat's series: (5a) calling up the entire genre to which the referent text belongs—the familiar class and pattern and all the recalled stories that belong to it—and (5b) situations in which a pattern, but no specific text, is recalled.

This revision of Porat's taxonomy suggests how allusions can do much more than alter the initial reading of a single element in the fiction-at-hand. They may alter the reader's experience and understanding of the text as a whole. Welty's reader, however, often is asked to do more, to work with the associations produced by several allusions, not just one.

When readers confront an allusion, they face something like a puzzle to be solved. They must decipher not only the reference itself, but also its relevance. Those readers are likely to ask certain predictable questions. They may want to know if the fictions involved run parallel, and if the referent texts act as either plot, genre, character, or motif "pointers." They may wonder which of the adapted textual patterns will be reenacted, which will be reproduced with an ironic difference, and which will be totally negated. They may look to see how the earlier text will complicate the meaning of the later one and if the later text will criticize or correct the earlier one. They may be attentive to submerged aspects of the text-at-hand which now take on new emphasis as a result of intertextual patterning, an interaction that brings the reader to realize effects hovering unarticulated in the juxtaposition of two articulated presences.

Characteristically, Welty disappoints predictions built on knowledge of referent texts. She relies on obstruction as a strategy for eliciting a desired response. When her allusions arouse expectations from which her tales diverge, meaning is located in the tension between the reader's literary memory and Welty's new text. That is, allusion emphasizes difference as well as similarity. Meaning is formulated in part by reference to and obstruction of expectations based on memory. These interactions sometimes silently comment on the source fictions and, in a sense, deconstruct them.

The process by which Welty leads the reader from allusion to a strategy for unraveling meaning can be seen clearly in "The Wide Net," a short work controlled by an allusive evocation of a genre other than the realistic short story, that is by mixing of genres. Genre is conventional; it is, as E. D. Hirsch put it, "a propriety which is, on the whole, socially considerate" of the author to observe (93). The reader who unexpectedly encounters a fiction extending generic conventions may feel as disoriented as a dinner guest whose host passes the evening without mentioning dinner. The visitor will not only be hungry but, like these readers, expectant and bewildered, too. To alter Hirsch slightly, readers also use their generic expectations as initial, prefabricated interpretive strategies. They may respond with irritation when genre expectations are frustrated, exactly as if they had been denied an expected courtesy. Welty's allusive evocation of more than one genre in a story, complicating a reader's interpretative process, is significant for a reader because, as Peter Rabinowitz has pointed out, "genres can be seen not only the traditional way as patterns or models that writers follow in constructing texts, but also from the other direction, as different packages of rules that readers apply in construing them, as ready made strategies for reading" (177).

"The Wide Net" builds on a generic mixing; it is a vernacular tale about a back-country couple's marital squabble that slips into the mythic tradition of the heroic quest. As she often does, Welty leads a reader to begin making meaning within the context of a "primary framework"—a term borrowed from sociologist Irving Goffman's discussion of the contextuality of interpretation (21). Then Welty guides a reader to suspect that this initial framing has been a misframing and to readjust that first interpretive strategy. The reader's reworking adds a layer to the interpretation which is still attached to the first frame and its meanings; the layers created by these multiple frameworks may subsequently interact.[2]

A reader meeting "The Wide Net" for the first time begins what appears to be a realistic short story about William Wallace Jamieson's bemused reaction to his wife Hazel's first pregnancy. This father-to-be is troubled by a feeling that he has lost Hazel to some mystery; he feels excluded and resents her acting as though she were about to deliver, although she is only three months pregnant. In response to the situation, he has slipped away to a carnival in Carthage, Mississippi, and then stayed out all night with two boys down the road. But when he returns home, he does not find a chastened, more attentive Hazel. Instead he spots a little letter announcing her intention not to put up with him, but to drown herself. In his distress, William Wallace turns for help to his friend Virgil Thompson, who has sat "on his neck" with him all the previous night, "done as much as he done, and come home at the same time" (174). Together the two organize and conduct a river-dragging party.

Students of mine sometimes say that in their first encounter with the story they loved reading "The Wide Net," but they wonder why the tone of the story eventually seems genuinely celebratory when it might be expected to be full of comic grief. They echo Virgil's question to William Wallace: "Was you out catching cotton-tails, or was you out catching your wife?" (172). It is entirely reasonable that when Hazel's husband gorges himself with fresh-caught fried fish, lapses into a sated sleep and wakes to dance with a catfish hanging from his belt, initial readers may feel startled, and either pleased or puzzled depending on their flexibility and their range of literary experience.[3]

One way to understand the tale's mid-stream generic transformation from a realistic tale to something else is through its allusions. When it begins, William Wallace has, after all, just spent the night with Virgil. And like Virgil's Aeneas who wandered from his duty and his destiny in Queen Dido's Carthage, William Wallace has strayed from husbandly devotion at a carnival in Mississippi's Carthage.

Welty transforms a realistic short story into one lightly laced with the heroic epic, and then transforms the epic form that she lightly evoked. Susan Gubar has said that while women writers tend to escape their strained relationships with some conventional literary forms through generic amalgamations,[4] she found that in putting together *The Norton Anthology of Women's Literature* she had not come across a woman writing the heroic epic. But it is clear that Welty is revising that form, transforming it precisely as it is gendered.

Virgil's *Aeneid* is not a single, privileged reference that readers must find evoked by the text in order to appreciate it. Nor is it a single key allusion that all studious readers must inevitably find. Michael Kreyling, for example, is helped by memories of Dante taking Virgil as a companion in his search for Beatrice, and later of the attitude of the madonna in Hazel's final gesture (*Eudora Welty* 19). It would be inaccurate to claim that Welty's tale re-creates any one epic. Rather the story evokes the generic elements of the mythic, heroic quest. Its comic tone is in part the product of a reader's barely conscious awareness of parody and transformation.

Consider, for example, William Wallace's band of men. As if we were in a Homerian epic, we find the clans of Dover represented in it: the eight giant Malones, the Doyles and their noisy dogs, Grady and Brucie Rippen who are tied to this search by their history (their father had drowned in the Pearl River), and two black boys, Sam and Robbie Bell. These troops stomp and paw each other, eager to go, attending while their leaders apply to wise Old Doc for permission to use the wide net; Old Doc himself plays the part of oracle. He is a seer who could foretell the day's outcome, but instead he only obliquely hints at it, not quite revealing fate's decree. He waits patiently for the inevitable to come to pass, and for the order of the universe to become as clear to others as it is to him. As Ruth Vande Kieft points out (57–58), there are also the ordeals which the questing hero survives. Like Aeneas who voyaged into the underworld, William Wallace dives to the deepest spot on the Pearl River, a spot "so dark that it was no longer the muddy world of the upper river but the dark, clear world of deepness" and returns from "the gloom of such depths" with an intuition of the "true trouble that Hazel had fallen into" (180). Later he faces the inhabitant of these depths, that river creature, the King of Snakes, and he stares him down. Next he directs his men through a storm which steals the goldenness of the day. Lashing its tail "through the air," this tempest breaks the river "in a wound of Silver," and fills the air with fragrance and a mystery reminiscent of Hazel's troubling mystery. Encountering this dragon-tailed storm, our hero founders on a sharp rock, opening a wound he later carries as a trophy of his quest. He reenters that town of Dover not obviously successful in his quest, but oddly triumphant.

Although the story shares several elements with the heroic epic, a reader making full sense of it must know that it also differs from them, and departs from expectations formed on knowledge of that genre. And this need to revise our expectations again, as in so many of Welty's works, brings us to the story's center. William Wallace, triumphant though he seems to be when he returns to Dover, has not in any obvious sense triumphed. That is, he has set out to find Hazel, but returns without her.

Unlike the traditional epic hero whose goal is clear, William Wallace's is not. For William Wallace needs, not to find Hazel, but to gain insight into what has possessed her and caused trouble between them. That is what Hazel, by writing her note, sends William Wallace to discover in the Pearl River. The effect of her suicide note is to send him into the natural world as it approaches its own "changing-time." And so Hazel leaves her husband to observe nature's cycle at this moment when, as Doc puts it, "any day now the change will come":

> It's going to turn from hot to cold, and we can kill the hog that's ripe and have fresh meat to eat. Come one of these nights and we can wander down here and tree a nice possum. Old Jack Frost will be pinching things up. Old Mr. Winter will be standing in the door. Hickory tree there will be yellow. Sweet-gum red, hickory yellow, dogwood red, sycamore yellow . . . Magnolia and live-oak never die. Remember that. Persimmons will all get fit to eat, and nuts will be dropping like rain all through the woods here. And run, little quail, for we'll be after you too. (176)

Standing on the verge of this ordered change and then immersing himself in the Pearl River, William Wallace intuits what Hazel must feel as she prepares to give birth: "the elation that comes of great hopes and changes, sometimes simply of the harvest time, that comes with a little course of its own like a tune to run in the head" (180). That is, he rediscovers the excitement that nature's changeful cycles can generate. This is what he celebrates finding. Welty has amalgamated the pattern of heroic epic to emphasize the powerful (and mysterious) cycles of nature over a powerful hero's conquest—and made a female revision of a literary form by blending elements of comic realism, pastoral, and epic. This accommodation of forms, one to the other, is appropriate to the story's content in which William Wallace comes to accommodate something female and puzzling.

Welty makes William Wallace wander into a harmony with nature that causes him to rejoice when he intended to drag the river for his wife's body. As he returns home from this odd experience, he hears the music of "the Sacred Harp Sing"—female music that seems to evoke an oblique and comic transformation of the Sirens' songs that attracted previous wanderers. William Wallace associates this celestial music permeating the woods with nature's female principle. "He [smiles] faintly, as he would at his mother, and at Hazel, and at the singing women in his life, now all one young girl standing up to sing under the trees the oldest and longest ballads there were." Then in the night sky, he sees a rainbow which looks to him "in the light of the moon . . . small and of gauzy material, like a lady's summer dress, a faint veil through which the stars showed" (187). Affected by his glad knowledge of the Pearl River's depths, the night sky, and the mysterious part that women play in mother nature's order, William Wallace walks back into his house. And there he finds Hazel awaiting his return from the ordeal she had conceived. Like some fairy-tale hero who has earned his heart's desire by successfully completing a series of tasks, William Wallace finds his life restored to routine domesticity. He feels relief, but also anger with Hazel who, coolly hidden in the closet, had watched him read her suicide note. Asserting himself against her mysterious and knowing superiority, he turns her upside down and spanks her. And she, responding unpredictably to his challenge, crawls into the crook of his arm. Then as she gazes into "the dark fields where the lightning bugs flickered," he stands beside her with a frown on his face, straining to see what she sees there in the natural world. And when, after a few minutes, she takes him by the hand and leads him into the house, "smiling as if she were smiling down on him" (188), a reader may feel that though William Wallace will never share Hazel's experience entirely, he may now better intuit the source and implication of her mystery.

Return then to the reader's initial notion that somehow in the course of the day William Wallace wandered from his purpose: to recover Hazel. That first impression needed revision, even though Welty appeared to confirm it in Virgil's question "was you out catching cotton-tails or was you out catching your wife?" As in the case of Aeneas, who to all first appearances was waylaid from his purpose and destiny in Carthage, the wandering of a hero may prove to be his destiny, the path by which he will arrive where he is going—in this case, by way of a river-dragging with the boys from the town.

Readers may not be entirely comfortable with "The Wide Net" until they consciously or, more probably, intuitively identify the genres which intertwine in it. This is not the case with *The Robber Bridegroom*, a fairy tale which evokes multiple sources and is more highly allusive than "The Wide Net." There, the tale does not discomfort the reader who neither senses nor recognizes its sources. But the reader who discovers the tale's allusiveness is rewarded when memories of fairy tale, history, legend, and myth interact with the text, and that reader may find the tale considerably darker than the one who reads without these.

The list of allusions which critical readers of *The Robber Bridegroom* have compiled in their commentary is long indeed. J. A. Bryant Jr. began a brief directory to these in his 1968 monograph, *Eudora Welty*:

In addition to the general shape of Grimm's story, suggestions and reminiscences of a number of other tales are discoverable here, among them "The Little Goose Girl," "Rumpelstiltskin," "Little Snow White," "The Fisherman and His Wife," "Beauty and the Beast," Charles Perrault's "Cinderella," and the Hellenic myth of Cupid and Psyche. Moreover, a great deal of American folklore and near-folklore gets worked into the narrative, the stories of Davy Crockett and Mike Fink, the atrocities of Big Harpe and Little Harpe, and tall tales about Indians, frontiersmen and bandits of the Natchez Trace. (17)

Many of the allusions in this tale resemble dark threads that run through the fabric of a light, bright text. There, in the brightness where rape is obscured by the colors of love and murder by those of marriage, these dark threads running across the story's most obvious pattern are also a part of its look. A reader's overall impression may be that the tale's fabric is colorful and celebratory, while it holds in its background the darker hues of a lament for lost innocence (the nation's as well as Rosamond's).

As a fairy tale, *The Robber Bridegroom* belongs, by Welty's own definition, to a genre that is "not innocent," but has "been to the end of experience and back" ("And They All Lived Happily"). Some readers have argued that Welty's story is too dark to be called a fairy tale,[5] underestimating Welty's respect for the dark side of the fairy tale genre and the extent to which fairy tale allusions are sometimes directly responsible for the dark coloring of Welty's tale. The fairy tale, in spite of its conventional ending, is a genre that regularly offers dramatic instruction in man's dual nature and dark side. Welty herself has described the fairy tale genre in this way:

> ogres who enjoy eating people show children very well in fantasy what will threaten them later on . . . We are all brothers, but some of us are loveless. If fairy tales stir the imagination toward benevolence with the "good" fairies, they can awaken respect for the power of the "bad" fairies. Without the old fairy tales, children today could easily think malice and ill will are nothing but a set of miniature, sanitized, plastic toys—"giants 'n' ogres"—that come free in boxes of cereal at the supermarket. ("And They All Lived Happily")

If fairy tales teach that "we are all brothers, but some of us are loveless," Welty's allusions in *The Robber Bridegroom*—to Grimm's and other old tales— are designed to carry news of this potential treachery. Her echoes of fairy tales emphasize familial lovelessness—the wife who does not love her husband, the mother who does not love her child. Her Salome, for instance, is an embodiment of the spirit of step-motherliness. She is a composite of three characters by Grimm: the never-satisfied, husband-abusing old woman from "The Fisherman's Wife"; the unnatural mother of "Hansel and Gretel" who, because she is unwilling to share her food with her children, sends them into the forest hoping they will never return; and the jealous queen of "Little Snow White," that terrible replacement for a loving mother who demands that her stepdaughter's heart be brought to her. In Welty's retelling, Salome resembles that jealous queen as she poisons Rosamond's metaphoric heart by infecting it with suspicion. And Salome, again like the jealous stepmother in Grimm's "Snow White," pays for her crime when she is coerced to dance herself to death—a detail of Grimm's original version lost to those of us who grew up with altered retellings. But in the original, as in Welty's tale, she "had to dance until she fell down dead to the ground" (*Frog King* 190). Allusions such as these act as character, plot, and motif pointers, guiding the reader to recognize quickly Welty's variations on the archetype.

Welty also spins the tale's thread of doubleness "out of the times" (*Eye* 310), that is, out of the American past. Evoking an American literary tradition, she creates the wilderness as a place of anarchic, if sometimes liberating, lawlessness and then establishes a parallel between it and the morally ambiguous settlement where greed is sated legally. She calls up American literature, legend, and history to darken the tapestry of her tale. She adapts, from the narratives of those who survived capture by Indians in the seventeenth and eighteenth centuries, a setting in which to uncover man's capacity for ungodly acts. She re-creates the wilderness of the Natchez Trace where little Wiley Harpe, her "Little Harp," once carried the detached head of his own brother Micajah—wanted dead or alive—in preserving, blue Mississippi mud, as if it were a bank check to be cashed when needed. Welty also adapts southwestern humor, particularly those violent yet beguiling tales that chronicle the adventures of strutting, law-defying Mike Fink, half-horse, half-alligator. Merrill Maguire Skaggs and Melody Graulich have both written on Welty's adaptation of this genre. Skaggs argues that Welty's combination of southwestern humor with the fairy tale reveals the extent to which both genres are about the use of "extravagance . . . to confront basic fears and anxieties" (97) and an assertion of wished-for invulnerability. And Graulich, looking at how southwestern humor is itself a genre which breaks out of narrative conventions, discusses how Welty breaks its conventions by dropping the conventional framing narrator's voice, often used to constrain the voice of the roarer, and by allowing her narrator to speak the language of fantasy. In one especially provocative remark Graulich suggests that Welty revises the gender of this genre, creating a female tall tale in which "power comes through emotional rather than physical strength" (289), a view perhaps paralleling my reading of "The Wide Net."

These two types of allusion—to the fairy tales and to the American folklore named by Welty's various commentators and specifically cited in Welty's own essay, "Fairy Tale of the Natchez Trace"—murmur below the composition's most optimistic tones; they whisper distress. Distress, lament, and the dark tones of this narrative have received much critical attention as the tale has been discussed as an American pastoral, "a putdown of mercantile probity" (French 186), a comic consideration of an historical change. Yet there is reason to give the female focus of Rosamond and her adolescent emotional discoveries centrality[6] and to emphasize three allusions which softly sound variations on the theme of the robber bridegroom. These allusions may be the most provocative of the group. For this fiction is one of Welty's many stories about a troubling love that reveals the need to transform a discovered separateness. Knowledge of these three source fictions, along with a perception of how Welty's tale differs from these, can guide a reader's developing understanding.

First and most obvious among these sources is Grimm's "The Robber Bridegroom" (*German Popular Tales*). In that tale a young woman is engaged to, but ultimately saved from, a dangerous lover who threatens her innocence and her life. The heroine wanders into the forest one day to spy on her suitor. There she is warned by a bird and an old woman "to turn back my bonny, turn away home" (the refrain that Welty borrows). In spite of this warning the girl proceeds and discovers her betrothed, cutting other girls into pieces and salting them. A finger, chopped off for the wedding ring on it, flies into the observing girl's lap. She escapes undetected with this evidence of the danger approaching with her own wedding night. At her marriage ceremony, she produces the severed finger from her bodice, exposing her groom's violence. Then this loveless, lawless bridegroom, who is clearly associated with the sexual experience that cuts off childhood and threatens chastity, is ultimately restrained and arrested.

Ominous potential parallels occur to the reader familiar with Grimm's terrible robber bridegroom. And although the comedy of Welty's variant clearly promises that these predictions will be transformed, the allusion may alter the reader's perception of Jamie. For, having compared him to Grimm's bride-groom, a reader searches him for a sinister potential. And what does a reader find? Like the robber bridegroom, Jamie does away with a young girl—but by transforming her into the wife he takes. He accomplishes this when, robbing Rosamond of all her clothing, he awakens in her imagination visions of his return for "that which he . . . left her . . . before" (65), effectively ending her girlhood. He is not threatening as is Little Harp—the menacing double who covets Lockhart's success, then kills the girl he thinks is Jamie's and finally mounts her in sadistic conquest on a food-littered table. Harp personates the fearsome aspects of Grimm's character; rapacious, he slices off his victim's finger, and it pops into our hidden heroine's lap. But this doubling of rob-ber bridegrooms whispers at least of a potential similarity between these two characters.

And that is the point that strikes Rosamond, although the reader who re-membered Grimm may have felt it first. The severed finger, token of Harp's cruel passion, awakens in Rosamond, not only a terror of Harp, but a mis-trust of her own Jamie's potential for lovelessness. In panic, she identifies so strongly with her violated double that she almost believes she is killed. This suddenly suspicious girl, daughter of Clement Musgrove, has been raised on the story of how her father's first loving mate gave way to another, self-ish, jealous and insatiably greedy. Familiar with the danger of her father's spouse, Rosamond is concerned that she does not know Jamie's true identity. Perhaps the lover who comes to her wearing a mask is more robber than bridegroom.

Rosamond's fear is also underscored by allusion, overt but rarely identi-fied,[7] to a ballad known as "Young Andrew," whose first stanzas Rosamond sings as she sits dreaming in her room and then again as she goes into the woods to meet Jamie:

The moon shone bright, and it cast a fair light:
"Welcome" says she, "my honey, my sweet!
For I have loved thee these seven long years,
And our chance it was we could never meet."

Then he took her in his armes-two,
And kissed her both cheek and chin,
And twice or thrice he kissed this way
Before they were parted in twin. (33)

Although these two stanzas are quoted in the text, the reader benefits who knows the unsung portion of this ballad. In it, Andrew persuades the girl who loves him to rob her father so they may marry. But later he unpredictably steals all her clothing as well as the money she has taken for his sake; abandoning her, he gives her the choice of going home naked or dying on the spot. When the jilted girl is sent off by the robber bridegroom who preferred to steal all she would have freely given, she returns home to her father. Her father, however, sets so much store on his gold that he leaves her to die naked on his doorstep, maimed by two loveless men.

Again, expectations based on this source will not be fulfilled. The ballad, like Grimm's fairy tale, will be transformed rather than re-created. But certainly the possibilities suggested by the ballad are evoked for a purpose. Although they do not accurately foreshadow Jamie Lockhart's behavior (since Jamie proves to be guilty of greed, but not of domestic treachery), they serve as motif pointers in another way. Rosamond's preoccupation with the ballad allows a reader to glimpse both her strategy for self-creation (that is, to fictionalize her way into her future) as well as her simultaneous yearning for romantic love and suspicion of it.

Rosamond at first uses the old ballad of betrayal to conjure up a lover (just as the ballad's heroine calls up her dream: "As I was cast in my ffirst slepe, / A dreadful draught in my mind I drew, / Ffor I was dreamed of a yong man, / Some men called him yonge Andrew'" [Child 432]). Singing aloud, she rehearses the notion of a romantic adventure and imaginatively explores the risk of love. Jamie finds "Rosamond singing so sweetly, as if she had been practicing just for this" (45–46). Then he and she borrow their interchange from the ballad's storyline. Jamie's interest in each successive layer of clothing, Rosamond's appeal "were you born of a woman?" (48) and Jamie's reply that he will have all, as well as Rosamond's story of the father and seven brothers who will want revenge, and her decision to go home naked rather than die on the point of a sword, all come from the original. In effect, when these two meet, they invent their lives along the ballad's lines. Singing the ballad and telling its story, Rosamond is educating herself to an idea of a potentially dangerous sexual union which she plans to disarm. This fictional exploration is part of the girl's education for marriage, and Welty's tale echoes Shakespearean comedies in which young men and women in forest settings educate themselves for union in plots rich in mistaken (that is, unrecognized) identities. This connection between Rosamond's singing of the ballad and her education for marriage is reinforced by Bernard Cook's discovery that in early southern Mississippi among families of means, the robber bridegroom fiction played a role in marriage ceremonies. After marriage was arranged, a ritualized abduction was enacted; the bridegroom and his party would ride on horseback to snatch the bride from her porch where she waited with her party. The ceremony, begun in ambush, would at last end in contractual vows.

On any reading it is obvious that Rosamond, filled with an adolescent eagerness for experience, is imaginatively set to turn whatever comes her way towards love. And that she—perhaps contradictorily—cannot help fearing the longed-for lover whom she cannot fully know. But the reader who misses Welty's allusion to "Young Andrew" of course does not recognize the couple's reenactment of the ballad, and so may not fully perceive Rosamond's habit of fitting her life to stories she knows. This character trait has earned her a reputation for lying, but the fictions that fall from her lips are neither snakes nor toads. They are instead the pearls of a romantic girl who lives with fantasy and reality interacting in her head. In this habit, she authors life while familiar with its literary sources and allusions, and uses her imagination (as it intersects with Jamie's) to transform robbery into love. The pessimistic expectations that a reader might base on "Young Andrew" are disappointed when Rosamond successfully recasts the melancholy ballad in a comic genre. And yet those discarded expectations are belatedly and unexpectedly fulfilled when her imagination, retaining the picture of love as separateness and vulnerability, generates suspicion and discord.[8]

The story's further development alludes to Apulieus's *The Golden Ass* and another tale that balances longing for love with the suspicion of love. There the story of Psyche and Eros is told to a frightened young woman who has dreamt of and feared being stolen from her bridal bed by a band of robbers. In the narrative told to calm and to instruct her, the young woman's fear is itself revealed to be more dangerous than the unknown lover.

In that story within a story, young Psyche is warned by her three jealous sisters that the mysterious lover who comes to her in the dark is a monster. The mortal girl allows this slander to breed suspicion. Soon she cannot overcome her apprehension. Her lover, Eros himself, warns her that he will leave her if she ever looks too closely at him. But Psyche, with her name that suggests the mind and its rationality, is unable to maintain unquestioning faith and turns a prying light onto Eros while he sleeps. When she does, a drop of her lamp's hot oil burns his shoulder, and the slumbering god of love awakens and departs. Only after arduous pursuit does Psyche regain Eros, to become his wife and a goddess.

In Welty's version, Salome[9] plays the jealous slanderer who seduces the young beloved to suspicion. Feeding Rosamond's mistrust of the masked lover who, for reasons of his own, is unwilling to reveal himself, Salome tells Rosamond

> I fear, my dear, that you feel in your bosom a passion for a low and scandalous being, a beast who would like to let you wait on him and serve him, but will not do you the common courtesy of letting you see his face. It can only be for the reason that he is some kind of monster. (123)

Rosamond, who has attentively heard her father wonder if his loving wife and his selfish wife are not perhaps the same woman, whose beauty he loved so well at first that for a time it obliterated her ugliness, carefully attends Salome's words. She is alarmed by her ignorance of her lover and has not yet recognized that this mystery of identity has nothing to do with berry stains. When she leaves her father and stepmother and returns to Jamie's den to see Little Harp assume Jamie's place and then assault her by proxy, she is "torn as she had never been before with an anguish to know [her own lover's] name and true appearance" (134). She betrays her promise to Jamie by removing his mask, and watches him flee.

But for Rosamond, whose anxieties about betrayal, about the failure of love, and about unknowable others have been released, this act of unmasking Jamie is not reassuring. And this is where Welty's tale surprises expectations based on a reader's knowledge of the Psyche/Eros story. Unlike Psyche, who finds Eros revealed beneath her lover's mask, Rosamond finds no answers in Jamie's face. Not the god of love, he is apparently robber, bridegroom, and still unknown. Rosamond's unrelieved perplexity over Jamie's nature disappoints expectations based on allusion to *The Golden Ass*. This characteristic deviation from expectation, here as elsewhere in Welty's fiction, signals to us the scene's thematic importance.

Rosamond has met Jamie in the wooded wilderness of her imagination and loved him without knowing him at a time when she was herself caught in change and eager for love. She knew him so little that when she was reintroduced to him outside of the romantic forest, she did not recognize him, nor did he recognize her. She could not see her dark lover in the orthodox caller, nor could he see his beauty in the silly girl. Their romance, perhaps nourished by their repudiation of everyday identities, thrived on their ignorance of one another. But when they lived together, the question of Jamie's identity plagued

Rosamond. In time she—who at first rejoiced in his successful theft of her love—grew disturbed by her inability to name her lover. Then "she would wake up out of her first sleep and study [Jamie's] sleeping face" only to find that "she did not know the language it was written in."

> She would look out the window and see a cloud put up a mask over the secret face of the moon, and she would hear the pitiful cries of the night creatures. Then it was enough to make her afraid, as if the whole world were circled by a band of Indian savages, and she would shake poor Jamie until he shouted up out of his sleep, and rouse him to see his eyes come open. (84–85)

Rosamond, who has uneasily come to dread her husband's unknown nature, does not precisely recognize what she fully feels—that her love has not so much been a discovery of another as a self-discovery. This is the rule rather than the exception in Welty's fictions. In "Livvie," for example, a girl is kissed by yet another robber bridegroom, one who steals her from a passionless marriage. Touched by him, she is "dazzled at herself . . . as he had been dazzled at himself to begin with" (236). Sexuality awakens Rosamond, like Livvie, not to her lover but to herself. Discoveries of sexual desire and personal identity mingle. In Welty's fiction, love often reveals the self's particular separateness as well as a similar quality intuited, but not exactly known, in the beloved.

Young Rosamond, however, knows little of such limitations and will not content herself to love the mysterious Jamie who is "visible and present" (86). She innocently feels she must know her lover's identity, which she assumes is simple and discernible, although hidden. But we readers, who know the complexity of his character more thoroughly than if he were an actual acquaintance, recognize that Jamie is not simple. He is robber and bridegroom, romantic and conventional, hero and businessman. When we first meet him, he simultaneously reveals himself as both hero and thief in the one gesture of saving Clement from Mike Fink. The fact of this doubleness is explained to Rosamond by her father, but she does not at first accept the explanation that Jamie is both bandit and lover. Only when in the course of time she removes Jamie's mask and sees for herself that faces reveal no mysteries and names untie no knots, does she, without another thought, accept the ambiguity she had resisted, only then does she decide to live with an imprecisely known, ambiguous nature, rather than live alone. She pursues the love that left her when she studied it too closely, regaining it in New Orleans, that city where "beauty and vice and every delight possible to the soul and body stood hospitably, and usually together, in every doorway" (182). And there she appropriately gives birth to Jamie's twins.

By having robbery and rape lead to fairy-tale love, Welty upsets those pessimistic expectations her reader may have built on knowledge of Grimm's "The Robber Bridegroom" and the ballad of "Young Andrew." Unlike Grimm's tale where the institution of marriage is dissolved by the threat of sexual violence, Welty's retelling seems to show lawlessness deferring to social order. The dangers discovered by Rosamond's literary predecessors seem at last resolved when her own romantic robber bridegroom kills his evil double "for the sake of [his] future and his love" (*Eye* 312). This done, the potentially predatory lover may become the prosperous husband and father of twins. Welty's fairy tale—rather than bringing news of lovelessness—seems again to be like a Shakespearean romance or a novel of manners in which lawlessness is eventually contained by a marriage contract.

But if this tale evokes older, more sinister tales only to transform them joyously, it also upsets whatever optimistic expectations may be built by allusions to *The Golden Ass*. Here fear cannot be cleared away by knowledge. The discomforting associations that are companions to this tale, the surprisingly dark contours that lurk in this coy fiction, are never wholly obliterated. For this tale about doubleness is neither simple, nor clearly optimistic. Its happily-ever-after resolution teases us, but leaves us with the problems of a love initiated by robbery and rape. And Jamie himself permits no one to ask of him what he is: a hero whose motto is "take first and ask afterward" (69) and who never alters his nature but only his appearance. If, at the story's conclusion, the bridegroom seems to part ways with the robber to become "a gentleman of the world . . . respected by all" (183), the fact is that Jamie has only washed his face and called on the thief to help the merchant, "enjoying all the same success he had ever had" (184–85). He is, then, as always, the hero inextricably entwined with the robber, "with the power to look both ways and to see a thing from all sides" (185).

Add to these ambivalences their context in a fairy tale so evidently built on stories that it reminds us that robbery and rape lead to love in fiction only, not in life.[10] Welty's allusions, having intensified the reader's awareness of being immersed in fiction, undercut the robber bridegroom's transformation with the aura of make-believe, and leave us uncertain of the fiction's optimism. This fairy tale, through the emphasis it places on human complexity, adjusts the genre it adapts. For as much as Welty respects Grimm's archetypal

rendering of love and lovelessness, she finds his fairy-tale promise of evil's
exile inadequate to her ambiguous America where good and evil are not so
distinct as fairies and ogres. In her tale, resolution is ambiguous—another
appearance which is not a reality.

If in *The Robber Bridegroom* Welty retells and implicitly comments on several old tales, "At The Landing," the closing story in the collection published
next, is itself a retelling of her *The Robber Bridegroom*. For Welty not only
alludes to twice-told tales, but also occasionally retells stories that she has
herself told before, transposing plots used once, performing them again—
with a difference—in other genres. When doubles such as these are brought
to Welty's attention, she often seems rather dismayed; her "did-I-do-that" tone
expresses a writer's concern for originality (a concern also disclosed in responses to questions about allusions). Her tone sometimes suggests that these
remarkably original and yet related tales are semi-conscious variations. But
story doubles—"double" here used unconventionally to suggest plots similar
in situation but performed in different story genres—exist in Welty's canon
and may be a mine for articles on the connectedness of her work. Pairs like
"Flowers for Marjorie" and "The Wide Net"—which treat two husbands' un-
easy responses to their wives' pregnancies—explore a single premise in two
distinct genres. *Delta Wedding* and *Losing Battles* are another example of this
sort of doubling; they each examine a family's use of story and ritual against
change; the earlier fiction develops that premise in a modern novel of manners peopled with relatively sober southern gentry, while the later one, evoking the southern tall-tale tradition, develops country folk and broad comedy.
*The Robber Bridegroom* and "At The Landing," written in fairly close sequence,
are another interallusive pair.

The later story is the earlier tale's situational twin, but born outside of the
fairy-tale genre. It too is set in and around Rodney's Landing, treats a rape
received as love and its heroine is Jenny Lockhart (her last name appears on
her mother's tombstone). This name—so close to Jamie Lockhart's—connects
the two fictions, urging a consideration of their relationship, the patterns they
share and how the later tale comments on the earlier one. This connectedness,
then, is how allusion (even what may be unconscious allusion) leads a reader
to create understanding "in relation to"—or in this instance, how the reader
may understand "At The Landing" as not *The Robber Bridegroom*.

Jenny is another adolescent girl who, dreaming of love, is attracted to
an unknown lover who rides through the woods on a red horse. And like
Rosamond, Jenny has lost her mother. But unlike the fairy-tale parent who

died romantically of a mother's grief when she lost her infant son, Jenny's parent more realistically died of a daughter's frustration when her father turned jailer. Raised by this severe grandfather who deprecated his daughter's raving as "a force of Nature and so beneath notice or mention" (242), young Jenny has grown within his confining restrictions and has had little enough to do with the female nature made emblematic by river water in this and other of Welty's fictions. (The river baptisms in "The Wide Net," "The Wanderers," and *Delta Wedding* all similarly emblematize an immersion in female nature.) When the story opens, the overly protective old man is himself dying. He comes to Jenny in his sleep to say that the river is rising ("It has come ...") and "made a complaint of it" (240). Anticipation of the day when she will be free to come and go trembles about her like "distant lightning" (242). She watches in the woods for a dreamt-of lover, but cannot imagine "what [is] to come" (244) until, like Rosamond when she sang "Young Andrew," Jenny conceives of separateness. Rosamond recognizes this potential source of pain from her father's stories and her favorite ballad. But Jenny perceives separateness in an observation of the life around her. Seeing Mag, she conceives of love, separateness, and the possibility that these lie in store for her, too.

Once noticed, the counterpoint of similarity and difference between the two stories is obvious. When high water comes—with its overtones of passion, birth, and baptism inextricably bound with change, danger, and death—Floyd saves Jenny. Then when her eyes are "clear upon him, [he violates] her" (251). Like Rosamond, Jenny has longed for the violation of her isolation, and she attempts to use the power of her imagination to create love. But like the girl in "A Memory," Jenny invents a love that is challenged by Floyd's actual presence.

> If she could have followed and found him then, she would have started on foot. But, she knew what she would find when she would come to him. She would find him equally real with herself—and could not touch him then. As she was living and inviolate, so of course was he, and when that gave him delight, how could she bring a question to him? ... Nothing in Floyd frightened her that drew her near, but at once she had the knowledge come to her that a fragile mystery was in everyone and in herself, since it was there in Floyd, and that whatever she did, she would be bound to ride over and hurt, and the secrecy of life was the terror of it. (245)

Intuiting without fully knowing Floyd's otherness, and projecting onto Floyd the vulnerable position his separateness creates for her (as the girl of "A

Memory" did as she "speculated endlessly on the dangers" [76] of her class-mate's home), Jenny hesitates to touch Floyd, fearing to find "him equally real with herself." She is drawn to something mythic rather than real in Floyd, who is for her—Brookhart and Marrs have pointed out—"charged with the river country's vitality and mystery" (89). For Jenny, Floyd is a mythic wanderer who counterpoints her confinement. For her as for a Welty reader who is rereading or reading out of chronological sequence, Billy Floyd is as much an Aeneus figure as King MacLain, and "At The Landing" may evoke *The Golden Apples* as well as *The Robber Bridegroom.* "In the long shadows," Floyd's fig-ure appears with "the gleaming fish" (243)—recalling the silver trout Yeats's Aeneus caught, which became a glimmering girl "who called him by his name and ran and faded through the brightening air" (22). Later Floyd is "golden in the road" (254)—an emblem of longing and desire whose name Jenny calls. But when Floyd finally grasps Jenny, she is taken not by the longed-for mythic lover, but by a wandering and dangerous beloved who "lived apart in delight" and about whom she has glimpsed something "used and worldly." Welty hu-morously underlines Floyd's doubleness when she juxtaposes Jenny's thought in the story before the flood that "there was something handled and used about Floyd, strong as an odor" (248), with the postmaster's comment aloud on flood slime.

Jenny Lockhart's encounter with Floyd echoes Rosamond's with Jamie Lockhart, but the contrast between Jenny who from her story's outset is con-fined in imagery of enclosure and Rosamond who roams outdoors, is critical.

> For all her life the shy Jenny could look, if she stayed in the parlor, back and forth between her mother's two paintings, "The Bird Fair" and "The Massacre at Fort Rosalie." Or if she went in the dining room she could walk around the table or sit on one after the other of eight needlepoint pieces, each slightly different, which her mother had worked and sewn to the chairs, or she could count the plates that stood on their rims in the closet. In the library she could circle an entirely bare floor and make up a dance to a song she made up, all silently, or gaze at the backs of the books without titles—books that had been on ships and in oxcarts and through fire and water, and were singed and bleached and swollen and shrunken, and arranged up high and nearly unreachable, like objects of beauty. (241)

Jenny is circumscribed by indoor spaces and limiting images, and then de-scribed with the language of passivity and obedience:

Jenny was obedient to her grandfather and would have been obedient to anybody, to a stranger in the street if there could be one. She never performed any act, even a small act, for herself, she would not touch the prisms. It might seem that nothing began in her own heart. (242–43)

In the house she lives an object among objects, enclosed and protected as they are. She can be called to obedience even by her grandfather's "little murmur" (242), and yet her stillness initially contains an unsurrender paralleling "the stillness and unsurrender of the still and unsurrendering world" (243) before the flood. She contains longings that resemble the prisms with which she is associated,[11] prisms reflecting a trapped elusive light, glimmering, but not reached for. The image of her relationship to these prisms is promising but passive; Jenny hears their music, sees their color, but fears reaching to touch them.

They gave off the faintest of musical notes when air stirred in any room or when only herself passed by, and they touched. It was her way not to touch them herself, but to let the touch be magical, a stir of the curtain by the outer air, that would also make them rainbows. (241)

Her attraction to these prisms implicitly resembles her attraction to Floyd, for whom she also fears to reach. There is, however, a contrast between the magical touch of the prisms—creating a faint music—and Floyd's touching of her—creating a slowly building cacophony.

The very heart of the contrast between Rosamond and Jenny is in their voices. Rosamond has the power to sing aloud, to retell old stories, to make them hers in ways she wishes, reshaping them to yield her story. From Rosamond's mouth, adventurous, authoritative lies fall "like diamonds and pearls" (39) while Jenny's is marked with silence. Jenny composes and sings a song "all silently." When she and Floyd walk together they hold berries in their mouths, not words. Jenny hardly speaks in this tale; her infrequent speech is characteristically reported. She only has three brief direct speeches, first to say "wake up, Grandpa" (240), next to say "go back" (244) to Floyd in an early encounter, and lastly to deny the accusation that she has been offensively silent: "I speak to you, Mag" (254). In the landing store, others pointedly speak to her in a conversational "exchange," but she does not respond. We are told that she knew she was not supposed to speak, and that eventually "in a kind of haste she whispered to the five old men" (249) of her grandfather's death.

At a critical moment she is reported to have said Billy Floyd's name. Later she is not able to speak to Floyd.

> "I ..." she began, and stopped ...
> She would like to tell him some strange beautiful thing, if she could speak at all, something to make him speak. Communication would be telling something that is all new, so as to have more of the new told back. The dream of that held her spellbound ... (251)

After "he violated her," Jenny attempts what the fairy-tale Rosamond comes closer to achieving: she attempts to transform the violation of her as the separateness with a story of love. Jenny's violation is an ambiguous flood that Floyd's name suggests, at once life's rush and violence. (This is the story of living "At The Landing"—that is, of living on high ground, out of life's water, until that water rises dangerously; the title, "At The Landing," and the town's name, "The Landing," suggest being *caught* on high ground rather than saved by it.) But unlike Rosamond's fairy-tale "rape," Jenny's violation indeed turns out to be rape. When Jenny attempts to speak and so to shape her story as Rosamond does by bringing her ballad to life, Jenny whispers over the sound of the lapping water. "Her words came a little louder and in shyness she changed them from words of love to words of wishing ... 'I wish you and I could be far way. I wish for a little house'" (251). But to communicate her desire to her mythic wanderer might be to confine him; she has already uncomfortably imagined him "caught and cornered in a little store," "trapped in the confined space with her between him and the door" (248). So Jenny does not speak too loudly and Floyd does not look around: "ideas of any different thing from what was in his circle of fire might never have reached his ears, for all the attention he paid to her remarks" (251). Unlike Rosamond's, Jenny's hesitant words have no transforming powers.

When Jamie Lockhart leaves Rosamond in the woods, that heroine goes home and scours her house until she is ragged and dirty. Having in that manner ordered her thoughts, she soon sets out after her lover. When in time she recognizes his nature as more complex and less perfect than she had pictured, she nevertheless claims him as he is. Jenny, when Floyd leaves her, also returns home to obsessively clean house and to put her feelings in place. Unlike Rosamond, however, Jenny hides, feeling troubled by beauty and ugliness alike because she is unwilling to discover the closeness of the two in Floyd. Her eventual response to this "shock of love" (253) is to shut down like a house with all its rooms darkened. The narrator tells us that to help her "someone would have to go slowly from room to room, slowly and darkly, leaving each one lighted behind, before going to the next" (254). Damaged, darkened, and yet without having admitted Floyd's double nature, Jenny sets out to follow him because she is unable to make "any way alone" (256). Jenny wonders:

> what more love would be like. Then of course she knew. More love would be quiet. She would never be so quiet as she wished until she was quiet with her love . . . It had been enough to make her desperate in her heart, the long search for Billy Floyd to give quiet to. (255)

When Jenny wanders among the fishermen asking for her lover, they are not concerned for her love, but put her inside a grounded boathouse. One by one they come in to rape her:

> she called out, she did not call any name; it was cry with a rising sound, as if she said "Go back," or asked a question, and then at the last protested. A rude laugh covered her cry, and somehow both the harsh sounds could easily have been heard as rejoicing, going out over the river in the dark night. (258)

Jenny's final cry is an inarticulate echo of her first words to Floyd, "go back," and her long silence is overwhelmed at the story's conclusion by the boatman's callous laughter. Their rude noise, shades distinct from a joyful noise, again conveys the ambiguity of Jenny's experience with Floyd, a missed celebration.

Unlike Rosamond, Jenny does not unmask emotional violence to recognize it as a real danger that she can nonetheless manage in a world where she had hoped to escape guardedness. Unfortunately the world that Jenny's grandfather had wanted her to fear and to withdraw from, proves to be worthy of fear. With no defenses other than evasion, Jenny can only extinguish all the lights in the house of her mind and hope the threat at its door will go away. In this state, Jenny "waits for Billy Floyd," her face hung with a smile "no matter what was done to her, like a bit of color that kindles in the sky after the light has gone" (258). Where Rosamond, who exists in a fairy-tale universe, can transform violation into deliverance, Jenny is overcome by the story of love with which she tries to shape experience. And she is silenced. The sound that readers are left with is not Rosamond's voice assuring her father that her story as she now authoritatively tells it, "is the truth" and not a lie ("all true but the blue canopy") (184). It is instead the inhumanly inarticulate "dull *pit*" (258) of boys' knives thrown at a tree, the sound of casual, unconcerned violence.

*The Robber Bridegroom* and "At The Landing," then, are variations written in the same time period. *The Robber Bridegroom* saw earlier publication, but "At The Landing" grew from a draft called "The Children" and dated 1934.[12] The two finished fictions significantly evoke one another in ways that emphasize difference. Welty has repeatedly worked toward this pattern with allusion, using it not only for the sake of building accurate character, plot, or motif predictors, but for establishing expectations that need adjustment and revision. As she leads readers to consider the difference between a literary memory and the fiction-at-hand, she pushes them toward a discovery of meaning. Her use of allusion does not create correspondence so much as transformation, which habitually restructures the intentions of the source fictions, causing the reader to revise initial predictions based on the allusion.

## Notes

1. Here I am thinking of insightful works that nevertheless fit a category Welty commented on by saying, "Anyone who attributes my stories to myths very specifically and thoroughly is overshooting it. I would rather suggest things" (Gretlund 203).
2. See Dawn Kendig's article for another application of Goffman to Welty.
3. Having noticed this response in readers, I was interested to see that the made-for-television version of *The Wide Net* offered an interpretive performance of William Wallace's catfish dance that was wild-with-grief. This interpretation is not, I think, true to the text, but to initial expectations that the text moves beyond.
4. In a keynote address for "Women, Society, and The Arts," Susquehanna University, November 3, 1989.
5. Kreyling, for one, citing folklorist Francis Lee Utley, argues that "this novel is properly a 'local legend' and not simply a 'fairy tale' because it has 'a cruelty and a directness . . . glossed over in the fairy tale'" ("Clement" 33). Marilyn Arnold is another who argues that Welty's tale is in conflict with "the shallowness of the fairy tale vision" (16). Arnold, however, shrewdly suggests the role that generic allusion may play in the reader's construction of the text, stating that "Welty creates standard expectations in the reader, but she does not fulfill them. Instead, she subverts, reverses, burlesques, and just generally scatters asunder the fairy tale's sacrosanct notions about the agenda for happily-ever-after living" (16).
6. Those who have given Rosamond rather more emphasis include Skaggs and Graulich. Skaggs's article extends Bruno Bettelheim's notions that fairy tales provide "a cultural escape valve" and that "the most important ingredient of all fairy tales is

the promise of success," to the genre southwestern humor and to Welty's tale. In making this extension, Skaggs tends to brighten Rosamond's story, suggesting that her happy ending transforms the anxieties suggested by the older plots of Grimm, Psyche and Eros, or frontier humor—a conclusion with which I cannot agree entirely.

7. "Young Andrew" appears as ballad no. 48 in Francis James Child's *The English and Scottish Popular Ballads*, vol. 1 (New York: Houghton, 1904). Gordon E. Sleuthang (in "Initiation in Eudora Welty's *The Robber Bridegroom*," *Southern Humanities Review* 7 [Winter 1973]: 77–78) is the only other critic I know who discusses Welty's use of this ballad.

8. The education which stories can provide is also a subject of Welty's autobiographical essay, "The Little Store." In it she remembers the moment when her own developing imagination, made bold by the news of "some act of violence" concerning the people who ran the neighborhood grocery store, strayed beyond her family's supervision.

9. Salome's name refers us to the Biblical character who traded a dance for the decapitated head of "the only man [she] ever loved" (this line from Oscar Wilde's version), a girl simultaneously awakened to sexuality and to a dangerously evil willfulness. The name strikes another allusive note.

10. As Rabinowitz points out in his discussion of narrative conventions, "undermining a conventional ending tends to stress the conventionality of that closure" (162–63), emphasizing the fictionality of that closure.

11. Is it coincidence that in *The Robber Bridegroom* "the prism light of day" diverts a redbird into his old song just before Jamie Lockhart rides up to rob Rosamond "of that which he had left her the day before"(63)?

12. Brookhart and Marrs discuss the development in their essay, "More Notes on River Country."

## Works Cited

Apulieus, Lucius. *The Golden Ass*. New York: Marvin, 1931.

Arnold, Marilyn. "Eudora Welty's Parody." *Notes on Mississippi Writers* 2 (Spring 1978): 15–22.

Brookhart, Mary Hughes, and Suzanne Marrs. "More Notes on River Country." *Welty: A Life in Literature*. Ed. Albert J. Devlin. Jackson: University Press of Mississippi, 1987, 82–95.

Bryant, J. A. *Eudora Welty*. Minnesota Pamphlet No. 66. Minneapolis: University of Minnesota Press, 1968.

Child, James Francis. *The English and Scottish Popular Ballads*. vol. 1. New York: Houghton, 1904.

Cook, Bernard. "Ritual Abduction in Early Mississippi." *Mississippi Quarterly* 36.1 (1982–1983): 72–73.

French, Warren. "'All Things Are Double': Eudora Welty as a Civilized Writer." *Eudora Welty: Critical Essays*. Jackson: University Press of Mississippi, 1983, 71–81.

Goffman, Irving. *Frame Analysis*. New York: Harper Colophon, 1974.

Graulich, Melody. "Pioneering the Imagination: Eudora Welty's *The Robber Bridegroom*." *Women and Western American Literature*. Ed. Helen Winter Stauffer and Susan J. Rosowski. Troy, NY: Whitson, 1982, 283–96.

Gretlund, Jan Nordby. "An Interview with Eudora Welty." *Southern Humanities Review* 14 (Summer 1980): 193–208.

Grimm, Jacob, and Wilhelm Grimm. "Little Snow White." *The Frog King and Other Tales of the Brothers Grimm*. New York: New American Library, 1964.

Grimm, Jacob Ludwig Karl. *German Popular Tales*. Philadelphia: Porter, 1869.

Gubar, Susan. Keynote address at "Women, Society, and the Arts." Susquehanna University, Selinsgrove, PA. November 1989.

Hirsch, E. D. *Validity in Interpretation*. New Haven: Yale University Press, 1967.

Kendig, Daun. "Realities in Sir Rabbit: A Frame Analysis." *Eudora Welty: Eye of the Storyteller*. Ed. Dawn Trouard. Kent, OH: Kent State University Press, 1989, 119–32.

Kreyling, Michael. *Eudora Welty: The Achievement of Order*. Baton Rouge: Louisiana State University Press, 1980.

———. "Clement and the Indians: Pastoral and History in *The Robber Bridegroom*." *Eudora Welty: A Form of Thanks*. Jackson: University Press of Mississippi, 1979, 25–45.

Porat, Ziva Ben. "The Poetics of Literary Allusion." *PTL: A Journal* 1 (1976): 105–28.

Rabinowitz, Peter. *Before Reading: Narrative Conventions and the Politics of Interpretation*. Ithaca, NY: Cornell University Press, 1987.

Skaggs, Menill Maquire. "The Uses of Enchantment in Frontier Humor and *The Robber Bridegroom*." *Studies in American Humor* 3 (October 1976): 96–102.

Vande Kieft, Ruth M. *Eudora Welty*. Rev. ed. Boston: Twayne, 1987.

Welty, Eudora. *The Robber Bridegroom*. New York: Harcourt, 1942.

———. "And They Lived Happily Ever After." *New York Times Book Review*. Part II. 10 November 1963: 3.

———. *One Time, One Place*. New York: Random, 1971.

———. *The Eye of the Story*. New York: Random, 1977.

———. *The Collected Stories of Eudora Welty*. New York: Harcourt, 1982.

———. "At The Landing." *Collected Stories*, 240–58.

———. "Livvie." *Collected Stories*, 228–39.

———. "A Memory." *Collected Stories*, 75–80.

———. "The Wide Net." *Collected Stories*, 169–88.

Yeats, William Butler. *Selected Poems and Two Plays of William Butler Yeats*. Ed. M. L. Rosenthal. New York: Collier, 1962.

# Natchez and Richard Wright in Southern American Literature

MARGARET WALKER ALEXANDER

The South has suffered many names and misnomers, including the Old South and the New South, the Confederate South, the antebellum South, the solid South, and the secessionist South. Today, I wish to speak of the historic South—that is, the South of history and fact—and the mythic or mythical South, a literary South of fantasy mixed with reality or fact.

Southerners who live in this region rarely think of its dual nature—fact and fiction, reality and fantasy—and, if we are mindful of this duality, we seldom, if ever, recognize or consider the effects of the region on our lives and our personalities. Southern literature illustrates this for us. The South is both an historical region and a mythical place, at least in the literature. Southern American literature, like all great world literature, is grounded in myth. We have only to look at Eudora Welty's story, *The Robber Bridegroom*, to see an illustration of this fact.

The historic events of the region are well known, but the elements of myth found in fantasy and taken from folk tales, legends, and gothic imaginations frequently puzzle and confound us. We squirm under the label of the Bible Belt, yet we live every day in terms of John Milton's theology and many fundamentalist beliefs from the King James version of the Bible. Violence seems to be native to the region from the days of the frontier, when the Native Americans lived and fought here, through the violence of the Civil War, the scourge of the Ku Klux Klan in the days of Reconstruction with its pattern of lynching and mob rule, to the days of the civil rights movement of the 1960s. Segregation was declared legally dead and unconstitutional on May 17, 1954, but the economic and political support systems of institutionalized and entrenched racism still distress and disturb us today.

*Southern Quarterly* 29.4 (1991): 171–76.

Natchez is a pivotal and historic point in the literary legacy that we now declare the Natchez Trace. The nation of the Natchez Indians began the legacy; the black slaves imported from Africa built the antebellum mansions which the French architects designed; those same slaves escaped through the underground railroad by the Natchez Trace and the Mississippi River to the banks of the Ohio and free soil. The Union soldiers broke the economic back of the cotton kingdom and devastated the land. Despite a century of lynching and mob rule by the Ku Klux Klan, the civil rights movement of the 1960s dictated another social revolution to free the people, black and white alike.

These are historic facts. What about the myths? John Pendleton Kennedy began the plantation tradition in southern American literature with his novel, *Swallow Barn*. The best examples of that tradition are Thomas Nelson Page with his trilogy of southern novels and Margaret Mitchell's *Gone with the Wind*. In this tradition, slavery is romanticized and glorified and the Old South is given mythical qualities which in fact it never possessed. The system is seen as benign and beneficial to all involved. The Greek state is revived and glorified as a slave state and utopia; agrarian culture—or agriculture—is considered superior to industry and business. The architecture is that of the Greek Revival. The War between the States was a crusade in which valiant knights went forth to rescue damsels in distress. But what about the slaves? According to myth, they were mindless pieces of property who loved their masters and never wanted to be free. As a matter of fact, the slavocracy included thousands of poor whites who hated the slave lords and the black slaves alike. Caste and class were as bitter a struggle as race.

If we read the books of the secessionists and abolitionists, we see this battle going on between races, classes, and nations. *Natchez on the Mississippi* by Harnett Kane describes this place. Stark Young's novel, *So Red the Rose*, describes the society and the system. The beautiful white ladies in crinoline skirts lived in the mansions but behind the mansions were the slave quarters with the threat of branding, beatings, killings, and fires.

The Confederate generals in their gray and gold uniforms were leading thousands of not-so-rich white men to death in the dirt and carnage of battle. Richard Wright's grandfathers were slaves in Mississippi, in Natchez. One became a sharecropper on Travellers Rest plantation, and one was a Civil War soldier who never got his pension. There were two Mississippis which William Faulkner and Shelby Foote have recorded as fiction and history and another Mississippi in Richard Wright's *Uncle Tom's Children*, *Native Son*,

*Black Boy*, *12,000,000 Black Voices*, and *The Long Dream*. Today in Natchez we pay homage to the myth of Mississippi in all these great southern writers.

The poverty of the region also has had its effects. Until the mid-twentieth century, the Industrial Revolution did not exist in Mississippi. There was no heavy industry and very little light and diversified industry. Suddenly in the 1950s, the industrial and the electronic revolutions hit Mississippi simultaneously with mechanized farming and computerized technology. What was the effect from 1917 to the 1950s on the minds of the people? Political demagoguery, substandard education and housing, and religious fundamentalism affected us all with a psychic wound of racism. Richard Wright, who was clearly a genius, was born in Natchez in 1908 and spent his early childhood here. He suffered all his life from that psychic wound of racism. He wrote sixteen books and the first four were written before he went to Paris. All four were influenced by Natchez and Mississippi. Only one book written in Paris was most affected by Mississippi and that was *The Long Dream*. I used to wonder when I read his first books from whence came all the violence and the horror. Years of study and research taught me. They came out of his deep-seated anger, neurotic anger and realistic anger against the system of segregation and the violent white racism he experienced here in Mississippi.

Early in his career, Richard Wright was further influenced by four great American writers. All four were southerners: Mark Twain, Edgar Allan Poe, H. L. Mencken, and William Faulkner. Wright believed (and I sometimes think he was right) that all Americans suffer from a form of paranoia. Black people suffer from delusions of persecution, some based on fact, and some on fantasy, while white people suffer from delusions of grandeur, a kind of God-complex.

White Americans believe they can fix the world. If only everybody looked and thought like them, the world would be a perfect place. That's a God-complex. The poor white people in the Ku Klux Klan believe that when God made this southern land, it was a kind of Eden, a physical paradise, until sin, death, and hell came into the garden. That the serpent brought sin, death, and hell into the garden and made Eve make Adam eat the apple and thus disobey God. They fell from grace and were punished, but the serpent also left children and according to the Ku Klux Klan, the children of the serpent were black people, Jews, and Catholics. How big a myth is that? They tell me the Arab or Moslem nations declare America is the Great Satan. That must be their myth. And the Black Muslims declare all whites are devils. Everybody's got his myth.

Faulkner made himself a system, but it was built on the myth of Christian redemption, and the New Critics have worn out that myth. Faulkner had more than a religious myth of Christian honor, he had a myth of racial superiority and inferiority which he grew up believing in Mississippi. It was a myth Richard Wright refused to believe. Their philosophies are diametrically different, but their symbology is the same. The folk roots of their fiction are in Mississippi, but they develop their symbolism in a very different way. For Richard Wright, Mississippi was no Garden of Eden, it was a racial hell. Faulkner believed the South was a ruined world. Slavery, miscegenation, and rising capitalism destroyed the pastoral paradise and ruined the Edenic South.

The world of fiction is one of myth, not history. Fiction blends fantasy with reality. Each enhances the other. Sometimes the fantasy of fiction seems as real as history, and sometimes the reality seems absolutely fantastic. When we read Ellen Douglas's fiction, we are caught up and enthralled in the racial myth and the social horror that a pastoral land of beauty breeds before our very eyes. Douglas, like Wright, was born in Natchez. Clearly, the fiction of Eudora Welty also illustrates the skillful blending of fantasy and reality while we hear the speech of the Mississippi Delta and see the land of myth and legend that the Natchez Trace truly and historically is.

Southern writers, like all other writers, seek to reflect their life and living in their literature. Life, however, is chaotic and the artist seeks to rearrange and order life into an artistic whole. Imagination works, therefore, with reality and creates a blend of fantasy and reality, thereby resulting in myth. When the artist is successful, the reader sometimes finds it difficult to separate myth and fantasy from fact and reality. This may be the greatest test, that fiction rings as true as fact. Southern American literature is a great component of all world literature. The great masters—Edgar Allan Poe, Mark Twain, William Faulkner, and Tennessee Williams—stand shoulder to shoulder with the greatest. Not the least of these is Richard Wright, native of Natchez, Mississippi. Despite the obstacles of extreme poverty and little formal education, coupled with a broken home, religious fanaticism, and the psychic wound of racism, Wright rose to world renown. He died thirty years ago in Paris, but today Natchez, the State of Mississippi, and the United States Department of the Interior honor this great author with an historic marker on the Natchez bluffs overlooking the Mississippi River. Wright leaves a proud literary legacy to his family, to his children's children, to his race—but most of all, to all humanity.

# The Mississippi Frontier in Faulkner's Fiction and in Fact

DON H. DOYLE

When William Faulkner was a struggling young writer in New Orleans his mentor and drinking companion, Sherwood Anderson, advised him to write about "that little patch up there in Mississippi where you started from" (Oates 47). But like most American writers and artists, Faulkner was trying to escape, not exploit, his provincial background. As a young man he fled to Canada to enlist with the Royal Air Force, to New Orleans to join a slightly bohemian literary circle, to Europe for a tour as an author in exile, and then to New York and, later, to Hollywood. In the end, he took Anderson's advice and retreated to that patch of land in Mississippi where he and his family had deep roots.

There he invented a place he called Yoknapatawpha County and, over the course of more than three decades, in a multitude of novels and short stories, he filled this place with fictional characters, some quite outlandish and incredible, others perverse and diabolical, but most either historically accurate or plausible. The saga of Yoknapatawpha dealt with universal themes bearing on the human condition, as Faulkner put it in his Nobel Prize address, with the "problems of the human heart in conflict with itself," with "love and honor and pity and pride and compassion and sacrifice" (*Portable* 723–24). But these themes were explored within a particular place and time, in northern Mississippi beginning about 1800 and extending into the mid-twentieth century. Faulkner's writing is *historical* because so many of the people and events, the language and customs, could only be found in this part of the world and in the particular time in which Faulkner set them.

Faulkner liked to tell inquisitive reporters and critics that he never bothered with research or that he just "made up" characters, as he said he did the Indians (Dabney 11n). This is not an entirely believable statement, however.

*Southern Quarterly* 29.4 (1991): 145–60.

There is too much correspondence between the dates, events, and people of the fictional Yoknapatawpha and the actual Lafayette County to believe that he was not a diligent student of Mississippi history. Much of what he knew of the past was informal, oral tradition, passed down to him by Mammy Callie and her husband, by his school teacher, Ella Wright, by his friend Phil Stone, or by the elderly men on the courthouse square whose stories held him transfixed. As Malcolm Cowley put it:

> The pattern was based on what he saw in Oxford or remembered from his childhood; on scraps of family tradition . . . on kitchen dialogues between the black cook and her amiable husband; on Saturday-afternoon gossip in Courthouse Square; on stories told by men in overalls squatting on their heels while they passed around a fruit jar full of white corn liquor; on all the sources familiar to a small-town Mississippi boy—but the whole of it was elaborated, transformed, given convulsive life by his emotions; until by simple intensity of feeling the figures in it became a little more than human, became heroic or diabolical, became symbols of the old South, of war and reconstruction, of commerce and machinery destroying the standards of the past. (vii)

This kind of oral tradition was strong in Mississippi, and Faulkner, born in 1897, was coming of age at a time when the early history of the county (founded a little over sixty years before he was born) was within living memory of the older residents. It is likely that Faulkner also made use of the numerous published historical books, journals, newspapers, and other sources he would have had at hand in Oxford. Faulkner was twenty years old in 1917 when Mississippi was celebrating its centennial of statehood, and was in his prime in 1936 when Lafayette County and Oxford were observing their centennials. These centennial observances brought considerable attention to the history of his state and locality, manifest in numerous books and newspapers and in unrecorded volumes of conversation around the courthouse square and family dining table.[1] We know, too, that Faulkner had developed an abiding interest in his own family's history in northern Mississippi and that his great grandfather was the model for Colonel Sartoris, the hero of his first Yoknapatawpha novel, *Flags in the Dust* (first published as *Sartoris*). Several Faulkner biographers and literary scholars have noted the parallels between Faulkner's fictional saga of Yoknapatawpha and the actual history of Lafayette County, and they support the notion that Faulkner was more than a casual student of his past.² The exploration of Mississippi's frontier history reveals both the richness and limitations of Faulkner's historical vision.

Mississippi's history extends surprisingly far back in time for an area so far from the eastern seaboard, where we all too easily assume that history (meaning white, European history) began. Most accounts of Mississippi's history, particularly those published before the early twentieth century when Faulkner was learning his history, devote long sections to the early French, Spanish, and British explorations and governance, along with lengthy treatments of the aboriginal cultures of the Natchez, Choctaw, and Chickasaw peoples. But the beginning of the American epoch in northern Mississippi's history is the story of white traders, soldiers, speculators, and settlers invading, conquering, contaminating, cheating, and finally removing the natives of the land.

The story of the Indians and their expulsion from Mississippi presented Faulkner, as it has historians before and since, with profound moral and historical problems of interpretation. Few modern historians have been tempted to embrace contemporary justifications for the policy of Indian removal, which rested on national chauvinism and racial arrogance, and which now seem wholly inconsistent with our democratic values. Andrew Jackson and his supporters spoke of righteous Americans fulfilling their manifest destiny to expand across the continent and fulfill God's design for a superior civilization which had to push aside the savage red man for a rich land he was simply incapable of developing.

For most Americans of European ancestry at least, a sense of compassion—and, no doubt, guilt—urges historians to adopt instead a remorseful history based on a romantic view of the Indians as nature's noble savages, virtuous and at one with nature, but naive victims of avaricious whites whose policies amounted to crimes against a race.

James Malone's *Chickasaw Nation: A Short Sketch of a Noble People*, published in 1922, was a source familiar to anyone interested in the Indians of northern Mississippi. Malone, who admitted to having "never personally met a Chickasaw Indian," was nonetheless fervent in his efforts to "pay a just, though tardy, tribute to their ancient heroes" (394). Malone's Chickasaws were "roaming the forests as the untutored children of nature" (170) when Europeans entered Mississippi and almost immediately began a process of corruption that doomed them to defeat. He cleverly joined this tragic story of decline and subjugation at the hands of whites to a story that cast the heroic Chickasaw as the allies of Anglo-Americans when they defeated the French in 1736 and thereby "determined that the English and not the French would dominated this continent" (170, 395).

William Faulkner never personally knew any Chickasaw Indians either, for they were all gone from northern Mississippi sixty years before he was born. Except for some mixed black and Indian people (whom Faulkner depicted in his character Sam Fathers), and except for the Indian place names like the Tallahatchie and Yoknapatawpha rivers which run through Faulkner's (real and fictional) county, there is nothing left of the Chickasaw nation in that part of Mississippi. In several short stories and in parts of his novels Faulkner re-created the Indians and their culture as it existed before the removal in 1837. His portrayal of the Indians, for the most part, avoided the usual romantic, sentimental view of the noble savage. In his story "Red Leaves," Faulkner seemed to have just the opposite intent when he has his Indians casually discussing cannibalizing their black slaves and hunting down one of them to be buried alive with his master who has died. It seems to have been Faulkner's purpose to show the Indians living by a moral code that was wholly remote and alien—but not necessarily inferior or superior—from that of whites.

Faulkner focuses on the confrontation between whites and Indians between about 1800, when his fictional whites first established a trading post in the area (it was much later in reality), and the 1830s when the Indians sell their land and leave Mississippi forever. The meeting of cultures had actually begun well over a century earlier and with consequences that were to determine the outcome of defeat and expulsion the Chickasaws later suffered. The Chickasaw nation extended from northern Mississippi north to western Kentucky and east to Middle Tennessee, but the heart of the nation was northern Mississippi, centered around the Chickasaw towns surrounding the present day Pontotoc, just east of what is now Lafayette County. In the contest between England, France, and Spain for control of the West, the Chickasaws had aligned with the English. Almost precisely a century before their expulsion, in May of 1736, Chickasaw warriors had cut to pieces two French armies sent to destroy them. The Chickasaws remained an unconquered people, and their resistance to the French was largely responsible for the eventual British dominance in the West, which was confirmed by the British victory in the French and Indian War ending 1763.

But the Chickasaw's fraternization with the British began an insidious process of subversion brought on by the mixing of blood and culture, the introduction of slavery and by the capacity of the Chickasaws to accommodate the invasion of whites. A Scots trader named James Logan Colbert entered

Chickasaw territory in 1729 and, over the course of forty years and three wives, he spawned a large brood of mixed bloods. The Colberts, along with a growing population of other mixed bloods, emerged by the end of the century as a dominant force in the economy and governance of the Chickasaw nation. This mixed-blood Colbert clique combined a shrewd Scotsman's savvy for bargaining with the legitimacy bestowed on them by the tribe as spokesmen for the Chickasaw nation. Though the full bloods, through chiefs Piomingo and Tishomingo, rebelled against the ascending power of the Colberts and the mixed bloods, the advance of white culture gave this latter group more leverage as interpreters—and as collaborators. Arrell Gibson in his authoritative book on the Chickasaws regards the Colberts and their clique with astonishment: "It is wondrous to behold the imagination, ingenuity, initiative, and unmitigated brass which this group of Chickasaws brought to the joyous business of integrating the [Chickasaw] nation's productive enterprises into a combine which they shrewdly managed" (134).[3] It is a shame Faulkner did not explore the possibilities these mixed bloods offered to his Yoknapatawpha saga, for Levi Colbert and his clan might have served as the Chickasaw counterpart to the infamous Flem Snopes and the omnivorous "tribe of Snopeses" who took over the county a century later.

Contact with the British and other Europeans also introduced the Chickasaws to black slaves, whom they bought or accepted as gifts and bribes in growing numbers. By the 1830s over 1,000 of the more than 6,000 people in the Chickasaw nation were black slaves. Slavery itself had not been introduced by whites, for the Chickasaws had enslaved other Indians captured in war with neighboring tribes or seized by raiding parties. Black slaves, however, were regarded as more prestigious because of their European associations, and they were owned largely by the rising mixed-blood element who employed them in clearing fields and raising cash crops, chiefly cotton, for a new commercial economy which intensified contact with whites. Bilingual slaves also came to serve as interpreters between white and Indian cultures and served thereby to promote the Chickasaw's acculturation, particularly among the mixed bloods (Gibson 124–25).

Faulkner acknowledged the presence of black slavery among the Indians, but he made a point of demonstrating a vast difference in the economic mentality of whites and Indians. In "Red Leaves" he describes the Indians "gathering in squatting conclave over the Negro question," complaining at the burden of having to keep their slaves working and sweating. Ruling out eating all of them, one Indian concludes "we must do as the white men do," which is to

"Raise more Negroes by clearing more land to make corn to feed them, then sell them. We will clear the land and plant it with food and raise Negroes and sell them to the white men for money." "But what will we do with this money?" another Indian asks. "They thought for a while" (*Portable* 63). Here Faulkner exaggerated the indifference of the Indian, at least the mixed-blood element, to commercial enterprise, for many were, in fact, quite diligently, clearing land, raising cotton, and buying slaves to employ in clearing still more land for cotton.

By 1800, when this confrontation began on a more intensive level, the Chickasaw nation (along with the Choctaws to the south) occupied a large unconquered wilderness between two extending arms of white settlement. To the north, Nashville stood at the lower edge of settlement that had advanced across the Appalachians into the Ohio, Cumberland, and Tennessee river valleys. To the south, Natchez represented an outpost of settlement that had thickened in the lower Mississippi valley and Gulf coast. The Natchez Trace originated as one of several Indian trails that crossed this vast land bridge. Americans had used this trail to transport mail by horseback, but with the expansion of trade from the Ohio River and its tributary valleys down the Mississippi, there was growing need for a wider, improved wagon road for the return trip overland. When Levi Colbert negotiated with U.S. officials in 1801, he allowed right of way for construction and travel along the proposed road, but he shrewdly forbade any white-owned accommodations—that was to be the monopoly of the Colberts and their clique who operated ferries across the rivers and taverns or "stands" along the way. As whites constructed other roads through the Chickasaw territory, the opportunities for Indian entrepreneurial activities grew apace, and the Colberts' mercantile combine seized every chance. When later treaties allowed that annual annuities be paid to the Indians, Chickasaw mercantile interests made sure these payments were made in gold and silver and not in blankets, guns, and other goods which could be sold at a profit in Chickasaw-owned stores (Gibson 134–35).

The exclusion of white traders were often justified by white missionaries and government officials in the Chickasaw territory as a way of protecting a pristine, primitive Indian culture from unscrupulous white swindlers and whiskey sellers. But this may be better understood as trade protection legislation, a concession to the calculating design of the Colbert clique. The subversion of what Faulkner's Indians called the "old way" took place rapidly with their own people, or the mixed bloods in their tribe, playing the lead role. Very rapidly the hunting and gathering economy of the Chickasaws gave way to an agricultural economy of corn and cotton. The old winter and summer houses of sticks and mud were abandoned in favor of log cabins with wood floors. Likewise, the Chickasaw towns were forsaken for dispersed farms. As trade with the white world increased, the Indians shed their breechcloths, leather garments, leggings, and moccasins for calico dresses, shirts, shoes and hats, and a variety of adornments of European finery, much of it imported to the Mississippi frontier along the Natchez Trace. Faulkner had one of his Indian characters, Ikkemottube, adopt the name of a steamboat captain and later the fateful name of Doom, a derivation from his French patron's term *du l'homme*, "of The Man." Doom trades cotton and slaves in New Orleans, travels to Paris with his French patron and brings back a pair of red-heeled slippers, which become an icon of leadership after he poisons his uncle, the chief, and assumes his place. Doom has his slaves drag an abandoned steamboat from the Tallahatchie through the forests and set it up on land as a house, where he sits in the saloon, surrounded by French souvenirs and fanned by a black slave. Other Indians and their slaves are adorned with ludicrous samples of Eastern and European imports—beaver hats, military amulets, parasols, and linen underwear.

The Indian appetite for consumption of goods and liquor was fostered with shrewd calculation by white officials. American trading posts gladly extended the Indians credit for the many goods they purchased, and government officials offered to retire the debt and provide more money for purchases in exchange for Indian land claims. Beginning in 1786 with the Treaty of Hopewell, a series of treaties carved away small and large parcels of the Chickasaw nation, all in exchange for monetary payments. In 1805 the Chickasaws ceded hunting lands north of the Tennessee River, in 1816 the area south of the Tennessee River to the west bank of the Tombigbee and 1818 all land north of the Tennessee state line. Now the Chickasaw nation was confined to northern Mississippi and a small portion of northwestern Alabama. Within this more restricted region game became more scarce, and more Indians were forced to turn away from the chase and adopt agriculture (Gibson 103–5).

The relative ease with which Andrew Jackson and other negotiators had persuaded the Indians to give up their land for money gave white officials confidence that the final step, complete removal to land west of the Mississippi River, would take place in due time. But the Chickasaws had now retreated to their homeland, the site of their towns, the graves of their ancestors and other sacred places. The mixed bloods, who as farmers had readily given up the unsettled hunting grounds to the north, now proved as immovable as the full bloods. When in 1826 the United States offered an equal area of land in the west in exchange for the Chickasaw homeland, Levi Colbert replied for his people: "the consequence may be similar to transplanting an old tree, which would wither and die away . . ." (Gibson 147).

Ultimately the strategy whites took was not to seduce the Indians with money or new land, nor was it to use military force to drive the Indians west—a strategy Jackson had applied to the Creeks and one that would become the policy of first resort west of the Mississippi. Instead, Mississippi in 1829 and 1830 simply abolished Chickasaw sovereignty and extended the laws of the state over all its inhabitants. Heavy fines and imprisonment were used to punish any tribal leaders who continued to exercise the powers of their office. Federal authorities, who had formerly guaranteed the Chickasaws' privileged status as a nation with certain autonomous powers of self government, stood back. President Jackson answered their appeals for protection with an icy reply: "you must submit . . . Your great father cannot, nor can congress, prevent it. The states only can. When then? Do you believe that you can live under these laws? That you can surrender all your ancient habits, and the forms by which you have been so long controlled?" (Gibson 154).

With that, the Chickasaws promptly began negotiating the terms of their removal. Mississippi's leading men celebrated at Parker's Hotel in Natchez "to testify their joy." They raised toasts to President Jackson: "He found one half our territory occupied by a few wandering Indians. He will leave it in the cultivation of thousands of grateful freemen." They also toasted the Chickasaws in language laden with unintended irony: "Our departing brethren, destined where they are going, to learn the right of individual property, and self government." And they toasted the "newly acquired Territory—the dawn of civilization now beams on its horizon. The wilderness shall blossom as the rose" (Gibson 157).

It was not until 1832 in the Treaty of Pontotoc Creek that the Chickasaws finally negotiated to have their land put up for sale at auction, and it was 1837 before the Chickasaw nation followed the Trail of Tears the other Indian tribes in the Southeast had taken before them to their new home in Indian Territory. Each Indian family had been allotted temporary homesteads which they now sold to whites for the best market price they could get, each transaction subject to the approval of designated Indian supervisors, usually the mixed-bloods who understood the business ways of the white man. Most of the Chickasaw cession was held by the tribe at large and sold at auction. The Indian land was purchased, not by the "thousands of grateful freemen" toasted earlier in Natchez, but by large land companies funded by distant speculators, notably eastern capitalists whose New York and Mississippi Land Company was the biggest player on the scene (Young ch. 6, 7).

The Indians who remained in the area must have been amazed as their tribal homeland was subdivided, sold and settled almost overnight. Swarms of surveyors, land locators, auctioneers, and interpreters poured into the area. Advertisements in newspapers across the country brought thousands of buyers to the federal land office at Pontotoc, the site of the great Chickasaw victory over the French one century before. Over 6.4 million acres were suddenly thrown open to sale. The land traders brought an estimated $1 million to Pontotoc in January 1836. A horde of merchants, tavern keepers, and swindlers of every stripe followed the land speculators and settlers to cheat the Indians out of their profits with cheap trinkets and watered liquor. Despite supervision by more savvy Indians, transactions were subject to all manner of chicanery. Many buyers used marginal down payments to secure land options and others traded goods of dubious value (Young 116). Faulkner's Jason Compson swapped with Chief Ikkemotubbe a race horse for a square mile of land that became the site of Jefferson (*Requiem* 12, 185). Another Faulkner character, Thomas Sutpen, apparently traded some gold coin of suspicious origin for the enormous parcel that became Sutpen's One Hundred in *Absalom, Absalom!* (38, 51).

For the Chickasaws these were the days of doom and dispossession, of drunken despair and bewildering negotiations over land they never thought of owning much less of selling. For the white land buyers these were the flush times of the Mississippi frontier, of speculative frenzy, of town booming, of wildly inflated credit and exaggerated profits. Many land sales were based on bank notes that became nearly worthless when the whole economy crashed in the Panic of 1837 following President Jackson's decision the previous year to put on the economic brakes and require hard money—gold or silver—for all future land purchases by any but the actual settlers (Young 164–67).[4]

Faulkner was fascinated with the early beginnings of his mythical county—its government, stores, hotels, and other institutions of white civilization, like schools and churches which were all quickly planted in Jefferson. He explored the creation of a new society in terms that were, on one level, like Biblical stories of creation and on another like hilarious backwoods tall tales. Two of the themes he explores in his tales of early Yoknapatawpha have special value to our historical understanding of how this new social order took shape on the Mississippi frontier. Faulkner seemed to understand that this formative stage of creating a new society was the essence of the American experience, and that in this protean act of initial creation, his community and the South became what it would be, for as Faulkner understood so keenly the past always bore down upon the present and lived within it always. ("The past isn't dead," he has one character say. "It isn't even past" [*Intruder in the Dust*].)

One of Faulkner's recurring themes is the introduction of law and government in defining the social order, sometimes reinforcing the privileges of caste and class and other times remedying the injustices that derive from these inequalities. In his stories about the construction of the jail and the courthouse in Yoknapatawpha, Faulkner described the coming of law and order to a lawless, violent frontier. The jail, first made of logs and secured with a huge iron padlock brought from Carolina by way of Nashville on horseback along the Natchez Trace, is used to incarcerate a small gang of bandits thought to be Wiley Harpe or Big Harpe and his band, or perhaps part of John Murrell's heinous gang of slave stealers and murderers. The Harpes and Murrell were actual outlaws whose gangs preyed on travelers on or near the Trace. Murrell was notorious for his practice of murdering victims, disemboweling them, and then filling the bodies with rocks and throwing them in the water where they would sink. The crude jail and padlock, in Faulkner's story, is not enough to hold this lawless band who quietly dismantle the log wall, stack it neatly to one side and take off in the night, apparently taking the padlock with them. To appease an officious United States post rider named Thomas Jefferson Pettigrew who had brought the lock to Mississippi by horseback and now wants to exact a ridiculous fine for its loss, the men of this Yoknapatawpha settlement decide to create a town and name it in his honor. Thus was born the town of Jefferson and the courthouse that became its symbol of government, the archives for its legal and, in time, historical records and the forum within which justice was meted out—in Faulkner's words: "the center the focus, the hub, sitting looming in the center of the county's circumference . . . tall as cloud, solid as rock, dominating all: protector of the weak, judiciate and curb of the passions and lusts, repository and guardian of the aspirations and the hopes . . ." (*Portable* 50).

The founding and naming of the town of Oxford was almost as arbitrary and as whimsical in historical fact as Jefferson's were in fiction. The settlement had begun around a log building operated as an Indian trading post by John J. Craig who, with John Chisholm and John D. Martin, had entered the area in 1835. They bought for $800 a section of land from the Indian woman Ho-kah who made her mark, an "X," on the deed, indicating she had "bargained, sold, deeded and conveyed" the land to them; two Chickasaw elders also signed the deed to affirm that "Ho-kah is able to take care of her own affairs" (WPA 225; Sobotka 29). Early in 1836 the state of Mississippi carved the Chickasaw cession into ten counties, including Lafayette County, and named four settlers within its boundaries to act as commissioners responsible for organizing a new county government. That March these commissioners called an election for the Board of Police, the main governing body of the county, and other officials were elected in April and June. The Board of Police, made up of large landowners, met in Craig's store and as one of its first acts of business (following inspection of the county and "mature deliberation") undertook to choose a site for the seat of government. John Craig and two partners had offered to donated fifty acres to the county, their scheme being that the larger section of land they owned surrounding the town site would rise greatly in value. On this land the county officials platted town lots surrounding a public square and sold the lots at public auction. This rude settlement staked out in the Mississippi wilderness was named, at the suggestion of pioneer Thomas Isom, after the ancient seat of learning in England in hopes that this pretense, this aspiration, would help attract the proposed state university then being discussed in Jackson. Of course, by 1848 this seemingly preposterous ploy bore fruit when the legislature selected Oxford for the new state university.

After the town was named and laid out in lots, the new government put up a temporary structure to serve as its meeting place and then took bids for a permanent courthouse and separate jail. The courthouse was to be a two-story structure fifty-two feet by forty feet, made with a thick stone foundation and hard brick walls topped by an octagonal cupola. It would take nearly four years to complete. The jail was built with a first-story dungeon to be built of hewn post oak logs, eighteen inches square and braced by iron bars, with a second story for debtors (restricted by state law to those involved in fraud) built in a similar fashion (Hathorn 44; Sobotka 29).

There was plenty of business for the courthouse and jail in a new country. The county seats of northern Mississippi became the forum for a swarm of lawyers who came west to serve a disorderly society filled with possibilities for the litigation of dubious land titles, false contracts and notes, and fraudulent deals of all kinds. In Oxford the establishment of the Federal District Court for northern Mississippi added to its role as a center of law.[5]

Beyond establishing the rudiments of law and government on the frontier, the early history of Faulkner's Yoknapatawpha and of northern Mississippi

was absorbed with laying the foundations of a new economy and the social hierarchy that would build upon it. His account of the early settlers
of Jefferson and Yoknapatawpha come fairly close to the actual history of
Lafayette County. There were store and tavern or hotel proprietors, a doctor,
and a cotton planter joined by an anonymous population of small and large
farmers, many of the latter with slaves. By 1840 the newly formed county had
drawn nearly 3,700 white people; it was a young, largely male population.
There were another 2,800 black slaves in the county by this time—44 percent of the over 6,500 total population (Hathorn 76–77). Almost overnight,
a former wilderness of Indian hunting grounds had been turned into a plantation economy based largely on slave labor. Much of the slave labor in this
early stage of development was being employed not in raising cotton or corn
but in clearing the fields and constructing houses. At first these plantation
homes were crude log cabins, then the rich put up more ostentatious mansions like the one Robert Shegog built in 1848 which Faulkner later bought
and called Rowan Oak. It would be several more years, after clearing and
planting the land, before the county's agricultural economy as a whole would
even be self-supporting let alone show a profit. The early settlers who became
cotton planters in Lafayette County had to be men of some means with slaves
enough to improve the land and capital enough to tide them over before the
rich profits from cotton began to flow (Hathorn 95–97).

But there were also men on the make who came to the frontier of the cotton South and to the primitive conditions of northern Mississippi to build
wealth with a swiftness that could never be duplicated in the older sections
of the eastern states or in the upper South. Our knowledge of the origins
and backgrounds of these men is obscure and was probably just as murky
to the early settlers who came to this frontier to start anew. One example is
Alexander Hamilton Pegues Sr. who was born in Marlborough District, South
Carolina, in 1808, left for Tennessee in 1834, and came to Mississippi with his
father about the time the land first opened for sale. He began inauspiciously
in a bachelor log cabin in the Woodson's Ridge area east of Oxford. Pegues
served as the district's first state senator from 1842 to 1850, and again in 1858.
By 1850 he had amassed an estate of more than 1,500 acres and by 1860 he
held 5,000 acres on which 150 slaves were employed. Others in the Pegues
family also owned large amounts of land and slaves by this time, and they
were the richest clan in the county by far. In 1856 Alexander Pegues moved to
Oxford from his plantation, about 7.5 miles outside town, and there put up a

large brick mansion that still stands on North Lamar Street. It was thought to be designed by Calvert Vaux of New York, known locally as the architect with the French-sounding name (Miner 95, 33; Hathorn 47, 103, 104, 107).[6]

It may have been Pegues, coming from a somewhat obscure background and rising abruptly to great wealth and notoriety, that suggested to Faulkner the character of Thomas Sutpen who figures in his most famous and haunting novel, *Absalom, Absalom!* Sutpen is a poor white from the mountains of Virginia who in his youth was insulted by the servant of a rich planter and, in his enduring rage over this humiliation, determines to build great wealth and begin a dynasty. His design is temporarily foiled in Haiti when he marries into a rich but racially tainted family, so he abruptly abandons his wife and son and comes to the frontier of Mississippi with a band of "wild" Haitian slaves and a captive French architect. Sutpen mysteriously swindles the Indians out of a hundred-square-mile domain of swampy land. Sutpen's One Hundred, his plantation, is "torn" out of the virgin land. He and his slaves work clearing and draining the swamps. They turn the forests into lumber, the mud into bricks, and out of these his French architect builds a grand plantation house, which he at first lives in as a crude, unfurnished camp barracks. After another mysterious absence, Sutpen returns with wagon loads of imported furnishings and finishes his mansion in grand style. Sutpen is a rough, violent man who drinks and gambles with the men who come to his house and who enjoys fist-fights with his slaves. But he marries the daughter of Goodhue Coldfield, a pious, eminently respectable, Methodist merchant in Jefferson, and Sutpen continues to pursue his design by producing a son and a daughter with Ellen Coldfield.

Sutpen, of course, is ultimately destroyed by his own arrogant design, and his destruction becomes, for Faulkner, a demonstration of the South's doom, a punishment for enslaving and exploiting others. Along with Sutpen there is the decline of the entire old order of wealthy owners of land and slaves, the pioneer generation of the Old South's frontier who, though they survive the war and even Reconstruction, slowly decay. Just as their ancestors had wrested the land from the Indians, now the remnants of the old order watch as a new breed, led by Flem Snopes and his ubiquitous relatives, enter Frenchmen's Bend and then the town of Jefferson, taking over the stores, the banks, the power company, and then the mansions with the white columns that had once been emblems of an earlier grandeur.

In his stories of Thomas Sutpen, the founding of Yoknapatawpha, and of the Indians who lived there before, Faulkner exaggerated and distorted that past in ways both grotesque and comical. But he did not distort it beyond recognition and not in ways that mislead the historians in their quest for the truth. Indeed, with his literary freedom combined with his knowledge of local history, Faulkner may have allowed his readers to understand a deeper level of historical truth.

## Notes

1. Among the published sources on Mississippi history available to Faulkner at the time were J. F. H. Claiborne's classic *Mississippi, as a Province, Territory, and State* (1880), Dunbar Rowland's multivolume works, the *Encyclopedia of Mississippi History* (1907) and *History of Mississippi: The Heart of the South* (1925), the *Publications of the Mississippi Historical Society* (1898–), the WPA's *Mississippi: A Guide to the Magnolia State* (1938) (from which Faulkner borrowed readily; see, Thomas L. McHaney, "Faulkner Borrows from the Mississippi Guide," *Mississippi Quarterly* XIX [Summer 1966], cited in Dabney, *Indians of Yoknapatawpha*, 35n), along with a few local histories, like Minnie Smith Holt, "Oxford, Mississippi" (1936) and several master's theses on Lafayette County history completed at the University of Mississippi, including John Cooper Hathorn, "A Period Study of Lafayette County from 1836 to 1860 with Emphasis on Population Groups" (1936) and Lucie H. Craig, "The Removal of the Chickasaw Indians" (1929). The Oxford *Eagle*, 10 December 1936, includes extensive historical accounts at the county's centennial. Earlier, in 1910, the *Eagle* published a series, "Early Recollections of Oxford." Joseph Blotner's *William Faulkner Library: A Catalog* (1964), however, shows very few historical works in Faulkner's possession at the time of his death.
2. Ward L. Miner, *The World of William Faulkner* (New York, 1952), and Elizabeth M. Kerr, *Yoknapatawpha: Faulkner's "Little Postage Stamp of Native Soil"* (New York, 1969), are two of the more comprehensive efforts at exploring the parallels between fiction and history in Lafayette County.
3. Gibson's book is the best modern account of the Chickasaw story.
4. Land sales in the Chickasaw cession revived in 1839 based on purchases by individual settlers or those who posed as such for large speculators.
5. For sketches of the law on the Mississippi frontier, see Joseph G. Baldwin, *Flush Times in Alabama and Mississippi* (1853; Baton Rouge, 1987), 47–48.
6. In 1860 Pegues's father, Malachi Pegues, owned 1,600 acres worth $1,500 and another, listed as T. E. B. Pegues, owned 2,420 acres worth $31,000.

## Works Cited

Cowley, Malcolm. Introduction. *The Portable Faulkner*. Rev. ed. New York: Random, 1967.

Dabney, Lewis M. *The Indians of Yoknapatawpha: A Study of Literature and History.* Baton Rouge: Louisiana State University Press, 1974.

Faulkner, William H. *Absalom, Absalom!* Rev. ed. New York: Random, 1987.

———. *Intruder in the Dust.* New York: Random, 1948.

———. *The Portable Faulkner.* Ed. Malcolm Cowley. Rev. ed. New York: Random, 1967.

———. *Requiem for a Nun.* New York: Random, 1951.

Gibson, Arrell M. *The Chickasaws.* Norman, OK: University of Oklahoma Press, 1971.

Hathorn, John Cooper. "A Period Study of Lafayette County from 1836 to 1860 with Emphasis on Population Groups." Thesis. University of Mississippi, 1936.

Kerr, Elizabeth M. *Yoknapatawpha: Faulkner's "Little Postage Stamp of Native Soil."* New York: Fordham University Press, 1969.

Malone, James H. *The Chickasaw Nation: A Short Sketch of a Noble People.* Louisville, KY: Morton, 1922.

Miner, Ward L. *The World of William Faulkner.* New York: Grove, 1952.

Oates, Stephen B. *William Faulkner: The Man and the Artist, A Biography.* New York: Harper, 1987.

Sobotka, C. John, Jr. *A History of Lafayette County.* Oxford, MS: Rebel, [1976].

Works Projects Administration. *Mississippi: A Guide to the Magnolia State.* Washington, D.C., 1983.

Young, Mary E. *Redskins, Ruffleshirts, and Rednecks: Indian Allotments in Alabama and Mississippi, 1830–1860.* Norman, OK: University of Oklahoma Press, 1961.

# Unlinking Race and Gender

## The Awakening as a Southern Novel

BARBARA C. EWELL

We do not typically think of *The Awakening* as a southern novel, which (set in Louisiana and dealing with many Reconstruction issues, such as the postwar role of women and life in the upper classes) it certainly is. At the same time, we do customarily regard Kate Chopin as a southern writer—despite the fact that she was from St. Louis (albeit in a family of southern sympathizers) and that she only spent the thirteen years of her marriage in the South and that much of her fiction (fully a third) is not specifically southern. But if Kate Chopin is not technically a southerner and *The Awakening* does not always "feel" like a southern novel, both writer and text were shaped by the very specific contexts of southern literature.

Perhaps what has diminished our sense of this famous feminist text as southern is the conflicted character of those contexts themselves. On the one hand, as Susan Donaldson so articulately argues, the canon of southern literature has been determinedly defined as "white, male, and conservative" (493). Donaldson traces what she calls the southern "project of imposing boundaries and exclusions" back from modernists like Allen Tate and John Crowe Ransom to antebellum critics like Henry Timrod and William Gilmore Sims (495). But such careful boundary-keeping—especially against women and African Americans—only exposes the "gender and racial anxieties they are meant to contain" (Donaldson 493). Such practices of exclusion simply reveal how profoundly southern literature resists enclosure in any carefully marked perimeters, how fundamental and unstable race and gender are in southern writing.

Naming the crucial links among race, gender, and notions of region has become a familiar practice in southern studies.[1] In numerous texts, writing by African Americans or by white women has been shown to challenge standard

*Southern Quarterly* 37.3–4 (1999): 30–37.

contours of southern identity and its explicit reflection of patriarchal values. For example, both the reevaluation of nineteenth-century local color and the attention to the slave narrative as a southern genre have exposed the gaps and fissures that everywhere disturb the serenity of the plantation myth underlying definitions of southern literature.[2] But if inserting an alternative notion of gender or race (or class or sexuality) into a text undeniably troubles its regional identity, the sheer persistence of southernness alone suggests that the ultimate effect is not as destructive as those who abhor racism or sexism or elitism might hope: literature turns out to be no easy feat, not least because of the complexity of the interrelationships on which a notion of region depends. The staggering appeal of southern mythology affirms just how coherently its pieces interlock and how many can be damaged or absent without seriously distorting its recognizability.

At the turn of the century, when Chopin was writing her own text about a southern woman, southernness was being sharply contested—as indeed were notions about women, about race, even class. The South in 1898 (when Chopin began to write her second novel) was just emerging from the wholesale reconstruction of its mythic (as well as its political) identity, although the exact contours of that reconfiguration were not altogether set. The effects of *Plessy vs. Ferguson* had legally, but not socially, rigidified the color line; the defeat of southern Populism in the elections of 1896 had practically but not completely dashed hopes for improving the lot of working-class southerners; and the racial compromises of the National American Woman Suffrage Association to attract southern support had not fully resolved the "woman question" in the region.[3] Chopin's own agenda as a writer could not but be shaped by these shifting and unstable contexts in which southern literature, indeed, the national identity itself, was being redefined. Examining just how Chopin negotiated these contexts and with what success is one way of gauging the southerness of her novel. But such an inquiry also exposes how Chopin's proposed interrogation of gender roles implicates a complex web of southern identity, one whose designs on women could not easily—if at all— be detached from notions of race and class. By employing a southern setting for her reconsideration of the ways that social roles limit female selfhood, Chopin also discloses how fiercely the fortresses of southern identity resist any challenge to its interlocking hierarchies.

Chopin was certainly conversant with the texts that had helped to shape southern consciousness. As we know from her notebooks and her biographers, her reading habits as a child were both conventional and wide-ranging.

Her best friend, Kitty Garesche, recalled that she particularly enjoyed *Ivanhoe* by Sir Walter Scott—the novelist whose romantic spirit and aristocratic trappings southerners eagerly incorporated into their fictional self-images. As an avid reader and an active contributor to the burgeoning literature of southern local color in the 1890s, Chopin would have understood, with no small degree of sympathy, the issues of southern identity and social conservatism that the genre encoded. (Her husband had after all been a member of New Orleans's reactionary White League.) She knew the work of Thomas Nelson Page (whose *Red Rock* was a bestseller in 1898) and Joel Chandler Harris (whose *Sister Jane* she reviewed in 1897 [*CW* 718–19]), as well as that of James Lane Allen (whose "exquisite" short novel "A Kentucky Cardinal" she approvingly mentions in 1894 [*Miscellany* 91]), Ruth Stuart (whom she met with great pleasure in 1897 [*CW* 711–12]) and many others, including George Washington Cable and Grace King, with whom she was often compared.

Among the representations most crucial to postwar fiction, and on whom southern regional identity most prominently depended, was of course the antebellum belle. As Anne Goodwyn Jones insists, "the southern lady is at the core of [the] region's self-definition; the identity of the South is contingent in part upon the persistence of its tradition of the lady" (4). As traced by contemporary scholars, the lineage of the belle lies both in the romantic traditions of Sir Walter Scott and in the domestic fiction by women that dominated mid-century canons. From Scott and other sectionalist writers (like Lord Byron and Jane Porter, whose *The Scottish Chiefs* was recalled by Kitty Garesche as one of hers and Katie's childhood favorites [Toth 51–52]), the belle obtained her aristocratic status. Placed on the pedestal of chivalric caste, she was relieved (theoretically at least) from the domestic drudgery assigned to most women of the world. In the South, slavery enabled upper-class (and many middle-class) white women to assume in fact the exceptional status of leisure conventionally reserved for nobility. Pointedly excused from any specific labor, the belle, as Kathryn Lee Seidel explains, became herself the culture's "object or work of art . . . the projection of her society's attitudes towards woman and sexuality, toward blacks and guilt, toward itself and its weakness and loss" (xv). But as Diane Roberts observes, this elevated "positioning within the political discourse" of southern feudalism also "placed her in the center of proslavery rhetoric" (6). Her leisure and refinement provided the chief evidence of aristocratic privilege, and the belle became the focus of any effort to defend or to discredit the South's peculiar institutions. Maintaining the privilege of the white woman became both a literal and figurative justification for slavery before the Civil War and for Jim Crow after it. The Lady was the South; as in other romantic traditions, her status and fate became identified with that of the region. Seidel traces this merging of the rhetorical image of the South as the Great Lady, fallen but still dignified, with the postwar version of the antebellum belle, who begins as spokesperson for the lost cause and gradually becomes its alter ego.[4]

The belle's other ancestry derived from the traditions of domestic fiction, with its powerful ideology of feminine culture. Writers like E. D. E. N. Southworth, Susan Warner, Dinah Mulock Craik, and Harriet Beecher Stowe (all familiar to Chopin) helped to construct an image of women as morally superior, functioning in a domestic sphere of her own, which served both to challenge and to support the public sphere of male power. As virgin, wife, and especially as mother, the Victorian lady epitomized the highest values of her culture. The southern belle was par excellence such a lady, defined by and destined for motherhood. But like her aristocratic status, that destiny made her a crucial site for white southern identity. As Roberts writes, if the body of the belle "provide[d] white heirs to the property[,] her chastity guarantee[d] racial purity" (186); a particular concept of gender thus explicitly maintained the privileges of class and white supremacy.

As in domestic fiction generally, motherhood in plantation ideology also assumed a spiritual cast, though not without significant contradictions. Like the "motherland" itself, the plantation mistress "mothers" all—even those persons who as chattel could be sold or abused. Such cruelty patently violated the regime of care that the idea of women's "domestic space" enshrines, so that, in a bitter irony, the nurturing work of women reinforced the patriarchal structures of a slave society. The ideal of womanhood both valorized the duties of the mother as caregiver and modeled a devout obedience to "higher powers," even those whose intrusions the home was supposedly a refuge. The sacredness of motherhood could in no way protect a woman's children, whether actual or metaphorical, from the cruel requirements of profit.

If the ethic of care disguised certain demands of the marketplace, it also concealed what Roberts neatly terms the "fissures in sexual decorum" that marked actual plantation life (188). For while motherhood was the special calling of the lady, the passage through sexual experience necessary for individual women to reach that elevated status was systematically effaced in nineteenth-century discourse on womanhood, markedly so in the South. White women were not supposed to be sexual; that physical and implicitly inferior task was imposed on "other," less pure, females: whores and black women (which in southern ideology were indistinguishable). The suppression of sexuality among "ladies" was central to the ideal of nineteenth-century motherhood. An influential tract on *The Functions and Disorders of the Reproductive Organs* (1857) by Sir William Acton intones, for example, that "a modest woman seldom desires any sexual gratification for herself. She submits to her husband, but only to please him; and, but for the desire of maternity, would far rather be relieved of his attentions" (qtd. in Roberts 188). Roberts also observes how "it was a southern gynecologist . . . who recommended that a patient who found intercourse 'painful' have sex while unconscious on chloroform so that she might conceive" and thus achieve her sacred duty of motherhood (189). This erasure of women's sexuality in a rhetoric of maternal worship ensured that no threatening female passion would unsettle the systems of marriage, family, and racial caste that their bodies were required to support. Not only in the antebellum period but even more emphatically after the war, when those institutions were being steadily pressured by large populations of ex-slaves and intensifying economic and political forces, that erasure proved a significant bulwark against unwanted social change.

Much Reconstruction fiction consciously constructed this view of self-sacrificing, asexual motherhood, reinforcing its potency as an ideal by merging female identities with southern regionalism. Since "true women" can exist only in and for their children (and the South can only live for its "true inheritors"), any sexual violation (which damaged the integrity of the racial or property lines insured by her purity) or sexual assertiveness (which manifested a threatening independence), necessarily results in the death of the lady, either figuratively or literally. Yankee ideas, black upstarts, and "outside agitators" all represented mortal, as well as moral, danger to the southern belle. Committed exclusively to the welfare of her children, she manifested an absolute, ahistorical identification with "traditional ways of life," even though those traditions defined away her selfhood almost as radically as it abolished the humanity and independence of the former slaves. Thomas Dixon's *The Clansmen* (1905), for example, among the most virulent of southern apologia, makes explicit this connection among woman, child, and region: the mother so identifies with her raped daughter that she leaps to death with her, indicating, as Roberts suggests, her clear preference for annihilation over the chaotic reality of Reconstruction in which such "violations" of social order have become so commonplace that neither the southern lady nor the traditional values of the motherland can continue to exist (190).

Chopin's first novel, *At Fault* (1890), which exploited many of the conventions of southern fiction, including its North-South romance structure and its focus on the belle, signaled the beginning of her own fictional exploration of female desire within the confining social and institutional contexts of the South. However, throughout her short stories of the next decade, she thoughtfully posed a variety of narrative answers to how women might achieve or maintain selfhood inside and against the rigid roles prescribed for them—not exclusively in southern contexts.[5] In that exploration, Chopin aligned herself with a new generation of women writers, many of whom, like Sarah Jewett, Mary Wilkins Freeman, Mary Catherwood, or Mary Austin, were using the conventions of local color to express their own conflicted responses to the positive, though restrictive, aspects of "domestic culture" and the need to articulate their emerging sense of independent female selfhood. Linda Dowling asserts that the rebellion against Victorian culture and the cult of motherhood was expressed by these writers "chiefly through sexual means—by heightening sexual consciousness, candor, and expression" (qtd. in Showalter 69). Female sexuality, the admissibility of passion for women, became the battleground for female selfhood, with motherhood emerging as an equivocal adversary.[6]

For southern writers, the admission of sexuality into women's experience, even in fiction, was particularly difficult. As numerous Reconstruction novels and tracts insisted, challenging the ideal of the belle challenged sectional loyalty as well.[7] Preserving the southern lady inviolate and impervious either to internal resistance or outside influences confirmed the South's regional fidelity to its old "verities" of caste and race. In posing the dilemma of her heroine explicitly in terms of motherhood (an issue that she had approached in several short stories, notably "Wiser than a God," "Regret," and "Athenaise"), Chopin knew that she was engaging head-on the central issue for many nineteenth-century women writers: how to reclaim women's displaced desire, so that she might, in Cynthia Wolff's terms, re-possess her own libido from her children (8) or, in Edna's terms, retain the "essential." As Elizabeth Fox-Genovese suggests, Chopin may well have thought that her explorations of female sexuality were less threatening to the southern social order than exploring women's social independence. In other words, as Fox-Genovese argues, Chopin may have believed that Edna's struggle—that every woman's struggle—was an individual matter, necessary for personal fulfillment, but only incidental to the larger social structures that constrained her (39): that the lady's release from the pedestal would not undo the society that put her there.

But by setting her novel in south Louisiana, Chopin, whether she meant to or not, was also engaging issues critical to southern identity. Given her resistance to being classified as a regionalist and the drift of her late fiction away from specifically southern settings, it is unlikely that she saw her new novel as part of the contemporary conversation on the fate of the South. She had already been there and done that in *At Fault*. But southern identity implied not simply a useful construction of womanhood, but also its complex interdependence on race and class, not all of which was Chopin equally prepared to challenge. As Margaret Ferguson analogously argues of Aphra Behn's *Oronooko*, Chopin's asymmetrical allegiances to woman's desire and white, upper-class privilege strikingly reveal the intricate interdependence of region upon constructions of race, class, and gender. Not necessarily intending to write a southern novel, but only to make use of its evocative locales, Chopin discloses the dependent relationship between what seems to be an individual woman's desire for "personal fulfillment" and the system of hierarchies that circumscribes any southern identity. The lady simply cannot escape being southern, just as Chopin's parable about seeking freedom from the restraints of gender ultimately cannot separate itself from the suppressions of race and class that its setting presupposes. Nonetheless, writing out of—or into—such contrary allegiances, Chopin successfully exploits those conflicting relationships toward her own ends: creating selfhood for her character and narrative authority for herself.

The creole South in which Chopin sets Edna's search represented a familiar fictional terrain, one whose exotic distances and conventional assumptions helpfully exaggerated the role of women that she wished to explore and critique. Chopin could rely upon audiences, northern and southern, to appreciate the importance of being a lady in the upper-class South—and creole society was, thanks to Cable, viewed as notoriously elitist and exclusive. But Chopin uses that elitism not only to undermine Edna's difference as an outsider (a "northern" southerner, whose radical ideas are specifically alien to the conservative creoles), but also to provide her with an economic mobility that in fact gives her choices. Edna's very presence on Grande Isle indicates her economic means to escape the heat and disease of New Orleans's summers, a status confirmed by the upper-class occupations she pursues in the city: entertaining the female relatives of Leonce's business associates, attending musical soirees at the Ratignolles or the race-track with her father and Alcee Arobin, participating in Leonce's decoration and travel plans. Mr. Pontellier's wealth underwrites Edna's leisure, though she begins to resist the constraints imposed by that ladyhood. That Edna wants to be an artist rather than a cultural artifact certainly affirms her agency, but that she can in fact "do it" demonstrates that even her presumed autonomy depends on her position in the same culture whose confinements she resists. When Edna begins to defy her conventional role, she has what Virginia Woolf knew was essential: a room of her own. As a southern mistress (rather than as, say, a single or lower-class woman), Edna can enlist the whole hierarchy of her household "in the service of art"; children, quadroons, housemaids—all take turns posing in the atelier as material for her self-expression (*CW* 19: 939). The very responsibilities that Edna experiences as encumbrances to her autonomy specifically enable her to explore it.

Edna's freedom assumes racial as well as economic caste. Unlike her contemporaries King and Stuart and most other southern writers, Chopin was not particularly engaged by southern sectionalism and the racist agenda of segregation that most defenders of the South supported. Even so, as Violet Harrington Bryan indicates, *The Awakening* tacitly approves the racial structures of southern society (58). The labor and presence of black people are systematically assumed in the novel. Edna's spiritual journey is directly supported by nameless black servants who care for her children and cook her meals and drive her carriages while she tries to figure out how to be a lady and still have a self. As Pamela Menke argues, Chopin's focus (not unlike Behn's) simply did not permit her to see the ways that the chafing suppression of her own "dark desires" depends upon the control of the same "dark people" who make possible her individual enfranchisement.

If the notion of female autonomy is not separate from southern contexts but in fact dependent upon them, even Chopin's focal issue—detaching "womanhood" from synonymity with selflessness—is complicated by southerness. Edna protests to Adele that she simply wants to preserve what is "essential" about her being. She would readily sacrifice the external and physical "self" that motherhood demands. ("Nobody has any right—except children perhaps. . . . Still, I shouldn't want to trample upon the little lives" [38: 995–96]), but she does not want to allow that sacrifice to exhaust her entire identity as a human being. But while Edna perceives sexual desire as the touchstone of a deeper selfhood, the *sine qua non* of existence, the novel itself retains alternative space for more conventional options. Though Edna pities the Ratignolles' life of "domestic harmony" as "appalling and hopeless ennui," Chopin clearly reserves more irony for Edna's vague longing for "life's delirium" than for Adele's apparently rich and sexually satisfied life (18: 938). Conspicuous in her fertility as well as in her marital content, Adele counters Edna's restless desire with an affirmation of the mother-woman that does not, in fact, exclude a satisfying female sexuality. If "[t]here are no words to describe [Madame Ratignolle] save the old ones" reserved for "the bygone heroine of romance and fair lady of our dreams" (4: 888), those words only half-conceal their sexual charge: "the spun-gold hair that comb nor confining pin could restrain. . . . two lips that pouted, that were so red one could only think of cherries or some other delicious crimson fruit" (4: 888). The perfect southern mistress perfectly congruent and even happy with her assigned place in creole society, Adele astutely recognizes Edna's own alienation and warns Robert, "She is not one of us; she is not like us" (8: 900). If Edna's difference does not indeed challenge the sufficiency of motherhood in meeting the needs of a fully human self, it nonetheless fails to discount the adequacy of that role for at least some women within the limited terms of creole society. The presence of Adele, desiring and desirable, as well as a source of unfailing good sense and sound advice, unsettles Chopin's own critique of conventional mother-womanhood.[8] When stretched across the narrow grid of region—or any other cultural space—the selflessness of women appears a perfectly comprehensible, even admirable, description of selfhood.

While Edna's central insistence on her "own way" exposes intolerable constrictions on southern places for women, it still cannot entirely deconstruct southern womanhood. The radical ambivalence of her suicide, together with the contradictory affirmations of southern hierarchy that the text incorporates, ultimately minimizes the effectiveness of Edna's revolt. Even her most dramatic attempt to move out of the social place assigned to her (like the novel's singular focus on gender) results in an ironic reaffirmation of the larger systems that define female status. The pigeon house is, after all, purchased with Edna's father's money and staffed by a black servant, and though Edna can invite Robert to resist a conventional relationship there, she cannot finally rescind his gentlemanly allegiance to patriarchal propriety—or stop him from leaving.

In posing her heroine's dilemma as essentially gendered, Chopin succeeded in undermining one version of the southern belle: the nurturing, selfless, undesiring female. But to construct her alternative in a specifically southern setting, Chopin also had to leave in place the economic and racial hierarchies that had made the belle central to southern ideology. Differences of race and class were critical to the exaggerated female identity that Chopin sought to challenge. Yet Edna's own difference from southern society remains equivocal. Her (admittedly incipient) version of autonomous selfhood still depends on the same hierarchies of class and race that support the conventional belle. By framing Edna's repression solely in terms of feminine desire and not also in terms of the racist hierarchies the belle is meant to protect, Chopin corroborates a modern critique of the South, one that insists on the interdependence of race and gender and class in defining regional identity—or any enclosed system. In its partiality, Edna's problem and her solution remain personal and unique—and thus safely marginal. At the end, Edna may seem to slough off the stifling roles that constrict her dream of an essential self, but her birth remains an act of individualism, itself enveloped by the figures of the South she has supposedly rejected. The voices of the sea are those that recall her to a very southern place of fathers and families, sycamores and cavalry officers, humming bees and musky pinks (*CW* 39: 1000).

Partiality inevitably limits the effectiveness of Chopin's interrogation, but it also enables her critique. For if Edna is not wholly outside the paradigms of southern culture, neither is she contained by them. Chopin's calculated use of southern womanhood does heighten Edna's dilemma, and the novel's insistence on the ownership of sexual desire as critical to human wholeness does conspicuously broaden the fictional territory of female identity. At the same time, Chopin's deployment of a southern locale in the interests of a problem she clearly understood to be "universal" reflects a notion of region as a far more significant space than its contemporary relegation to "mere local color" would admit.

Unfortunately for Chopin's own authority as a writer, neither of these achievements were much appreciated by her early readers. Precisely because Edna was a southerner, her concerns (like all regional matters) could be all the more easily dismissed by literary history as merely the plight of another aberrant southern "other"—certainly "not one of us." And even when the importance of the South as a site for examining issues of national concern was acknowledged, it was race, not gender that engaged modern attentions. Indeed, southern writing has remained markedly resistant to images of female autonomy even though it has not infrequently challenged the erasure of black people's individuality. If southern writers considered the problem at all, they continued to isolate and privatize women's resistance to oppressive social roles, failing to perceive their function in supporting white supremacy or sectional loyalty, matters which even many southern white women continued to sympathize with or defend. If Chopin could not see the systemic links between racism and sexism, she was hardly alone. But she was unique in appreciating how damaging to white women were the narrow role of the southern belle and the loss of sexuality to female identity. By writing about that dilemma as applicable to "all" (white upper-class) women, Chopin thus not only profoundly revised the place of female desire, but she also expanded regional writing beyond sectionalism, opening the way for the next century's renderings of women as autonomous subjects and the South as the site of this nation's most searing self-examinations. Neither the southern novel nor the southern woman could ever be the same.

## Notes

1. The best recent contribution to this discussion is Jones and Donaldson's *Haunted Bodies*. See especially their introduction, "Rethinking the South through Gender" (1–19). See also the essays in Humphreys.
2. On reassessing southern local color, see Taylor and Ewell.
3. See Ayers for fuller explication of these issues.
4. Seidel shows how the belle merely articulates the southern perspective in early works like William DeForest's *Miss Ravenel's Conversion* (1867), but functions more and more allegorically in novels like DeForest's *The Bloody Chasm* (1881), or Page's very popular *Red Rock* (1897), or Cary Eggleston's rather obvious *Dorothy South* (1902); Seidel, 23ff.
5. See "Mrs. Modry's Reason," "A Shameful Affair," "Lilacs," "Her Letters," "The Kiss," "Fedora," and "An Egyptian Cigarette," among others.
6. Earlier in the century, the role of motherhood had been, in Harriet Stowe's words, "the 'Woman Question' of the day" (Showalter 14). But instead of trying to bring maternal virtue to the "public sphere," the new women writers of the 1890s were asking if motherhood itself were not an obstacle to creativity and personal fulfillment.
7. Thomas Nelson Page's nostalgic anatomization in *The Old Dominion: Her Making and Manners* (1908) is one of the most explicit versions of this identification (see Roberts 8–9).
8. Certainly Chopin's affirmation of motherhood in numerous short stories, like "Athenaise," "Regret," or "A Matter of Prejudice," together with her own evident personal satisfactions in the role, reinforce the ambiguity in Edna's desire for autonomy. See Chopin's comments about her own first experience of motherhood (*Miscellany* 92).

## Works Cited

Ayers, Edward L. *The Promise of the New South: Life after Reconstruction*. New York: Oxford University Press, 1992.

Bryan, Violet Harrington. *The Myth of New Orleans in Literature: Dialogues of Race and Gender*. Knoxville: University Press of Tennessee, 1991.

Chopin, Kate. *The Complete Works*. Ed. Per Seyersted. Baton Rouge: Louisiana State University Press, 1969.

———. *A Kate Chopin Miscellany*. Ed. Per Seyersted and Emily Toth. Natchitoches: Northwestern Louisiana State University Press, 1979.

Donaldson, Susan V. "Gender, Race, and Allen Tate's Profession of Letters in the South." In Jones and Donaldson. 492–518.

Ewell, Barbara C. "Changing Places: Women and the Old South; or What Happens When Local Color Becomes Regionalism." *Amerikastudien / American Studies* 42.2 (1997): 157–79.

Ferguson, Margaret W. "Juggling the Categories of Race, Class and Gender: Aphra Behn's *Oronooko*." *Women's Studies* 19 (1991): 159–81.

Fox-Genovese, Elizabeth. "*The Awakening* in the Context of the Experience, Culture, and Values of Southern Women." *Approaches to Teaching Chopin's "The Awakening."* Ed. Bernard Koloski. New York: MLA, 1988: 34–39.

Humphries, Jefferson, ed. *Southern Literature and Literary Theory*. Athens: University of Georgia Press, 1990.

Jones, Anne Goodwyn. *Tomorrow Is Another Day: The Woman Writer in the South, 1859–1936*. Baton Rouge: Louisiana State University Press, 1981.

Jones, Anne Goodwyn, and Susan Donaldson, eds. *Haunted Bodies: Gender and Southern Texts*. Charlottesville: University Press of Virginia, 1998.

Menke, Pamela. "The Catalyst of Color and Women's Regional Writing: *At Fault, Pembroke*, and *The Awakening*." *Southern Quarterly* 37.3–4 (1999): 9–20.

Roberts, Diane. *Faulkner and Southern Womanhood*. Athens: University of Georgia Press, 1994.

Seidel, Kathryn Lee. *The Southern Belle in the American Novel*. Tampa: University of South Florida Press, 1985.

Showalter, Elaine. *Sister's Choice: Tradition and Change in American Women's Writing*. Oxford: Clarendon, 1991.

Taylor, Helen. *Gender, Race, and Region in the Writings of Grace King, Ruth McEnery Stuart, and Kate Chopin*. Baton Rouge: Louisiana State University Press, 1989.

Toth, Emily. *Kate Chopin*. New York: Morrow, 1990.

Wolff, Cynthia Griffin. "Un-utterable Longing: The Discourse of Feminine Sexuality in *The Awakening*." *Studies in American Fiction* 24 (1996): 3–22.

PART V

## 2000S

# "When Is an Ocean not an Ocean?"
# Geographies of the Atlantic World[1]

JAMES TAYLOR CARSON

Poetry is a nice place to start thinking about a different way to imagine the past, a way that can bring into focus a horizon that scholars too often have turned away from in silence.[2] "The stone had skidded arc'd and bloomed into islands," Kamau Brathwaite mused more than thirty years ago in his poem "Calypso." And behind that stone, in the middle of the concentric rings that formed around the points where it had touched the water only to resume its flight again, he saw whole worlds rising to the surface: Cuba, Jamaica, Grenada, and Guadeloupe. Islands. Plantations. Masters. Sugarcane. Blood. It is easy and almost intuitive to hear the words Cuba or Grenada and imagine them as places on a map. Jagged little configurations of shades of brown and green and yellow that darken with the rising elevations they depict surrounded by counterpoint shades of blue reaching out away from the pale Caribbean basin past the continental shelf and into the azure of the open Atlantic. But if places have objective knowable qualities they also have their deeply subjective sides, and these tend to be easy to forget. We often take geography to be an immutable fact when in both its physical and cultural forms, it is the product of dialogues, contests, and accommodations, contact between substances as disparate as eternal stone and the primordial sea.[3]

The Atlantic World wound its way into many places. The ports of England bustled with cargoes from far away. Coffle trails snaked along the Senegal and Gambia rivers to the sea. Men burrowed holes in a hillside to seek the silver of Potosí. And the cowboys of Chota, Coweta, and Tallassee tended cattle in ways not dissimilar to the ways they had hunted deer once upon a time. Such places began in an ocean that afforded opportunities for the peoples of Europe, Africa, and what came to be called the Americas to become involved in one another's lives. The same body of water has also given scholars

*Southern Quarterly* 43.4 (2006): 16–45.

an organizing principle around which to arrange the variety of histories of exploration, conquest, colonization, and resistance that created the Atlantic World. But the meaning of the Atlantic and the way we understand its importance to the past rest on a particular view of geography. After all, who would dispute the question that David Armitage posed recently: "Is not an ocean," he asked, "a natural fact?"[4]

The answer, however, is not as straightforward as it would seem. To reply that an ocean is not a natural fact might beggar belief, but it is not. It is a cultural proposition that carries with it any number of insights, assumptions, and blind spots. All too often, geographers John Paul Jones and Wolfgang Natter have argued, historians relegate space to "an inert horizontality" and, in effect, substitute a seemingly natural understanding of space for the multiple cultural constructions that tied past people to past places.[5] What was the Australian outback to the English and the Irish, for example, was to the Pintupi an enduring landscape that, like all life, had been born of the Dreaming. What was the Pacific Ocean to British navigators was, for the inhabitants of the island of Tanna, a road to other islands and nearby peoples. What agents of the Colonial Office in West Africa took to be trees were to other people the repositories of spirits and sacred charters to the land. And what we take today to be the Atlantic Ocean has been to other people in other times the salty seed of life, the river of the world, and the abode of the Leviathan.[6] "It is only through culture," anthropologist Bernard Cohn has suggested, "that we construct nature, not the other way around."[7]

Calling the Atlantic Ocean a natural fact obscures the degree to which it and the Atlantic world that surrounded it were different things to different people. To reconstruct the histories and geographies of the Atlantic World, we must set aside the inert horizontality of fact that Jones and Natter identified and confront the vastness of the cultural places and spaces that were contained within it. Nature, in this case the fact of the ocean, was not the setting for the creation of the Atlantic World but rather the basis of the differences between its founding peoples and the places they made for themselves. "Places," philosopher Edward S. Casey reminds us, "not only are, they happen."[8] In this essay I will explore how acts of placemaking, in particular those related to water and to the sea, informed the colonization of, in this particular case, one small corner of the Atlantic World, the colonial American South.

My intention is not to supplant the concept of the Atlantic World but to make space for alternate conceptions of the ocean that made the creation of this world possible. But there is more to it than the simple recognition of past perceptions of landscape. J. G. A. Pocock, writing about British history some years ago, argued for the need to find ways to talk about plural or multicultural histories; to divest ourselves of ethnocentrisms and nationalisms that entailed, as he put it, "a high degree of commitment to a single and uniting point of view."[9] Any attempt to recover the variety of past peoples and their practices must therefore be implicated in the consideration of current debate about multiculturalism. Building on the work of such creole theorists as Brathwaite, Édouard Glissant, and Raymond Relouzat, Rex Nettleford has identified the Americas as a space uniquely situated in terms of its human past to challenge notions of exclusive authorship and to unsettle one culture's claim to epistemological preeminence over others.[10]

The founding peoples of the colonial American South—the first people, the invading people, and the enslaved people—held particular views about how the world they inhabited was constructed, how it operated, and what it meant. For first people the sea was a large body of water that held a place of particular significance in their cosmologies. From the Woodland peoples of what became the province of Virginia to the Mississippian mound builders of present-day Georgia, Alabama, Mississippi, and Louisiana, water was the primeval force of creation; the source of the chaos, decay, and life that made human existence so precarious and dangerous. Only the light of the sun counterbalanced the flow of water and provided people with the safety and the order they needed to go about their daily lives. Coming from across the sea placed Europeans in the world of water and presaged, for the first people at least, the turmoil and destruction that the invaders visited upon the land. The Spanish, French, and English adventurers who set sail to find their fortunes saw the ocean in a similar light. From Classical antiquity to the early Renaissance scholars and theologians had depicted the ocean as a world river that separated "civilization" from antipodean realms where men's mouths were in their bellies, where people with the heads of dogs cavorted with cannibals and other beasts, and where so-called "ethiops" suffered their skin to be burned black by the rays of the equatorial sun. The founding of Virginia, South Carolina, Georgia, and Louisiana put the explanatory powers of Christian cosmology into play on the land and sustained the belligerent acquisition of land. And with the control of land came the need for labor.

The Africans and descendants of Africans who had labored in the West Indies brought their own conception of the Atlantic into the South. Like the other founding peoples, water was for them a marker of instability, transition, and alterity. Kongolese and other peoples of western Africa believed that the souls of the dead had to traverse the world sea to reach the afterlife on the other side. And it was not an easy voyage, for the white spirits that dwelled beneath the waves savaged whatever souls they could catch. With the disruptions of the slave trade, European factors came to be seen as predatory spirits who held the shore of the sea and threatened to consume all who disembarked from its shores. For those people who survived the middle passage from the land of the living to the land of the dead, they arrived in a world that for them was as close to hell as one could get.

Colonization in the South was as much a collision of competing geographies as it was of competing societies, and the existence of different kinds of geographical knowledge makes the modern historiographical assertion of an Atlantic Ocean as a natural fact difficult to sustain in light of recent work in epistemology, environmental studies, and humanist geography. What examples drawn from the early colonial history of the South can show is first, how different peoples understood the Atlantic, and, second, how such understandings influenced the course of contact. If cultural conceptions of the sea impelled the history of colonization then the assertion of an objective natural fact, the Atlantic Ocean, has the potential to efface such plural notions of ocean and to superimpose a normative or perhaps even hegemonic historiographical logic on the more variegated set of past beliefs and practices that made the places of the Atlantic World the historical "happenings" that they were.[11]

The ocean or, even more generally, water, embodied for each of the South's founding peoples strangeness, unpredictability, and danger—the source of life and chaos, wisdom and sin. Some years ago a landscaper in present-day Brevard County, Florida, turned up human bones along with the sod he was excavating from a place the locals called Windover pond. Eight thousand years before, however, the water hole had been a site of great and somber importance to a different group of people. For about one thousand years, humans wrapped their dead in cloth made from plant fibers, sank the corpses into the shallow pond, and staked the cloth to the pond's bottom to ensure their loved ones stayed submerged. But no ancient stake could hold against the metal teeth of a Caterpillar. Clearly such ponds were crucial sites for hunting and living. But, in light of later beliefs about origins in mother earth, about the life-giving powers of water, and about the bodies of the dead constructing claims to land for the present and future, it is possible that those who had left their dead at the bottom of the pond carried in their heads and hearts a belief system that would become more readily apparent in pottery motifs, ornamental designs, and public architectures in later millennia as their descendants learned to temper, to coil, and to fire clay; to hammer cold copper, and to heap the earth in the form of great mounds to mark their position between the sun and its sky and the earth and its waters.[12]

Such was the thinking that informed the layout of a site called Poverty Point in present-day northeastern Louisiana, the South's first large mound center. The people situated their mounds and homes in reference to relationships between the sun, the earth, and the horizon that had probably preoccupied the people for ages. Six concentric sets of octagonal ridges encircled the village center and aisles radiated out from the center and cut through the ridges. From the sky it looked like the Sun had dropped a pebble in a pond or a spider had woven a great web. A giant mound in the shape of a bird dominated the skyline. The ridge sat seventy-five feet above the alluvial plain and suggested the broad outlines of a story that posited an opposition of sky and earth and which found expression in the ceremonial and burial mounds that placed the deceased in the watery underworld while bringing the living closer to the Sun.[13]

Across present-day Georgia and neighboring portions of Florida, South Carolina, North Carolina, Tennessee, and Alabama, groups of people began marking their pottery with serpent designs embedded in counterclockwise spirals representing water and swirling in a direction away from the sun that moved across the sky in clockwise fashion. The placement of bird figures in spirals, perhaps figurative winds, that turned clockwise bolsters the notion that somehow snakes and water and birds and the sky constituted the endpoints of a complicated continuum of beliefs about place and space and where the people located themselves. Societies such as those that gathered at the mound sites we know today as Pinson or Kolomoki or McKeithen expanded and contracted over time owing to unclear fluctuations in trade and the food supply and the vagaries of political and social life. What is clear, however, is that new kinds of societies emerged out of the growing populations of this woodland world that were qualitatively different from anyone who had come before. The new people drew upon indigenous political models but the real impetus for their new social formations came from the mound builders and maize growers of Cahokia, a site near present-day St. Louis, Missouri.[14]

Archaeologists call the new people Mississippians, and one of the most conspicuous symbols Mississippian leaders used to express their power was an equilateral cross enclosed by a circle. The motif appeared on all sorts of elite objects, from shell ornaments to decorative pots. The cross's arms marked the four positions of the sun during the passage of each day, and the circle set off the orderly place of the cross from the disorderly, watery, space of the sea. The two arms that also divided the top half of the circle, the Upperworld of the sun, fire, and birds, from the bottom half, the Underworld that was home to the moon, water, and serpents, marked the space where the people struggled to live between the endpoints of their cosmos.[15]

Across the waters that surrounded the first people's world lived another people who also saw the cosmos in terms of circles and crosses and birds and snakes. As the seeds and the knowledge to grow wheat and other cereals moved out of the valleys of the Tigris and the Euphrates rivers into southern and central Europe people began to write their impressions of the world on the pottery they used and the fetishes they honored. Incised or painted crosses depicted the four cardinal points of the world, the passage of time, and the rhythms of life while black snakes crawled across the curved surfaces of their bowls, connoting the mysterious powers of life and water. Depictions of birds brought to life the sky world that, in conjunction with the waters of life, brought health and prosperity to the world of humans. Babylonians looked beyond the Bitter Waters surrounding their land to the quarters of the sun, the houses of the winds, and the ends of the earth. And when they looked to the sky their eyes followed a great staircase that had descended from the gods to the earth they inhabited. Germanic craftsmen embossed circular sheets of gold to depict their own take on the cosmos while other societies projected vertical dimensions onto the sacred circle. From Mesopotamia to Scandinavia people imagined a great tree of life standing in the middle of the world with its roots sinking to the depths of the earth and its branches reaching toward the heavens while the sea encircled it all.[16]

Greeks sat astride the great roads that carried the caravans, armies, and embassies that bound Europe and Asia. An astronomer in Asia Minor, Thales of Miletus, pondered many of the same mysteries that had preoccupied the Babylonians, and later generations of philosophers located in his teachings the first stirrings of something new, something outside of the circle that had expressed the perfection and divinity of their world for so long. They proposed that the one-dimensional circle which appeared in Babylonian rock carvings and Germanic dials, when taken together with such structures as the cosmic staircase or the tree of life, may have in fact depicted the earth as a three-dimensional sphere. Aristotle added later that a spherical heaven revolved around the spherical earth. The size of the earth, however, was infinitesimal in comparison to the surrounding heavens. Other continents, beyond the sight of the known world, he surmised, probably shared the watery surface of the earth.[17]

The thinkers of Classical and Hellenistic Greece gave way to the leading lights of Rome in due time, but the Greeks' original works continued to set the parameters of cosmological and geographical thinking. Posidonius, a Syrian, opened an academy in Rhodes where he and his pupils revived and revised Aristotle's work on climatic zones. Just as with the form of the world, Aristotle followed the early Pythagorans who had divided the terrestrial globe into five bands according to temperature and habitability. Two barren frigid zones covered the extreme ends of the world and one equally desolate torrid zone circled the earth at the equator. Only savages dwelled in these inhospitable spots. Between the northern and southern frigid zones and the torrid zone of the equator stretched temperate lands that were home to temperate people like the Greeks and Latins. At either pole, Pliny wrote, stood a polar zone that was so cold, wet, and dark that the inhabitants had "white skins and long light hair." Around the center of the earth ran a torrid zone that was so hot, dry, and bright that its inhabitants suffered from scorched hair and burned skin under the unmediated rays of the sun. Perhaps it was these people Pliny had in mind when he ascribed to man the destiny to command all others.[18]

While the Roman Empire crumbled, the dissemination of Classical knowledge did not stop. Conquests, population movements, disease, and recovery all had a hand in transforming a medieval landscape. At a time when trade caravans carried news of Cathay and when Christians battled Muslims over the walled cities of the Holy Land, however, the Great Chain of Being provided the means whereby European Christians could recall the ancient antipodes and situate foreign folk in a broader cosmos. Again, Classical authors set the precedent. Pliny the Elder, for example, pieced together the portions of his *Historiae naturalis* on exotic people and monsters from Classical accounts reaching back to the early fifth century BCE. His stories of Amazons, man eaters, and dog-headed people who lived beyond the sea captured the medieval imagination while it pulled the far transoceanic horizons into sharper focus. Solinus, who had relied heavily on Pliny, reported nations of monstrous people near Ethiopia and Arabia. The Blemmyes of Libya, he wrote, were born headless but could see and speak through the eyes and mouth in their chests while Alphonse de Saint Onge's *Cosmographie* recapitulated Solinus's recapitulation of Pliny. To the men with eyes and mouths in their chests he added a race of cyclopes on the margins of the known world. Cosmas Indicopleustés reported in the mid-sixth century that in the unknown lands on the other side of the world, the antipodes, the "antichthoniens" lived upside down.[19]

Christian scholars used tales of monsters and the explanatory power of the Great Chain of Being to map a kind of moral hierarchy over land and sea. A biblical genealogy supplanted the Classical division of the world into three continents—Asia, Africa, and Europe—and imputed to the founding inhabitants of each region certain moral qualities. Noah's sons Shem, Ham, and Japheth, the argument went, had each colonized a separate continent. Shem traveled across the Caucasus Mountains where he sired the wild races of Asia while Japheth fathered the temperate people of Europe. Ham, though, who had been cursed for seeing his father naked, took his bane to Africa where he spawned a race of dark-skinned people. Classical authors had rarely associated dark complexions with monsters, but Church fathers read blackness, darkness, and sinfulness into the skins that, in the words of Bartholemew Anglicus, had been "roasteth and toasteth" by the sun. The antipodal people whom Classical authors believed stood upside down owing to their placement across the sea became, in Christian hands, people whose pigment and morality were also inverted. Classical explanations for dark skin persisted— proximity to the sun ranked high in various explanations for the blue or black skins of Ethiopians—but popular editions of the adventures of Marco Polo and John Mandeville added poor diet, nakedness, and hard toil to the list of the curse's symptoms.[20]

Others projected the postdiluvian world in so-called T/O maps on which medieval scholars drew a circle, the "O," a remnant of the Babylonians' and Aristotle's perfect sphere, and placed a *tau* cross within the circle, the "T," that harkened back to the decorations on the first pots thrown by European farmers as well as the puncture wounds Christ suffered when he was fixed to the cross. The cross of the "T" divided the earth into the three known continents separated by three bodies of water, the Don and Nile rivers and the Mediterranean sea, while the ocean surround all three and provided the map with its perfect and self-contained circularity. When read through the genealogies of Shem, Japheth, and Ham, however, such maps established a chronological and moral encoding of what was otherwise a Classical formulation of the great land masses. It established the earth as the Father's stage where the world's ultimate salvation unfolded, a world ready to be staked out, carved up, and delivered to the Him. "And the fear of you and the dread of you," the Book of Genesis told the faithful, "shall be upon every beast of the earth, and upon every fowl of the air, upon all that moveth upon the earth, and upon all the fishes in the sea; into your hand are they delivered." What the Church Fathers had done was to replace earlier models of the world in which men and the earth were at the gods' mercy with the Great Chain where men became as gods ruling the land and the sea as He ruled them from the heavens. In this way, those who possessed the power to control the earth became civilized while those who were a part of it became savages and barbarians. The promise of such domain, however, came at a steep price. "And surely your blood of your lives will I require," the Father covenanted, "at the hand of every beast will I require it, and at the hand of man; at the hand of every man's brother will I require the life of man."[21]

The Crusades against the Muslim rulers of the Holy Land put such notions of space in motion and sparked important transformations in the medieval view of the Christian world and the seas that surrounded it. While abroad the nationalities of western and southern Europe projected a Christian identity, long-distance traveling and diplomacy, military strategy, and lines of supply required a kind of detailed navigational knowledge that the moralizing of the *mappae mundi* and the T/O maps could not provide. While the mapmakers of Christian Europe increasingly crafted exquisite depictions of their place at the navel of Christ's crucified body, sailors and navigators in Italy and Catalonia crafted an entirely different set of maps born of a faith all their own in currents, winds, and promontories. Their charts afforded detailed topographic knowledge and place names along the Mediterranean coast, measured and scaled distances by sea between points, and charted various features that were necessary to the successful navigation of the Mediterranean, Black, and Red Seas. Portolan maps, after the Italian word *portolano*, "a collection of written sailing directions," improved upon Ptolemy's struggles with proper projection and scale and offered a less theological, more commercial vision of the Mediterranean world. As one sailor from Genoa boasted, portolan charts were "the true description of the world of the cosmographer . . . from which frivolous tales have been removed."[22]

The portolan charts that were so useful for navigating the inland seas, however, were useless in opening the uncharted waters of the open Atlantic that lay beyond the Pillars of Heracles. With King Jão I's conquest of the Moroccan fortress Ceuta on the shore of North Africa in 1415, however, the Portuguese Crown began to gaze toward the open ocean for a way to circumvent the overland gold trade of the Maghreb that linked West Africa to the Mediterranean. The base at Ceuta emboldened the Portuguese, for their

possession of the town put them in direct contact with Tuareg traders working out of Fez and scattered outposts in the Moroccan interior where slaves
from Bilad al-Sudan—the land of the blacks—were purchased for service in
the homes and courts of Egypt, Iraq, and Turkey. In addition to knowledge of
the money to be made in trading West African slaves as well as ivory and gold,
Tuareg merchants gave the Portuguese a name for the place. Where Greeks
and Romans had discussed the sunburned Ethiops of Africa, the Portuguese
set their sights on "Gineus." Inspired by the Holy Father's promise to repay
one converted soul a hundred times over, Jão's son, Dom Henrique, pushed
his sailors past Madeira in 1414 to the Canary and Azores Islands, then to the
Cape Verdé Islands in 1444. A little more than a decade after Henrique's death,
a Lisbon merchant named Fernão Gomes reached the land called Guinea and
landed on a shore he named Costa da Mina where his crew sank a wooden
cross into the surf that fringed this antipodean land.[23]

The Africans who met the Christians and who enjoined them in various
trade and diplomatic relationships, of course, possessed their own notions
of how the world fit together and where the ocean belonged in the grander
scheme of things. Clothing, for example, mapped the world and carried the
cosmos into quotidian life. Yoruba-speaking women wore cloth the color of
the soil and of the dark clouds that brought rain to the earth while their counterparts in the kingdom of Kongo agreed that black cloth marked the power
to give life. Men across West Africa, however, wore white clothing; it evoked
purity, rain, semen, the sea, or death, to display their own complementary
powers and place in the world. Where black and white came together life
emerged. Before burying their ancestors, for example, Kongolese men put on
white cloths to mourn the dead while women smeared their faces and chests
with black dust to counter the power of death and to reconfirm their own
powers of life.[24]

Others expressed similar relationships through the symbol of the circle
and the cross that the Mississippians and early Europeans had known so well.
From the Gold Coast to the Kongo, people mapped the forces that structured
their lives as an equilateral cross in line with the sun. Its four arms traced
the fundamental relationships of the sun and the moon and the sky and the
earth. Each arm of the cross marked one of the four positions of the sun during the day. Its upper half expressed masculinity while the lower half invoked
femininity, and the horizontal line that bisected the cross, the *kalunga* line,
marked the horizon where the surface of the undersea world that was home
to powerful spirits met the sky and framed the world the people inhabited.

They would either draw the map on the ground or form a circle around a wooden cross and dance counter-clockwise around the figure in imitation of the sun that ordered their world. Women might invoke the moon in such dances by dancing in the opposite direction, and thus express the total system in which the people lived. The dances brought the land alive to send the spirits of the dead into the sea and onto the next stage of life, to offer aid in some way to the people of this world, or to reproduce the social and spatial order that made their lives meaningful. Others traced the patterns of the dances in their hair, shaving away all but enough to trace crosses or concentric circles on their scalps. Warriors too painted crosses on their bodies before going off either to defend their own sacred circle or to destroy the circle of another.[25]

The trade in enslaved people altered the cosmologies the people of West Africa used to explain their world and the ground began to reflect the new movements of people as they traveled out of the villages and into the cargo holds of the ships on the coast. People assigned the slavers a particular color, white, and a particular place of origin—the world of the dead. One German explorer of the Guinea Coast inquired as to why corpses were painted white before burial; he learned that their bodies would travel to a land of "Whites."[26] Some years later, at El Mina, a local woman identified a European who was visiting the post as the reincarnation of her husband. "She said it was me," the stunned visitor declared, "and I was her deceased husband, who had become white through death."[27] While in the Kongo two small white children from the land of the dead visited a young girl named Doña Beatriz Kimpa Vita. After her encounter with the twins Beatriz undertook training in the spiritual arts and captured people's attention when the spirit of St. Anthony possessed her in order to redeem the kingdom and to restore the balance of the Kongo world that had been lost to civil strife and slaving. Beatriz framed the world of the slave trade in reference to her land. Whereas her people, she revealed, had come from an ancestral fig tree named n'sanda, the Europeans who had beset the kingdom had crawled out of fuma, a white clay-like mineral associated with the watery realm of the dead.[28]

Before the slave trade, the spirits of the dead, people believed, descended a mountain and crossed the kalunga line into a body of water. After crossing the water, they reached the foot of another mountain where the soul passed into the afterworld. As slavers worked their way into BaKongo consciousness, however, they came to inhabit the bottom of the body of water and the lower slopes of the second mountain. By seizing the realm below the kalunga line that was home to the powerful forces of life and death, white spirits devoured

African flesh, cut off access to the afterlife, and circumscribed the power and reach of the ancestors. Such spirits broke the circle, set adrift the cross, and ruptured the lines of kinship that had made Kongo society meaningful and whole.[29] Adaptations to the presence of the slave trade were not, of course, limited to the Kongolese. Captives who passed through Ardrah in the Bight of Benin believed that their captors were fattening them in the pens for sale to cannibals. Growing up in Fante country, Ottobah Cugoano remembered being told as a child that "white people" ate Africans. Olaudah Equiano recalled upon boarding the slave ship that delivered him to the Americas, "I was now persuaded that I had gotten into a world of bad spirits, and that they were going to kill me." After fainting from fright, the young Equiano regained consciousness and asked his fellow captives "if we were not to be eaten by those white men with horrible looks, red faces, and loose hair [?]"[30]

Christopher Columbus made possible the commingling of the South's founding peoples as well as the clash of geographies that ensued. With the patronage of Isabella the Catholic, queen of Castile, and her husband King Fernando of Aragón, he carried Castile's expansionist impulses into the west, an unknown but wholly anticipated region that medieval cosmographers had associated with health, happiness, and paradise. Indeed, as Columbus tracked the expanses of the open Atlantic during the three voyages he made to the Indies, he thought himself closer and closer to a holy paradise that sat atop not the spherical earth of Aristotle and Ptolemy but one that was pear-shaped or, better yet, pendulous like a woman's breast. The cyclopes, cannibals, and other inversions of the natural order that had inhabited the antipodal lands since antiquity, however, were another matter altogether.[31] To his sovereigns, the "lovers and promoters of the Holy Christian Faith, and enemies of the false doctrines of Mahomet and of all idolatries and heresies," Columbus pledged fealty and promised to continue across the seas what the assault on the Alhambra had finished on land.[32] Whether with a bite of the pear or a grasp at the breast, Columbus promised to take ownership of a western paradise that medieval clerics had regarded as all but closed to any but the divine.

The great sailor navigated the western seas by dead reckoning, inferring what was not known—his actual position—from what was known—the speed at which he was moving and his ship's relationship to the path the sun traced in the sky. The rhumb lines, compass roses, and meridians of the portolan charts he and others used to ply the Mediterranean and the shores of western Africa were of no use in the open Atlantic, and the farther he sailed, the more his own mind determined the relationships of wind, sun, and water that bore him westward over the waters. The same system of navigation showed him his way through the worlds he entered in the Indies. Only, to locate himself on the ground, he looked not to the sky but to histories, geographies, medieval compilations, and his own memories to position what he had found in relationship to what he knew. Marco Polo had already named the land for Columbus who sought in vain Cathay, Quinsay, and Chipangu.[33] The dwellings he spied through his eyeglass reminded him of the tents Moorish soldiers pitched on their campaigns. Pliny the Elder explained for him why the trees he saw were so large while Ptolemy and Aristotle enabled him to correlate latitude and skin color. Pierre d'Ailly's 1483 compilation *Imago mundi* provided a T/O map that forced Columbus to reconcile what he saw with what the Bible taught, and a host of other authors who crowded his shelves prepared him to believe that beyond the island that came to be called Cuba, he would find, he wrote, "one-eyed men, and others, with snouts of dogs, who ate men."[34]

But dead reckoning could only suggest links between fixed objects and fluid positions. The navigator's most primitive craft could not weave new things and old referents into a meaningful order. Without the aid of a portolan chart to guide him, he simply could not take in the entirety of what he had seen. Just a few days after sighting trees unlike anything to be seen in the Mediterranean, Columbus confronted the limits of the world he had known. "But that I do not recognize them," he confided to his diary, "burdens me with the greatest sorrow in the world." Rather than yield to his own crisis of confidence, however, he made his own fate and his own world all the while believing that He had handed him both. Wherever his crews made landfall ringing axes felled trees, cross-cut saws hewed timbers, and carpenters assembled crosses to plant on the beaches as if to cower the forests, to bring order to the bays, rivers, and plains that opened before them, and to make real what they had imagined.[35]

The wooden crosses, Latin prayers, and linen flags that accompanied each ceremony of possession situated the places he saw within a mental map of dominion that Columbus revised every time he rounded a point or sounded a shoal. And the knowledge he sustained through the names he bestowed on the land bent the unfathomable origins of the place he had entered to the known genealogy of the Creation and the Crown that he served. As the days passed into weeks, though, the world he crafted moved farther and farther from what he might have read in Pliny or Aristotle, seen in the *mappae mundi* that hung on the walls of churches of Genoa, Lisbon, or Seville, or measured in the portolan charts that stopped short on the near shores of the Canaries.[36]

The people posed a particular challenge. He called them "Indios," a term that reflected his own erroneous assumption about where he was and who he was seeing. But the meanings he attached to the term as he navigated the island seas came to denote so much more than a people who inhabited the Indies. The edenic qualities the navigator attributed to the islands he surveyed suggested that Columbus wondered whether or not the Fall or the Flood had ever happened there. If they had not, the Indians were an antipodean people who had lived outside of time as he understood it. And if they had their innocence, their poverty, simplicity, and, ultimately, degradation made them ideal candidates for redemption before the One True Faith in vassalage to the Crowns of Castile and Aragón. As he reported to his sovereigns, the Indians were "fit to be ordered about and made to work, plant, and do everything else that may be needed, and build towns and be taught our customs," and, lastly, "to go about clothed."[37]

The men of Jamestown too sought to fashion a world on the other side of the sea that they could master, and their vision hewed close to Columbus's original line. The land's potential remained untapped for it had not been inhabited by, John Smith wrote, "industrious people" who could draw from the land both pleasure and profit. To begin to wrest the land from those he argued who "make so smal a benefit of their land," Smith initiated a number of claims. The crosses he and his men erected on river shores and by waterfalls extended the grip of the faith across the wide sea. If no cross was to be had they improvised and carved them into tree trunks or secreted notes or small brass crosses into hollow limbs and trunks to demonstrate to all who followed that "Englishmen had beene there."[38]

More than a century and a half later, another group of invaders expanded upon General James Oglethorpe's intent to dedicate the colony of Georgia to "a Christian, moral and industrious way of life." Sir Robert Montgomery, an early booster of Georgia, described the colony as "Paradise with all her virgin beauties." But the nubile garden did not belong to the people who had made her. Georgia was nothing less, Montgomery declared, than "our future Eden." To erase any doubts in the minds of his readers, he calculated that the new settlements occupied the same latitude as the Promised Land.[39] Even Oglethorpe remarked that the land Creek women farmed would "produce almost everything in wonderful Quantities with very little Culture."[40] Another visitor to Georgia went so far as to applaud the "spontaneous" wealth that sprung from the soil.[41] Abundant oak trees pointed colonizers toward champion land where they could produce raw silk, potash, flax, hemp, cattle, and fowl with little or no effort.[42]

The notion of paradise on the other side of the sea, however, was unsustainable and led to the importation of Africans to do the hard work associated with pulling a living out of the land. The captives who were crammed between decks on slave ships suffocated in the reek of vomit, feces, urine, and blood. Such poor men, women, and children, one ship captain wrote, had "a more dreadful apprehension of Barbados than we have of hell."[43] In addition to the horrible living conditions, inhumane treatment, poor food, and bad water, the passage severed their connections to the ancestors, to the spirits, and to the worlds they had made together. Captives on the slave ships looked on in horror as the slavers, wise to local notions that only intact bodies could make the journey below the water to the afterlife, knowingly mutilated some captives to cow the others into submission. Captives watched with horror as one ship's captain beheaded a man accused of killing a crewman and threw the body across the *kalunga* line into the ocean. Without his head the man had no chance of finding the afterworld where his ancestors awaited and with his death an entire family tree fell into the sea and sank to the bottom.[44]

But out of these early fragments comes a story that, while taking different turns depending on where the enslaved people were placed, followed a fairly common narrative. Enslaved people stumbled out of the holds at the end of social life and on the edge of death. Relationships that reached back to their homelands or that had been forged in the holds could come undone in the sales. The effort to reconstitute their former homes or the homes of their forebears took place almost immediately, however, and was an important part of their broader struggle to make new families and new communities under the worst of circumstances. The cycles of the moon had to be recalibrated for both planting and birthing, new seasons had to be overlaid atop old calendars, new medicines had to be fashioned from unfamiliar plants, and the screeches of owls and colors and patterns of snakes' skins had to be added to extant lists of omens. The Cooper river in South Carolina, for example, became home to a water spirit whose ability to read the future, alter the weather, and protect the people merited a number of gifts. On the bottoms of the pottery pieces that people threw into the river potters traced the circle and cross maps that both first people and enslaved people shared as a basic cosmological referent and that brought the *kalunga* line to the plantations of the South. People left similar pots filled with food in the graveyards that were adjacent to their villages. The water-borne spirits that relied upon such gifts to sustain them were thereby able to remain in the land and, within a generation, to transform the land of death into a land of life for the enslaved.[45]

But this land of life was a hard place and the great cosmic endpoints of the Africans' cosmos continued to inform their lives and the world they made together. In 1710 an enslaved man who lived in Goose Creek parish, South Carolina, claimed to have seen sin where before he had seen only slavery, and he foretold a day of judgment. To the man who owned him he prophesied that "a dismal time" was coming and that "the Moon would be turned into Blood, and there would be death and darkness." The owner called in an Anglican minister to give counsel while fleet feet and colorful pettiaugers carried up the paths and waterways of the countryside word that an angel had come and spoken to a man, to one of them, and that the angel had revealed to him a book and would raise fires to signal the approach of the end. In his doom, however, lay the creation of something new, a world reserved for the righteous. In some respects, the man's creed fit within the millennial traditions of Christianity, but the new place he envisioned also reached back to the towns and homes of both Africa and the first nations where people associated the moon with blood, women, the sea, chaos, and the creation of new life.[46]

Far from simply representing discontent with slavery, such conspiracies and revolts actually represented the culmination of the enslaved people's abilities to reconstruct out of their received African practices and the exigencies of their Atlantic world a place that had meaning and purpose for them. And that world was not the land of Shem nor was it a plane that held the middle ground between the Sun and the Earth. It was a hell inhabited by white cannibals who had seized control of the sea that the enslaved people made humane, to the best of their ability, by creating places for themselves in their homes, in their markets, and on the paths that connected them within a broader space of coercion, servitude, and inhumanity. Clearly the revelation of the blood moon that the Goose Creek man had seen was widespread and a regular feature of the enslaved people's cosmology which parents and preachers handed down to the generations that followed.

When the prophecy of the blood moon reached the Cherokees, worlds began to overlap and merge. In 1751 a trader named Richard Smith reported to South Carolina officials that "some Negroes" had told Old Warrior of Keowee that there were far more enslaved people than free people in South Carolina.

The logic of the situation, the men explained, was clear. "For the sake of lib-erty," they argued, the Cherokees should join them in plotting against the colony. The Carolinians caught one of the ringleaders, Phillip John, who had offered the Cherokees the role of the sword wielded by avenging angels. "The Indians," he informed his captors, "were to be concerned in the extermina-tion of the white people from the face of this earth." Did John believe, as had his forebears, that white people belonged at the bottom of the sea? The plot stunned the colony, especially when the invaders learned that the Cherokees planned to hold off until the maize was in before sending warriors to "assist in killing all the Buckraas."[47]

Eight years later Philip John made trouble again and was, Governor William Lyttelton wrote to his superiors in London, "tried whip'd & branded for endeavouring to stir up sedition among the Negroes." John preached that the end was nigh, and he drew a *kalunga* line across Carolina and placed "the white people" under the ground where the dead dwelled. A sword he saw would slaughter the cannibals and shine "with their Blood." "There should be no more White Kings, Governors or great Men," he promised, "but the Negros shou'd live happily & have laws of their own." Even being whipped and burned did not stop John from spreading his gospel as his vision shot through the backstreets and the urban markets and took its place in the culture of slavery.[48]

The links John drew between African cosmology and the place of white spirits within it were not lost to the first people either. Rappahanocks had called the men who had come to found Virginia "strangers," people who had "come from under the world, to take their world from them."[49] Powhatan cosmographers shared similar conceptions of the strangers that placed their origins in the world of water and chaos. After John Smith's capture during a foray into the forest a party of warriors brought him back to a town where a party of warriors enclosed him in a house. Seven men entered the dwelling one morning painted in the colors of their world, red for war and blood, black for death, and white for life and peace. Around the fire that blazed in the cen-ter of the floor, its smoke trailing out of a hole in the ceiling up to the Sun in the sky, they danced, shook their rattles, and sang, and at the end of the song one of them sifted between his fingers a line of ground maize with which he traced a circle around the fire. Beyond the circle of cultivation represented by the pale yellow grains of meal, the dancers laid concentric circles of whole kernels of maize, perhaps to stand for the fields that surrounded their towns or the towns that comprised their confederacy. The farther the mapmakers got from the fire, however, the less domesticated their world became, and they scattered small sticks amongst the kernels to connote the forests that bounded their world and that had also been the first thing the Company had felled in the construction of their fort.[50]

"They imagined the world to be flat and round," Smith concluded from the ceremony, ". . . and they in the middest." But his own conception of his own people's place was not so different. When the leader Opechancanough inquired after Smith about his ivory compass, Smith obliged him by drawing on an intellectual tradition that reached back to Pliny the Elder, Aristotle, and even old Thales of Miletus. The sun, Smith explained, ordered the universe and marked the predictable rhythms of time. It chased the moon in an endless cycle of days. If he understood Smith, Opechancanough probably nodded in agreement. Against the immutability of the sun's celestial order, Smith went on, planets embodied change, mortality, and imperfection because of the erratic movements they followed through the sky. To emphasize the point, Smith traced their imperfect orbits across the sky with his finger, and Opechancanough followed. Each planet in Smith's universe brought a unique mixture of heat, cold, dryness, and moisture to bear on the earth, which when combined with air, fire, soil, and water produced the variability of human life, and he related how the globe was covered with a variety of nations and people of different colors all separated by the sea.[51]

The concepts of space and place enacted by the dancers who visited Smith that morning in Pamaunk or demonstrated by Smith in the conversation around his compass each made room for other kinds of people, albeit in different ways and for different reasons. To the dancers, Smith had a place in their world sitting on the edge of their map by the shores of the sea while, for Smith, the Powhatans and the English were bound to one another as antipodeans, forever locked in cosmological opposition across an ocean of water and a sea of civilization. The leaders of a first nation who met Oglethorpe in 1735, like those who had met Smith, pinned the newcomers' origins in the sea. To the *nokfilaki*, "people of the ocean foam," a group known as the Kasihtas mapped their world and instructed the English as to their proper place in it. They had crawled from out of a hole in the ground, they explained, a mother cave, the source of the world's water, and had fought their way across many red rivers to arrive at their present home. While offering the Englishman a white token of peace to mark the opening of a clear bright path between the two peoples, they, at the same time, drew Oglethorpe and his followers into their own landscape so that they could share the same world. In pointing out to the Georgians how best to conduct themselves in this new relationship, the chief reminded Oglethorpe that in the past his people had never shirked from setting aside their white feathers when outsiders violated the balance of their relationship. At such times, the people had, the men informed Oglethorpe, painted their hatchets red and marched to war down crooked paths against former friends who, through their ungrateful behavior, had shown they truly were people from under the world, from beneath the sea.[52]

Obtaining supplies of maize, beans, and venison required ongoing efforts at cultivating and maintaining relationships. Gift giving, smoking of the calumet, and pledging friendship enabled Pierre Le Moyne, Sieur d'Iberville, to both integrate La Louisiane into broader regional networks of power and to situate first Biloxi and then New Orleans as important nodes in those networks. But it took practice and effort to make it happen. Under the deer moon, for example, the first moon of their calendar, a real and true people known as the Natchez welcomed Iberville to their country. The body of their leader, the Great Sun, mapped his people's world in the blue tattoos of the sun and serpents that covered his arms, legs, and chest. As a group of men bore the Sun to meet Iberville, the visitors understood the degree to which land and power fused in the body and the lineage of the man before him. The living map welcomed Iberville to his world with gifts, a white cross to evoke the sun's power and the sanctity of the chief's place, and a pearl, an object from the watery world of the sea, that situated the explorers in the same in-between place that his people called home.[53]

A sacred fire burned in the temple that sat atop a mound adjacent to the Great Sun's home. Inside lay the cane boxes that held the bones of the deceased Suns that had preceded him, tying his family's line to the original Mother, the earth. Wooden eagles perched on the roof, watching the world on behalf of the sky. Outside of the temple, the chief performed his own sense of place and space. The architecture of his home and the mound, his body's markings, and the cross and the pearl came to life as each morning he shouted to the west, lit his pipe, and blew smoke to the four points of the cross. His visitors shared in the pipe ceremony letting their clear voices fly into the air to take wing toward the west, signaling their own concurrence, if for only a moment, in the poetics of his place and space, his in-between. When the Great Sun instructed his guests to blow smoke to the sky, the earth, and, lastly, the horizon that separated the two and that marked the in-between world where he and his guests lived, he held out the promise that they too could come out of the water and belong to this world.[54]

The sense of belonging that each founding people extended to the other whether it was in chains, as cannibals, or at the stem of a pipe was rooted in each people's notion of the world they inhabited. Without understanding the different cultural constructions of, in a narrow sense, the Atlantic Ocean, or, in a broader sense, the Atlantic World, it is impossible to understand how such cultures operated in space and produced the kinds of societies they did. Moreover, if we discount the meaning of different cultural constructions of past spaces then we discount as well the depth of their meaning. Asserting that the Atlantic Ocean is a natural fact is, then, more than just another instance of proclaiming the inert horizontality that Natter and Jones identified. It is a cultural position not unlike that taken by the Genoese merchant who characterized portolan maps as the truth minus the frivolous tales. When we consider the ocean to be a fact, then we risk characterizing water serpents, the *kalunga* line, and visions of Eden as also frivolous when they should instead be seen as foundational to the creation of the Atlantic World. When Brathwaite's stone skipped across the water's surface it left widening circles that then reached the limits of their energy, faded, and disappeared. The movement in the acts of creation he suggested in his poem "Calypso" was as integral to the making of places as they were to the making of history, and if we lose our sense of balance between the past and its places, then we risk silencing the voices that can tell us about the making of the Atlantic World. If we recognize the formation of Atlantic World societies in the processes of contact and colonization then we must also recognize the disparate geographies which brought that world into being as truths of their own kind.

## Notes

1. The author would like to thank Professor Bernard Bailyn and the members of the Atlantic History Seminar meeting at Harvard University for their support and comments and Mary Rita Holland for her musely advice.
2. Federico Garcia Lorca, *A Season in Granada* (1998), 119.
3. Edward Kamau Brathwaite, "Calypso," in *The Arrivants* (1973), 48; Christopher Norris, *Language, Logic, and Epistemology* (2004), 4–9, 150, 181; Ivana Markova, *Dialogicality and Social Representation* (2003), 82; and Lisa M. Dolling, "Dialogue as Praxis: Philosophical Hermeneutics, Historical Epistemology, and Truth" (2003), 38–40.
4. David Armitage and Michael J. Braddick, "Introduction" (2002), 1.
5. Wolfgang Natter and John Paul Jones III, "Signposts toward a Poststructuralist Geography" (1993), 167.

6.  Fred R. Myers, *Pintupi Self* (1986), 11; Joël Bonnemaison, *The Tree and the Canoe* (1994), 105; Carola Lentz and Hans-Jürgen Sturm, "Of Trees and Earth Shrines: An Interdisciplinary Approach to Settlement Histories in the West African Savanna," *History in Africa* (2001), 145; and Barry Cunliffe, *Facing the Ocean* (2001), ch. 1.

7.  Bernard Cohn, *An Anthropologist among the Historians and Other Essays* (1987), 43.

8.  Edward S. Casey, "How to Get from Space to Place in a Fairly Short Stretch of Time: Phenomenological Prolegomena" (1996), 27.

9.  J. G. A. Pocock, "British History: A Plea for a New Subject," *Journal of Modern History* (1975), 616.

10. Édouard Glissant, *Introduction à une poétique du divers* (1995); Raymond Relouzat, *Tradition orale et imaginaire créole* (1998); Rex Nettleford, "The Caribbean: Crossroads of the Americas" (1994), 8; and Norris, *Language, Logic, and Epistemology*, 186.

11. Bernard Bailyn, *Atlantic History* (2005), 61; Pocock, "British History," 605; David Baker and Willy Maley, "An Uncertain Union (A Dialogue)" (2004), 11; and Paul Gilroy, *The Black Atlantic* (1993), 15.

12. Jerald T. Milanich, *Archaeology of Precolumbian Florida* (1994), 72–73.

13. Charles Hudson, *The Southeastern Indians* (1976), 67–68.

14. Frankie Snow, "Swift Creek Design Investigations: The Hartford Case" (1998), 76–78; Karl T. Steinem, "Kolomoki and the Development of Sociopolitical Organization on the Gulf Coastal Plain" (1998), 188; David G. Anderson, "Swift Creek in Regional Perspective" (1998), 296–97; Richard Jefferies, "The Swift Creek Site and Woodland Platform Mounds in the Southeastern United States" (1994), 82; Vernon James Knight, "Feasting and the Emergence of Platform Mound Ceremonialism in Eastern North America" (2001), 311–21.

15. Claudine Payne and John F. Scarry, "Town Structure at the Edge of the Mississippian World" (1998), 30, 43–46; and Milanich, *Precolumbian Florida*, 355.

16. Marija Gimbutas, *The Goddesses and Gods of Old Europe* (1982), 91–112; Catherine Delano Smith, "Cartography in the Prehistoric Period in the Old World: Europe, the Middle East, and North Africa" (1987), 87–91; R. V. Tooley, *Maps and Map-Makers* (1987), 3; Karen Louise Jolly, *Popular Religion in Late Saxon England* (1996), 27–28; and Alasdair Whittle, *Neolithic Europe* (1985), 235.

17. J. B. Harley and David Woodward, "The Foundations of Theoretical Cartography in Archaic and Classical Greece" (1987), I, 134–44; Aristotle, *The Complete Works of Aristotle*, ed. Jonathan Barnes (1984), vol. 1: "On the Heavens," book 1, ch. 9, 461–63, book 2, ch. 4, 473, book 2, ch. 11, 480; "On the Universe," ch. 3, 628.

18. Harley and Woodward, "The Foundations of Theoretical Cartography," 136, 145; Harley and Woodward, "Greek Cartography in the Early Roman World" (1987), I, 168–69; Pliny the Elder, *The Natural History of Pliny the Elder*, trans. John Bostock and H. T. Riley, 2 vols. (1890, 1893), 1: book 2, ch. 68, 111 and ch. 80, 110–11 from which the quote is taken; and ibid., 2: book 7, ch. 1, 118.

19. John B. Friedman, *The Monstrous Races in Medieval Art and Thought* (1981), 7; Seymour Phillips, "The Outer World of the European Middle Ages" (1994), 46; Julius

Solinus, *The Excellent and Pleasant Worke of Julius Solinus Polyhistor* (1587), chs. 42, 43; William Cohen, *The French Encounter with Africans* (1980), 5; Cosmas Indicopleustés, *Topographie chreìtiennee* (1968), vol. 1, book, 1, 284; and Bartholemew Anglicus, *Medieval Lore*, ed. Robert Steele (1893), 75.

20. Phillips, "The Outer World of the European Middle Ages," 28–29, 44–45; Isidore de Séville, *Étymologies*, ed. and trans. Marc Reydellet (1984), book 9, 42; Indicopleustés, *Topographie*, book 2, ch. 24, 328–30; Gustav Jahoda, *Images of Savages* (1999), 26–29; Cohen, *French Encounter with Africans*, 9; and Anglicus, *Medieval Lore*, 75.

21. Woodward, "Medieval *Mappaemundi*" (1987), I, 334–41; Evelyn Edson, *Mapping Time and Space* (1999), 4–17; Rhonda Lemke Sanford, *Maps and Memory in Early Modern England* (2002), 5–6; Norman Joseph William Thrower, *Maps & Civilization* (1996), 42; John Hale, *The Civilization of Europe in the Renaissance* (1993), 15; Frank Lestringant, *Mapping the Renaissance World* (1994), 23; Anthony Pagden, *European Encounters with the New World* (1993), 6; and Genesis 9:5, *King James Bible*.

22. David Woodward, "Reality, Symbolism, Time and Space in Medieval World Maps," in *Annals of the Association of American Geographers* (1985), 510–15; Joyce E. Chaplin, "Race" (2002), 158; Woodward, "Medieval *Mappaemundi*," 340–41; Tooley, *Maps and Map-Makers*, 10–15; and Tony Campbell, "Portolan Charts from the Late Thirteenth Century to 1500," *History of Cartography* (1987), 371–75 and, as quoted, 372.

23. J. D. Fage with William Torduff, *A History of Africa*, 4th ed. (2002), 218–36; Thomas Astley, "The First Voyage of the Portugueze to the East Indies," in *A New General Collection of Voyages and Travels*, 4 vols. (1968), I, 10–12; E. Savage, "Berbers and Blacks: Ibadi Slave Traffic in Eighth Century North Africa," *Journal of African History* (1992), 351–53; A. Ryder, *Benin and the Europeans, 1485–1897* (1969), 24; Jerry Brotton, *Trading Territories* (1998), 58–63; and Ivor Wilks, "Wangara, Akan, and Portuguese in the Fifteenth and Sixteenth Centuries. I. The Matter of Bitu," *Journal of African History* (1982), 335.

24. Elisha P. Renne, *Cloth That Does Not Die* (1995), 3–11, 23–25, 38, 42–43, 69; Philip D. Curtain, "The Lure of Bambuk Gold," *Journal of African History* (1972), 624; Astley, "The Kingdoms of Koto and Popo," in *New General Collection*, III, 6; John K. Thornton, *The Kongolese Saint Anthony* (1998), 161; Robin Law, "Problems of Plagiarism, Harmonization and Misunderstanding in Contemporary European Sources: Early (Pre-1680s) Sources for the 'Slave Coast' of West Africa," *Paideuma* (1987), 347–48; Anne Hilton, *The Kingdom of Kongo* (1985), 10; quote from Astley, "The Third Voyage of the Sieur Brüe up the Sanaga, Made in the Year 1715," *New General Collection*, II, 129; and Astley, "An Account of the Jalofs," in ibid., 255–60.

25. B. W. Hodder and U. I. Ukwu, *Markets in West Africa* (1969), 128; Michael A. Gomez, *Exchanging Our Country Marks* (1998), 148–49; Sterling Stuckey, *Slave Culture* (1987), 11–14; Jean Barbot, *Barbot on Guinea*, eds., P. E. H. Hair, Adam Jones, and Robin Law (1992), II, 494; and Pieter de Marees, *Descriptions and Historical Account of the Gold Kingdom of Guinea (1602)*, eds. and trans. Adam Jones and Albert von Dantzig (1987), 89.

26. Adam Jones, ed., 'Andreas Josua Ulsheimer's Voyage of 1603–4,' "German Sources for West African History, 1599–1669," *Studien zur Kulturkunde* (1983), 31.

27. Michael Hemmersam's Description of the Gold Coast 1639–45,' in ibid., 104.

28. Wyatt MacGaffey, "The Cultural Roots of Kongo Prophetism," *History of Religion* (1977), 183–87; Thornton, *Kongolese Saint Anthony*, 26–27, 110–11.

29. Gomez, *Exchanging Our Country Marks*, 135–47.

30. Barbot, *Barbot on Guinea*, II, 639; Ottobah Cuguono, "Thoughts and Sentiments of the Evil and Wicked Traffic of the Slavery and Commerce of the Human Species" (1971), 150; Olaudah Equiano, *The Life of Olaudah Equiano, or Gustavus Vassa the African Written by Himself*, ed. Paul Edwards (1988), 22.

31. Mary W. Helms, "Long-Distance Contacts, Elite Aspirations, and the Age of Discovery in Cosmological Context" (1992), 167–69.

32. Christopher Columbus, *The Diario of Christopher Columbus's First Voyage to America, 1492–1493*, trans. Oliver Dunn and James E. Kelley, Jr. (1989), 19; David J. Weber, *The Spanish Frontier in North America* (1992), 20; Anne McLintock, *Imperial Leather* (1995), 21–22; Margarita Zamora, *Reading Columbus* (1993), 143–44, 174.

33. Robert Finley, *The Accidental Indies* (2000), 60–61; Phillips, "The Outer World of the European Middle Ages," 25.

34. Columbus, *Diario*, 69, 91–93, 145, quote on 133; Ashis Nandy, Zia Sardar, and Merryl Wyn Davies, *Barbaric Others* (1993), 53; Pagden, *European Encounters with the New World*, 47–48; Peter Mason, *Deconstructing America* (1990), 18.

35. Alfred W. Crosby, *The Columbian Exchange* (1972), 9; Miguel Angel Ledero Quesada, "Spain, circa 1492: Social Values and Structures" in Stuart Schwartz, ed., *Implicit Understandings*, 98–100; McClintock, *Imperial Leather*, 24; Zamora, *Reading Columbus*, 176; Columbus, *Diario*, 111,157.

36. Columbus, *Diario*, 235; Mclintock, *Imperial Leather*, 28; Jamaica Kincaid, *My Garden (Book)* (1999), 155; and Mason, *Deconstructing America*, 17.

37. Robert F. Berkhofer, Jr., *The White Man's Indian* (1979), 3; Ter Ellington, *The Myth of the Noble Savage* (2001), 12; Johannes Fabian, *Time and the Other* (1983); Columbus, *Diario*, 235–37.

38. John Smith, "A Map of Virginia. With a Description of the Countrey, the Commodities, People, Government and Religion," *Complete Works of Captain John Smith*, ed. Philip L. Barbour (1986), I, 144, 160; Smith, "The Generall Historie of Virginia, New-England, and the Summer Isles (1624)," in ibid., II, 172; and Smith, "A True Relation," in ibid., I, 33–35.

39. As quoted in Betty Wood, *Slavery in Colonial Georgia, 1730–1775* (1984), 5–7; Sir Robert Montgomery, "A Discourse Concerning the Design'd Establishment of a New Colony to the South of Carolina in the most Delightful Country of the Universe (1717)" (1972), 5–8.

40. James Oglethorpe, "A New and Accurate Account of the Province of South Carolina and Georgia (1732)," in *Most Delightful Country*, 124.

41. Montgomery, "A Discourse Concerning the Design'd Establishment of a New Colony," 15.

42. Oglethorpe, "A New and Accurate Account of the Province of South Carolina," 124; Thomas Nairne, "A Letter from South Carolina (London, 1710)" (1989), 37; Edward Bland, "The Discovery of New Britaine (1650)" (1911), 9–12.

43. Gomez, *Exchanging Our Country Marks*, as quoted, 159.

44. Voyage of the Hannibal, 1693–1694," in Elizabeth Donnan, ed., *Documents Illustrative of the History of the Slave Trade to America* (1930), I, 403–6; William Snelgrave, *A New Account of Some Parts of Guinea and the Slave-Trade (1734)* (1971), 184; and William D. Piersen, "White Cannibals, Black Martyrs: Fear, Depression, and Religious Faith as Causes of Suicide among Slaves," *Journal of Negro History* (1977), 147–59.

45. Leland Ferguson, *Uncommon Ground* (1992), 10–16, 26, 110–12; Ferguson, "'The Cross Is a Magic Sign': Marks on Eighteenth-Century Bowls from South Carolina" (1999), 118–19; Patricia Samford, "The Archaeology of African-American Slavery and Material Culture," *William and Mary Quarterly* (1996), 102–5.

46. Morgan, *Slave Counterpoint*, 456; and Francis Le Jau to the Secretary, 1 February 1710, in Frank J. Klingberg, ed., *The Carolina Chronicle of Dr. Francis Le Jau, 1706–1717* (1956), 70.

47. Deposition of Richard Smith, 12 July 1751, in William L. McDowell Jr., ed., *Colonial Records of South Carolina* (1958), I, 103, and, as quoted, Thomas Hatley, *The Dividing Paths* (1993), 111–12.

48. William Lyttelton to the Board of Trade, 1 September 1759, box 10, William Lyttelton Papers, William L. Clements Library, University of Michigan, Ann Arbor, Mich.

49. Smith, "Generall Historie," 172–78; and Martin D. Gallivan, *James River Chiefdoms* (2003), xi.

50. Smith, "True Relation," 59; Smith, "Generall Historie," 149–50; Frederick Gleach, *Powhatan's World and Colonial Virginia* (1997), 109–21; and Gregory A. Waselkov, "Indian Maps of the Colonial Southeast: Archaeological Implications and Prospects" (1998), 209–10.

51. Smith, "Generall Historie," 147; Smith, "True Relation," 47; Joyce E. Chaplin, *Subject Matter* (2001), 120–24; and Lestringant, *Mapping the Renaissance World*, 21.

52. Charles M. Hudson, *Conversations with the High Priest of Coosa* (2003), 9; Claudio Saunt, *A New Order of Things* (1999), 14–17.

53. Pierre Le Moyne, Sieur d'Iberville, *Iberville's Gulf Journals*, trans. and ed. Richebourg Gaillard McWilliams (1981), 125; Dumont du Montigny, *Memoires historiques sur la Louisiane* (1753), I, 139; and Jean-Baptiste Bénard de la Harpe, *Journal historique du l'établissement des Français á la Louisiane* (1831), 28.

54. Pierre-François-Xavier de Charlevoix, *Journal d'un voyage fait par ordre du roi dans l'Amerique Septentrionale* (1994), II, 800–815; Antoine Simon Le Page du Pratz, *Histoire de la Louisiane* (1758), III, 15–18; Montigny, *Memoires historiques*, 159–60; and Bénard de la Harpe, *Journal historique*, 29.

# Works Cited

Anderson, David G. 1998. "Swift Creek in Regional Perspective." In *A World Engraved: Archaeology of the Swift Creek Culture*. Eds. Mark Williams and Daniel T. Elliott. Tuscaloosa: University of Alabama Press, 274–300.

Anglicus, Bartholemew. 1893. *Medieval Lore: An Epitome of the Science, Geography, Animal and Plant Folk-Lore and Myth of the Middle Ages*. Ed. Robert Steele. London: Elliot Stock.

Anonymous Plantation Diary. ca 1820. Mississippi Department of Archives and History, Jackson, Mississippi.

Aristotle. 1984. *The Complete Works of Aristotle: The Revised Oxford Translation*. Ed. Jonathan Barnes. 2 vols. Princeton: Princeton University Press.

Armitage, David and Michael J. Braddick. 2002. "Introduction." In *The British Atlantic World, 1500–1800*. Eds. David Armitage and Michael J. Braddick. New York: Palgrave, 1–10.

Astley, Thomas, ed. 1968. *A New General Collection of Voyages and Travels Consisting of the Most Esteemed Relations Which Have Been Hitherto Published in Any Language*. 4 vols. London: Frank Cass and Company Limited.

Bailyn, Bernard. 2005. *Atlantic History: Concept and Contours*. Cambridge, MA: Harvard University Press.

Baker, David and Willy Maley. 2004. "An Uncertain Union (A Dialogue)." In *Archipelagic Identities: Literature and Identity in the Atlantic Archipelago, 1550–1800*. Eds. Philip Schwyzer and Simon Mealor. Burlington, VT: Ashgate, 8–24.

Barbot, Jean. 1992. *Barbot on Guinea: The Writings of Jean Barbot on West Africa, 1678–1712*. 2 vols. Eds. P. E. H. Hair, Adam Jones, and Robin Law. London: Hakluyt Society.

Bascom, William R. 1951. "Yoruba Food." *Africa* 21.4: 41–53.

Berkhofer, Robert F., Jr. 1979. *The White Man's Indian: Images of the American Indian from Columbus to the Present*. New York: Vintage Books.

Bénard de la Harpe, Jean-Baptiste. 1831. *Journal historique du l'établissement des Français á la Louisiane*. New Orleans, LA.: A. L. Boimare.

Bland, Edward. 1911. "The Discovery of New Britaine (1650)." In *Narratives of Early Carolina 1650–1708*. Ed. Alexander S. Salley. New York: Charles Scribner's Sons, 1–19.

Bonnemaison, Joël. 1994. *The Tree and the Canoe: History and Ethnogeography of Tanna*. Trans. Josée Pénot-Demetry. Honolulu: University of Hawaii Press.

Brathwaite, Edward Kamau. 1973. "Calypso." In *The Arrivants: A New World Trilogy*. Oxford: Oxford University Press.

Brotton, Jerry. 1998. *Trading Territories: Mapping in the Early Modern World*. Ithaca, NY: Cornell University Press.

Campbell, Tony. 1987. "Portolan Charts from the Late Thirteenth Century to 1500." In *History of Cartography: Volume 1: Cartography in Prehistoric, Ancient and Medieval Europe and the Mediterranean*. Eds. J. B. Harley and David Woodward. Chicago: University of Chicago Press, 371–463.

Casey, Edward S. 1996. "How to Get from Space to Place in a Fairly Short Stretch of Time: Phenomenological Prolegomena." In *Senses of Place*. Eds. Steven Feld and Keith H. Basso. Santa Fe, NM: School of American Research Press, 13–52.

Catesby, Mark. 1731. *The Natural History of Carolina, Florida and the Bahama Islands*, 2 vols. London: Benjamin White.

Chaplin, Joyce E. 2001. *Subject Matter: Technology, the Body, and Science on the Anglo-American Frontier, 1500–1676*. Cambridge, MA: Harvard University Press.

———. 2002. "Race." In *The British Atlantic World, 1500–1800*. Eds. David Armitage and Michael J. Braddick. New York: Palgrave, 154–72.

Charlevoix, Pierre-François-Xavier de. 1994. *Journal d'un voyage fait par ordre du roi dans l'Amerique Septentrionale*, 2 vols. Montréal, Canada: Les Presses de l'Université de Montréal.

Cohen, William. 1980. *The French Encounter with Africans: White Response to Blacks, 1530–1880*. Bloomington: Indiana University Press.

Cohn, Bernard. 1987. *An Anthropologist among the Historians and Other Essays*. Delhi, India: Oxford University Press.

Columbus, Christopher. 1989. *The Diario of Christopher Columbus's First Voyage to America, 1492–1493*. Trans. Oliver Dunn and James E. Kelley, Jr. Norman: University of Oklahoma Press.

Cosmas, Indicopleustés. 1968. *Topographie chreìtiennee*. Trans. Wanda Wolska-Conus. 2 vols. Paris, France: Éditions de Cerf.

Covington, Levin. ca. 1820. Levin Covington Diary. Mississippi Department of Archives and History, Jackson, Mississippi.

Crosby, Alfred W. 1972. *The Columbian Exchange: Biological and Cultural Consequences of 1492*. Westport, CT: Greenwood Publishing Co.

Cuguono, Ottobah. 1971. "Thoughts and Sentiments of the Evil and Wicked Traffic of the Slavery and Commerce of the Human Species." In *Three Black Writers in Eighteenth Century England*. Eds. Francis D. Adams and Barry Sanders. Belmont, CA: Wadsworth Publishing Company, Inc., 125–58.

Cunliffe, Barry. 2001. *Facing the Ocean: The Atlantic and Its People, 8000 BC–AD 1500*. Oxford: Oxford University Press.

Curtain, Philip D. 1972. "The Lure of Bambuk Gold." *Journal of African History* 13.4: 623–31.

Dolling, Lisa M. 2003. "Dialogue as Praxis: Philosophical Hermeneutics, Historical Epistemology, and Truth." In *Constructivism and Practice: Toward a Historical Epistemology*. Ed. Carol C. Gould. New York: Rowman and Littlefield, 8–40.

Donnan, Elizabeth, ed. 1930. *Documents Illustrative of the History of the Slave Trade to America*. Vol. 1, *1441–1700*. Washington, D.C.: Carnegie Institution of Washington.

Dumont du Montigny. 1753. *Memoires historiques sur la Louisiane*, 2 vols. Paris, France: C. J. B. Bauche.

Edson, Evelyn. 1999. *Mapping Time and Space: How Medieval Mapmakers Viewed Their World*. London: British Library.

Ellington, Ter. 2001. *The Myth of the Noble Savage*. Berkeley: University of California Press.

Equiano, Olaudah. 1988. *The Life of Olaudah Equiano, or Gustavus Vassa the African Written by Himself*. Ed. Paul Edwards. Essex, Great Britain: Longman.

Fabian, Johannes. 1983. *Time and the Other: How Anthropology Makes Its Object*. New York: Columbia University Press.

Fage, J. D., with William Torduff. 2002. *A History of Africa*. 4th ed. New York: Routledge.

Ferguson, Leland. 1992. *Uncommon Ground: Archaeology and Early African America, 1650–1800*. Washington, D.C.: Smithsonian Institution Press.

———. 1999. "'The Cross Is a Magic Sign': Marks on Eighteenth-Century Bowls from South Carolina." In *"I Too Am America": Archaeological Studies of African-American Life*. Ed. Theresa A. Singleton. Charlottesville: University Press of Virginia, 116–30.

Finley, Robert. 2000. *The Accidental Indies*. Montréal, Canada: McGill-Queen's University Press.

Friedman, John B. 1981. *The Monstrous Races in Medieval Art and Thought*. Cambridge, MA: Harvard University Press.

Gallivan, Martin D. 2003. *James River Chiefdoms*. Lincoln: University of Nebraska Press.

Gilroy, Paul. 1993. *The Black Atlantic: Modernity and Double Consciousness*. London: Verso.

Gimbutas, Marija. 1982. *The Goddesses and Gods of Old Europe: Myths and Cult Images*. London: Thames & Hudson, Ltd.

Gleach, Frederick. 1997. *Powhatan's World and Colonial Virginia*. Lincoln: University of Nebraska Press.

Glissant, Édouard. 1995. *Introduction à une poétique du divers*. Montréal, Canada: Presses de l'Université de Montréal.

Gomez, Michael A. 1998. *Exchanging Our Country Marks: The Transformation of African Identities in the Colonial and Antebellum South*. Chapel Hill: University of North Carolina Press.

Hale, John. 1993. *The Civilization of Europe in the Renaissance*. London: Fontana Press.

Harley, J. B. and David Woodward. 1987. "The Foundations of Theoretical Cartography in Archaic and Classical Greece." In *History of Cartography: Volume 1: Cartography in Prehistoric, Ancient and Medieval Europe and the Mediterranean*. Eds. J. B. Harley and David Woodward. Chicago: University of Chicago Press, 134–45.

———. 1987. "Greek Cartography in the Early Roman World." In *History of Cartography: Volume 1: Cartography in Prehistoric, Ancient and Medieval Europe and the Mediterranean*. Eds. J. B. Harley and David Woodward. Chicago: University of Chicago Press, 168–69.

Hatley, Thomas. 1993. *The Dividing Paths: Cherokees and South Carolinians through the Era of Revolution*. New York: Oxford University Press.

Helms, Mary W. 1992. "Long-Distance Contacts, Elite Aspirations, and the Age of Discovery in Cosmological Context." In *Resources, Power, and Interregional Interaction*. Eds. Edward M. Schortman and Patricia A. Urban. New York: Plenum Press, 167–69.

Hemmersam, Michael. 1983. 'Michael Hemmersam's Description of the Gold Coast 1639–45.' In "German Sources for West African History 1599–1669." Ed. Adam Jones. *Studien zur Kulturkunde* 66: 97–133.

Hilton, Anne. 1985. *The Kingdom of Kongo*. Oxford: Clarendon Press.

Hodder, B. W. and U. I. Ukwu. 1969. *Markets in West Africa: Studies of Markets and Trade among the Yoruba and Ibo*. Ibadan, Nigeria: Ibadan University Press.

Hudson, Charles M. 1976. *The Southeastern Indians*. Knoxville: University of Tennessee Press.

———. 2003. *Conversations with the High Priest of Coosa*. Chapel Hill: University of North Carolina Press.

Jahoda, Gustav. 1999. *Images of Savages: Ancient Roots of Modern Prejudice in Western Culture*. London: Routledge.

Jefferies, Richard. 1994. "Swift Creek Site and Woodland Platform Mounds in the Southeastern United States." In *Ocmulgee Archaeology, 1936–1986*. Ed. David J. Halley. Athens: University of Georgia Press, 71–83.

Jolly, Karen Louise. 1996. *Popular Religion in Late Saxon England: Elf Charms in Context*. Chapel Hill: University of North Carolina Press.

Kincaid, Jamaica. 1999. *My Garden (Book)*. New York: Farrar Strauss Giroux.

Knight, Vernon James. 2001. "Feasting and the Emergence of Platform Mound Ceremonialism in Eastern North America." In *Feasts: Archaeological and Ethnographic Perspectives on Food, Politics, and Power*. Eds. M. Dietler and B. Hayden. Washington, D.C.: Smithsonian Institution Press, 311–33.

Law, Robin. 1987. "Problems of Plagiarism, Harmonization and Misunderstanding in Contemporary European Sources: Early (Pre-1680s) Sources for the 'Slave Coast' of West Africa." *Paideuma* 16: 337–58.

Ledero Quesada, Miguel Angel. 1994. "Spain, circa 1492: Social Values and Structures." In *Implicit Understandings: Observing, Reporting, and Reflecting on the Encounters between Europeans and Other Peoples in the Early Modern Era*. Ed. Stuart B. Schwartz. Cambridge: Cambridge University Press, 96–133.

Le Jau, Francis. 1956. *The Carolina Chronicle of Dr. Francis Le Jau, 1706–1717*. Ed. Frank J. Klingberg. Berkeley: University of California Press.

Le Moyne, Pierre, Sieur d'Iberville. 1981. *Iberville's Gulf Journals*. Trans. and ed. Richebourg Gaillard McWilliams. Tuscaloosa: University of Alabama Press.

Lentz, Carola and Hans-Jürgen Sturm. 2001. "Of Trees and Earth Shrines: An Interdisciplinary Approach to Settlement Histories in the West African Savanna." *History in Africa* 28: 139–68.

Le Page du Pratz, Antoine Simon. 1758. *Histoire de la Louisiane*. 3 vols. Paris, France: DeBure.

Lestringant, Frank. 1994. *Mapping the Renaissance World: The Geographical Imagination in the Age of Discovery*. Trans. David Fausett. Cambridge: Polity Press.

Lorca, Federico Garcia. 1998. *A Season in Granada: Uncollected Poems and Prose*. Trans. and ed. Christopher Maurer. London: Anvil Press.

MacGaffey, Wyatt. 1977. "The Cultural Roots of Kongo Prophetism." *History of Religion* 17.2: 177–93.

Marees, Pieter de. 1987. *Descriptions and Historical Account of the Gold Kingdom of Guinea (1602).* Eds. and trans. Adam Jones and Albert von Dantzig. Oxford: Oxford University Press.

Markova, Ivana. 2003. *Dialogicality and Social Representation: The Dynamics of Mind.* Cambridge: Cambridge University Press.

Mason, Peter. 1990. *Deconstructing America: Representations of the Other.* London: Routledge.

McDowell, William L., Jr., ed. 1958. *Colonial Records of South Carolina: Documents Relating to Indian Affairs, May 21, 1750–August 7, 1754.* 2 vols. Columbia: South Carolina Archives Department.

McLintock, Anne. 1995. *Imperial Leather: Race, Gender and Sexuality in the Colonial Conquest.* New York: Routledge.

Milanich, Jerald T. 1994. *Archaeology of Precolumbian Florida.* Gainesville: University Press of Florida.

Montgomery, Sir Robert. 1972. "A Discourse Concerning the Design'd Establishment of a New Colony to the South of Carolina in the most Delightful Country of the Universe (1717)." In *The Most Delightful Country of the Universe: Promotional Literature of the Colony of Georgia, 1717–1734.* Ed. Trevor R. Reese. Savannah, GA: Beehive Press, 3–31.

Morgan, Philip D. 1998. *Slave Counterpoint: Black Culture in the Eighteenth Century Chesapeake and Lowcountry.* Chapel Hill: University of North Carolina Press.

Myers, Fred R. 1986. *Pintupi Self: Sentiment, Place and Politics among Western Desert Aborigines.* Washington, D.C.: Smithsonian Institution Press.

Nairne, Thomas. 1989. "A Letter from South Carolina (London, 1710)." In *Selling a New World: Two Colonial South Carolina Promotional Pamphlets.* Ed. Jack Greene. Columbia: University of South Carolina Press, 33–73.

Nandy, Ashis, Zia Sardar, and Merryl Wyn Davies. 1993. *Barbaric Others: A Manifesto on Western Racism.* Boulder, CO: Pluto Press.

Natter, Wolfgang, and John Paul Jones III. 1993. "Signposts toward a Poststructuralist Geography." In *Postmodern Contentions: Epochs, Politics, Space.* Eds. John Paul Jones III, Wolfgang Natter, and Theodore R. Schatzki. New York: Guilford Press, 165–204.

Nettleford, Rex. 1994. "The Caribbean: Crossroads of the Americas." In *Crossroads of Empire: The Europe-Caribbean Connection 1492–1992.* Ed. Alan Cobley. Cave Hill, Barbados: Department of History, University of the West Indies, 1–14.

Norris, Christopher. 2004. *Language, Logic, and Epistemology: A Model-Realist Approach.* Hampshire, NY: Palgrave Macmillan.

Oglethorpe, James. 1972. "A New and Accurate Account of the Province of South Carolina and Georgia (1732)." In *Most Delightful Country of the Universe: Promotional Literature of the Colony of Georgia, 1717–1734.* Ed. Trevor R. Reese. Savannah, GA: Beehive Press, 115–56.

Pagden, Anthony. 1993. *European Encounters with the New World: From Renaissance to Romanticism.* New Haven: Yale University Press.

Payne, Claudine, and John F. Scarry. 1998. "Town Structure at the Edge of the Mississippian World." In *Mississippian Towns and Sacred Spaces: Searching for an Architectural Grammar*. Eds. R. Barry Lewis and Charles Stout. Tuscaloosa: University of Alabama Press, 22–47.

Phillips, Seymour. 1994. "The Outer World of the European Middle Ages." In *Implicit Understandings: Observing, Reporting, and Reflecting on the Encounters between Europeans and Other Peoples in the Early Modern Era*. Ed. Stuart B. Schwartz. Cambridge: Cambridge University Press, 23–63.

Piersen, William D. 1977. "White Cannibals, Black Martyrs: Fear, Depression, and Religious Faith as Causes of Suicide among Slaves." *Journal of Negro History* 62.2: 147–59.

Pliny the Elder. 1890, 1893. *The Natural History of Pliny the Elder*. 2 vols. Trans. John Bostock and H. T. Riley. London: George Bell & Sons.

Pocock, J. G. A. 1975. "British History: A Plea for a New Subject." *Journal of Modern History* 47.4: 601–21.

Relouzat, Raymond. 1998. *Tradition orale et imaginaire créole*. Martinique: Ibis Rouge Éditions.

Renne, Elisha P. 1995. *Cloth That Does Not Die: The Meaning of Cloth in Bùnú Social Life*. Seattle: University of Washington Press.

Ryder, A. 1969. *Benin and the Europeans, 1485–1897*. New York: Humanities Press.

Samford, Patricia. 1996. "The Archaeology of African-American Slavery and Material Culture." *William and Mary Quarterly* 53.1: 87–114.

Sanford, Rhonda Lemke. 2002. *Maps and Memory in Early Modern England*. New York: Palgrave.

Saunt, Claudio. 1999. *A New Order of Things: Property, Power, and the Transformation of the Creek Indians, 1733–1816*. Cambridge: Cambridge University Press.

Savage, E. 1992. "Berbers and Blacks: Ibadi Slave Traffic in Eighth Century North Africa." *Journal of African History* 33.3: 351–68.

Séville, Isidore de. 1984. *Étymologies*. Ed. and trans. Marc Reydellet. Paris, France: Société d'éditions.

Smith, Catherine Delano. 1987. "Cartography in the Prehistoric Period in the Old World: Europe, the Middle East, and North Africa." In *History of Cartography: Volume 1: Cartography in Prehistoric, Ancient and Medieval Europe and the Mediterranean*. Eds. J. B. Harley and David Woodward. Chicago: University of Chicago Press, 54–102.

Smith, John. 1986. *Complete Works of Captain John Smith*. 2 vols. Ed. Philip L. Barbour. Chapel Hill: University of North Carolina Press.

Snelgrave, William. 1971. *A New Account of Some Parts of Guinea and the Slave-Trade (1734)*. London: Frank Cass & Co.

Snow, Frankie. 1998. "Swift Creek Design Investigations: The Hartford Case." In *A World Engraved: Archaeology of the Swift Creek Culture*. Eds. Mark Williams and Daniel T. Elliott. Tuscaloosa: University of Alabama Press, 61–98.

Solinus, Julius. 1587. *The Excellent and Pleasant Worke of Julius Solinus Polyhistor*. London: Charlewood.

Steinem, Karl T. 1998. "Kolomoki and the Development of Sociopolitical Organization on the Gulf Coastal Plain." In *A World Engraved: Archaeology of the Swift Creek Culture*. Eds. Mark Williams and Daniel T. Elliott. Tuscaloosa: University of Alabama Press, 181–96.

Stuckey, Sterling. 1987. *Slave Culture: Nationalist Theory and the Foundations of Black America*. New York: Oxford University Press.

Thornton, John K. 1998. *The Kongolese Saint Anthony: Dona Beatriz Kimpa Vita and the Antonian Movement, 1684–1706*. Cambridge: Cambridge University Press.

Thrower, Norman Joseph William. 1996. *Maps & Civilization: Cartography in Culture and Society*. Chicago: University of Chicago Press.

Tooley, R. V. 1987. *Maps and Map-Makers*. London: B. T. Batesford Ltd.

Ulsheimer, Andreas Josua. 1983. 'Andreas Josua Ulsheimer's Voyage of 1603–4.' In "German Sources for West African History, 1599–1669." Ed. Adam Jones, *Studien zur Kulturkunde* 66: 18–43.

Waselkov, Gregory A. 1998. "Indian Maps of the Colonial Southeast: Archaeological Implications and Prospects." In *Cartographic Encounters: Perspectives on Native American Mapmaking and Map Use*. Ed. G. Malcolm Lewis. Chicago: University of Chicago Press, 205–22.

Weber, David J. 1992. *The Spanish Frontier in North America*. New Haven: Yale University Press.

Whittle, Alasdair. 1985. *Neolithic Europe: A Survey*. Cambridge: Cambridge University Press.

Wilks, Ivor. 1982. "Wangara, Akan, and Portuguese in the Fifteenth and Sixteenth Centuries. I. The Matter of Bitu." *Journal of African History* 23.3: 333–49.

Wood, Betty. 1984. *Slavery in Colonial Georgia, 1730–1775*. Athens, GA: University of Georgia Press.

Woodward, David. 1985. "Reality, Symbolism, Time, and Space in Medieval World Maps." *Annals of the Association of American Geographers* 75.4: 510–21.

———. 1987. "Medieval *Mappaemundi*." In *History of Cartography: Volume 1: Cartography in Prehistoric, Ancient and Medieval Europe and the Mediterranean*. Eds. J. B. Harley and David Woodward. Chicago: University of Chicago Press, 286–370.

Zamora, Margarita. 1993. *Reading Columbus*. Berkeley: University of California Press.

# The Southern Way of Death

## The Meaning of Death in Antebellum White Evangelical Culture

RANDY J. SPARKS

> I could just remember how my father used to say that the reason for living
> was to get ready to stay dead for a long time.
> —William Faulkner, *As I Lay Dying*

Since Philippe Aries published his pathbreaking study of attitudes toward death in Western culture, studies of the topic have proliferated, but despite that outpouring of scholarship, relatively few studies have focused on the American South. What is perhaps even more surprising is that few scholars have explored the impact of evangelicalism on the cultural attitudes surrounding death and dying. Even scholars as sophisticated as Aries himself ignore the most powerful religious movement of the eighteenth and nineteenth centuries and its transforming effect on society and culture. While death is a common denominator in human experience, anthropologists have found that the responses it evokes are incredibly various. Death rituals, then, throw "into relief the most important cultural values by which people live their lives and evaluate their experiences. Life becomes transparent against the background of death, and fundamental social and cultural issues are revealed."[1] An examination of white southern religion and the culture of death reveal the ways evangelical southerners understood death and dying. As evangelicalism spread to more and more southerners during the antebellum period, it provided the lens through which southerners viewed the final stage in the cycle of life. Evangelicalism shaped the social and cultural patterns surrounding death and provided the rituals that marked the occasion.

"Our people die well," said John Wesley. Scholars of death and dying agree that Western attitudes surrounding the end of life changed in the late eighteenth and early nineteenth centuries, and they have generally ascribed

---

*Southern Quarterly* 44.1 (2006): 32–50.

this change to the impact of the Romantic movement. But the rising tide of evangelicalism should not be overlooked in this regard, particularly in the southern United States where the movement had a profound social and cultural impact. Beginning with tiny churches and a handful of members in the colonial period, evangelical churches expanded rapidly in the South after the Revolution, particularly after the outbreak of the Great Revival in Kentucky in 1801. Like wildfire, revivals spread across the region and brought tens of thousands of converts into the rapidly growing Methodist, Baptist, and Presbyterian churches. While it is difficult to determine church membership across the South with any degree of accuracy, local studies have found that evangelicalism spread rapidly throughout the antebellum period. While evangelicalism began as a religion of the plain folk in the colonial South, it moved up the socioeconomic ladder and converted more and more members of the planter elite as the nineteenth century progressed. In some areas up to two-thirds of white families had some evangelical church affiliation on the eve of the Civil War, and planters played a prominent role in church leadership.[2]

As Wesley's quote suggests, evangelicals faced death in a different way from the non-converted, and as the evangelical ethos spread, their beliefs permeated southern society. The certainty of death and judgment was a constant theme for evangelical ministers. Preachers used their most graphic oratorical skills to paint the torments of the damned, the "rush of agony!," and the horrors that awaited "the lost spirit in hell." The famous Methodist evangelist Lorenzo Dow, who frequently preached at camp meetings across the South, told his audience that "Eternity is the country to which all are travelling; sleeping or waking, they progress with unremitting speed . . . there are two places of destination . . . one being attended with ineffable pleasure, the other with weeping, wailing and gnashing of teeth." Such sermons had the desired effect; one minister looked back on his conversion and reported that from the age of nine or ten he had "serious . . . fears when reflecting on death and eternity . . . [and] the fear of punishment." Until his conversion, he thought that everyone suffered from the same "sense of guilt and . . . tormenting fear of hell and the wrath of God."[3]

In the South, a region plagued by high death rates and diseases, natural disasters and epidemics contributed to the region's distinctiveness. Evangelicals interpreted these disasters as visitations of divine justice, and they advised southerners to heed these warnings. An 1804 funeral sermon for a Charleston, South Carolina, minister included references to a hurricane in that year that devastated the low country and to a yellow fever epidemic in that same year.

According to the author, yellow fever epidemics ravaged Charleston almost every year. Yellow fever also swept through the lower Mississippi Valley with alarming regularity. In 1840 the members of the Vicksburg (Miss.) Presbyterian Church lamented that "Disease & death entered almost every family. For six long and gloomy weeks we bore the dead to their graves in almost one continual stream." After a tornado left hundreds dead in Natchez a Methodist minister asked "when will this people learn righteousness and serve the God of heaven [?]" No wonder that southerners saw themselves as "living in the midst of a mighty charnel house. We are the vast funeral procession, moving with ceaseless course to the chambers of death. Our earth is our great sepulchre."[4]

Even evangelical worship services were colored by their fascination with death and dying. A common feature of camp meeting and revival services was calling up mourners, those sorrowful would-be converts whose name reflected the grieving of death, as did the uncontrollable weeping that some of them experienced as they sought salvation. Other converts were so powerfully overcome by the Holy Spirit that they collapsed as if dead. Though most closely associated with the Great Revival and the early evangelical movement, such emotional conversions continued throughout the antebellum period and intensified during the revival of 1856. At a Mississippi camp meeting in that year, "many were prostrated at the altar like men slain in battle, and the rigid muscles, the icy hand, and the pallid countenance (like death!), told that the work of the . . . Spirit was powerful within." Evangelicals frequently referred to their conversion as the New Birth, but by the 1840s conversion was often associated with death rather than birth. The members of one Baptist church declared in their church covenant, "we have been voluntarily buried by baptism & . . . raised up from the emblematical grave." In 1851 a preacher at a Georgia revival rejoiced that he had baptized converts "into the watery grave . . . ," while a report of an 1859 revival in Mississippi proclaimed "Thirty-one Died—26 Buried!"[5]

Evangelical ministers were willing and eager to conjure up vivid pictures of the fiery pit of hell as a warning to the godless, but they more often focused on the joyous "triumphant death" that awaited the converted. Presbyterian Daniel Baker, in a published series of revival sermons, called on mourners to rejoice in the death of a faithful loved one, and recounted the story of "a beloved female member" who rejoiced as death approached, "I am in great pain, but O! I am happy! very happy!"[6] A Methodist newspaper article explored the apparent inconsistency in an expression common among southern evangelicals; "I Thank God That I Was Born to Die." This sentiment, found in a popular hymn and "heard so often in the class-room and the love-feast, as well as at the death-scene," was described as "peculiar to Christianity" since no other religion "has ever been able to . . . create in the mind a thankfulness to God for the prospect of death." Triumphant death scenes were among the most common features of the evangelical press. Sophia Hays (ca. 1827–1910), as a young Sunday School teacher, recorded reading a "delightful" "little Sabbath School-Book" in which the heroine struggled to find salvation, and did so "in the entire surrender . . . into the hands of her Savior." Predictably, her death soon followed, and though she suffered terribly in her final weeks, her anguish seemed more like "a constant triumph" as she enjoyed "the blessed realization of her Savior's presence." This eighteen-year-old paragon met her death with joy.[7]

It would be simple to dismiss such reading material as sentimental melodrama, but for evangelicals like Sophia Hays, such materials were an important part of their quest for spiritual growth. Sophia Hays's diary, like that of many evangelical women, was also a book of meditation that reveals its author's search for spiritual autonomy, or what one scholar has labeled a process of self-fashioning. Sophia expressed her fears that "death will find me before I have accomplished scarcely any thing that I design." The death of friends and acquaintances was another occasion for soul-searching. She wrote that "Death & burial are ever solemn occasions and should awaken in our minds the deepest & most serious reflections." At Mr. Cary's funeral, the minister spoke "on the duty & importance of making speedy preparations for an event which must come to all before a great while, and might come very soon. He repeated an expression made by him whose remains lay before us, . . . that the only thing worth living for was the salvation of the soul, and made an earnest appeal to the spectators to apply it to their consciousness," a quote that could have been drawn directly from William Faulkner.[8] Reflecting another common theme in evangelical attitudes, Sophia expressed her desire to be united with her family in eternity. "How . . . I wish to see my brothers and sisters all claim the promise of eternal life," she wrote, "that we might . . . [be] united in a home of . . . never ending happiness." Sophia shared her spiritual strivings with her sister, Matilda Boyd, and urged her to join in the quest. She wrote, "If we would be really happy we must endeavor to do our duty, and . . . seek assistance from above." After a serious illness, she reported to her sister that "I hardly hoped to live still I was not unhappy in view of death.... Oh my dear Sister, above all things make sure of that hope which will prepare you for the dying hour."[9]

Sophia's faith would often be tested. In 1851 she fell in love with J. Sidney Hays, a Presbyterian minister, but their life together was marked by tragedy. In 1854 their infant son died shortly after his birth, and she fell ill with a fever that nearly ended her life. While Sophia was still too ill to write, the Reverend Hays wrote Sophia's sister to inform her of the situation. "Our hearts are sad," he wrote, "And yet why should we mourn? He is safe ... in heaven. We shall go to him when our warfare is over." Within a few years, Sidney Hays was also dead.[10]

Sophia Hays's story illustrates many central themes surrounding the southern way of death and dying. First, it is important to note the central role women as mothers and nurses played in death rituals and the ways in which women's self-perceptions were influenced by evangelical responses to death. As one evangelical newspaper put it, "the couch of the tortured sufferer, ... the cross of the neglected Savior—these are the scenes of a woman's excellence." Since women usually nursed the sick, they were frequent witnesses of death-bed scenes. Mahala Roach described such an event in her diary; "Our dear, good, gentle Christian friend Mrs. Magee died this morning ... I had the great privilege of being with her in her last hours—of joining with her pure soul, in prayer, and witnessing a triumphant Christian death bed!"[11] These scenes were a powerful testimony of faith and devotion, a source of strength and comfort to those who witnessed them. No doubt the importance of these scenes in the lives of evangelicals account for Wesley's boasts that Methodists died well. Clearly, in these settings, dying women actually ministered to those around them. Robert Alexander was summoned to the bedside of "Old Mother Wynne." When he arrived he found the preacher there along with "a number of ladies." The group "had prayer & a delightful meeting." He reported that "the old Lady's *Resigned to Heaven[']s will*, seems very Happy." Louisa C. Lawrence, who faced death at the young age of twenty-four, spent her time in "prayer and praise, and earnestly exhorted her afflicted friends" to meet her in heaven. These exhortations often made a deep impression on those who heard them; one writer referred to death bed scenes as "a bright star guiding my wayward feet in the narrow path." An article in the religious press noted that many converts could "trace their first serious impressions ... to the time when death entered their family circles."[12]

Given the choice, many contemporary Americans would probably choose a quick death rather than a lingering one, but antebellum southerners looked on sudden deaths with foreboding. The obituary of Emily Dowsing is a case in point. Ms. Dowsing died suddenly, alone in her room, a parting that greatly distressed her friends and relatives: "she died alone . . . she was not permitted to give her parting blessing to her weeping friends and kindred and assure them of her happy exit." In a similar case, Ann E. Gillespie mourned the death of her sister "under circumstances peculiarly distressing. She was called to die far from home and friends." Southerners dreaded being condemned to a solitary death, robbed of the comfort of friends and family and unable to demonstrate their faith and courage in the face of death.[13]

Ideally, death was a public ritual, one where friends and family joined together in what amounted to a deeply religious worship service. Few aspects of antebellum southern life give more vivid testimony to the depth of female friendships than these moving scenes. Sophia Laborde found comfort in "the kindness and attention of friends" as she lay dying. Mahala Roach described the death of her close friend, Jennie Auguste. After spending time at her friend's bedside, Mrs. Roach returned "to see my poor Jennie, and assist in laying her out." Women, generally the friends of the deceased, were responsible for preparing bodies for burial. Mrs. Roach's assistance extended even further, however, for Jennie died in childbirth. Mrs. Roach, recently a mother herself, nursed her dead friend's infant from her own bosom until a wet nurse could be found. On many occasions Mrs. Roach performed the sad duty of preparing the bodies of her friends' deceased children for burial. For example, when the daughter of Mrs. March died, Mrs. Roach "assisted to wash and dress the little angel." Her friend Mrs. Burwell sent for her when her young daughter died; Mrs. Roach "went up at once, saw the lovely little 'sleeper'—dressed her, and did all I could for the parents." On other occasions Mrs. Roach dressed the pulpit of the Baptist Church in white for a funeral and put flowers around a child's body, intended not only to beautify the scene but to help cover the odor of death. In her grief, she asked, "If I am not too wicked, too sinful—may I hope that the strength I have to bear this blow has been given me by God?" When Christmas came a few months later, she wrote, "the memory of our Angel child has chastened the joy of the day, but not saddened it too much—for we know she is . . . beyond our ideas of happiness." The close friendships like that between Mahala Roach and Jennie Auguste are examples of "true" or "sacred" friendships that developed between antebellum evangelical women in the North and the South. True friends nurtured one another in faith, and this culture of friendship, based in part on female piety, transcended the nuclear family and promoted close emotional bonds beyond the circle of kin. When Mrs. Roach's young daughter Sophy died in 1857, her kindness was repaid as friends gathered around her. Sophy was buried in a family burial ground carefully maintained by Mrs. Roach's mother-in-law.[14]

When possible, southern women carefully tended the graves of family members. Along with parting gifts from dying loved ones or commemorative jewelry, caring for graves kept memories alive and "became a powerful means of compensating for the losses of separation." J. P. Drake visited the grave of his brother Edmund's child and reported "that Aunt Betsy had planted Camomile over his grave and we planted four Rose bushes around." When Dr. John Ker notified his daughter, Sarah E. Butler, that he was forced by financial setbacks to sell the family plantation, her chief regret was that "the *graves* of my *Grandmother*, of her husband & son—of my brothers & sisters, had passed into the hands of those of cared not for them—I felt as if my heart were breaking."[15] Men were sometimes more skeptical of these rituals of death than were women. Mrs. Roach's husband, James, for example, found the care his mother lavished on the graves of her deceased family members excessive. He wrote, "rode up to Grandma & found her as usual at grave yard. This mock regard for the dead is getting quite fashionable, to the neglect of the living."[16]

Another feature of death-bed scenes involved the presence of slaves who were summoned to the bedside along with family and friends. When Mrs. Elizabeth Bullock lay dying, she spent her final moments "in prayer for her husband, her children, her brothers and sisters, and her servants. All . . . received a parting exhortation." As twenty-one year old Thomas H. Wade lay dying of typhoid fever he "prayed fervently for the mercy of God upon his soul, upon his relatives, for his friends in the room, bade them farewell . . . The servants were called in, whom he bade farewell, and exhorted them to meet him in heaven." When Nancy A. Brown fell ill, "her praying friends, . . . especially aunt Lebby, (colored sister) prayed for her recovery, but all in vain." She died happy and charged her family and friends to join her in heaven. Mary Ann Raney "continued, while she had strength, to exhort friends, neighbors, servants, all to meet her in heaven."[17] The inclusion of slaves in these ritualized settings drew on the popular perception among white southerners, and among evangelicals in particular, that slaves were a part of the extended family who were expected to join in the death-bed rites.

Historian James Oakes tied white southerners' obsession with death to their guilt over slavery, but such an interpretation has little to support it. By the antebellum period, southern evangelicals had abandoned their antislavery position, and after 1830 actively embraced Biblical proslavery. They insisted that slave-owners carry out their duties to their slaves, and Christianizing them was among those duties. A Methodist newspaper explained that the "Duties of Christian Masters" included teaching slaves "the power of the gospel . . . in giving them victory over the fear of death." It may be that evangelical masters who had failed to perform their duties might face death with guilt over slavery, but such sentiments cannot explain the southern attitude toward death. Far from promoting guilt over slavery, evangelical proslavery offered the prospect of perfecting the institution and thereby assuaging whatever guilt slave-owners may have felt.[18]

The lives of Sophia Hays and Mahala Roach illustrate a tragic reality in the lives of most southern families; the loss of an infant or child. Historians estimate that children under five accounted for as much as 40 percent of the total death rate in nineteenth-century America. Evangelicals had conflicting views on the nature of infants that shaped their attitudes toward infant death. On the one hand, they held a traditional Christian view that children "are conceived in sin, and shapen in iniquity." On the other, they regarded infants as pure and without sin, with "no accountability, no individuality." The latter view became increasingly common and gave evangelicals who lost children a certainty of their infants' salvation. David Stannard argued that high infant mortality rates made Puritan parents less attached to their infants. That theme emerges among southern evangelicals; for example, Methodist minister William Winans warned that "It is . . . a dictate of human prudence, as well as a precept of our holy religion, that we 'Set not our affection on things which are upon earth' . . . we should not allow our regard to cling to them [children] with so eager . . . an embrace as to render it painful to give them up." Winans and his wife experienced the death of a child after a painful illness. He described the contradictory feelings his daughter engendered; "We felt that she might be the ornament and solace of our declining age, but we felt, too, that she *might* embitter the last draughts of our existence . . . He who sees the end from the beginning . . . put an end to the perplexity of our anticipations, by taking her to Himself . . . We feel her loss with bitterness." John C. Calhoun responded in a similar vein when his young daughter died in 1815; he wrote, "Providence may have intended it in kindness to her and ourselves."[19]

The frequent publication of consolation literature in the evangelical press for parents who lost infants and children, much of it aimed specifically at mothers, suggests that most parents formed close bonds to their infants and, like Winans, mourned with bitterness. Indeed, some evangelicals blamed the death of their children on the intense love they felt for them. As one woman wrote to a friend whose young daughter died, "since 'Death loves a shining mark,' perhaps God has taken the little loved one from your arms, as an idol from your heart ... often ... our affection for an earthly object becomes stronger than that for our Savior." When Isham Howze's son fell ill he, too, feared that his deep affection might lead to his son's death; he prayed, "I fear not for his Soul, ... for he is thy child. But ... forsake *me* not, in taking him from me. Let me not love him too idolatrously; but O let him live to support my declining years." Poems like "The Dying Infant" and "Mother's Comfort in the Infant's Death" filled the evangelical newspapers and offered solace to grieving mothers.[20]

Perhaps the chief comfort evangelicals found was their conviction that they would be reunited with their deceased loved ones in what historian Ann Douglas referred to as "domestic heaven," a reunion that included both family members and true friends. A typical article in the evangelical press assured readers that "We Will Know Each Other After Death." Such assurances were a common feature of death-bed scenes. One woman recalled the death of her "beloved girlfriend" who assured her from her death bed; "I am going to Heaven: do not weep ... You will come there, and father and mother, and Jesus will make us all happy." As seventeen-year-old John F. Gilmore lay suffering in his final illness, his friends gathered around him; he "told them he was going to Heaven ... and expected them to meet him there." The prevalence of the image of reunification after death can be explained in part by the high morbidity and mortality rates in the antebellum period, but also by the high mobility among antebellum southerners. Benjamin Drake, separated from his family for over forty years, wrote his brother "that I now abandon the cherished idea of seeing all my brothers once more in the flesh, but it is joyful to hope to meet them all in *heaven*." Another family member, Albrittain Drake of North Carolina, wrote his grandmother in Kentucky who he had never met; "Dear grand mother[,] as I know according to nature['s] courses you cannot live much longer ... if I never see you on earth I hope to meet you in heaven ther[e] to be parted no more[;] may God grant it is my prayre [*sic*]." Southerners cut off from family members yearned to rejoin them. When Nancy M. Robinson married in 1833 she prepared to leave her family and join her husband on an isolated farm; she wrote, "I will never be happy any more away from my family." In a similar vein, Mary Perkins asked her "Dear Sister Louisa[,] what are we to do? . . . if we were to be separated from our family we could not be happy."[21] As evangelicals placed more and more emphasis on the hope of reuniting loved ones after death, they became increasingly convinced that it was possible to commune with the dead. One Methodist newspaper assured its readers that "There is a fellowship between us and the happy dead." Cases of "Spiritual Recognition" were not uncommon in death scenes, especially with children whose mothers died before them. As the young Mary E. Ross lay dying she heard "sweet music" and saw her dead mother by her bedside; the child said, "I know you have come for me, mother!" In one typical case a young girl lay surrounded by "weeping neighbors assembled to see the little child die." In the final moments of her life a "brightness, as if from the upper world, burst over the child's colorless countenance . . . 'Mother!' she cried," as she breathed her last. A "distinguished divine" who witnessed the scene said, "If I had never believed in the ministration of departed ones before, I could not doubt it now."[22]

Evangelicals clung to the promise of being united in the afterlife; that belief served as a powerful means of conversion, helped bind family members and friends more closely to one another and deepened emotional ties. D. Lipscomb, for example, pleaded with his wife to remain true to her faith; "my dear wife[,] let us try to live more devoted & faithful to God. In life or in death it will be better for us and our . . . example will tell the more strongly upon our children & family . . . They must be . . . christians, so that we may all get to heaven together."[23] While evangelical men certainly hoped to reunite with loved ones after death, women carried the primary burden of spreading religious beliefs in their families. When Mary Mason's husband died without having converted, she poured out her guilt to her uncle, John Ker: "God knows how much I . . . reproach myself for . . . neglecting to lead his thoughts heavenward." Mothers were held even more responsible for the souls of their children; as one religious newspaper warned, "how nearly does the destiny of a child lie in a mother's hands." Historians have suggested that as the nineteenth century progressed, the idea that mothers were responsible for the health of their children and that human agency could ensure an infant's survival replaced the idea that the child's fate was in the hands of Divine Providence. The authors were quick to point out that their conclusions did not apply in evangelical families, and evidence here suggests that southern evangelical women took greater personal responsibility for their infants' well-being, but that chiefly lay in their role as spiritual rather than physical nurturers.[24]

As the central role of wives and mothers suggests, the rituals surrounding death were highly gendered. Obituaries with their vivid descriptions of death scenes and the funeral sermons were frequently published and widely circulated; these publications served as prescriptive literature which casts gender roles into high relief. At times, obituaries and sermons stated their purpose clearly as when Benjamin M. Palmer encouraged the mourners at Josiah Smith's funeral to profit from his example "by fashioning [their] lives after the same evangelic model upon which his was framed." Pious women were also held up as models; when Mary Carter died at the advanced age of eighty-four her church praised her "as an ornament and bright example of piety and devotion." In general, both men and women were praised for their piety, their usefulness, their devotion to family, and their church work. Evangelical women were not expected to be mere adornments, and their virtues set them apart from the idealized southern belle. Only men, however, were noted for their patriotism and their professional character. While men's educational background was more likely to be noted in obituaries, evangelical women were often praised for their "wisdom." Many of the male virtues celebrated in obituaries reflected the popular southern images of masculinity, those praising honor, professional success, and patriotism, for example, but others were at odds with southern conceptions of male honor and virility. When evangelicals praised William Fisk McGehee as "Pure and modest as a woman" or the Reverend William Hamilton Watkins as "gentle as a woman" they were clearly attempting to redefine evangelical masculinity. Most obituaries did not go as far as these in emasculating faithful men. Hezekiah Harrington was more typical of the evangelical male ideal. A South Carolina native, he was a faithful member of the Methodist Church for over fifty years. He spent hours every day engaged in reading the Scriptures and singing and praying with his family; "His religion, though serious, was not of the sour and gloomy kind." His tastes were simple, and he had "a contempt of all display." A model husband and father, "In his family he was kind, without being indulgent." He felt a sense of responsibility for the welfare of his slaves, and took an interest in their moral and religious improvement. Historians have found that northern consolation literature highlighted gender differences and stressed boundaries between the male and female spheres. So, too, did southern consolation literature, though when compared to the sharply defined southern male and female ideals outside the evangelical fold, evangelicals sought to redefine those ideals and mediate, to some degree, between dualities.[25]

Beginning in the nineteenth century, evangelicals moved away from their weak antislavery stance and worked hard to reconcile evangelicalism and slavery as a way of reaching out to slaveholders. After the 1820s, their efforts paid off handsomely as more and more members of the planter elite joined their ranks. Evangelicals challenged the traditional attributes of southern manhood grounded in honor between men and nurtured and tested in such activities as drinking, fighting, and gambling at taverns, race tracks, dances, political rallies, court days, and other public events. Instead, evangelicals celebrated a new masculinity, a "holy honor," based on sobriety, piety, and nonviolent behavior. These evangelical planters found new outlets for their leadership abilities and a new sense of community with like-minded men by leading churches, Sunday Schools, missionary and tract societies, temperance societies, and other benevolent enterprises. When Georgia planter Hardy Durham died in 1860 at age seventy-two, he was praised because he "achieved position and fortune . . . not, as is too frequently the case, by a ruthless disregard of the rights and interests of others," but rather through "generous impulses" and "beneficence." Evangelical efforts to convert planters "was crowned with stunning success." In one Georgia county, for example, most rich families were connected to an evangelical church in 1860.[26]

By the end of the antebellum period, then, white southerners of all classes and both genders were gathered into the evangelical fold and shared a world view defined by their faith. Evangelicalism fundamentally shaped the southern way of death and surrounded the deathbed with a complex and highly ritualized culture. The evangelical obsession with death mirrored and reinforced other forces at work in the antebellum period, but the central role of death and dying among evangelicals suggests that their remarkable success can partly be explained by their ability to convert the terrors and grief surrounding death and dying to a sense of triumph and rejoicing. It is hardly surprising that the idealized earthly family had a perfected heavenly counterpart where evangelicals could live in eternal familial bliss, a belief made even more potent by the frequent separation of southern families. Increasingly, as the antebellum period progressed, evangelical ministers celebrated the household as the fundamental building block of southern society and religious life. They stressed the heavy responsibilities placed upon the head of the household for the salvation of his dependents. In a typical statement of the theme, Daniel

Baker said, "thou who art the head of your family . . . come into the ark! . . .
the responsibility of a parent is great." He looked forward to the day of resur-
rection when he foresaw "a family—a whole family! . . . all radiant and happy,
ascending to the skies together." The evangelical celebration of family religion
increased throughout the antebellum period, and was widely disseminated
through sermons, associational letters, Sunday Schools, and the evangelical
press, by far the largest producers of print media in antebellum America. That
sacred evangelical home imposed heavy duties on fathers, but it also elevated
the nurturing role of evangelical mothers who were largely responsible for
the conversion of the entire family. Beyond the family, evangelicalism encouraged close, emotional sacred friendships between men and women outside
the family circle. The consolation literature that figured so prominently in the
religious press helped foster these new gender and familial roles. The evangelical absorption with death was tied directly to these emotional bonds and
the prospect of their continuation into eternity. David Stannard found that
Puritans faced death with fear and ambivalence rooted in a theology that
emphasized human depravity and the inability of individuals to secure their
salvation. The evangelical promise of salvation to all who sought it domesticated death and truly robbed it of its sting. Their faith enabled them to face
death with confidence, to die well, their hopes focused on "sweet heaven . . .
the Christian's rest! the pilgrim's home! the dwelling place of love, of glory,
and of God!"[27]

## Notes

1. In this essay I follow Donald Mathews's definition of "evangelical" and include Bap-
   tists, Methodists, and Presbyterians. See Mathews (1977: xvi–xvii). Quotation from
   Peter Metcalf and Richard Huntington (1991: 25); see also Philippe Aries (1981).
   Gary Laderman gives brief attention to evangelicalism in his book *The Sacred Remains: American Attitudes Toward Death* (1996), which, despite its title, is focused
   on the North; see especially pages 54–62; see also Laderman (1995: 27–52). Similarly, James J. Farrell pays brief attention to evangelicalism and antebellum attitudes
   toward death, but his work also focuses on the North; see *idem* (1980: 35–43). To
   cite another example, Nancy Schrom Dye and Daniel Blake Smith focus on elite
   northern women and make only passing reference to evangelicalism as an exception to their argument; *idem* and *idem* (1986: 329–53).
2. Wesley quoted in *New Orleans Christian Advocate*, 5 September 1851. On evangelical growth see Jon Butler (1990: 268–70); Samuel Hill, ed. (1984: 486–87); Ernest
   Trice Thompson (1963: I; 175, 433); Frederick A. Bode (1994); Sparks (1994: 76–114).

3. Rev. Lorenzo Dow (1856: 471). The Mississippi Baptist Association warned that "There is a radical and essential difference between the righteous and the wicked; . . . and this distinction holds among men both in and after death . . . the wicked will be adjudged to endless punishment, and the righteous to endless joy"; "Minutes of the Mississippi Baptist Association, 1843" in Albert E. Casey, ed. (1948; II: 366); Daniel Baker (1846: 147); Norvelle Robertson Sr., "Autobiography" (Mississippi Department of Archives and History [hereinafter cited as MDAH]).

4. Todd L. Savitt and James Harvey Young, eds. (1988); George Buist (1804: 28–31); Church History (ca. 1840), First Presbyterian Church of Vicksburg Records (MDAH); Elijah Steele to B. M. Drake, 11 May 1840, Drake Papers (ALS, Cain Archives, Millsaps College, Jackson, Miss. [hereinafter cited as Cain Archives]); *Liberty Advocate* [Miss.], 19 August 1841; James Oakes (1982: 110–11); Jack Larkin (1988: 72–73, 76, 78–85). An 1853 outbreak, for example, killed nearly a third of New Orleans's 100,000 residents. Larkin notes (81) that "Very likely the most dangerous place in the United States was New Orleans."

5. *New Orleans Christian Advocate*, 8 November 1856, 26 May 1855; Church Covenant [c. 1842], Academy Baptist Church Records (MDAH); *Mississippi Baptist*, 2 September 1858, 22 September 1859; *Tennessee Baptist*, 1 May 1847; Bode (1994: 722).

6. Baker (1846: 35).

7. *New Orleans Christian Advocate*, 14 June 1851; Sophia Boyd Hays Diary, 13 March 1858, Hays-Ray-Webb Collection (Special Collections, Mississippi State University, Starkville, Miss.).

8. Hays Diary, February, March 1858. The concept of "self-fashioning" was formulated by Stephen J. Greenblatt (1980).

9. Sophia Boyd Andrews to Matilda Boyd, ALS, 21 December 1851; 18 January 1854; 1 October 1852; 31 December 1852. As 1852 drew to a close she sent her sister a new year's letter: "my dear Sister," she wrote, "our only hope of true happiness is in the religion of Christ . . . Often when we expect to be most happy, we may be most miserable." For similar examples, see Jean Friedman (1985: 5).

10. Sophia was left to care for a son whose illnesses also caused her distress. After he contracted a fever, she wrote, "Were he taken from me . . . Nothing could bring consolation but the unvanishing promise of God, and a clear hope of future happiness"; Hays Diary, 25 April 1858.

11. Mahala P. H. Roach Diary, 29 May 1855, Roach-Eggleston Collection (TMs., Southern Historical Collection, University of North Carolina at Chapel Hill, NC [hereinafter cited as SHC]).

12. Alexander Diary (MDAH), 24 November 1861; *New Orleans Christian Advocate*, 15 July 1854, 4 February 1854; *Mississippi Baptist*, 23 July 1857, 4 February 1858, 15 July 1858 (quotation). Similarly, as Julia Whit lay dying, "weeping friends and relatives would crowd the room to listen to her peaceful and unearthly counsel."

13. *New Orleans Christian Advocate*, 10 April 1852; Ann E. Gillespie to Dr. John Ker, 6 December 1836 (ALS, Ker Papers, SHC). The author of Mrs. Ann McClure's funeral sermon lamented that she was "suddenly doomed to die—'to be taken away with a stroke'"; John Douglas (1859: 8).

14. *In Memory of Sophia Parsons Laborde* (ca. 1841: 7); Roach Diary, 10–13 December 1856, 9 March and 27 August 1858, 15 June 1860; Irene Quenzler Brown (1987: 370–71, 374–75); Roach Diary, 28 August 1857, 3 April 1860.

15. Brown (1987: 375); J. P. Drake to Edmund Drake, ca. 1840s (undated TMs., Arrington Papers, SHC); Sarah E. Butler to Dr. John Ker, 25 November 1849 (ALS, Ker Family Papers, SHC); Sarah Hunt to "My Dear Jennie," 19 April 1860 (ALS, Hughes Family Papers, SHC). Sarah Gayle of Alabama expressed similar sentiments; see Elizabeth Fox-Genovese (1988: 11).

16. Roach was also put off by another funeral custom; "I was pained to see the folly of casting hat bands into his grave," he wrote, after attending a friend's funeral, "and thought it would have been suitable if the pall bearers had pitched their hats." Colonel Thomas C. Billups, a wealthy Methodist planter, disliked the crowded, emotional death-bed scenes, and gave his family careful instructions; "When I am dying I do not wish my family and friends to crowd round my bed—be seated and quiet, that I may die easy and in peace." James Roach Diary, 13 March and 12 May 1858 (TMs., Roach-Eggleston Collection, SHC); *New Orleans Christian Advocate*, 6 October 1866.

17. *New Orleans Christian Advocate*, 26 June and 24 July 1852; *Mississippi Baptist*, 5 October 1859, 8 November 1860.

18. Oakes (1982: 110–17); *New Orleans Christian Advocate*, 4 May 1859.

19. Dye and Smith (1986: 330); Laderman (1996: 24–25); *New Orleans Christian Advocate*, 3 April 1851, 13 November 1852; *South-Western Religious Luminary*, October 1836; Substance of a Funeral Sermon Occasioned by the death of Miss Mary Magruder . . . 23 September 1829, Winans Funeral Sermons (Winans Papers, Cain Archives); Winans to Benjamin Drake, 28 August 1835 (ALS, Drake Papers, MDAH); David E. Stannard (1974: 19–20). Calhoun quoted in Bertram Wyatt-Brown (1982: 136).

20. *Mississippi Baptist*, 8 April 1858. Isham Howze Journal, 27 February 1854 (MDAH); *New Orleans Christian Advocate*, 31 May and 7 June 1851.

21. Ann Douglas (1975: 65); Laderman (1996: 60–61); *New Orleans Christian Advocate* 6 August and 10 September 1853; *Mississippi Baptist*, 23 July 1857; Benjamin Drake [in Nashville] to William Drake [in Kentucky], 12 May 1858 (ALS, Mary Jones Arrington Papers, SHC); Albrittain J. Drake to Mrs. Ruth Drake, 25 September 1841 (ALS, ibid.); Nancy M. Robinson Diary, 28 July 1833 (MDAH); Mary Perkins to Louisa Winston, 10 April 1847 (ALS, Winston Papers, MDAH); Lewis Saum (1974: 481). As Sophia Laborde died she regretted her separation from her family, especially her mother, and said, "Oh! If my dear mother knew how sick I was, I know that nothing would keep her from me"; *In Memory of Sophia Parsons Laborde* (7). For other examples see Friedman (1985: 5); Fox-Genovese (1988: 10, 16–17). Nancy Robinson's fears materialized, and she confided her loneliness to her diary: "I am sad to night, sickness preys in my frame I am a lone & more than 150 miles from any near relative . . . a stranger and unknown."

22. *New Orleans Christian Advocate*, 26 April 1851, 15 November 1856; Robinson Diary, 8 July 1853 (MDAH). For other examples see Saum (1974: 494–95). It was only a

short step from such scenes to attempts to reach the dead. While southern women may not have been as involved as northern women in spiritualism, some actively participated in attempts to contact the dead. Nancy McDougal Robinson, for example, identified "Sister Sarah Posey" as "a Medium," and with her help tried unsuccessfully to raise a table and speak to deceased parents and siblings. On spiritualism see Ann Braude (1989).

23. Duncan to Ker, 24 January, 2 February, and 15 February 1830 (ALS, Mary Susan Ker Papers, SHC).

24. As Donald Mathews wrote, mothers became "the person primarily responsible for family religion because it was she who came to have the primary responsibility for religious nurture"; Mathews (1977: 101); Mary Mason to John Ker, 3 July 1837 (Ker Papers); *New Orleans Christian Advocate*, 21 June 1851, and see also 9 April 1852. Cf. Dye and Smith (1986: 342–46). Joanna Bowen Gillespie (1985) found that religious women in both the North and South continued to rely on Providence to understand almost every aspect of their lives through the early decades of the nineteenth century; see also Fox-Genovese (1988: 17–20, 28).

25. Benjamin Morgan Palmer (1826: 24); Obituary of Mary Carter, Bogue Chitto [Miss.] Baptist Church Records, September 1860 (MSU); Brown (1987: 368–69). The Reverend L. Rush in his funeral sermon for Mrs. Henrietta M. M'Coll intended to "set forth the excellencies of the deceased . . . to make them beneficial to the living"; Rush (1838: 2). See also obituary of McGehee in *New Orleans Christian Advocate*, 7 September 1859; T. L. Mellen, ed. (1886: 24); Hezekiah Harrington obituary in *New Orleans Christian Advocate*, 2 July 1853; Douglas (1975). These general conclusions are based on a sample of over eighty obituaries published in the *South-Western Religious Luminary*, 1836; the *Mississippi Baptist*, 1857–1860; the *New Orleans Christian Advocate*, 1850–1860; and the *Tennessee Baptist*, 1847, broken down evenly by gender.

26. Bertram Wyatt-Brown (1982) explored the concept of honor among the planters, and argued that elite southern men placed little stock in evangelical religion or its precepts, though he altered that conclusion somewhat in his later work (1989). Other scholars have found that planters linked evangelicalism, honor, and the southern martial tradition, especially as the antebellum period progressed, though tensions between evangelicalism and southern honor persisted. On "holy honor" see Edward Crowther (1992: 620); Bode (1994: 744), for second, third and fourth quotations; Janet Moore Lindman (2000); Robert M. Calhoon (1988: 144–46). On the leadership of the planter elite in evangelical churches and benevolent societies see Bode (1994); John W. Quist (1996).

27. Baker (1846: 206–7, 319); David E. Stannard (1973: 1305, 1317). On the evangelical press see Nathan O. Hatch (1989: 142–46).

# Works Cited

Aries, Philippe. 1981. *The Hour of Our Death*. New York: Knopf.

Baker, Daniel. 1846. *A Series of Revival Sermons*. Philadelphia, PA: W. S. Martien.

Bode, Frederick A. 1994. "The Formation of Evangelical Communities in Middle Georgia: Twiggs County, 1820–1861." *Journal of Southern History* 60.4: 711–48.

Braude, Ann. 1989. *Radical Spirits: Spiritualism and Women's Rights in Nineteenth-Century America*. Boston: Beacon Press.

Brown, Irene Quenzler. 1987. "Death, Friendship, and Female Identity During New England's Second Great Awakening." *Journal of Family History* 12.4: 367–88.

Buist, George. 1804. *A Discourse Delivered September 25, 1804 at the Funeral of the Reverend James Malcomson; Formerly Minister of the Original Presbyterian Church of Williamsburg and Late Minister of the Second Presbyterian Congregation of Charleston*. Charleston, SC.

Butler, Jon. 1990. *Awash in a Sea of Faith: Christianizing the American People*. Cambridge, MA: Harvard University Press.

Calhoon, Robert M. 1988. *Evangelicals and Conservatives in the Early South, 1740–1861*. Columbia: University of South Carolina Press.

Casey, Albert E., ed. 1948. *Amite County, Mississippi, 1699–1865*. 3 vols. Birmingham, AL: Amite County Historical Fund.

Crowther, Edward. 1992. "Holy Honor: Sacred and Secular in the Old South." *Journal of Southern History* 58.4: 619–36.

Douglas, Ann. 1975. "Heaven Our Home: Consolation Literature in the Northern United States, 1830–1880." In *Death in America*. Ed. David E. Stannard. Philadelphia: University of Pennsylvania Press, 49–68.

Douglas, John. 1859. *A Funeral Sermon Occasioned by the Death of Mrs. Ann F. McClure: Preached at Chesterville, SC*. Charleston, SC.

Dow, Rev. Lorenzo. 1856. *History of the Cosmopolite: Or the Writings of Rev. Lorenzo Dow*. Cincinnati, OH: H. M. Rulison.

Dye, Nancy Schrom, and Daniel Blake Smith. 1986. "Mother Love and Infant Death, 1750–1920." *Journal of American History* 73.2: 329–53.

Farrell, James J. 1980. *Inventing the American Way of Death, 1830–1920*. Philadelphia, PA: Temple University Press.

Fox-Genovese, Elizabeth. 1988. *Within the Plantation Household: Black and White Women of the Old South*. Chapel Hill: University of North Carolina Press.

Friedman, Jean. 1985. *The Enclosed Garden: Women and Community in the Evangelical South, 1830–1900*. Chapel Hill: University of North Carolina Press.

Gillespie, Joanna Bowen. 1985. "'The Clear Leadings of Providence': Pious Memoirs and the Problems of Self-Realization for Women in the Early Nineteenth Century." *Journal of the Early Republic* 5.2: 197–221.

Greenblatt, Stephen J. 1980. *Renaissance Self-Fashioning: From More to Shakespeare*. Chicago: University of Chicago Press.

Hatch, Nathan O. 1989. *The Democratization of American Christianity*. New Haven, CT: Yale University Press.

Hill, Samuel, ed. 1984. *Encyclopedia of Religion in the South*. Macon, GA: Mercer University Press.

*In Memory of Sophia Parsons Laborde, 1806–1841*. ca. 1841. Charleston, SC.

Laderman, Gary. 1995. "Locating the Dead: A Cultural History of Death in the Antebellum Anglo-Protestant Communities of the Northeast." *Journal of the American Academy of Religion* 63.1: 27–52.

———. 1996. *The Sacred Remains: American Attitudes Toward Death, 1799–1883*. New Haven: Yale University Press.

Larkin, Jack. 1988. *The Reshaping of Everyday Life, 1790–1840*. New York: Harper and Row.

*Liberty Advocate* [Mississippi].

Lindman, Janet Moore. 2000. "Acting the Manly Christian: White Evangelical Masculinity in Revolutionary Virginia." *William and Mary Quarterly* 57.2: 393–416.

Mathews, Donald. 1977. *Religion in the Old South*. Chicago: University of Chicago Press.

Mellen, T. L., ed. 1886. *In Memoriam: Life and Labors of the Rev. William Hamilton Watkins, D.D.* Nashville, TN.

Metcalf, Peter and Richard Huntington. 1991. *Celebrations of Death: The Anthropology of Mortuary Ritual*. Cambridge: Cambridge University Press.

*Mississippi Baptist*.

*New Orleans Christian Advocate*.

Oakes, James. 1982. *The Ruling Race: A History of American Slaveholders*. New York: Vintage Books of Random House.

Palmer, Benjamin Morgan. 1826. *Good Men the Protection and Ornament of a Community. A Sermon Delivered in the Independent or Congregational Church in Charleston, Feb. 19, 1826, on the Occasion of the Death of Josiah Smith, Esq. Eldest Deacon*. Charleston, SC.

Quist, John W. 1996. "Slaveholding Operatives of the Benevolent Empire: Bible, Tract, and Sunday School Societies in Antebellum Tuscaloosa County, Alabama." *Journal of Southern History* 62.3: 481–526.

Rush, Rev. L. 1838. *A Sermon on the Death of Mrs. Henrietta M. M'Coll Wife of Reverend J. W. M'Coll*. Charleston, SC.

Saum, Lewis. 1974. "Death in the Popular Mind of Pre–Civil War America." *American Quarterly* 26.5: 477–95.

Savitt, Todd L., and James Harvey Young, eds. 1988. *Disease and Distinctiveness in the American South*. Knoxville: University of Tennessee Press.

*South-Western Religious Luminary*.

Sparks, Randy J. 1994. *On Jordan's Stormy Banks: Evangelicalism in Mississippi, 1773–1876*. Athens: University of Georgia Press.

Stannard, David E. 1973. "Death and Dying in Puritan New England." *American Historical Review* 78.5: 1305–30.

———. 1975. "Death and the Puritan Child." In *Death in America*. Ed. David E. Stannard. Philadelphia: University of Pennsylvania Press, 9–29.

Thompson, Ernest Trice. 1963. *Presbyterians in the South, Volume One: 1607–1861*. Richmond, Va.: John Knox Press.

*Tennessee Baptist*.

Wyatt-Brown, Bertram. 1982. *Southern Honor: Ethics and Behavior in the Old South.*
    Oxford: Oxford University Press.
————. 1989. "God and Honor in the Old South." *Southern Review* 25.2: 283–96.

# Africa and the American South

## Culinary Connections

ROBERT L. HALL

O ne result of the Atlantic slave trade and other aspects of what Alfred W. Crosby called the "Columbian exchange," in addition to the forced migration of people and diseases, was the movement of food crops.[1] These consisted of a combination of crops originally domesticated in Africa and crops indigenous to other continents that had reached Africa before Columbus's voyages (mainly coming from Asia) or which did so during the first century or so after the opening of the New World to European colonial expansion (including such significant American domesticates as maize, manioc, and the peanut). Thus the African culinary tastes at the time of the massive forced migration—probably the largest in world history up to that time—constituted a fusion of food stuffs originating from every part of the Earth. The purpose of this essay, however, is to explore briefly what food crops and culinary habits were (or could have been) introduced into the Western Hemisphere from Africa. Emphasis is on the influence of Africans and their foodways in the Southern states, defined as the eleven former Confederate states plus the four slaveholding states that remained loyal to the Union during the Civil War. As recently as 1910, on the eve of an upsurge of black migration out of the South, nearly 90 percent of the African American population still lived in the former Confederate states and 73 percent in rural areas.[2]

There are two basic ways to approach the issue of African influences on Southern foodways. One is to emphasize the basic food crops that were either domesticated in Africa or, though domesticated elsewhere, had become incorporated into the diets of Atlantic Africa before the captives were shipped to the Americas. A second approach, rather than focusing on crops and ingredients of African origin, stresses how ingredients (regardless of their ultimate locus of domestication in the case of plants) were prepared and seasoned.

*Southern Quarterly* 44.2 (2007): 19–52.

## African Agricultural Origins and Dispersals

Farming economies have a long history on the African continent.[3] Indeed the subsistence economies of most of the source areas for the Atlantic slave trade were primarily agricultural. Africans in several regions played significant roles in developing agriculture, domesticating plants, and dispersing food plants and culinary styles to other parts of the world.[4] In the most extensive and most recent list of Africa's contributions to the diets of New World populations, Judith A. Carney identifies three geographical areas where "agricultural domestication unfolded": the East African savanna, the West African savanna, and the tropical rain forest of West and Central Africa.[5] For example sorghum was domesticated in the East African savanna, watermelon and African rice (*Oryza glaberrima*) in the West African savanna, and white guinea yams, yellow guinea yams, the oil palm, tamarind, okra, cowpeas (black-eyed peas), and pigeon peas were domesticated in the tropical rain forests of West and Central Africa.[6]

Plant material preserved in a cave at Shongweni, Natal, South Africa (excavated in 1971) and dated to the third millennium BCE include finger millet (*Eleusine coracana*), *Pennisetum typhoides*, *Sorghum bicolor*, *Citrullus lunatus*, and *Lagenaria siceraria*. Pollen from the oil palm (*Elaeis guineensis*) is found at excavated sites of the Kintampo culture of the Brong-Ahafo region of central Ghana—the earliest archaeological expression of a food-producing economy in West Africa south of the Sahel. In fact, the incidence of oil palm pollen increased in the Lake Bosumtwi core area about 1650 BCE.[7] At Karkarichinkat in present-day Mali evidence dating to the second millennium BCE has been found for *Pennisetum Americanum* (bullrush millet) and *Brachiaria deflexa* (Guinea millet). On the animal side of the food ledger, footprints found in the Laetoli flats of Tanzania of what is believed to be guinea fowl have been dated to 3.6 million years ago. The prints were probably made in damp volcanic ash and then covered and hence preserved by later showers of volcanic ash from an active volcano nearby.

Although yams were widely consumed in Africa on the eve of European overseas expansion, the major environmental zone for yam cultivation was located in the moist woodlands and savanna of West Africa.[8] Today four major varieties of yams are cultivated in West Africa: *Dioscorea cayenensis*, *D. rotundata* (white guinea yam), *D. bulbifera*, and *D. alata* (greater yam). The first two were almost surely domesticated in Africa. The third may have been domesticated in both Africa and Asia and the fourth was domesticated in

Asia. D. G. Coursey suggests that in West Africa yams were gradually domesticated. "Protoculture" involving the removal of wild plants to more convenient, accessible, or advantageous locations in or near settlements developed nearly five thousand years ago. Then, about four thousand years ago, through the interaction of "protoculturalists" and Neolithic grain-crop cultivators influenced by Southwest Asian cultural patterns a "cross-fertilization of ideas" took place resulting in "the development of a yam-based agriculture in something approaching its present form."[9] As we shall see, yams (whether of the African or Asian variety) were frequently provisioned on slave ships particularly when the involuntary African passengers were known to have come from yam-eating societies.[10] William Smith, who traveled to Africa during the 1730s, found yams to be among the major root crops cultivated in both the Gambia and at Cape Coast on the Gold Coast.[11] It is significant that numerous persons engaged in the slave trade distinguished among the several groups of African captives according to their principal dietary staples. The British trader Henry Ellis, for instance, commented:

> Those from the Gold Coast, who are accustomed to Freedom and inhabit a dry Champain Country and feed on nutritious and solid Aliments, such as Flesh, Fish, Bread of Indian Corn &c are healthy and robust; little subject to Mortality; very hardy and turbulent, as well as much disposed to rise on the White People . . . Those from the Grain Coast, which is also elevated, live chiefly upon Rice, Plantains, Potatoes &c are less hardy than Gold Coast Slaves, but somewhat more so, than those from Angola, whose Situation and Mode of Living is in many Respects similar. But the Slaves from Bennin, Bony, & the Calabars, where the Soil is low, moist, and marshy, and the Common Food nothing else than Yams, Plantain, Cassava, Potatoes, and other soft and succulent vegetables, are of all others on the African Coast, the most weakly and delicate.[12]

Wet rice of the species *Oryza glaberrima* was probably first domesticated on the middle Niger about 1500 BCE, with a secondary cradle of domestication between the Sine-Salum and the Cassamance Rivers. Africans whose ancestors had lived in Jenne-Jeno [Mali], the oldest Iron Age city in Africa south of the Sahara, would have been accustomed to eating catfish and perch as well as rice and beef. The animal bones, grain fragments, and utensils found by archaeologists at the site indicate that between 100 and 1200 CE "everyone in this part of town dined nutritiously on catfish, perch, rice, beef, and presumably milk." According to Roderick and Susan McIntosh, annual silt-bearing floods of the Niger River yielded huge surpluses of rice, making it one of Jenne's major exports. Peter H. Wood, John Michael Vlach, Karen Hess, and Judith A. Carney are among the scholars who argue that South Carolina's early economic success owed a great deal to the contributions of black slaves and their agricultural knowledge—especially their knowledge of rice cultivation.[13]

The beginnings of European exploration and colonization of the New World took new food imports from the Americas and the East that were added to the acquired tastes of populations in Atlantic Africa. One of the most important of these imports from the Americas was maize. First documented in the African regions of most direct interest to the Portuguese during the early sixteenth century, maize was also included among the items loaded onto the slave ships as provisions and it was destined to become a regular part of the food rations dispensed to slaves by their masters in the antebellum South.[14]

Previously my own research has concentrated on edible plants, particularly (but not exclusively) domesticated crops, but recently I have begun to pay more attention to the animal products consumed by West and West-Central Africans and their scattered descendants. Thinking of the Nigerian context, Elizabeth Isichei identified four distinct entities for profitable historical analysis in the realm of food production: the yam complex (most closely identified with the Igbo and such other present-day Nigerian groups as the Yoruba), the cereal complex, later plant accessions, and animal husbandry.[15] Although most emphasis has been placed thus far on food crops and medicinal plants, there are glimpses in the written and archaeological record of what kinds of meats (both domestic and wild) were consumed in West and Central Africa during the era of the slave trade. For instance Nicholas Owens, who lived on the Gambia for many years, included meats in his description of what the peoples in that region ate:

> Their diet is rice, palm oil and small fowls at their common meals. Other times they have wild deer, monkeys, elephants, alligators, and several kinds of fish and birds, but the most particular kind of food is large worms that grow in trees close to the water, some exceeding three inches long and as thick as a man's thumb, of colour white and hideous to behold.[16]

While monkeys and elephants were absent from the new environment encountered by African forced migrants to the Western Hemisphere, deer, alligator, fish, and birds were in the habitat of many parts of the South and captives from the Gambia, for example, would have been familiar with these animals and with techniques for catching them.

## Provisioning the Middle Passage

The pathways of diffusion and the specific timing of the entry of common African food crops into the British colonies of North American have not been worked out fully, but provisioning of slave ships did not militate entirely against the persistence of some previous African food preferences, both in terms of foodstuffs and food preparation techniques. Before about 1695 most black newcomers to the British colonies of North America, even those arriving in Southern colonies, arrived via the West Indies and undoubtedly brought with them African-influenced foodways that had developed in what Thomas Marc Fiehrer has called the circum-Caribbean area.[17] A turning point was reached during the window of time between 1695 and about 1720 after which the bulk of the black newcomers for the duration of slave importation into North America would come directly from Africa with no stopovers or seasoning in the West Indies. Also between 1700 and 1780 about twice as many Africans as Europeans were shipped from the Old World to the Chesapeake and the Lowcountry. By the early 1700s when southern colonies from the Chesapeake to the Carolinas began to import the bulk of their Africans directly from Africa, European companies experienced in the slave trade had already begun to pay closer attention to the provisioning of these enslaved Africans during the Middle Passage. Such companies as the Royal African Company and the South Sea Company had learned that although some European foods were acceptable to the Africans, they fared better when the holds of slave ships were provisioned with their customary food. Provisioning records of the Royal African Company between 1705 and 1723 reflect this. At the company's factory in Whydah in 1705 corn, yams, malagueta pepper, and palm oil were recommended as suitable items. In 1707 the Royal African Company advised its agents at Cape Coast to supplement supplies of beans taken on in London with fifty chests of corn, forty pounds of malagueta pepper, twenty pounds of palm oil, two bushels of salt, and twenty gallons of rum for every one hundred slaves. When the Royal African Company agreed to "slave" one of the ships of the South Sea Company carrying 340 enslaved Africans the contract called for the following: fourteen bushels of salt, 280 chests of corn, 170 pounds of malagueta pepper, and seventy gallons of palm oil. Such provisions are typical of items loaded on the slavers. In addition, depending in part on the slavers' perception of whether the captives came from rice-eating or yam-eating societies, large quantities of rice or yams would be provisioned. Prominent among Africans who preferred yams were those shipped from the port of Calabar in what is now Nigeria. "The Calabar slaves," wrote James Barbot, Junior, "value this root above any other food, as being used to it in their own country." The records of such slave ships as the *Arthur* (1678), the *Elizabeth* (1754), the *Friend* (1768), and the *Othello* (1768–1769) indicate that significant quantities of yams were provisioned along with lesser quantities of plantains, limes, pepper, palm oil, and "gobbagobs" (goobers or peanuts). Not only did yams "take up so much room," as John Barbot (uncle of James Junior) observed, but also on longer voyages they sometimes rotted before they could be consumed. According to John Barbot's estimate, more than 100,000 yams had to be loaded for a cargo of 500 Africans—more than 200 yams per person.[18]

Having sketched the African food crops introduced into North America, I turn now to the second approach mentioned near the beginning of the essay, moving beyond the ingredients to the preparation and seasoning of these and other foods for consumption.

Charles W. Joyner insists that "food played a role in slave culture beyond mere sustenance . . . It had immense cultural and ideological significance: the choice of particular foods and particular means of preparation involved issues of crucial importance to the slaves' sense of identity."[19] The possibility of continuity of African food preparation techniques even during the Middle Passage itself is suggested by several observations. That African women prepared much of the food during the voyage is suggested by an entry from the journal of the ship *Mary* for Monday, June 20, 1796: "The Women Cleaning Rice and Grinding corn for corn cakes."[20] Even more explicit and detailed was the observation of George Pinckard, a physician who was aboard a North American vessel carrying enslaved Africans from "Guinea" to Savannah, Georgia, during the late-1790s. Their meals, too, consisted mainly of boiled rice and in a letter to a friend he gave the following description of how the rice was prepared:

> Their food is chiefly rice which they prepared by plain and simple boiling. At the time of messing they squat round the bowl in large bodies, upon their heels and haunches, like monkies, each putting his paw into the plat-

ter to claw out with his fingers. We saw several of them employed beating the red husks off the rice, which is done by pounding the grain in wooden mortars with wooden pestles, sufficiently long to allow them to sing while beating in mortars placed at their feet. This appeared to be a labor of cheerfulness. They beat the pestle in time to the song and seemed happy; yet nothing of industry marked their toil, for the pounding was performed by indolently raising the pestle and then leaving it fall by its own weight.[21]

All of the food items such as corn or rice were usually mixed with a sauce of meat or fish or with palm oil, product of an indigenous African plant and a constant and widely sought element in many traditional African cuisines. Once survivors of the Middle Passage reached plantation America, the meals they consumed in the fields commonly consisted of boiled yams, eddoes (or taros), okra, callaloo, and plantain, all seasoned generously with cayenne pepper and salt.

According to Charles W. Joyner, "slave cooks not only maintained cultural continuity with West African cuisine but also adapted the African tradition creatively to the necessities and opportunities of a new culinary environment."[22] There was what Joyner, using a linguistic analogy, has called "the African culinary grammar"—a set of implicit rules by which a bundle of ingredients is transformed into food deemed fitting for human consumption.[23] Joseph G. Brand, Morley R. Kare, and Michael Naim argue that "food habits are one of the last characteristics of a cultural group to disappear as the culture changes."[24] Yet Africans had to adapt and change their foodways creatively as they encountered new environments. In this process they both influenced and were influenced by the foodways of Europeans and Native Americans.

A significant part of "the African culinary grammar" alluded to by Joyner resides in the condiments and seasonings used to prepare foods. Many African traditional dishes are characterized by "bitey" or "hot" seasoning with red peppers, malagueta pepper, and other sources of hotness.

## The Emergence of Sub-Regional Styles in the Colonial and Revolutionary South

If it remains generally true, as John K. Thornton observed in 1996, that "historians have not yet fully investigated the implications of this regional diversity for the development of African-American culture," the exploration of the role of this sub-regional diversity in shaping the food habits and cooking and seasoning techniques of African Americans is in its infancy.[25] Enslaved African newcomers to the British colonies of North America (1619–1775), to the United States (1775–1810), to Spanish-held Louisiana (1719–1743 and 1777 to the early 1800s, including the ever so brief period when it was French-held) arrived through identifiable "nodes of import" to use John K. Thornton's apt phrase.[26] For the British colonial era in continental North America, the major sub-regional distinction in the South among what W. E. B. Du Bois called "the Planting Colonies" was between the Chesapeake and South Carolina.[27] These Southern sub-regions received African captives during different (though sometimes overlapping) time spans and from a different mix of regional origins in Africa. South Carolina, for example, experienced rhythms of African importation in which importation not only ebbed and flowed but in which the preponderant places of origin changed from one time period to another. True to the general pattern in the colonial South, the vast majority of the people of African descent carried into South Carolina came directly from Africa. The African origins of 63,400 individuals imported between 1733 and 1807 were summarized by William S. Pollitzer as follows:

| | |
|---|---|
| Senegambia | 20% |
| Windward Coast | 23% |
| Gold Coast | 13% |
| Whydah, Benin, Calabar | 4% |
| Congo | 17% |
| Angola | 23% |
| (Congo-Angola combined | 40%) |

Between March 1735 and March 1739, a period studied intensely by Peter H. Wood, almost 70 percent of the incoming Africans whose coastal origins in Africa were indicated in the import duty records and the *South Carolina Gazette* had been shipped from Angola.[28] During the 1740s, the decade following the Stono Rebellion, very little importation of Africans occurred at all and when importation resumed beginning in 1750 the main African sources for captive laborers shifted away from Angola. From the 1750s through the 1780s, when South Carolina suspended the oversea slave trade, Senegambia, the Windward coast, Sierra Leone, and the Gold Coast, taken together, surpassed Angola as a main source area with a noticeable increase in the importance of the Gold Coast as a place of origin during the 1780s.[29] Then, as we shall see later, when South Carolina reopened the trade in 1804, Angola resumed its prominence as a place of shipment for the last massive legal infusion of almost 40,000 Africans.

The region designated simply as Chesapeake (subsuming arrivals at various ports in both Virginia and Maryland) ranked tenth out of the seventeen most important "American ports of disembarkation" between 1662 and 1867 in a sample of voyages contained in the W. E. B. Du Bois Institute Slave Trade Data Base. The 288 ships in the sample that arrived in the Chesapeake during those years brought in an average of 210 slaves per ship.[30]

The patterns of distribution of newly arrived Africans in colonial Virginia, for example, can be characterized with some specificity. These patterns, I would argue, have implications for the introduction and distribution of African foodstuffs, food preparation, and seasoning techniques and of the African women who were responsible mainly for passing on and adapting these foodways. Allan Kulikoff, Douglas B. Chambers, and others have recognized that the largest group of Africans shipped to the Chesapeake region during the eighteenth century were from the Bight of Biafra (roughly 40 percent of the total for 1700 to 1800) and a plurality of those shipped from Biafra were yam-cultivating Igbo-speaking peoples.[31] Lorena S. Walsh has made astute and provocative observations of spatial and temporal patterns in the slave trade to the Chesapeake: slaving vessels from certain British home ports (London, Bristol, Liverpool) frequenting particular African coastal shipping points and they, in turn, delivering their black cargoes to certain specific Chesapeake ports.[32] Such fine-grained analysis of regional patterns, African origins, and particular Chesapeake destinations undoubtedly has implications for the culinary history we are trying to reconstruct, but we are only beginning to tease them out.[33] Most African newcomers to Virginia before about 1750 would have resided in the tidewater region, but, as Philip D. Morgan and Michael L. Nicholls have indicated, ". . . in the years after 1750 most Africans brought to Virginia were taken up the James [River] to be sold at ports like Bermuda Hundred. Most were then marched into the interior, where planters eagerly sought their labor on newly settled piedmont plantations."[34]

Morgan has suggested that there probably were regional differences in the amount and composition of animal protein consumed by eighteenth-century slaves with protein rations being "much stingier" in the Lowcountry than in the Chesapeake. The analysis of faunal remains at eighteenth-century sites in the Chesapeake indicates that in addition to hog meat—the main source of animal protein for most slaves—some captives also ate beef and mutton. Fish were also a significant source of animal protein; usually such smaller species as catfish, herring, and bass.[35] Thus in terms of the consumption of animals, the bulk of the animal protein consumed by slaves in the Chesapeake—based on the limited evidence available—was derived from domesticated rather than wild animals. In the Chesapeake sites that have been excavated, wild animals constituted less than 5 percent of the animal bones found.

In the South Carolina and Georgia Lowcountry, on the other hand, not only were slave owner–dispensed rations thinner on the whole, but there was also a relative lack of domestic meat supplied to them by their owners. Archaeological evidence indicates that slaves on coastal plantations in the Lower South exerted considerable efforts to augment their diets.[36] John Komlos's analysis of the heights of runaway slaves reported in advertisements published in newspapers between 1720 and 1770 reinforces the notion that Carolina slaves got the short end of the nutritional stick despite their obviously valiant efforts to supplement plantation rations. Clearly, Komlos observed "slaves residing in the Lower South were shorter than those in the Upper South."[37] Thus out of sheer necessity, if nothing else, Lowcountry slaves during the eighteenth century may have had to be more enterprising in supplementing their diets. Also many Lowcountry enterprises, especially the rice plantations, operated on the task system rather than the gang system that was associated with tobacco cultivation during the colonial period and which would later be employed in cotton cultivation. Not only was there the necessity to augment their diets through their own efforts, but there was the greater possibility of gaining considerable control over their own time under the task system. Morgan states that "probably no group of slaves could match those of the Lowcountry for the amount of time spent fishing and hunting."[38] Just as African-born females were able to continue many of their culinary ways during the Middle Passage and upon their arrival in North America, so African-born males shipped to South Carolina or Georgia did not leave their hunting and fishing skills behind. Nor did they become cultural amnesiacs as a result of even so horrible a journey as their transatlantic voyage. Morgan cites the example of Titus, a newcomer to South Carolina from Africa who spoke no English and had ritual scars down each side of his face. In 1775 he disappeared from a Santee River plantation and his master thought he had gotten lost "as he was out hunting."[39] Lowcountry slaves also engaged in chemical fishing similar to that practiced by the Djuka band of maroons in Surinam who made use of sinapou (*Tephrosia toxicaria*) and damned up tidal pools and inlets as well as catching fish using a line and a hook.[40] Archaeological evidence from eighteenth-century South Carolina and Georgia Lowcountry sites supports the notion that a significant proportion of the animal protein in the diets of slaves in the region—in contrast to their Chesapeake contemporaries—was obtained from wild rather than domesticated species. These included opossum, raccoon, deer, rabbit, turtle, mullet, topgaffsail, and catfish.

Similarly, as Morgan indicates, "Lowcountry slaves cultivated a much greater range of plants, including many more African varieties, in their own plots and gardens than did Chesapeake slaves."[41] During the eighteenth century white planters and European travelers visiting the Lowcountry observed Africans and their American-born progeny cultivating, preparing, and consuming the following African domesticated plants: Tania or tannier, millet, sorghum, sesame, African peppers, okra, black-eyed peas, and watermelon.

In certain parts of West Africa, especially Senegambia, sesame is called *benne*. Eighteenth-century Lowcountry slaves also called it "Benni" or "benyseed" and not only made soups and puddings containing sesame, but also used sesame oil on salads. Writing in the 1780s C. Bryant noted that blacks in South Carolina raised "large quantities of it [sesame], being very fond of the seeds, and make soups and puddings of them, as with rice and millet. They parch them over the fire, and with other ingredients stew them into a hearty food. The seed in Carolina is called 'oily grain' it yielding oil very copiously."[42] Today tourists visiting Charleston, South Carolina, will find individually-wrapped candies made of molasses and sesame seeds called benne candy or benniseed candy. In her letter book Eliza Lucas mentioned African peppers which she called "Negro pepper."[43] And during his American travels between 1785 and 1787 Luigi Castiglioni saw Africans in the Lowcountry cultivate "an annual herb with mallowlike flower . . ., which was brought by negroes from the coast of Africa and is called okra by them."[44] Although the plant, *Hibiscus esculenta*, is known by many different names in Africa, the word okra is almost identical in sound and meaning to *ókrò* in the Igbo language.[45] Writing in 1783 Anthony Stokes stated: "in the Rice Colonies . . . the Negroes in General have Rice, Indian-corn, potatoes or black-eyed pease sufficient to subsist them."[46] Despite the stereotypical identification of African Americans with watermelon, there is a kernel of truth to the linkage between the people's and the food's African origins. Geographers and botanists generally agree that the watermelon plant was first domesticated in West Africa and that it constitutes one of Africa's several original contributions to the world's storehouse of foodstuffs. It is not clear, however, precisely when and how African-domesticated watermelon came to be cultivated and consumed in North America, but by the early 1730s, Virginians of both races had grown fond of it.[47] According to the Englishman William Hugh Grove, who visited Virginia in 1733, the Virginians he knew "chiefly Esteem the Water Melon, which is green, as bigg as a Pump[k]in, smoothe, not furrowed. They Eat it as an apple, but in my opinion [it is] too flatt and Waterish. They say [eating] it hurts no one, even in fever."[48] African Americans are reported to have called the fruit watermillon rather than watermelon and George Krapp wrote: "The Negro's watermillon for watermelon was common English usage everywhere in America as late as the first quarter of the nineteenth century."[49] As Jessica Harris states, "Once rooted in this hemisphere, African plants such as okra, black-eyed peas, and watermelon went on to become emblematic of the food of Africans in the North American Diaspora."[50]

In some instances American plants were substituted for similar African plants as appears to have happened with the sweet potato. As writers such as Jessica B. Harris and Raymond Sokolov have been at pains to point out, sweet potatoes and yams are not the same thing; although they are both tubers they are not of the same species or even of the same genus. Beyond that relatively little has been said about the ubiquitous sweet potato which in much of southern cooking seems to have substituted for what was the yam niche in Old World African diets. Beyond the fact of this substitution nothing has been said about the world travels of the sweet potato and few explanations have been offered for why the substitution for true yams may have been attractive or advantageous. The ideas of the French writer Magulonne Toussaint-Samat whose monumental *History of Food*, originally published in French in 1987, did not appear in English translation until 1992, is helpful here. According to Toussaint-Samat, "the sweet potato comes from the equatorial forests of America," which has been common enough knowledge. But it may be less commonly known that it reached Polynesia about 2,000 years ago. To those who thought that the sweet potato was introduced into Africa near the beginning of the era of the Atlantic slave trade she says "we now have to put that date back several centuries, without knowing how or why it got there."[51] This raises the possibility that the sweet potato reached Africa in pre-Columbian times via the Melano-Polynesian connection from Ecuador or Columbia to the Pacific archipelagos to Malaysia and South-East Asia or to East Africa via Madagascar or by several different paths. Did American-derived sweet potatoes, ground nuts, peppers, and cassava diffuse to Africa in a cluster sometime before 1492 as the coconut palm, the banana tree, and taro (eddoes) appear to have done? Leaving aside the question of whether, how, or why the sweet potato reached Africa before the beginning of the Atlantic slave trade, Toussaint-Samat offers a persuasive reason why, when Africans from the yam zones reached North America, it slipped into the diets so readily and held its ground so effectively.

On October 12, 1774, even before the outbreak of hostilities in the American Revolution, the first Continental Congress discontinued the overseas slave trade, with that prohibition to go into effect on December 1 of the same year. The only holdout among the thirteen colonies was Georgia which did not adopt the resolution until the summer of 1775.[52] During the Revolution South Carolina and Georgia were loci of a disproportionate share of the fighting and experienced significant losses of their enslaved populations through a combination of warfare, disease, being carted off with the British army, or being evacuated with slaveholding Loyalists. Thus, once the war ended, Patriot slaveholders were eager to make up for the losses in their labor force by reopening the overseas slave trade. When they did so, however, importation from the West Indies was no longer permitted. This may have been because one result of successful revolution was that, as Stephen J. Goldfarb has suggested, "the United States was not part of the British imperial system."[53] And it may also have been, in part, because the West Indies were perceived to be rife with revolt. Virginia and Maryland abolished the overseas slave trade at the state level in 1778 and 1783 respectively. North Carolina levied a prohibitive import duty in 1786. In 1787, before the gathering of the Constitutional Convention in Philadelphia, South Carolina had temporarily suspended the trade. As the convention met, Georgia was the only state to have a legalized overseas trade in enslaved Africans. Georgia, which had not legalized slavery until 1750 and did not experience its first direct importation of Africans until 1766, began to impose restrictions in 1793 and closed off the trade altogether in 1798.

Even within South Carolina the demand for slaves from abroad was not uniform throughout the state. Lowcountry slaveholders were much less in need of additional laborers than the upcountry farmers. After the expiration of the initial five-year moratorium imposed in 1787, Lowcountry representatives in the state legislature were able to resist the demands of upcountry representatives to reopen the trade. Instead a series of extensions of the prohibition, two years at a time, was passed (in 1788, 1790, 1792, 1794, 1796, 1798, 1800, and 1802) amounting to an official fifteen-year suspension of the trade.

As indicated by Ira Berlin, who may have done as much as any living historian to sensitize us to the significance of regional variation and change over time in slavery and African American culture, "at the beginning of the nineteenth century, the great mass of slaves lived along the Atlantic seaboard, cultivated tobacco or rice, and practiced a variety of religious faiths derived from Africa."[54] In 1803, as the expiration of the initial twenty-year constitutional shield protecting the overseas slave trade from federal interdiction approached, South Carolina reopened the trade with a flurry of activity, importing almost 40,000 Africans over a four-year period. Since, by that time, Lowcountry planters (whose political representatives in the state legislature had resisted reopening the trade) had a sufficient and self-reproducing slave population, most of these newcomers were destined to be transported to the Upcountry of South Carolina or reshipped to Louisiana. The closer to the end of the legal transatlantic slave trade the greater the concentration of the newcomers' origins in the Kongo-Angola area of Central Africa. Thus while African-born people in the Chesapeake had diminished to virtual demographic insignificance by the turn of the nineteenth century, South Carolina—especially the Upcountry—and Louisiana (recently acquired from Napoleon Bonaparte's France) received a massive infusion of Bantu-speaking African newcomers.

By 1810 probably more than 80 percent of the enslaved black population in the United States lived between the Delaware and Savannah rivers, in Maryland, Virginia, North Carolina, or South Carolina, and the regional varieties of culture and cuisine between the Chesapeake and the Carolinas were still distinct. After 1810 the enslaved population experienced a massive involuntary relocation that Berlin describes as the Second Great Migration—the first, presumably, being the transatlantic slave trade. After a concise but thorough review of the history, evidence, and statistical methods used to develop estimates of the volume of this forced internal migration, Steven Deyle, author of the most recently published book on the domestic slave trade concluded:

> ... between 1820 and 1860 at least 875,000 American slaves were forcibly removed from the Upper South to the Lower South and that between 60 and 70 percent of these individuals were transported via the interregional trade [as opposed to traveling with migrating slave owners].[55]

This Second Great Forced Migration, otherwise known as the domestic or internal slave trade, resulted not only in the break-up of households, families, and kinship groupings and the geographical redistribution of the enslaved

African American population but also an acceleration of the commingling of the previously distinct sub-regional styles of African American cuisine. Concentrating on foods and their preparation may be a useful way to trace the fusion and transformation of African peoples into African Americans and help us advance the task of answering the question posed by Sterling Stuckey in the preface to his *Slave Culture* (1987): "How was a single people formed out of many African ethnic groups on the plantations of the South?"[56]

Although there is little agreement on the actual numbers involved, there is no doubt that the clandestine importation of "illegal aliens" from Africa to the United States continued to occur after Congress outlawed the overseas slave trade in 1807 (effective January 1, 1808). As late as the 1850s such slave ships as the *Clotilde* and the *Wanderer* (which arrived in 1858) landed Africans in Alabama, and South Carolina and Georgia, respectively. In the early twentieth century Charles J. Montgomery, a University of Chicago anthropologist with linguistic training, tracked down and interviewed seven survivors from among the 400 or so Africans obtained by the *Wanderer* near the mouth of the Congo River (Zaire) in West-Central Africa.[57] He took down word lists including samples of African counting systems. Significantly, in light of our focus, the list contained words referring to such foodstuffs as corn (*massa*) and manioc (*madeoka*). Most interesting of all was the word for peanuts or groundnuts—*goobas* or *nguba*—which by the 1850s had become common currency in the regional dialects of both blacks and whites in many parts of the rural South.

Because of now widely recognized health disparities between African Americans and Euro-Americans, "soul food" has come to be viewed as "unhealthy" in some quarters. We sometimes forget that traditional diets in what was once an overwhelmingly rural and agricultural region emphasized fresh foods derived from plant sources. As we have seen in the discussion of African foodways during the era of the Atlantic slave trade, many of the foods that we have come to identify with Southern cuisine were either domesticated in Africa (black-eyed peas, okra, sorghum, pigeon peas, leafy greens, watermelon, and sesame) or had been adopted before the arrival of Europeans in Africa during the early fifteenth century (turnips, cabbage, eggplant, cucumbers, onions, chick peas, dates, figs, kidney beans, and lentils). Others, introduced into Africa after 1500 CE—like tomatoes, chili peppers, maize, and cassava—had become significant sources of nutrients for many Africans in the catchment areas for the slave trade well before significant numbers of them were being transported directly into the British colonies of North America.

Folklorist Darryl Cumber Dance described the persistence of preferences for African foods among Africans in the United States:

African foods such as yams, watermelon, legumes, okra, and grains remained popular with Africans in America, as did wildlife such as deer, rabbits, squirrels, birds, and (of course) opossums. As in Africa, the African American's meals were predominantly vegetarian (this not so much by choice as circumstance).

While acknowledging that African American cooking "is certainly a derivative of African cuisine," Dance went on to say, "it largely developed as a result of the exigencies of life as a slave."[58] This statement suggests the necessity of shifting the focus of the essay slightly at this point from pre-American diets, foodstuffs, and food preparation techniques to some of the dietary "exigencies of life as a slave" to which Dance referred. Having already discussed some of the continuities and discontinuities and the transformation of African foodways observable during the colonial and early national periods, the concluding section of this essay concentrates on the antebellum period—roughly from 1820 to 1860.

In the brief compass of ten pages in his magisterial *Roll, Jordan, Roll: The World the Slaves Made* (1974) Eugene D. Genovese, under the heading "Kitchens, High and Low," offered a welter of astute insights into the role that slave diets and black cooks played in the shaping of what came to be known as Southern cooking. He began his discussion by citing the rather crude observation about food in Washington, D.C., made by the Ohio abolitionist senator, Benjamin F. Wade. In 1851 Wade complained that food in the nation's capital "is all cooked by niggers until I can smell and taste the nigger." Genovese commented that "Southerners themselves [referring apparently to white Southerners] have tended to discuss the subject [southern cooking] with greater respect, not to mention delicacy." He suggested that southern cooking "has undeniably been our most impressive regional cuisine" but noted that the praise heaped upon it had all too often been given to "Old Missus."[59]

What foods did the slaves eat? How did they prepare their foods? To what extent were they dependent on rations doled out by slave owners? Was there much variety in their diets? Were their diets nutritionally adequate to the amount and vigor of the work required of them? How did the food preparation techniques of black cooks preparing food for white consumption influence the palate of white Southerners?

At a very general level, discussions of slave diets usually revolve around how much slaves got to eat or how varied their diets were. The launching pad and reference point for much of this discussion over the last three decades was the brief discussion of "Food, Shelter, and Clothing" in *Time on the Cross* (1974) by Robert William Fogel and Stanley L. Engerman.[60] At one point they stated: "the nutritional content of the slave diet was quite high."[61] While acknowledging the possibility that this was so, Richard Sutch, a stringent critic of Fogel and Engerman, suggested that if it was so it was not necessarily because the rations provided by the slaveowners were adequate or nutritionally balanced. By going beyond rations, slaves struggled mightily and intelligently to make their diets nutritious.[62] In their characteristically provocative fashion Fogel and Engerman made the bold statement that "the belief that the typical slave was poorly fed is without foundation in fact."[63] They then proceeded to try to explain how such an erroneous view could have developed. A major factor, they believed, may have been "a misinterpretation of the instructions of masters to their overseers."[64] These instructions often mentioned only corn and pork in the typical daily amount of two pounds of corn and one half-pound of pork per adult. Ascertaining the quantity of food slaves consumed, to say nothing of its nutritional adequacy or balance, requires going beyond food allotments recorded in these written instructions. Furthermore, Fogel and Engerman argued that other food items which the slaves may have received did not usually appear in these minimalist (usually handwritten) instructions to overseers. So why were rations of corn and pork such central items of the plantation routine that they were almost religiously mentioned in written instructions to overseers and these other food-related items were seldom mentioned? Simply put, Fogel and Engerman offer two reasons:

1) While corn and pork "did not constitute the totality of the slave diet, they were the core of the diet on most plantations" because corn and pork could be stored and made available fresh for distribution year around, whereas vegetables were less easily stored and, hence, were primarily available on a seasonal basis.

2) While beef, chicken, dairy products, and Irish potatoes "had to be consumed soon after they were slaughtered or harvested (because they were difficult to preserve for later use) pork and corn were kept in store for the full year."[65]

These are both valid points worth considering, but focusing on "planta-tions" (meaning the larger sized slaveholdings in a small selection of the Parker-Gallman statistical sample from antebellum federal censuses for ex-ample) and on explaining the presence or absence of certain items from the written instructions of the masters to their overseers is problematic. This is what I call the Phillipsian fallacy (after the distinguished early twentieth-cen-tury historian of slavery, Ulrich Bonnell Phillips). Twenty slaves was usually the threshold that distinguished "planters" from farmers who owned some slaves. Considering that roughly half of the enslaved black people lived in units smaller than twenty, the typicality of assertions derived from examining a very small number of very large plantations is not to be taken for granted.

Focusing too intently on the food consumption patterns of adults in bond-age, regardless of the size of the units in which they were held, results in understating the devastatingly poor nutritional patterns and health status afflicting enslaved children. Some of the nutritional woes of slave children, in turn could be traced to mothers suffering from one or another nutri-tional deficiency. One of the most common forms of malnutrition is called Protein-Calorie Malnutrition (PCM), which particularly affects young chil-dren because their protein needs are much greater relative to their size than the needs of adults or of school age children. One of three forms of PCM is "kwashiorkor." Although the first clinical descriptions of the disease were not made until the early 1930s by Dr. Cicely Williams, it appears to have existed among young rural black children during the slavery era. Interestingly, the name of the disease derives from a word in the Ga language of Ghana and it means "the sickness which the older child gets when the next baby is born." Also, leaving aside favorable assessments of the "adequacy" of the diet of adult slaves as reflected in comparisons of completed adult heights of United States slaves with European peasantry, northern white urban dwellers, and southern white farmers, enslaved African Americans experienced and witnessed stag-gering levels of infant mortality compared to any other group with which one might choose to compare. According to Richard H. Steckel, newborn slave children weighed, on average, less than 5.5 pounds and infant mortality rates were in the range of 30 to 35 percent![66] Risk factors associated with neonatal deaths (birth to one month) have primarily to do with circumstances of the mother during the pregnancy and post neonatal deaths (one month to one year) are affected by breast-feeding and weaning practices, diet and other as-pects of infant care.

Attempts to gain perspective on diet and nutrition among American-born African Americans enslaved in the American South have resulted in numerous comparisons with other groups including enslaved African-born people, slaves in the Caribbean and Brazil, their adult English contemporaries, their white southern contemporaries, and even contemporaneous Russian serfs. As previously suggested by John Komlos's effort to extend the record of slave heights back into the eighteenth century using advertisements for runaway slaves in colonial newspapers, one of the central bodies of evidence used in these various comparisons has been the height that adults slaves achieved. Economic historians consider height to be closely related to nutrition. Southern slaves were an inch shorter than American whites generally, suggesting that whites had only a slight nutritional advantage over their enslaved black contemporaries, but Southern slaves averaged more than two inches *taller* than Trinidad-born slaves and nineteenth-century Englishmen. But the relative nutritional position of enslaved southern blacks does not look so rosy when regional differences among whites are considered or when they are compared with whites in their own region. Southern white males had a height advantage over northern white males and a very robust height advantage over their enslaved southern black male contemporaries.[67]

Kenneth F. Kiple's sophisticated, if also rather technical discussion of slave diet, points out that determining nutritional adequacy is more complicated than ascertaining the gross amount of caloric intake. Starting with caloric intake, Kiple, too, articulated the consensus among scholars alluded to by Fogel and Engerman: "Today most scholars agree that by the nineteenth century the majority of slaves enjoyed a sufficient intake of calories."[68] Balanced nutrition requires a sufficiency not only of protein from animal and other sources but adequate intake of a whole series of vitamins and minerals. In some instances deficiencies of certain specific vitamins and minerals can cause illness and in severe instances even death. As Nevin S. Scrimshaw put it, "even relatively mild degrees of specific nutritional deficiencies reduce resistance to most infections and increase their prevalence and severity."[69] Bleeding gums were frequent among the enslaved suggesting a low yield of Vitamin-C from the diet due in part to the reduced yield of Vitamin-C from vegetables that were boiled or simmered extensively and oxidation from cooking in iron pots. To the extent that eye afflictions were prevalent in the slave population deficiencies in Vitamin-A and, perhaps, riboflavin may have been common. Pellagra-like symptoms suggest deficiencies in niacin and so on. To the extent that

there was a higher incidence of lactose intolerance among the slave population than among some other populations is the extent to which other sources
of complete protein and calcium would have been necessary.[70] The combination of having darker complexions and seasonal cycles of overcast weather
and indoor work may have militated against the bodily production of opti-
mum levels of Vitamin-D although, historically, this probably became a more
severe problem for the darker complexioned African Americans of the post-
slavery era who migrated en masse to the cities of the North and Midwest beginning with the First World War. Vitamin-D is also considered to be critical
for the absorption of calcium and magnesium. Recent research has suggested
that sunshine and calcium may help guard against colorectal cancer and a
deficiency in Vitamin-D intake has been implicated as a possible risk factor
in several other types of cancers.[71]

In light of the earlier discussion of why sweet potatoes may have been a
judicious substitute for yams in slave diets and recipes (what I have called the
yam niche) Fogel and Engerman make the extremely telling assertion that
"while both slaves [in 1860] and free men [in 1879] ate large quantities of potatoes, slaves consumed virtually nothing but sweet potatoes, although most
of the potatoes consumed by free men [again in 1879] were white."[72] Sweet
potatoes are high in calcium and rich in Vitamin-A.

When we turn from a critical look at evidence derived from slave heights,
fertility rates, archaeological evidence, and manuscript census returns describing atypically large plantations to examine anecdotal evidence derived
from published slave narratives and interviews with former slaves, we find
that each of these bodies of evidence also poses methodological and interpretative difficulties. T. Lindsay Baker draws almost exclusively on the WPA
Slave Narratives to analyze Texas African American foodways and Josephine
Beoku-Betts draws heavily from the Slave Narrative Collection—largely
conducted by white interviewers—in discussing slave diets and food preparation in the South Carolina Lowcountry, but caution is necessary when
considering the former slaves' evaluation of their diets.[73] In a quantitative
analysis of the WPA Narratives which takes the race of the interviewer into
account, Paul D. Escott found that ex-slaves interviewed by whites recalled
having received much better diets under slavery than those interviewed
by African Americans. Six hundred seventy-one former slaves included in
Escott's analysis rated the food they had received as slaves. While a higher
proportion of those interviewed by blacks rated the food "same as master"
(11.5 percent versus 6 percent), over twice as many of those interviewed by

blacks characterized the food they received as inadequate (19 percent versus 9 percent). The widest discrepancy between the former slaves interviewed by blacks in the proportion who rated their food as good, 72 percent of those interviewed by whites compared with only 46 percent of those interviewed by blacks. Generally Escott found that "former slaves were more likely to reveal to black interviewers than to white ones negative feelings about their treatment and masters and their willingness to act upon those feelings."[74] Thus in the hypothetical and counterfactual scenario in which the majority of the WPA interviewers had been black, the former slaves' ratings of food may have been quite different and quite a bit less positive than the actual available responses in interviews which, overwhelmingly, were conducted by white interviewers.

A major health problem for African Americans today is hypertension and cardiovascular disease. One of the first things that a person with hypertension is told is to lay off of salt. There is some evidence that salt may not have been as readily available during slavery days as it is today when most pre-packaged and processed foods contain staggeringly large amounts of sodium. An account of "Slave Days in Florida," in *The Florida Negro* suggests that salt was at a premium:

> One commodity seems to have given both master and slave great cause for worry—salt; the master, because of the expense and trouble often necessary to secure it, and the slave because he so frequently went without it.
>
> In many cases it was obtained from boiled sea water; so great would have been the cost of purchasing it that one plantation owner near Monticello used to take a team and a slave and travel 40 miles to the Gulf and there boil down a week's supply. The process was slow and laborious.[75]

Margrett Nickerson, who had been a slave on William A. Carr's plantation in Leon County, Florida, remembered: "We done de cookin' in de fiahplace in iron pots, an' de meals wuz plenty of peas, greens, cornbread, burn' co'n fur coffee. Sometime de marster bot coffee fur us; we got water fum de open well. Jes 'fore de big gun fiahed dey fotched my pa fum de bay whar he wuz makin' salt; he done hear dem say de Yankees is comin' an' he sure wuz glad."[76]

Without doubt corn and pork were staples of the diets of slaves. The corn was often served in a corn meal mush: "Supper usually consisted of corn meal in some form, meat—white salt pork—on some occasions, coffee of parched corn, and sometimes potatoes or some green vegetable . . . The corn meal might be mush or bread." If it was mush, "it would be boiled with whatever scraps of meat or vegetable might be available, in a large pot out of which the whole family was served. If corn bread, it would have to be baked in the top of an iron spider, a large pan with a compartment over it in which coals could be heaped."[77]

Some recipes for corn pone or hot water cornbread have been passed down across generations. Sandra Y. Govan, whose mama's recipe for corn pone is reprinted in Daryl Cumber Dance's anthology, *From My People* (2002), succinctly describes the chain of transmission of the recipe across four generations of women in her family reaching back to a great grandmother who had been a slave:

> I acquired my taste for this special treat while watching my mother mix and make the bread and listening to her tell stories while she cooked of growing up on her family's farm in Ruston, Louisiana. She acquired her taste from watching her grandmother, who had been a slave, bake the bread on an open-hearth fireplace skillet.[78]

There has been considerable discussion of what the slaves ate during the period between 1820 and 1860, how much they ate in terms of volume or caloric intake, how much variety there was in their diets, and how nutritionally adequate their diets were. These discussions have led to explorations of the links between nutrition and height, fertility, and patterns of disease.

The exigencies of the Civil War probably meant food shortages for both enslaved African Americans and free white civilians in the Confederate states of America but little systematic study of the impact of the war on southern diets has been conducted. How the transition from slavery to freedom affected the diets of the freed people and their progeny is also beyond the scope of this essay. Because most African Americans remained in the rural South through the early twentieth century and continued to do physically demanding agricultural labor, the energy they expended and hence their caloric and nutritional needs are not likely to have diminished in comparison to slavery days. And while, quite naturally, some changes in foodstuffs and food preparation techniques occurred, there was a good deal of continuity in both during the remainder of the nineteenth century. For example, my own maternal grandmother, who was born in about 1886 in Albemarle County, Virginia, and lived there all seventy-two years of her life, was during most of my early childhood still using an outhouse, pumping water from a well and cooking on a wood burning stove. With the Great Black Migration to cities of the North, Midwest, and later the West, geographically mobile black southerners would become the carriers and ambassadors of Southern foodways generally. At some point along the line—many would say that not until as late as the 1960s—what black migrants once called simply "Southern food" or "down home cooking" was transformed into "soul food" and, according to such scholars as Tracy Poe, became an integral component of an emergent black urban identity.[79]

Theresa A. Singleton, an archaeologist of slavery and plantation life concerned about how we interpret objects found during excavations, identified two aspects of culture, what she calls "value culture" (customs, beliefs, and values "presumably influenced by an African heritage") and "reality culture." The latter, which Singleton defined as "those aspects of slave life largely influenced instead by external forces, especially social control inherent in a slave society" closely resembles what Daryl Cumber Dance characterized as "the exigencies of slavery." Singleton says that food-related objects found at archaeological sites can often be understood from both perspectives. She believes that what foods slaves ate was "determined to a large extent by a reality culture where the boundaries of what they ate were set by a combination of what food the slave owner provisioned and what they were able to forage." But she also considers foodways associated with the preparation and serving of food to be aspects of "value culture."[80]

To conclude, much assertion and counter-assertion exists about what enslaved African American Southerners ate, how much they ate, how it was prepared, and when it was consumed but very little systematic work has been undertaken. The time has come for someone or a team of researchers to examine systematically all slave testimony (fugitive slave narratives, autobiographies, newspaper and magazine articles, and interviews) and prepare a compendium of what enslaved blacks had to say about their diets under slavery. This effort should include indications of the size of the unit on which the slave narrator lived to the extent that is possible.

This essay was meant to be merely an extensive prolegomena to that sorely needed history of slave diet and nutrition. Only when we have sketched regionally specific profiles of what the African ancestors of African Americans ate and how they prepared it and what their American-born descendants ate and how they prepared it can we produce a nuanced depiction of the relative roles of African influences and the constraints of slavery and poverty in the development of African American and southern cuisine.

# Notes

1. Philip D. Curtin (1969: 70). Elsewhere I have explored in considerable detail what food crops Africans ate in the various regions that supplied captive laborers for the Western Hemisphere. See Robert L. Hall (1991), and (forthcoming 2007).
2. Robert L. Hall (1975).
3. See Christopher Ehret (1979).
4. Richard B. Sheridan (1972: 16n6).
5. There are numerous lists of "foods brought from Africa" or "foods coming from Africa." For example, Cathleen Baird Huck listed the following nineteen foods "coming from Africa" or trees "brought to the Americas from Africa": 1) yams, 2) millets, 3) sorghums, 4) rice, 5) cow peas or black-eyed peas, 6) okra, 7) gourds, 8) watermelons, 9) fluted pumpkins, 10) groundnuts, 11) malaguetta, 12) Benin pepper, 13) oil palm, 14) raffia palm, 15) kola shea butter, 16) locust bean, 17) akee, 18) baobob, and 19) silk cotton. Huck (1994: 4–7).
6. Judith A. Carney (2001: 378).
7. Ann Brower Stahl (1986).
8. Although this essay is not the place to delve deeply into the nexus between yam cultivation, the incidence of the sickle cell trait, and resistance to malaria, the physical anthropologist, Frank B. Livingstone, noted that "The cline in the frequency of the sickle cell trait coincides with this spread of yam cultivation": in Livingstone (1958), reprinted in M. F. Ashley Montagu, ed. (1962), quoted material on 290.
9. D. G. Coursey (1976: 402).
10. Some scholars, Patrick Manning for example, are convinced that the vernacular names by which yams and other food crops are known in Africa may constitute tools for the understanding of history by helping to determine when various populations adopted new food crops. This, in turn, illuminates both population fluctuations and the degree of Africa's involvement in the world economy at any give time. See Manning's comments in Nuala McGeogh and Joseph Souza (1989).
11. William Smith (1744). For a view of the use of yams among the Yoruba of present-day Nigeria, see William R. Bascom (1977).
12. cited in Daniel C. Littlefield (1981: 17n27).
13. Peter H. Wood (1974); John M. Vlach (1978), esp. 8; Karen Hess (1992); Judith A. Carney (2001).
14. See James C. McCann (2005), esp. chapter 2, "Naming the Stranger: Maize's Journey to Africa," 23–48.
15. Elizabeth Isichei (1983); Bascom (1977: 82–85). The paper from which this segment is extracted appears in full in Bascom (1951).
16. Nicholas Owen (1930), cited in Oliver Ransford (1971: 17).
17. Thomas Marc Fiehrer (1979: 26). A broader term is used by Dan Rose in (1974: 202–16).
18. James Barbot and John Casseneuve, "An Abstract of a Voyage to Congo River or Zair, and to Cabinde, in the Year 1700," and John Barbot, "A Supplement to the

Description of the Coasts of North and South Guinea," in Churchill's *Voyages*, vol. 5, both reprinted in Elizabeth Donnan (1930–1935, I: 463; II: 14–15), respectively.

19. Charles W. Joyner (1984: 239, 106).

20. Journal of the ship *Mary*, 20 June 1796; the ship sailed from Providence, Rhode Island, on 22 November 1795, intending to secure a cargo of slaves in Africa and carry them to Georgia, one of the few states where the overseas slave trade was still legal (Georgia did not abolish the trade until 1798). Excerpts from the journals were published in Donnan (1930–1935, III: 363–71).

21. George Pinckard, M.D. (1806), quoted in George Francis Dow, ed. (1927: xxviii, xxiv). What Dr. Pinckard perceived as indolence could easily be seen by others as efficient use of human effort, or as a form of resistance.

22. Joyner (1984: 106).

23. Ibid., 91.

24. Joseph G. Brand et al., (1980: 105).

25. Thornton (1996: 53).

26. See Ira Berlin (1981: 122–36). The period between 1968 and 1977 witnessed the beginning of a veritable revolution in writing about slavery that has continued unabated over the ensuing decades. For a review of the earlier literature to 1977 see Stanley L. Engerman (1979); some of the works reviewed by Engerman contained references to the feeding of slaves. See also Randall M. Miller and John David Smith, eds. (1988, and repr. ed. 1997) for many succinct articles (most having judiciously selected suggestions for further reading), written by leading specialists in the field of slavery studies; most relevant here is the lengthy entry on "Diet" by Kenneth Kiple, 186–91. Excellent published book-length syntheses of a massive revisionist body of work include Peter J. Parish (1989), and Peter Kolchin (1993). For a brief encapsulation of my view of the slave trade to North America, including an estimate that "over 500,000 Africans were imported into what became the United States between 1565 and 1807," see entry "Slave Trade," in John Mack Faragher, ed. (1990: 395–96).

27. On the transition to a majority black labor force in early colonial Carolina, see Russell R. Menard (1987). Observations made by Richard S. Dunn suggest that even more refined geographical distinctions could be made within the broad subregion generally termed the "Chesapeake." Willing to view the Chesapeake as "a single region—geographically, economically, and psychologically"—during the period before the American Revolution, Dunn argues that such singularity "began to fragment in the years following the Revolution," adding that there was "a growing divergence between developments in the upper and lower Chesapeake, between black life in Maryland and black life in Virginia"; Dunn (1983: 52). Although this divergence may have had dietary and nutritional implications for enslaved African Americans, I will not pursue that issue here.

28. Wood (1974).

29. David Richardson (1991).

30. David Eltis et al. (1999: 27).

31. Allan Kulikoff (1986); Douglas B. Chambers (2005) and see especially his Appendix A, "New Virginia Slave Trade Statistics, 1676–1775," 193–97.
32. Lorena S. Walsh (2001).
33. Stacy G. Moore (1989).
34. Philip D. Morgan and Michael L. Nicholls (1989: quote on 211).
35. Diana C. Crader (1984); see also Crader (1990). It should be noted that most of the faunal remains excavated from Chesapeake sites have been located either at Thomas Jefferson's Monticello or George Washington's Mount Vernon, and are often domestic- or house-slave sites.
36. Elizabeth Reitz et al. (1985).
37. John Komlos (1994: 103). If there is a caveat in this regional comparison, it is that African captives from West/Central Africa (the Congo-Angola region) tended to be shorter, on the whole, than Africans shipped from other parts of the Atlantic coast, particularly those from Upper Guinea (Mande, Wolof, Fulbe). Given the relatively small proportion of persons shipped to the Chesapeake who were derived from West-Central Africa and the relatively large proportion of Africans arriving in the Carolinas from the Congo-Angola area, the different mix of origins may have contributed to the shorter average heights of runaways from the Lower South.
38. Philip D. Morgan (1998: 138).
39. Ibid., 138.
40. For a good modern eyewitness account of how *sinapou* is still used for "chemical fishing" by the Djuka, see S. Allen Counter and David L. Evans (1981: 159–61). The bush-dwelling Djuka Maroons call the plant *neku*. The plant, found in both Africa and South America, stuns the fish by temporarily blocking their breathing apparatus but has no toxic effect on humans who might later consume fish caught in this manner.
41. Morgan (1998: 141).
42. C. Bryant (1783).
43. Elise Pinckney (1972: 28).
44. Luigi Castiglioni (1983: 171–72).
45. Chambers (2005: 40).
46. Anthony Stokes (1783), quoted in Betty Wood (1984: 237*n*43).
47. Mark Wagner (1981).
48. Gregory A. Stiverson and Patrick H. Butler III, eds. (1977: 34–35).
49. George Krapp (1926: 281).
50. Jessica B. Harris (2001).
51. Magulonne Toussaint-Samat (1993: 65).
52. While it is possible that between 1 December 1774 and the summer of 1775 Georgia may have continued to import Africans, most scholars as early as W. E. B. Du Bois have accepted the notion that the prohibition of the Continental Congress (the Association) was observed.
53. Stephen J. Goldfarb (1994: quote on 23).
54. Ira Berlin (1998: xxiv).

55. Appendix A, "Total Slave Migration, 1820–1860, and Percentage of Migration Attributable to the Interregional Slave Trade," in Steven Deyle (2005: 283–89, esp. 289).
56. Sterling Stuckey (1987: viii).
57. Charles J. Montgomery (1908).
58. Darryl Cumber Dance (2002: 422).
59. Eugene D. Genovese (1974: 540–49).
60. Fogel and Engerman (1974: 109–17).
61. Ibid., 11.
62. Richard Sutch (1976).
63. Fogel and Engerman (1974: 109). As was pointed out by Robert H. Abzug in his introduction to a festschrift volume honoring Kenneth M. Stampp and his *The Peculiar Institution* (1956), it was one of the first thoroughly researched full-scale reinterpretations of slavery since Ulrich Bonnell Phillips's *American Negro Slavery* (1918), and furthermore was "researched mostly in segregated archives": Abzug (1986: 2). These were, therefore, archives to which black would-be scholars of slavery in Stampp's generation were either denied access or, if they had access, it was under racial restrictions. It may appear churlish of me to observe that Stanley L. Engerman, in the diet and nutrition portions of his summary of "new evidence" on the realities of slavery (published in 1979 but treating publications through February 1977), in the rare instances when the work of black scholars of slavery such as Leslie Howard Owens (1976) were cited, their views were treated as marginal, not in keeping in the consensus view, or often discounted as in "for a dissenting view see . . .": Engerman (1979).
64. Fogel and Engerman (1974: 110).
65. Ibid., 110, 111, respectively.
66. Richard H. Steckel (1986).
67. On slave heights see Robert A. Margo and Richard H. Steckel (1982), and Gerald C. Friedman (1982).
68. Keneth F. Kiple (1988: 186).
69. Nevin S. Scrimshaw (1989: quote on 11).
70. The argument that the average daily amount of milk consumed by adult slaves was smaller than that of the adult white males is made in Nicholas Scott Cardell and Mark Myron Hopkins (1978).
71. This is not the place to pursue fully what I call the Vitamin-D factor in the health of African Americans and others. I am exploring this matter in a paper in preparation entitled, "Disease in the African Diaspora: The Role of the Atlantic Slave Trade." A suggestive study by Cedric Garland of the University of California at San Diego School of Medicine and his brother Francis Garland at the Naval Health Research Center found that people living in southern and western states with higher levels of exposure to sunlight had a significantly lower death rate from colorectal cancer than those living in the less sunny states. And a study of male employees at Western Electric Company's Chicago facility found significantly higher rates of colorec-

tal cancer (nineteen years after the original dietary data were collected from 1957 through 1959) for men with the lowest dietary intake of Vitamin-D and calcium compared with men having the highest dietary intake of those substances (38.9 per 1,000 versus 14.3 per 1,000 respectively). See Garland and Garland (1980).
72. Fogel and Engerman (1974: 113).
73. T. Lindsay Baker (1996); and Josephine A. Beoku-Betts (1994). Charles W. Joyner (1971; in Finkelman vol. 15, 1989) also drew extensively from the WPA Slave Narrative Collection.
74. Paul D. Escott (1979: 10).
75. Gary W. McDonough, ed. (1993: 22).
76. Ibid., 31.
77. Ibid., 20–21.
78. Sandra Y. Govan's recipe for corn pone in Dance (2002: 447).
79. Tracy N. Poe (1999).
80. Theresa A. Singleton (1991: esp. 158).

## Works Cited

Abzug, Robert H. 1986. "Introduction." In *New Perspectives on Race and Slavery in America:Essays in Honor of Kenneth M. Stampp*. Eds. Robert H. Abzug and Stephen E. Maislich. Lexington: University Press of Kentucky, 1–7.

Baker, T. Lindsay. 1996. "More Than Just Possum 'n Taters: Texas African-American Foodways in the WPA Slave Narratives." In *Juneteenth Texas: Essays in African-American Folklore*. Eds. Francis Abernathy, Patrick Mullen, and Alan Govenar. Denton: University of North Texas Press, 95–128.

Barbot, James, and John Casseneuve. [1700]. "An Abstract of a Voyage to Congo River or Zair, and to Cabinde, in the Year 1700." In *Documents Illustrative of the History of the Slave Trade to America*, 4 vols. Ed. Elizabeth Donnan. Washington, D.C.: Carnegie Institution of Washington, D.C., 1930, I, 463.

Barbot, John. [1700]. "A Supplement to the Description of the Coasts of North and South Guinea." In *Documents Illustrative of the History of the Slave Trade to America*, 4 vols. Ed. Elizabeth Donnan. Washington, D.C.: Carnegie Institution of Washington, D.C., 1939, II, 14–15.

Bascom, William R. 1951. "Yoruba Cooking." *Africa* 21.2: 125–37.

———. 1977. "Some Yoruba Ways with Yams." In *The Anthropologist's Cookbook*. Ed. Jessica Kuper. London: Routledge, Kegan Paul, 82–85.

Beoku-Betts, Josephine. 1994. "'She Make Funny Cake She Call Saraka': Gullah Women and Food Practices Under Slavery." In *Working Toward Freedom: Slave Society and Domestic Economy in the American South*. Ed. Larry Hudson. Rochester, NY: University of Rochester Press, 211–31.

Berlin, Ira. 1981. "The Slave Trade and the Development of Afro-American Society in English Mainland North America, 1619–1775." *Southern Studies* 20.2: 122–36.

———. 1998. "Introduction: Slavery as Memory and History." In *Remembering Slavery: African Americans Talk about Their Personal Experiences of Slavery and Emancipation*. Eds. Ira Berlin, Marc Favreau, and Steven F. Miller. New York: The New Press, xiii–xlvii.

Brand, Joseph G., Morley R. Kare, and Michael Naim. 1980. "Restraints in Accepting New Foods: Relationships among Taste, Acceptability, and Digestion." In *Nutrition, Food, and Man: An Interdisciplinary Perspective*. Eds. Paul G. Pearson and J. Richard Greenwell. Tucson: University of Arizona Press, 105–23.

Bryant, C. 1783. *Flora Diaetetica: Or History of Esculent Plants*. London: B. White.

Cardell, Nicholas Scott, and Mark Myron Hopkins. 1978. "The Effect of Milk Intolerance on the Consumption of Milk by Slaves in 1860." *Journal of Interdisciplinary History* 8.3: 507–13.

Carney, Judith A. 2001. *Black Rice: The African Origins of Rice Cultivation in the Americas*. Cambridge, MA: Harvard University Press.

———. 2001. "African Rice in the Columbian Exchange." *Journal of African History* 42.3: 377–97.

Castiglioni, Luigi. 1983. *Viaggio: Travels in the United States of America, 1785–1787*. Syracuse, NY: Syracuse University Press.

Chambers, Douglas B. 2005. *Murder at Montpelier: Igbo Africans in Virginia*. Jackson: University Press of Mississippi.

Counter, S. Allen, and David L. Evans. 1981. *I Sought My Brother: An Afro-American Reunion*. Cambridge, MA: M.I.T. Press.

Coursey, D. G. 1976. "The Origins and Domestication of Yams in Africa." In *Origins of African Plant Domestication*. Eds. Jack R. Harlan, Jan M. J. de Wet, and Ann B. L. Stemler. The Hague, Netherlands: Mouton, 383–408.

Crader, Diana C. 1984. "The Zooarchaeology of the Storehouse and the Dry Well at Monticello." *American Antiquity* 49.3: 542–58.

———. 1990. "Slave Diet at Monticello." *American Antiquity* 55.4: 690–717.

Curtin, Philip D. 1969. *The Atlantic Slave Trade: A Census*. Madison: University of Wisconsin Press.

Dance, Darryl Cumber. 2002. *From My People: An Anthology*. New York: W. W. Norton.

Deyle, Steven. 2005. *Carry Me Back: The Domestic Slave Trade in American Life*. New York: Oxford University Press.

Donnan, Elizabeth. 1930–1935. *Documents Illustrative of the History of the Slave Trade to America*, 4 vols. Washington, D.C.: Carnegie Institution of Washington, D.C.

Dow, George Francis, ed. 1927. *Slave Ships and Slaving*. Salem, MA: Marine Research Society.

Dunn, Richard S. 1983. "Black Society in the Chesapeake, 1776–1810." In *Slavery and Freedom in the Age of the American Revolution*. Eds. Ira Berlin and Ronald Hoffman. Urbana: University of Illinois Press, 49–82.

Ehret, Christopher. 1979. "On the Antiquity of Agriculture in Ethiopia." *Journal of African History* 20.2: 161–77.

Eltis, David, David Richardson, and Stephen D. Behrendt. 1999. "Patterns in the Transatlantic Slave Trade, 1662–1867: New Indications of African Origin of Slaves Arriving in the Americas." In *Black Imagination and the Middle Passage*. Eds. Maria Diedrich, Henry Louis Gates Jr., and Carl Pedersen. New York: Oxford University Press, 21–32.

Engerman, Stanley L. 1979. "The Realities of Slavery: A Review of Recent Literature." *International Journal of Comparative Sociology* 20.1–2: 46–66.

Escott, Paul D. 1979. *Slavery Remembered: A Record of Twentieth Century Slave Narratives*. Chapel Hill: University of North Carolina Press.

Fiehrer, Thomas Marc. 1979. "The African Presence in Colonial Louisiana: An Essay on the Continuity of Caribbean Culture." In *Louisiana's Black Heritage*. Eds. Robert R. Macdonald, John R. Kemp, and Edward F. Haas. New Orleans: Louisiana State Museum.

Friedman, Gerald C. 1982. "The Height of Slaves in Trinidad." *Social Science History* 6.4: 482–515.

Garland, Cedric F., and Frank C. Garland. 1980. "Do Sunlight and Vitamin D Reduce the Likelihood of Colon Cancer?" *International Journal of Epidemiology* 9.3: 227–31.

Garland, Cedric F., et al. 1985. "Dietary Vitamin D and Calcium and Risk of Colorectal Cancer: A 19-Year Prospective Study in Men." *Lancet*. 9 February: 307–9.

Genovese, Eugene D. 1974. *Roll, Jordan, Roll: The World the Slaves Made*. New York: Alfred A. Knopf.

Goldfarb, Stephen J. 1994. "An Inquiry into the Politics of the Prohibition of the International Slave Trade." *Agricultural History* 68.2: 20–34.

Hall, Robert L. 1975. "'Come Out from Among Them': Black Migration, Urban Culture and Human Geography." *Research Reports in Social Science*. Florida State University: Institute for Social Research, 61–84.

———. 1990. "Slave Trade." In *The Encyclopedia of Colonial and Revolutionary America*. Ed. John Mack Faragher. New York: Facts on File, 395–96.

———. 1991. "Savoring Africa in the Americas." In *Seeds of Change: Five Hundred Years after Columbus*. Eds. Herman J. Viola and Carolyn Margolis. Washington, D.C.: Smithsonian Institution Press, 161–72.

———. Forthcoming 2007. "Food Crops, Medicinal Plants, and the Atlantic Slave Trade." In *African American Foodways: History and Culture*. Ed. Anne Bower. Urbana: University of Illinois Press.

Harris, Jessica B. 2001. "Same Boat, Different Stops: An African Atlantic Culinary Journey." In *African Roots / American Cultures: Africa in the Creation of the Americas*. Ed. Sheila S. Walker. Lanham, Md.: Rowman & Littlefield Publishers, 169–82.

Hess, Karen. 1992. *The Carolina Rice Kitchen: The African Connection*. Columbia: University of South Carolina Press.

Higgins, Robert W. 1964. "Charles Town Merchants and Factors Dealing in the External Negro Trade, 1735–1775." *South Carolina Historical Magazine* 65: 205–17.

Huck, Cathleen Baird. 1994. "The Diet of American Slaves and Its Influence on American Foodways." *Food for Thought* (Spring): 4–7.

Isichei, Elizabeth. 1983. *A History of Nigeria*. London: Longman.

Joyner, Charles W. 1971. "Soul Food and the Sambo Stereotype: Foodlore from the Slave Narrative Collection." *Keystone Folklore Quarterly* (Winter): 171–78. Repr. in Paul Finkelman, ed., *Articles on American Slavery*, vol. 15, *Medicine, Nutrition, Demography, and Slavery*. New York: Garland Publishers, 1989.

———. 1984. *Down By the Riverside: Slave Folklife in a South Carolina Slave Community.* Urbana: University of Illinois Press.

Kiple, Kenneth F. 1988. "Diet." In *Dictionary of Afro-American Slavery.* Eds. Randall M. Miller and John David Smith. New York: Greenwood Press, 186–91.

Kolchin, Peter. 1993. *American Slavery 1619–1877.* New York: Hill and Wang. Repr. 2003.

Komlos, John. 1994. "The Height of Runaway Slaves in Colonial America, 1720–1770." In *Stature, Living Standards and Economic Development: Essays in Anthropometric History.* Ed. John Komlos. Chicago: University of Chicago Press, 779–802.

Krapp, George. 1926. "The English of the Negro." In *Readings from American Mercury.* Ed. Grant C. Knight. New York: Books for Library Press, Inc., 279–92.

Kulikoff, Allan. 1986. *Tobacco and Slaves: the Development of Southern Cultures in the Chesapeake, 1680–1800.* Chapel Hill: University of North Carolina Press.

Littlefield, Daniel C. 1981. *Rice and Slaves: Ethnicity and the Slave Trade to Colonial South Carolina.* Baton Rouge: Louisiana State University Press.

———. 1990. "The Slave Trade to Colonial South Carolina: A Profile." *South Carolina Historical Magazine* 91: 68–99.

Livingstone, Frank B. 1958. "Anthropological Implications of Sickle Cell Gene Distribution in West Africa." *American Anthropology* 60.3: 533–62. Repr. In M. F. Ashley Montagu, ed., *Culture and the Evolution of Man.* Oxford: Oxford University Press, 1962, 271–99.

Margo, Robert A., and Richard H. Steckel. 1982. "The Height of American Slaves: New Evidence on Slave Nutrition and Health." *Social Science History* 6: 516–38.

McCann, James C. 2005. *Maize and Grace: Africa's Encounter with a New World Crop, 1500–2000.* Cambridge, MA: Harvard University Press.

McDonough, Gary W., ed. 1993. *The Florida Negro: A Federal Writers' Project Legacy.* Jackson: University Press of Mississippi.

McGeogh, Nuala, and Joseph Souza. 1989. "What Yams Can Tell Us About Africa." *History Newsletter and Job Search.* Department of History, Northeastern University (Winter-Spring).

Meaders, Daniel C. 1975. "South Carolina Fugitives as Viewed Through Local Colonial Newspapers with Emphasis on Runaway Notices, 1732–1801." *Journal of Negro History* 60.2: 288–319.

Menard, Russell R. 1987. "The Africanization of the Lowcountry Labor Force, 1670–1730." In *Race and Family in the Colonial South.* Eds. Winthrop D. Jordan and Sheila L. Skemp. Jackson: University Press of Mississippi, 81–108.

Miller, Joseph C. 1976. "The Congo-Angola Slave Trade." In *The African Diaspora: Interpretive Essays.* Eds. Martin Kilson and Robert Rotberg. Cambridge, MA: Harvard University Press, 76–113.

Miller, Randall M., and John David Smith, eds. 1988. *Dictionary of Afro-American Slavery*. New York: Greenwood Press.

Montgomery, Charles J. 1908. "Survivors from the Cargo of the Negro Yacht Wanderer." *American Anthropologist* 10: 611–23.

Moore, Stacy G. 1989. "'Established and Well Cultivated': Afro-American Foodways in Early Virginia." *Virginia Cavalcade* 39.2: 70–83.

Morgan, Philip D. 1998. *Slave Counterpoint: Black Culture in the Eighteenth-Century Chesapeake & Lowcountry*. Chapel Hill: University of North Carolina Press.

Morgan, Philip D., and Michael L. Nicholls. 1989. "Slaves in Piedmont Virginia, 1720–1790." *William and Mary Quarterly* 46.2: 211–51.

Owen, Nicholas. 1930. *Journal of a Slave Dealer*. London: Routledge.

Owens, Leslie Howard. 1976. *This Species of Property: Slave Life and Culture in the Old South*. New York: Oxford University Press.

Parish, Peter J. 1989. *Slavery: History and Historians*. New York: Harper and Row.

Pinckard, George, M.D. 1806. *Notes on the West Indies*. London: Longman, Hurst, Rees, and Orme.

Pinckney, Elise. 1972. *The Letterbook of Eliza Lucas Pinckney, 1739–1787*. Chapel Hill: University of North Carolina Press.

Poe, Tracy N. 1999. "The Origins of Soul Food in Black Urban Identity: Chicago, 1915–1947." *American Studies International* 37.1: 4–33.

Pollitzer, William S. 1958. "The Negroes of Charleston (S.C.): A Study of Hemoglobin Types, Serology, and Morphology." *American Journal of Physical Anthropology* 16: 241–63.

Ransford, Oliver. 1971. *The Slave Trade: The Story of Transatlantic Slavery*. London: John Murray, Ltd.

Reitz, Elizabeth, Tyson Gibbs, and Ted A. Rathbun. 1985. "Archaeological Evidence for Subsistence on Coastal Plantations." In *The Archaeology of Slavery and Plantation Life*. Ed. Theresa A. Singleton. New York: Academic Press, 163–91.

Richardson, David. 1991. "The British Slave Trade to Colonial South Carolina." *Slavery and Abolition* 12.3: 125–72.

Rose, Dan. 1974. "Detachment: Continuities of Sensibility among Afro-American Populations of the Circum-Atlantic Fringe." *Journal of Asian and African Studies* 9.3–4: 202–16.

Scrimshaw, Nevin S. 1989. "Completing the Food Chain: From Production to Consumption." In *Completing the Food Chain: Strategies for Combating Hunger and Malnutrition*. Eds. Paula M. Hirschoff and Neil G. Kotler. Washington, D.C.: Smithsonian Institution Press, 1–17.

Sheridan, Richard B. 1972. "Africa and the Caribbean in the Atlantic Slave Trade." *American Historical Review* 77.1: 15–35.

Singleton, Theresa A. 1991. "The Archaeology of Slave Life." In *Before Freedom Came: African-American Life in the Antebellum South*. Eds. Edward D. D. Campbell Jr., and Kym S. Rice. Charlottesville: University Press of Virginia, for the Museum of the Confederacy, 155–75.

Smith, William. 1744. *A New Voyage to Guinea*. Reprint. London: Frank Cass, 1967.

Stahl, Ann Brower. 1986. "Early Food Production in West Africa: Rethinking the Role of the Kintampo Culture." *Current Anthropology* 27.5: 532–36.

Steckel, Richard H. 1986. "Birth Weights and Infant Mortality Among American Slaves." *Explorations in Economic History* 23.2: 173–98.

Stiverson, Gregory A., and Patrick H. Butler III, eds. 1977. "Virginia in 1732: The Travel Journal of William Hugh Grove." *Virginia Magazine of History and Biography* 85.1: 18–44.

Stokes, Anthony. 1783. *A View of the Constitution of the British Colonies in North America and the West Indies, with a Supplementary Index*. London: B. White.

Stuckey, Sterling. 1987. *Slave Culture: Nationalist Theory and the Foundations of Black America*. New York: Oxford University Press.

Sutch, Richard. 1976. "The Care and Feeding of Slaves." In *Reckoning with Slavery: A Critical Study in Quantitative History*. Eds. Paul A. David, Herbert G. Gutman, Richard Sutch, Peter Temin, and Gavin Wright. New York: Oxford University Press, 231–301.

Thornton, John K. 1996. "African-American Origins." In *Encyclopedia of African American Culture and History*. Eds. Jack Salzman, David Lionel Smith, and Cornel West. vol. 1. New York: Macmillan Library Reference, 53–58.

Toussaint-Samat, Maguelonne. 1993. *History of Food*. Cambridge, MA: Blackwell Reference.

Vlach, John M. 1978. *The Afro-American Tradition in Decorative Arts*. Cleveland, OH: Cleveland Museum of Art.

Wagner, Mark. 1981. "The Introduction and Early Use of African Plants in the New World." *Tennessee Archaeologist* 6: 112–23.

Walsh, Lorena S. 2001. "The Chesapeake Slave Trade: Regional Patterns, African Origins and Some Implications." *William and Mary Quarterly* 58.1: 139–70.

Wood, Betty. 1985. *Slavery in Colonial Georgia, 1730–1776*. Athens: University of Georgia Press.

Wood, Peter H. 1974. *Black Majority: Negroes in Colonial South Carolina from 1670 through the Stono Rebellion*. New York: Alfred A. Knopf.

# Harriet Jacobs at Home in Incidents in the Life of a Slave Girl

ANNE BRADFORD WARNER

In critical studies of Harriet Jacobs and her slave narrative, *Incidents in the Life a Slave Girl* (1861), she is often positioned in one of two groups; either she is examined in the body of antebellum slave narratives, almost all of which have male authors, or she is placed in a chronology of important writings by black women, most of whom, in the antebellum era, are northern. Her fit is, in both cases, a little off; in each case some significant part of her identity is de-emphasized because of her almost unique situation in the history of African American writing—as African American, southern, female, literate, and publishing before the Civil War. I believe she was fully aware of the unique combination of experiences that informed her story and that she made a point of her difference. In particular, her articulated vantage point on the white and black southern communities in Edenton, North Carolina, was distinctive because she was a woman, a mother, and a former slave—writing. Jacobs had a view of family and community not mirrored in male slave narratives and a view of the South not mirrored in works by northern black women.

It is my argument here that Jacobs was self-consciously southern-identified and that she constructed for her northern readers a radically new portrait of a southern home. Although she participated fully in the antislavery polemic that showed the slave-owning southern states as fallen, blighted, and full of perversity, she also introduced a view of the southern, African American folk community as organized, functional, and rich with its own cultural legacies and traditions. Jacobs's home—such an important theme in her narrative—remained, in significant ways, the home of her grandmother in Edenton, the Edenton to which she could not foresee a return while slavery existed. Despite her flight from this town in 1842, *Incidents* documents Jacobs's culturally

*Southern Quarterly* 45.3 (2008): 30–47.

specific southern and African American home community in a way rarely presented in writing before the Civil War.

From the beginning of her work, Jacobs emphasizes the authority inherent in the southern experience. As Frances Smith Foster points out in her discussion of Jacobs's uses of authority,[1] the autobiographer uses an epigraph, not from a northern abolitionist, but from a southern woman—an unnamed North Carolina woman whom Angelina E. Grimké, a white North Carolinian abolitionist, quoted in the *Appeal to the Christian Women of the South* (1836), and with whose comments on northerners' ignorance about slavery Grimké disagreed. The text of the epigraph asserts, "Northerners know nothing at all about Slavery. They think it is perpetual bondage only. They have no conception of the depth of degradation involved in that word, SLAVERY; if they had, they would never cease their efforts until so horrible a system was overthrown."[2] The epigraph on Jacobs's title page draws attention to the southern experience of slavery, validating a southern insight into its nature over a depiction by northern abolitionists. Disagreeing with Grimké's notion that northern abolitionists have a full appreciation of the "degradation" of slavery by positioning the anonymous North Carolina woman's statement as an epigraph, Jacobs emphasizes southern identity and experience, even effacing race, as Foster points out. Thus, Jacobs makes southernness a type of authority and also distinguishes between the lived experience of a place and a discourse about it, whether that discourse be abolitionist rhetoric or sketches from casual social observation.

## N. P. Willis and The Honorable Miss Murray: Misrepresenting Slavery

Jacobs's writing, no doubt, responded to the popular idealized and false pictures of the southern culture represented, in part, by the work of The Honorable Amelia Matilda Murray, whom Jacobs mentions in *Incidents*, or even by the travel vignettes of Jacobs's own employer.[3] While Jacobs wrote her narrative in the attic of his large estate, Idlewild, in the Hudson River Highlands,[4] Nathaniel Parker Willis sustained himself through the publication "of fashionable news and fashionable literature" in the *Home Journal*.[5] His family and servants all became part of his material in these sketches, as did the places to which he traveled. His observations about contented slaves in *A Health Trip to the Tropics* (1853), for instance, must have been a bitter pill to

Jacobs. As she writes to Amy Post, the complicated circumstances that compelled Jacobs to write in secret at night have, at the center, an apprehension of
Willis's displeasure: "Mr. W[illis] is too proslavery he would tell me that it was
very wrong and that I was trying to do harm or perhaps he was sorry for me
to undertake it while I was in his family."[6]

During the 1850s, Willis eagerly sought a readership in the proslavery
South. His travel to the South and his observations of it created a "fiction"
against which Jacobs wrote her "facts."[7] In a letter written about his visit to
Lexington, Kentucky, Willis extols one "advantage" of slavery—the lack of
suburbs—unlike the "purgatory of shanties" that line the road from the "interior grandeur" of northern cities: "The labouring classes live in the suburbs
of towns at the North. At the South they live, *each with his master*, and either
in compulsory cleanliness or in dirt hidden from the public eye."[8] This theme
of living with the master in an extended family is reinforced as Willis walks
through Lexington, still noting the absence of suburbs: "The merry black
faces, with numberless ebony babies, which I had seen in the group at the
side entrance of every house as I came along, were instead of this nuisance
[northern laborers] I missed—*negro comfort well distributed instead of white
wretchedness in a heap.*"[9] Willis's observations about slavery in the South mirror his own complacent commentaries about the mainly African American
servants that staff Idlewild. Willis's observation sustains a perverse fiction;
it cannot approximate lived experience. His insistence on the "merry black
faces" and "*negro comfort*" promotes the lie and, by doing so, diminishes the
credibility of the African American witness to slavery.

Jacobs explicitly invokes the authority of lived experience in *Incidents*
where she discusses the travel writing of "The Hon. Miss Murray."[10] Converted
to a proslavery stance during her visit to the American South, Amelia Matilda
Murray, a lady-in-waiting to Queen Victoria, was forced to resign her station
in 1856 because of the public position she presented in *Letters from the United
States, Cuba, and Canada*.[11] Murray's unexpected and outspoken defense of
slavery dramatizes the dangers inherent in observation. In some of her last
letters, Murray assures her readers that she has not been "hoodwinked and
cheated into an advocacy of southern institutions, when, wholly unknown
and unsuspected, [she has] seen with [her] own eyes, and heard with [her]
own ears."[12] In fact, presenting Topsy as the "reality" of the southern culture
and Uncle Tom as the "myth," Murray comments that Harriet Beecher Stowe
might have been fairer if she had "lived for some months among the institutions and the people which, in *Uncle Tom*, she thoughtlessly, perhaps not

intentionally, vilified."[13] This accusation about failed perceptions also forms a salient theme in *Incidents*. Certainly for Jacobs the accurate portrayal of any slave by any of these prominent writers was doubtful; whether proslavery or abolitionist, these writers demonstrate a class and race bias that regulates their perception. Jacobs offers this corrective for Murray:

> A small portion of my experience would enable her to read her own pages with anointed eyes. If she were to lay aside her title and, instead of visiting among the fashionable, became domesticated, as a poor governess, on some plantation in Louisiana or Alabama, she would see and hear things that would make her tell quite a different story. (185)

Thus, Jacobs refutes Murray's fictions of "happy darkies"; in the Edenton chapters Jacobs explains the dynamics of the dominant social order that make the appearance of the slaves' well-being plausible to visitors. It is Jacobs's agenda not only to demonstrate the degree of degradation female slaves were subjected to and activate northern women on behalf of these slaves, but also to re-present the ethos of the African American family and home in the South. *Incidents* is the antidote to these pictures of slaves as mindless and carefree children, unconcerned with an orderly existence and incapable of serious, self-motivated productivity. Willis, Murray, and even Stowe help to perpetuate these reductive and demeaning types, and Jacobs responds by rectifying these "fictional" images.

Thus, in *Incidents*, Jacobs delivers a revisionist portrait of her southern home, against the popular sentimental sketches of the "extended" southern family. Jacobs addresses the northern reader's understanding of sexual abuses in the slavocracy by dramatizing the "degradation" discussed in the Grimké passage. At the same time that the reader witnesses the deepening perversity and social decline that characterize the "family of Flints," Jacobs focuses on the power and function of the African American family and community; in this community, the reader finds the values mirrored in much women's writing of the period—industry, restraint, and piety. When Jacobs went north in 1842, she left a family, a community, and, even more importantly, a culture that had been marginalized and rendered invisible to most audiences of her time. She ends her narrative with a description of her longing for "a hearthstone of [her] own" and the "solace" she finds in the "tender memories" of her grandmother. The narrative ends without the recovery of the home and community that constitute the "light fleecy clouds floating over a dark and troubled sea"

(201). The portrait of this African American home and community stands in contrast to the bitter picture of the slavocracy, its cant, its silences, and its perversions. This is a portrait only a southern slave could draw. Jacobs implies, as Anna Julia Cooper would state thirty years later, "the 'otherside' has not been represented by one who lives there."[14] Jacobs's authority rests upon her being a southern slave and a woman.

Among the many cultural tasks *Incidents* accomplishes, one is the portrayal of a highly organized subculture with a productive life of skilled work, political understandings, communication networks, and significant religious traditions. Many of these features, as Jean Fagan Yellin has pointed out, shape Jacobs's position of agency or empowerment; her experience of her home shaped her reflection, articulateness, and activism. We can see influential features of her cultural landscape in several parts of her text, *Incidents in the Life of a Slave Girl*: first, the reader is introduced to a skilled, hardworking family, whose members share a home; second, the text presents a multigenerational family tradition of striving toward freedom and arguing about the ethics of stealing oneself; third, events suggest the rich community of the Underground Railroad and the maroon culture that coexist invisibly with the white town culture; and finally Jacobs portrays the highly developed, multicultural religious beliefs and practices that characterize the slave community. By looking first at the traditional contexts for women's writing and then examining the distinctive southern environment of *Incidents*, one can see the deliberateness with which Jacobs constructs her southern identity.[15]

## Antebellum Slave Narratives and the Gendered Community

The Linda Brent of Jacobs's *Incidents* differs greatly from other narrators of popular slave narratives appearing in the 1850s when Jacobs was writing hers. Though her narrative shares much with the works of, for instance, Frederick Douglass and William Wells Brown, as well as with the writing of her own brother, John S. Jacobs, Linda/Harriet is no picaro—she does not, like many male heroes, wander from place to place, living by her wits in a chaotic universe. She is thoroughly anchored in her community. This difference, usually viewed as determined by the interests and identity politics of gender, also makes Jacobs's writing far more centered in a particular time, place, and culture. Though the attachment to family is sometimes remarkably strong in the more traditional male slave narratives, frequently the narrator's family is so undermined that the attachment is never formed, and rarely do these narratives depict a stable, highly organized folk culture as it exists in Edenton in Jacobs's narrative.

Frederick Douglass's comments about the slave culture he observes on the eastern shore of Maryland offer a dramatic contrast to the commentary in Jacobs. In Douglass's two slave narratives published before *Incidents*, he considers the activities of the holidays from Christmas to the New Year. He observes to his northern reader, in a voice attuned to abolitionist puritanism, that, at Jubilee time, "only those wild and low sports, peculiar to semi-civilized people, are encouraged."[16] Often in the invective against the wrongs done to slaves and the brutality of chattel slavery, the traditional slave narrative focuses on the brutalization and victimization perpetrated upon the slave in a life relieved only by individual kindnesses—not by a systematic operation of folk values aimed at interpreting and responding to slavery. For Douglass and other slave narrators, the cultural folk practices may temporarily relieve or protect the hero, but the slave community is rarely presented as having order and agency. Jacobs differs from many of her fellow fugitive slave narrators in her portrayal of the culture, though she is often identified through this genre.

The remarkable popularity of Jacobs's text since Jean Fagan Yellin's 1987 edition of it has resulted in the inclusion of *Incidents* in many studies of black women's writing, the second context in which she frequently has appeared. The works of Hazel Carby, Valerie Smith, Joanne Braxton, and Frances Smith Foster, for instance, located Harriet Jacobs/Linda Brent as a key figure in establishing the themes to follow in later works by black women: legal resistance to economic and sexual exploitation, rhetorical methods for claiming authority and personhood, the compelling moral demands of motherhood, and the active, conflicted link between feminism and abolition.

Writing from the North herself, Jacobs shares the antislavery argument that characterizes the speaking and writing of many black women of the period. Like others, Jacobs conducts the economic critique of slavery as it profits from children who follow the condition of the mother; she dramatizes her outrage at the Fugitive Slave Law which caused tens of thousands of fugitives to relocate, and she pleads for, first—then demands—the right of women to have a voice. She also has significant themes in common with the African American women writing spiritual autobiographies and responding to the call to preach, as her slave narrative is deeply engaged with spiritual concerns and spiritual vision. However, Jacobs is distinctive in her carefully constructed portrait of the southern African American religious community.

Carla Peterson's *"Doers of the Word": African-American Women Speakers & Writers in the North (1830–1880)* teases out one very important distinction between Jacobs and other African American women speaking or writing in the antebellum North: Jacobs's "narrative of retrospection" becomes a means of "creating community." Peterson discusses Jacobs's isolation in the North, caused in part because of the economic limitations and legal vulnerability of women, especially fugitives, in the 1840s and 1850s. Moreover, Peterson interprets the figure of Jacobs's grandmother, Aunt Martha, to represent "the promotion and maintenance of community values."[17] Thus, "Without a hearthstone of [her] own" in the North, Jacobs portrays a home in Edenton.[18]

## Domesticity and Productivity

Home, the terrain for domestic fiction, is often characterized as the place of relative quiet and stability in a larger world of unbridled competition. The longstanding concept of separate spheres, certainly reflected in women's literature of the 1850s, encourages that historical representation of the American home as a communal refuge and retreat from a hostile marketplace. The abrupt shifts of fortune that characterize the plots of domestic fiction were a reality of the nineteenth-century marketplace. To some extent, Jacobs also acknowledges that sacredness of home, especially the sacredness of a home protected by law and inviolable—in contrast to the domiciles of slaves. However, it was the case with Linda, as with all slaves, that the public sphere of the marketplace formed a part of her intimate family life. The intrusion of the marketplace into the most private affairs of the slave is played out in many ways, including the tendency of popular literature to present a slave's abode as lacking the capacity for order and productivity. *Incidents* makes it clear that the labor of the slave, especially of the female slave, is a sustaining feature of many homes, indeed, of the entire community.

At both the beginning and ending of *Incidents*, Jacobs establishes the primacy of housekeeping and of the home, the first as a measure of character and the second as a lifelong goal. The narrative frames these themes—holding that the quality of a person may be measured in her competence in making an orderly home, and that a household that sustains its members shapes human happiness. In the first chapter, "Childhood," Jacobs describes her parents as "they lived together in a comfortable home" (5). With her mother's death, Jacobs wrote, "My home was now to be with [my mother's] mistress; and I found it a happy one" (7). Also, in this first chapter, intelligence, competence, and thrift characterize Jacobs's descriptions of her father and maternal grandmother; each was much valued by the community as a competent worker. About Aunt Martha, the narrator comments, "She became an indispendable personage in the household, officiating in all capacities, from cook and wet nurse to seamstress" (6). Thus the virtues of housekeeping open the narrative. In the Edenton chapters, Aunt Martha, Aunt Nancy, and Linda earn credit for their competence as housekeepers—the first making order in her own home, the latter two bringing order to the homes of their owners.

As a free woman and the town baker, Aunt Martha/Molly Horniblow, represents the very essence of domestic craft in *Incidents*. Having gained the respect of important people in Edenton, Aunt Martha gained her freedom at the age of fifty,[19] and soon "By perseverance and unwearied industry, she was . . . mistress of a snug little home, surrounded by the necessaries of life" (17). This home on King Street is at the center of the narrative. From it, Aunt Martha provides the town with crackers and preserves. In it, Linda/Harriet found almost seven years of refuge and protection as a fugitive, even though she suffered terribly from exposure and limited movement. Finally, in the last full chapter Harriet Jacobs wrote, at the request of L. Maria Child, her editor, the house was featured as the target of the illiterate militias in the wake of Nat Turner's rebellion. In this powerful chapter, inserted as Chapter XII, "Fear of Insurrection," Jacobs presents the resentment of the rural whites finding "colored people living in comfort and respectability," and notes that she prepared the house for display—making "arrangements of them with especial care" (63). In the details, Jacobs suggests the signs of a genteel life: linens, flowers, silver, preserves, and letters. In the last written chapter, Jacobs describes the home her grandmother had—still the object of Jacobs's longing.

## The Family Tradition of Freedom

The grandmother's "snug little home," surrounded by the necessaries of life, is first featured in chapter four, "The Slave Who Dared to Feel Like a Man." Like the chapter, the home is apparently filled with debate over Aunt Martha's acceptance of God's will and her "legal" struggle to purchase the freedom of her children and grandchildren—especially as those values contrast with the rebellion of young William/John S. Jacobs, who fought with his master, Nicholas/James Norcom. With such debate establishing the theme, the focus of this chapter moves to the repeated escapes of Aunt Martha's son, Benjamin/ Joseph, who was caught and jailed for months, refusing to humble himself, until finally he escaped to New York. Benjamin becomes the example for the attitude of resistance and the cost of isolation; he sets the standard for the chapter. Benjamin's resistance, William's escape, and Linda's "sass" to her owner all show the changing attitudes of young slaves yearning for freedom. Linda/Harriet, reflecting on her own misery and persecution from both the Flints/Norcoms, comments, "The war of my life had begun; and though one of God's most powerless creatures, I resolved never to be conquered" (19).

The family and near neighbors to this household continually respond to Aunt Martha's religious acceptance of her family's condition and her prayers for their patience and safety with oppositional points: Uncle Phillip calls upon his mother to say a prayer of gratitude for Benjamin's freedom. Aunt Aggy faults Aunt Martha for weeping over William's/John's escape, likewise telling her to get down on her knees. Though Harriet had advised her brother to be "good and forgiving" (19) of the wrongs done him by his master, she is aware of her own feelings of rebellion.[20] *Incidents* is the story of this rebellion.

Such discussion over the ethics of escape or acceptance of one's condition, over theft and deception, over the possibility of violent resistance and punishment, occurs often in *Incidents*. This kind of debate provides a window into the moral and intellectual life of the African American slave family—especially as it acknowledges the young slaves' understanding of Aunt Martha's feelings without agreeing with them. The narrative shows the dialogue of those struggling to understand the moral condition of slavery through the embrace of family and faith in the midst of decisions about risk and separation. The narrative reflects the unwillingness of the young slaves in the family to bow to the will of their owners. This family, struggle as it may, carries an open and candid debate; it operates with considerable awareness of the choices to be made and their implications. The experience of slavery, not the intervention of others, provides this awareness. William comments about the abolitionists encouraging his escape that "he needed no information they could give him about slavery to stimulate his desire for freedom" (136).

Jacobs comes from a family with the capacity to measure oppression and resolve to act in resistance—a family in which the younger generation does not resolve to resist and escape. Jacobs dramatizes the painful prospects in both continued enslavement and risks for escape in the dialogues among the young slaves, especially. This southern home, tortured as it is by slavery, conveys both the intellectual and emotional resources for endurance, and resistance. This is a family of slaves who refuse to be brutalized: "We all concluded by saying, 'He that is willing to be a slave, let him be a slave'" (26). This family, then, is one image of a southern home—carefully contrasted in the narrative with the treacherous silences and repression of ethical debate or action in the Flint/Norcom household.

The Flint/Norcom home is described early in Jacobs's narrative as a place of cruelty, deception, whispers, and lies. The lascivious Dr. Flint, the reader is told, was father of eleven slaves, whose mothers feared the consequence of speaking of their father. Jacobs writes, "The secrets of slavery are concealed like those of the Inquisition" (35). Not only having to resist Dr. Flint's sexual pursuit, young Linda is also victimized by Mrs. Flint's constant prodding, with whispered questions about Flint in the middle of the night. The pathology of silence and secrets is intensified by the displacement of anger and the dehumanized behavior of the mistress: Mrs. Flint's "nerves were so strong, that she could sit in her easy chair and see a woman whipped till blood trickled from every stroke of the lash" (12). In Jacobs's repeated use of the phrase, the "patriarchal institution," it is clear that she means both the larger society and the structure of the home in which she was enslaved. The Norcom correspondence also reveals the rigid discipline of the family's patriarch, who was years older than his wife, as he instructs his daughter in her values and behavior on January 13, 1838:

Our duties to parents & children, the duties of wives to their husbands, of husbands to their wives; & our duties, as Masters to our Slaves, & of Slaves to their Masters are called Social or Domestic duties, chiefly because they respect the most beneficial effects on our household establishments, & are calculated to make us happy at home to give us a relish for what we see & enjoy everyday; & to make us contented in ourselves & in our families. In my next letter I shall begin with the first of that class of duties called domestic duties, and say something first of the duties which parents owe their children, & the duties of children to parents. In treating of this class of duties, you will soon perceive, that, on a due performance of them, all peace, social order, domestic happiness & quiet essentially depend. It is therefore, not only our highest duty, but our greatest interest to cultivate & practice them; continually to recommend their observance; & by our example to show their essential operation.[21]

The surface of order and natural authority conveyed in this letter is the result of rigid structures enforced upon family and slaves, structures which hardly conceal the deep violations of humanity that shape the culture. The popular portraits of slavery as an idealized extended family are deeply eroded in this contrast, where the slaveholders deceive and silence one another while exploiting their power over the unfortunate slaves.

## "New Perils": Sailors, Maroons, and The Underground Railroad

Another powerful impact of this narrative involves not only the narrator's painful restriction and "captivity," but also a powerful sense of the network of communication that reaches beyond family, beyond Edenton, to the waterways, to the ports in the North. Edenton had a community that carried the news and, often, carried runaways. Even Aunt Nancy's husband was a free black seaman. Aunt Nancy, who constantly urges Linda/Harriet to obtain her freedom, makes the connection to this web of support for fugitives. Her spirit and her name itself represent the African American rendering of the African trickster, Anansi.[22] Among the sailors assisting Linda/Harriet and others is her friend Peter, who arranges hiding in Snaky Swamp and passage north later. The name itself connects with several rebellious figures—for instance, the African Petro Lemba, which brings violent healing in Vodun, when gentler spirits have failed.[23] More emphatically, it may echo the maroon leader General Peter II, in Isle of Wight County, Virginia, a figure who tried to unify the maroon community and support insurrectionist activities in the area near Edenton.[24] The figures of the maroon, as Peter, and the trickster, as Aunt Nancy, convey a code or signal for those who have ears to hear. Movement and escape constitute much of the plot. The shifting escape plans of African Americans in Edenton, especially the narrator's own plans (e.g. her ability to get information about connections in the North), show an active Underground Railroad as well as a powerful, invisible maroon community.

In *Incidents*, another figure that suggests the existence of an invisible underground in the South is Linda/Harriet herself, in her sailor's disguise, walking past familiar citizens of Edenton unrecognized. After the night in Snaky Swamp, Peter escorts Linda/Harriet to her hiding place in her grandmother's house. Linda comments, "I passed several people whom I knew. The father of my children came so near that I brushed against his arm; but he had no idea who it was" (113). This circuitous escape from hiding in her "dismal hole" (113) to the arrival in Philadelphia seven years later indicates a system of information that reached from Edenton to New England, and beyond. Jacobs's home contained an almost invisible network of support for runaways and for delivering news to their families. Embattled as it was, this home presented a very supportive and well-organized community.

## The Shaping of Traditions: "Christmas Festivities"[25]

The last and most important feature of the home Jacobs constructs for the readers of *Incidents* is its complex and orderly spiritual tradition. In the first section of the narrative, as Linda/Harriet recalls her interactions with the Flints/Norcoms, Biblical references abound. But as Linda decides upon her escape and begins her life in hiding, the reader encounters a powerful combination of Christian practices and African folk religion. The graveyard scene that spurs Linda/Harriet toward escape dramatizes the narrator's spiritual experience: the narrative implies the presence of the ancestors. As Linda/Harriet visits this sacred place, she observes "a black stump, at the head of [her] mother's grave . . . all that remained of a tree [her] father had planted" (90). She hears her father's voice urging escape as she passes "the wreck of the old meeting house" (91). As Kim Connor argues, the scene evokes both Christian and African spiritual traditions, combining the two. "Linda's response to this sacred place and the presence of spirits . . . indicates her faith went beyond the simple rudiments of Christianity as presented by the slaveholders; it encompasses an African concept of God as an indwelling spirit."[26] This scene suggests the fuller features of the religious home Jacobs locates through her retrospection.

An even stronger dramatization of this spiritual complexity occurs in the "Christmas Festivities" chapter. Only a few pages long, this chapter is the second that features Jacobs's years in hiding and signals her embrace of a folk religious tradition in addition to Christianity. Most importantly, this chapter, narrated by the concealed and suffering Linda Brent, is structured to give the northern female reader a sequenced look at conventions surrounding a southern Christmas: a visit from Santa Claus, an African American folk ritual called Johnkannau, and a Christmas feast presented to men in the community who play an essential role in the capture and punishment of fugitive slaves.

This sequence and Jacobs's treatment of it not only embrace a nontraditional religious practice, but also imply a systematic critique of the way in which cultural values and social opinion are constructed in the United States.

In the opening paragraph of this chapter, the "imprisoned mother" observes her son in the new clothes she has made for him and overhears his conversation:

> I heard Benny ask a playmate whether Santa Claus brought him any thing. 'Yes,' replied the boy; 'but Santa Claus ain't a real man. It's the children's mothers that put things into stockings.' 'No, that can't be,' replied Benny, 'for Santa Claus brought Ellen and me these new clothes, and my mother has been gone this long time.' (118)

Jacobs uses the children's statements to give the reader important information about home and tradition. Readers know Santa Claus is not "a real man"; of course, he is "the children's mothers" in a disguise that crosses race and gender. In fact, Jacobs is probably acknowledging that Santa Claus is a myth borrowed and reconstructed by New York literati, especially including Washington Irving, to give a new, domestic emphasis to the Christmas holidays—which were often celebrated in the streets by unruly crowds.[27] Having seen this myth developed while she worked for publisher N. P. Willis in New York, Jacobs saw in her own southern home another, older, more authentic folk practice, the Johnkannaus. Even Norcom offers praise of the Johnkannaus in his letters from Edenton; they form the center of the holiday festivities: "We have had a very dull and lifeless season. Had it not been for the John Koonahs that paraded through the town in several successive gangs Christmas Day would have [passed] without the least manifestation of mirth or . . . hilarity."[28] From both perspectives one sees that the African-adapted ritual has become a part of the holiday practices and social structures of Edenton.

The "Christmas Festivities" chapter presents the children's conversation about Santa Claus and then features the second ritual, the Johnkannau ritual, as the "greatest attraction" of the Christmas holiday. Jacobs describes the large groups or bands involved in this carnival ritual, each constituted of one hundred plantation slaves; they pour through this small North Carolina town during the morning hours of Christmas Day, making music, dancing, and singing well-rehearsed songs at the homes of the white townspeople. The routinely required deference of the slave is abandoned in this tradition. The slaves, in rhyme and song, make demands for money or rum; those whites who refuse are ridiculed, also in prepared, traditional songs. Jacobs offers details about the constumes, the African instruments, and the lyrics in this many-voiced performance of the Johnkannaus.[29] This scene depicting the African American folk celebration, with its inversion of the order of the slavocracy, shows the centrality of African American ritual to the town's traditions. It shows resistance to the status quo not only within the slave community but within *Incidents* itself. Of the Johnkannaus Jacobs says, "It is seldom that any white man or child refuses to give them a trifle" (119) and "Without them, Christmas would be shorn of its greatest attraction" (118). The care with which Jacobs describes the revelry—as rehearsed, coordinated, and ritually significant—constitutes an important message to her northern reader. The details of the costumes and instruments and sheer numbers of participants convey the dramatic force of the ritual, yet she supplies other details about the ultimate civility of the event: "Not a door is left unvisited where there is the least chance of obtaining a penny or a glass of rum. They do not drink while they are out, but carry the rum home in jugs, to have a carousal" (119). Unlike Douglass, who characterizes the slaves' revelry as a dissipation that leads to self-disgust, Jacobs suggests a ritual that has its own order; she hints, perhaps, at an order older than the domestic celebration of Christmas stockings and children's gifts. She describes, in her home, the power and civility of the African American folk values in Edenton. She sees Christian religious tradition and African folk ritual functioning side by side.

These two central scenes—in the graveyard and on Christmas Day—are supported by many other uses of folk practices and religious vision. For instance, at the beginning of her escape, Linda/Harriet depended on healing provided by "an old woman who doctored among the slaves" (98) for a terrible snakebite. The cure of cankered vinegar belonged to the wisdom of folk culture. The narrator, in hiding, had a vision of her children as she lay concealed in the attic space, and at the very time at which they were sold into greater safety, bought by Sands/Sawyer: The reader, Jacobs says, may call this "the superstition of slaves" (107). It is clear that Jacobs's own experiences of religion, and especially, of American Spiritualism in her stay with Isaac and Amy Post in the North, allowed her a new, affirming view of slave religion and spiritual practices. Her work shows the natural intertwining of folk practices with more traditional faith that characterizes southern black religion. Jacobs recognized the essential nature of African spiritualism in the culture of Edenton—and its distinctive blend with Christian practices. Extending the work of scholars of African-adapted religion in America—Sterling Stuckey,

Robert Farris Thompson, Albert J. Raboteau, and others—John Kucich argues that many strains of spiritualism have figured into the American culture. He identifies the Anglo-European strains of belief in witchcraft and possession, Native American shamanism, and African American traditions of ancestor worship and spirit communication as figuring strongly into the spiritualist movement of the 1850s.[30] The cultural work of *Incidents* then includes situating the power of this African-adapted ritual in relation to southern Christianity. As historians and literary critics are doing now, Jacobs was able to align and present various expressions of spiritualism; with the understatement that characterizes much of her commentary in *Incidents*, Jacobs includes features of spiritualism that resonate with her experiences at Rochester—spirit voice and vision—with African-identified practices for celebration, healing, burial, and ancestor worship. This rich spiritualism, which "had long been simmering in the ante-bellum American culture," reveals Jacobs's view of the southern shape of religion, a creative and ongoing combination of traditional Christian structures and African traditional religion—subtly informed by the rapidly developing phenomenon of American Spiritualism.[31] In the course of her representation of religion, Jacobs demonstrates the cultural complexity of the African American spiritual practices in contrast to the frequently reductive and dishonest uses of the Bible in the enslaving community.

## Conclusion

Jacobs's vision of Edenton conveys two worlds, white and African American, that exist in a haunting parallel. From the vantage point of the African American folk community, both worlds were visible, and the work of Jacobs's narrative is to make both of them visible to a broader audience. The parts of *Incidents* set in Edenton thus constitute a powerful antislavery text, conveying the perversion of decent values caused by chattel slavery. However, embedded in this retrospective narrative is an embrace of the southern African American folk community, highlighting the traditional structures of the culture—the debate, the connected and resistant community, and the multicultural religious practices. This is a home with far more civil order and civility than the slavocracy that surrounds it but does not "see" it. Jacobs ends her narrative with an observation of her own homelessness. Finally, her predicament is not only an issue of her economic situation as nurse to N. P. Willis's children, but also a lament upon the southern home that is lost to her through the construction of slavery. Her description of the folk culture in Edenton conveys that there was much of value left behind. This home community includes the grandmother's household and the spirit of support and intelligent debate that informs it, but Jacobs goes beyond the household to the extensive network of support from the larger black community, and to the sustaining rituals and institutions of the slave culture.

## Notes

1. Frances Smith Foster (1993: 110).
2. See both Harriet Jacobs (1987: title page), and Angelina E. Grimké (1836: 52); Grimké e-book edition transcribed by Lloyd Benson and proofed by Ryan Burgess, Department of History, Furman University, online at http://history.furman .edu/~benson/docs/grimke2.htm (Accessed 7 July 2007).
3. Jean Fagan Yellin cites Amelia M. Murray's travel writing, *Letters from the United States, Cuba, and Canada* (1856); see Jacobs (1987: 307n5).
4. T. Addison Richards wrote an extensive, illustrated article entitled "Idlewild, The Home of N. P. Willis." Praising both the man and his manor, the author demonstrates the extent to which the domestic environment dominated the literary landscape. See Richards (1858: 145–66).
5. Henry Beers (1885: 287).
6. Jean Fagan Yellin included this letter: Jacobs writes to Amy Post, "as yet I have not written a single page by daylight" in March 1854; quoted in Jacobs (1987: 254); see Isaac and Amy Post Family Papers (IAPFP), University of Rochester.
7. Jacobs (1987: 1).
8. Nathaniel Parker Willis (1853: 237).
9. Ibid., 240.
10. Jacobs (1987: 185).
11. Ann Beebe (1997).
12. Jacobs (1987: 288).
13. Ibid., 265.
14. Anna Julia Cooper (1892), quoted in Foster (1993: 5).
15. Jacobs, in the preface "by the author," explains, "I have concealed the names of places, and given persons fictitious names. I had no motive for secrecy on my own account, but I deemed it kind and considerate toward others to pursue this course." Child, in her introduction, also comments, "The names of both persons and places are known to me; but for good reasons I suppress them" (1987: 3, 5). In the case of *Incidents* the preservation of anonymity serves not only as an opportunity to protect the fugitives and those who assisted them, but also to invite the use of symbolic names to reinforce the roles of certain figures. In the remainder of this essay both fictional and real names of individuals will appear.

16. Frederick Douglass (1855: 156).
17. Carla Peterson (1998: 163, 164).
18. Jacobs (1987: 201).
19. Ibid., 11, 12.
20. Christina Accomando (2001) explores Jacobs's multiple arguments concerning United States law.
21. Norcom, Dr. James and Family Papers. PC 73.1–73.3, January 13, 1838. North Carolina State Archives.
22. Aunt Nancy in Jacobs's narrative is Betty, one of Molly Horniblow's five children. A wife, but never a mother herself, Betty was prevented from living with her husband of twenty years and died in 1842. Her health—in part, because of repeated stillbirths—was deeply eroded by her service to Mary Matilda Norcom. Jacobs (1987: 101–2, 143–47, 261$n$7, 263$n$7, 279$n$1).
23. Robert Farris Thompson (1983: 179–81).
24. Hugo Prosper Leeming (1995: 252–55).
25. For an earlier, extended exploration of the Johnkannau ritual and the religious syncretism in *Incidents*, see Anne Bradford Warner (1996).
26. Kimberly Rae Connor (1994: 62).
27. For an extended examination of the ways in which Christmas traditions shifted toward the domestic, aided by the adoption of Santa Claus, see Stephen Nissenbaum (1997).
28. Norcom, Dr. James and Family Papers, PC 73.1–73.3, January 13, 1838.
29. Jacobs (1987: 118–20).
30. John J. Kucich (2004: 1–35). Major figures who have done extensive research into African-retention and African-adapted religious rituals in United States culture include Robert Farris Thompson (1983); Albert J. Raboteau (1978); and Sterling Stuckey (1987).
31. Quotation, Kucich (2004: 107).

## Works Cited

Accomando, Christina. 2001. *"The Regulations of Robbers": Legal Fictions of Slavery and Resistance*. Columbus: Ohio State University Press.

Beebe, Ann. 1997. "'Statements made with fidelity and accuracy ought to be welcome': The Honorable Amelia Murray's Letters from the United States, Cuba, and Canada." From *Snapshots from Abroad: A Conference on Travel Writing*. University of Minnesota, November 15. Abstract accessed online: http://english.cla.umn.edu/travelconf/abstracts/Beebe.html.

Beers, Henry. 1885. *American Men of Letters: N. P. Willis*. New York: Houghton Mifflin.

Braxton, Joanne M. 1989. *Black Women Writing Autobiography: A Traditon Within a Tradition*. Philadelphia: Temple University Press.

Carby, Hazel V. 1987. *Reconstructing Womanhood: The Emergence of the Afro-American Woman Novelist*. New York: Oxford University Press.

Connor, Kimberly Rae. 1994. *Conversions and Visions in the Writings of African-American Women*. Knoxville: University of Tennessee Press.

Cooper, Anna Julia. 1892. *A Voice from the South*. Xenia, OH: Aldine Printing House.

Douglass, Frederick. 1855. *My Bondage and My Freedom*. New York: Miller, Orton & Mulligan.

Foster, Frances Smith. 1979. *Witnessing Slavery: The Development of Ante-Bellum Slave Narratives*. Westport, CT: Greenwood Press.

———. 1993. *Written by Herself: Literary Production by African American Women, 1746–1892*. Bloomington: Indiana University Press.

Grimké, Angelina E. 1836. *An Appeal to the Christian Women of the South*. New York: New York Anti-Slavery Society.

Jacobs, Harriet. 1987. *Incidents in the Life of a Slave Girl: Written by Herself*. Ed. Jean Fagan Yellin. Cambridge, MA: Harvard University Press. Orig. publ. 1861.

Kucich, John. 2004. *Ghostly Communion: Cross-Cultural Spiritualism in Nineteenth-Century American Literature*. Hanover, NH: Dartmouth College Press.

Leeming, Hugo Prosper. 1995. *Hidden Americans: Maroons of Virginia and the Carolinas*. New York: Garland Publishing, Inc.

Murray, Amelia M. 1856. *Letters from the United States, Cuba, and Canada*. New York: Putnam.

Nissenbaum, Stephen. 1997. *The Battle for Christmas*. New York: Vintage.

Peterson, Carla L. 1998. *"Doers of the Word": African-American Women Speakers and Writers in the North (1830–1860)*. New Brunswick, NJ: Rutgers University Press.

Richards, T. Addison. 1858. "Idlewild, the Home of N. P. Willis." *Harper's New Monthly Magazine* 16.92, 145–66.

Raboteau, Albert J. 1978. *Slave Religion: The "Invisible Institution" in the Antebellum South*. New York: Oxford University Press.

Stuckey, Sterling. 1987. *Slave Culture: Nationalist Theory and the Foundation of Black America*. New York: Oxford University Press.

Thompson, Robert Farris. 1983. *Flash of the Spirit: African & Afro-American Art & Philosophy*. New York: Random House.

Warner, Anne Bradford. 1996. "Carnival Laughter: Resistance in *Incidents*." In *Harriet Jacobs and Incidents in the Life of a Slave Girl: New Critical Essays*. Eds. Deborah M. Garfield and Rafia Zafar. New York: Cambridge University Press, 216–32.

Willis, Nathaniel Parker. 1853. *Health Trip to the Tropics*. New York: C. Scribner.

# James Agee, Walker Evans, and the Dialectic of Documentary Representation in Let Us Now Praise Famous Men

JOSEPH MILLICHAP

> For in the immediate world, everything is to be discerned ... and all of
> consciousness is shifted from the imagined ... to the effort to perceive
> simply the cruel radiance of what is.
> —James Agee, *Let Us Now Praise Famous Men*

Like most Americans during the 1930s, including many of his colleagues in Southern letters, James Agee was attracted to photography. In 1936, a documentary project in rural Alabama with photographer Walker Evans confirmed Agee's interest in this newly pervasive art form. A powerful compilation of his literary depictions and Evans's photographs of tenant farmers at last appeared as *Let Us Now Praise Famous Men* in 1941. Southern writers such as Eudora Welty, Zora Neale Hurston, Richard Wright, and Erskine Caldwell were involved with similar hybrids, so much so that the photo-book provides a convenient lens for reviewing the connection of photography and literature in the period. Although intriguing examples such as Welty's unpublished "Black Saturday" (1935), Hurston's *Tell My Horse* (1937), and Wright's *12 Million Black Voices* (1941) languished, a similar collaboration by the then better-known Caldwell and Margaret Bourke-White, *You Have Seen Their Faces* (1937), mounted the best-seller lists. Despite the economic depression, photography burgeoned as a popular pastime during the decade, while it also became a significant influence on the creation and interpretation of both social documentation and modern art.[1]

In his "Preamble" to *Let Us Now Praise Famous Men* Agee stated flatly that "the camera seems to me ... the central instrument of our time" (26).[2] As if to confirm his claim, Agee's collaboration with Evans has emerged as the

*Southern Quarterly* 48.1 (2010): 81–99.

most highly regarded of the era's photo-books. This respect is recently exemplified by the selection of *Let Us Now Praise Famous Men* as "The Best Work of Southern Nonfiction of All Time" in a poll of Southern writers and critics conducted by the *Oxford American* in 2009. The book has become so esteemed, in my view, because its dialectic of visual and verbal art exemplifies the larger issues of cultural representation during the Depression that recent criticism has rediscovered in the efforts of the decade's finest artists and writers. In *Dancing in the Dark: A Cultural History of the Great Depression* (2009), for example, Morris Dickstein traces "the tension in the 1930s between a resurgent naturalism and a subterranean modernism, between a desire to bear witness to the social fact and an insistence on the individual character of all witness, all perception" (41) through myriad examples in fine art and popular entertainment.[3] The visual and verbal texts comprising *Let Us Now Praise Famous Men* prove both complementary and conflicted; Evans's photographs of the rural South evolve from the realism and naturalism of New Deal documentary toward modern art, while Agee's literary effort to realize the representative individuality of these tenant families reveals the anxious subjectivity of a persistent American modernism.

∾

There are on this hill three such families I would tell you of: the Gudgers, who are sleeping in the next room; and the Woods, whose daughters are Emma and Annie Mae; and besides these, the Ricketts, who live on a little way beyond the Woods.
—James Agee, *Let Us Now Praise Famous Men*

The importance of *Let Us Now Praise Famous Men* in the recent critical reconsideration of the 1930s derives not just from the overall dialectic of documentary and modernism found in its visual and verbal intertextuality, but from the particular characteristics of its subject matter. Agee and Evans gathered their raw material during the summer of 1936 in Hale County, Alabama, a three-week sojourn that now appears as unique as their intertextual reactions to it through the literary and photographic aspects of Depression-era documentary. *Let Us Now Praise Famous Men* began as an assignment Agee readily accepted as one of his duties as a writer at *Fortune*, the glossy business magazine launched by Henry Luce just as the previous decade ended. The staff included writers like Archibald MacLeish and Dwight Macdonald, so that creative perspectives on topical assignments were not only accepted but encouraged.

Agee's prescribed subject would be the plight of the Southern tenant farmer, which President Roosevelt proclaimed the nation's number one problem during his 1936 reelection campaign, yet the writer had considerable latitude on the means to achieve his reportage. Agee could choose his photographer to illustrate the article, and he contracted with a New York friend, Walker Evans, who was then employed by the now famous photographic section of the Farm Security Administration or FSA. Roy Stryker, the legendary director of the FSA documentary unit, eagerly granted Evans a temporary leave in order to have section work published in *Fortune*; his only condition was that the rights to all of the photographs would remain the property of the agency.[4]

The collaboration of Agee and Evans, now formidable figures in historical considerations of American literature or photography, on this single documentary project seems extraordinary three quarters of a century later. We must remember, however, that both men were very young and as yet unproven in 1936. Born in 1909, Agee was only four years out of Harvard, a fledgling writer with but a handful of articles at *Fortune* and one book, *Permit Me Voyage* (1934), a slim volume in the Yale Younger Poets Series.[5] Evans was only six years senior to his literary collaborator, and he had little higher education, few publications of his photographs, and no extended work experience until he signed on with the FSA in 1935.[6] Despite its initial failure, *Let Us Now Praise Famous Men* marked the maturation of both artists; now with its later fame, the book remains in many ways the high point in their careers and canons.[7]

Agee and Evans knew each other through mutual friends in Manhattan's creative set, including Hart Crane in the years directly before the poet's suicide in 1932. Evans met Crane when they each lived near Brooklyn Bridge, a nineteenth-century structure that would become the central symbol in the poet's American epic *The Bridge* (1930). Their friendship was strengthened by each man's interest in the other's art. Evans had first aspired to be a writer, influenced by the examples of Gustave Flaubert, Henry James, and James Joyce.[8] Crane had experience as a graphic artist, and he emphasized the visual aspects of the great American artifice in his epic poem. In turn, their friendship led to the first publication of Evans's photographs, three medium-distance shots of Brooklyn Bridge in the first edition of Crane's great work. Although they also knew each other, Agee's relation to Crane was more literary than personal.

The poet was a major influence on the young writer's work, and the title of Agee's first poetry collection, *Permit Me Voyage*, derives from a visionary sequence titled "Voyages" in Crane's first collection, *The White Buildings* (1926). Like Crane, Agee emphasized visual imagery in his writing, and he shared with him a keen interest in the motion picture as a developing American art form.

Agee and Evans, however, were very different in their personal and professional identities despite their mutual interests. Agee was idealistic, impulsive, and often romantic in his literary vision, while Evans was realistic, reserved, and reticent in his approach to his photographic art. Still, the pair complemented each other almost perfectly in both personality and practice, so much so that each of them could accept the other's vision and integrate it with his own. Agee and Evans had taken individual documentary journeys through the South on earlier writing assignments for *Fortune* and photographic expeditions for the FSA; now the committed young writer proposed immersion in their new subject matter by living with a tenant family for a summer's cotton season. The normally detached photographer not only took up this challenge, but, after Agee was frustrated in his initial inquiries, Evans made the actual connection with the tenant families through his FSA experience and contacts. They were soon accepted by not just one but three interrelated families, so that Agee could observe life on an Alabama tenant farm as a boarder with them. The pragmatic Evans gave their project his best efforts during the working days, but spent his nights in the boarding houses and small hotels of nearby towns.[9]

This close and extended contact with each other and with their subjects is one thing that makes this documentary collaboration by Agee and Evans unique among so many others undertaken during the Depression decade. At the same time, these same conditions make it the most problematic in many ways as well. Although he was eager to take on this assignment, its inherent difficulties worried Agee from the outset. Describing the projected journey to Father Flye, a friend and mentor since prep school, Agee confessed his "considerable doubts of the ability to bring it off," in a way that would satisfy either his employer or himself.[10] If some self-doubt in his daunting circumstances was understandable, in Agee's case it seems exacerbated by an unrelenting fear of failure that had haunted him from his father's accidental death when he was yet a small boy. Recent critics view Agee's plan for a documentary expedition into the southern hinterlands as a quest to reconnect with his father's rural roots in east Tennessee, and the close personal union Agee then enjoyed with the tenants then becomes an attempt to restore his own fragmented family life.

These tensions involving Agee's professional and personal purposes also affected the others in the project, most of all his photographic collaborator Evans, but also the subjects of their dual documentation. If Evans initially shared Agee's enthusiasm for all the places and people they were sent to record, then he seemed to withdraw slowly from them all, even as his partner's commitment continued to intensify. In *Let Us Now Praise Famous Men*, Agee's attitudes toward Evans's photographic documentation became ever more conflicted. Although the writer believed the pictures were infused with something like Keats's truth and beauty, his anxiety about his own literary task may have derived from the immediate development of the photographer's images. In his "Preamble," Agee goes so far as to declare that "If I could do it, I'd do no writing at all here. It would be photographs" (28). Yet the striking pictures Evans captured also could prove stark and pitiless in their candid revelations of tenant life in the cotton South, as Agee's description toward the conclusion of a final photo shoot with the families demonstrates: "Walker setting up the terrible structure of the tripod crested by the black square heavy head, dangerous as that of a hunchback, of the camera; stooping beneath cloak and cloud of wicked cloth, and twisting buttons; a witchcraft preparing, colder than keenest ice, and incalculably cruel" (311).

Little wonder that these interrelated tenants—in reality the Burroughs, Fields, and Tengle families of the Mill's Hill community in Hale County, Alabama—also were confused by what they perceived as such bizarre activities on the parts of both these outsiders. Although the adult tenants must have understood and even supported the public goals of the project in the first place, they too started to draw back instinctively from Evans's professional assignment and Agee's personal mission. One obvious locus of anxiety all around was the sexual tensions created by these two attractive young men, both of whom were later considered to be womanizers. Indeed, Agee confesses his attraction to the tenant women, both single and married, with utter candor throughout his account of the summer. The father of one family joked about the effect of the documentarians on his female charges, but he also declined to board either of them in his house. Protocols for the treatment of human subjects did not exist universally in that era, and questions regarding the subjects' agency in the project haunt *Let Us Now Praise Famous Men*, especially given the two young outsiders' image as "Government men" (310) in the eyes of the tenants.

These problems become one focus of a much later photo-book, *And Their Children after Them* (1989), the collaboration of journalist Dale Maharidge and photographer Michael Williamson. Subtitled "The Legacy of *Let Us Now Praise Famous Men*," this documentary revisited the same area a half-century after Agee and Evans to trace the effects of their earlier effort. One legacy Maharidge and Williamson discovered was a lingering resentment among many of the surviving tenants and their progeny. Agee's revelations had caused local embarrassment early on and created wider notoriety later as *Let Us Now Praise Famous Men* emerged from obscurity in the 1960s and after. The most important findings of the new book concerned ongoing social and economic disparities long after the end of the cotton culture that determined the lives of these tenant farmers. In this regard, the later text proves much superior to the earlier one, as neither Agee nor Evans seem to have any real sense of the historical, cultural, or economic development of cotton in the South. Like its model, *And Their Children after Them* is a powerful document, as evidenced by the Pulitzer Prize it won in 1989.

∽

Against time and the damages of the brain
Sharpen and calibrate. Not yet in full,
Yet in some arbitrated part
Order the façade of the listless summer.
—James Agee, *Let Us Now Praise Famous Men*

My epigraph here is the first stanza of the "Verses" dedicated to Walker Evans that forms one of Agee's several attempts at an introduction to *Let Us Now Praise Famous Men* (21). In Agee's final ordering of the volume, the poem follows almost directly after the gathering of thirty-one photographs that became Book One, and it makes an important, if oblique comment on Evans's pictures. Even the writer's charge to his photographer again suggests a conflicted response to the new visual art form. If its scientific calibrations are capable of at least partially organizing the inchoate impressions absorbed during their long, hot summer, then its frozen order invokes only the "façade" of that experience, the anxious faces of the tenant folk or the worn fronts of their buildings. Such is the conflicted nature of the "part" achieved by some sort of arbitration between Agee and Evans in regard to the gathering of photographs that now serves as the visual introduction to *Let Us Now Praise Famous Men*.

Reconstructing the exact nature of the accord the two collaborators reached is impossible at this point, of course. Agee does insist that, "The photographs are not illustrative" (8), or not connected directly with the texts as in most published examples of the photo-book, including those by Caldwell, Hurston, and Wright mentioned above. In his "Preface," Agee also asserts that the visual and verbal texts "are coequal, mutually independent, and fully collaborative" (8). The photos will become Book One of their collaboration, therefore, while his written texts will form Book Two. Agee also remarks on the "fewness" (8) of the examples, and later he alludes to "photographs for which there is no room in this volume" (178), probably implying that their publishers cut the photo selections to contain costs. The first edition in 1941 opens with thirty-one photographs; for the 1960 edition five years after Agee's death, Evans dropped five and then added thirty-six to double the selection to sixty-two examples, though even this larger number includes fewer than half of the pictures still extant.

In both editions of *Let Us Now Praise Famous Men*, as well as in two early notebooks of the Alabama photographs preserved at the Library of Congress, Evans arranges his materials by analogy with family albums.[11] He considers the Burroughs, Fields, and Tengle families each in turn, moving from the parents to their children and other dependents with interspersed pictures of their homes and possessions. In the 1941 edition, this arrangement is bracketed by a portrait of the landowner at the opening and three documentary shots, two of a nearby crossroads hamlet and one of the town that was their county seat. Evans retains this general pattern of organization in the 1961 edition, though he adds fourteen pictures to the family albums and seventeen to the contextual images of Alabama's hamlets, towns, and cities. Thus, the overriding principle of Evans's organization in the visual Book One is topical and spatial, while Agee's order in the verbal texts of Book Two is topical and narrative.

Within this spatial ordering, Evans presents sixteen individual portraits and four group pictures, one farm house exterior and seven interiors, as well as the three shots of neighboring hamlets and towns. If the numbers vary in the 1961 edition, the two notebooks, and the FSA files, then the ratio of the sorts of shots stays roughly the same. Both Evans and Agee focus on people, especially the three families they encountered during that Alabama summer.

These persons, whether as individuals or as groups, always are represented in context, for even the tightest close-ups are arranged against the weathered boards of their homes. The group pictures and the interior shots create other contexts, of course, while the final three photos open out into other parts of the Alabama cotton belt. Yet these are for the most part not the contextual markers of much iconic FSA documentary photography found in eroded fields, abandoned farms, or migrant camps. Evans was indifferent to the aims of New Deal programs, asserting "*No politics* whatever," to Stryker; rather, he aspired to making photographic art out of the elemental American experience.[12]

In the photographs that became Book One of *Let Us Now Praise Famous Men*, Evans treated the matter of 1930s documentary with a formal regard he derived from modernism in the arts, including literature. In visual terms, this meant that he rejected a prior aesthetic inherited from the nineteenth-century pioneers of photography and extended into the twentieth by traditional practitioners such as Alfred Stieglitz. This initial phase of photographic art came to be called "pictorialism," for the most part because of its connections with the traditional graphic arts in terms of serious subject matter and self-conscious style.[13] Pictorial photography becomes analogous, in my view, to the late romanticism against which literary modernists reacted at the beginning of the twentieth century. Several differing movements toward a "pure" photography emerged as a loosely organized counter-aesthetic emphasizing the autonomy of the subject and the artistic restraint of the practitioner. In literary terms, connections with realism and naturalism seem obvious, but analogies with the modernist aesthetic in American poetry practiced by Robert Frost, William Carlos Williams, Marianne Moore, and Hart Crane prove more salient.

If these modernist poets preserve various continuities with the past, they simultaneously reveal an insistent focus on a very real American present. Williams famously defined this new poesis in a short, disjunctive poem with a suitably tentative title, "A Sort of a Song" (1954): "Compose. (No ideas / but in things) Invent!"[14] Williams's twentieth-century *ars poetica* proves particularly appropriate to Evans's pictures because the poet wrote an early and enthusiastic review of the photographer's first book publication, *American Photographs* (1938). The volume was essentially the accompanying catalogue of a retrospective exhibition of Evans's photography at the Museum of Modern Art introduced by his friend Lincoln Kirstein, and some historians of photography consider it the most influential single work in the American canon. Williams's review of the collection in the *New Republic* was entitled "Sermon with a Camera," and it traces Evans's vision in the vernacular matter transformed by photographic art. Clearly Williams recognized a kindred spirit in Evans, another modern artist who demonstrated the pertinence in the American present of Horace's classical dictum "ut pictura poesis" ("as is visual art so is poetic art," in my own loose rendering of the Latin).[15]

*Let Us Now Praise Famous Men* would not appear for another three years, but Evans's selection from his previous decade's work in *American Photographs* included almost a third derived from his eighteen months with the FSA, with nearly a third of those images taken during his three weeks in Hale County. Although he abandoned the family album arrangement found in his Library of Congress notebooks and both versions of Book One, Evans included several examples of his three sorts of subjects—individual portraits and group pictures, farm house exteriors and interiors, as well as neighboring places. Evans's later friend John Szarkowski, the first director of photography at the Museum of Modern Art, remembers that the photographer always wanted his work to be "literate, authoritative, transcendent."[16] Perhaps more than any other part of Evans's canon, the iconic images that developed from his documentary project with Agee in Alabama achieve the lofty standard he set for himself.

∾

One reason I so deeply care for the camera is just this. So far as it goes . . . and handled cleanly and literally in its own terms . . . it is, like the phonograph record and like scientific instruments and unlike any other leverage of art, incapable of recording anything but absolute, dry truth.
—James Agee, *Let Us Now Praise Famous Men*

Just as his collaboration on the documentary project that became *Let Us Now Praise Famous Men* provided the catalyst for the creation of Evans's finest photographs, those iconic images leveraged Agee's artistic achievement during their time together into the best single endeavor of his varied canon. Agee had seen Evans's first proofs before they left Alabama, and he continued to be impressed by more polished prints and the positive response they received, especially in the Museum of Modern Art retrospective and its catalogue volume. High praise of *American Photographs* began with Lincoln Kirstein's introduction to the book, in which he compared Evans's work with that of established literary figures including prose by Stephen Crane, John Dos Passos, and Ernest Hemingway, as well as poetry by Hart Crane, William Carlos Williams, and Ezra Pound. Reviews of both the show and the book were surprisingly wide-ranging and almost universally positive; for example, even Eleanor Roosevelt praised it highly in her syndicated newspaper column.[17] Friends of both Evans and Agee joined this chorus of praise, but with more artistic insight. Thomas Dabney Mabry discovered an ethical dimension inherent in Evans's documentary art—"a power which reveals a potential order and morality at the very moment that it pictures the ordinary, the vulgar, and the casually corrupt."[18] William Carlos Williams penetrated the artistic psychology of Evans's photographic images: "It is ourselves we see, ourselves lifted from a parochial setting. We see what we have not heretofore realized, ourselves made worthy in our anonymity."[19] All this critical success surely set a lofty standard for Agee to contemplate as he stared at his still unfinished manuscript.

Therefore, it should be noted that Agee's major revisions took place during 1939, the year after Evans's *American Photographs* retrospective. Their joint project then in progress as "Three Tenant Families" next became the book published two years later as *Let Us Now Praise Famous Men*. Agee's poetic new title derived from the Christian apocrypha, and it represents how his work evolved from a documentary study of tenant farming to a modernist intertext focused on the re-creation of tenant life in visual and verbal art.[20] Because Evans's photography challenged Agee's literary imagination, the conflicted responses in his new chapters reveal a creative anxiety. This artistic *agon* becomes more clear even while his photographic references emerged as an important focus within the loose organization of *Let Us Now Praise Famous Men*.

Just as Evans's arrangement of his topical matters in Book One roughly approximates the spatial boundaries of their Alabama setting, so Agee's narrative organization generally follows the chronology of their stay. Like modernist novels both men admired, narration here is far from straightforward. Agee makes several awkward attempts at a start, meanders about his topics in the development of his book, and concludes abruptly without a real resolution. A "Preface," three epigraphs, and a table of "Persons and Places" precede two pages of contents Agee hopefully names "Design of the Book." It lists some eighteen additional sections, including another introductory gathering consisting of "Verses," "Preamble," and "All Over Alabama." The seemingly logical organization of the succeeding parts "One," "Two," and "Three" is complicated when Agee parallels other parts he names "July 1936," "Colon," and "Intermission." He counterpoints the factual matter in these parts with longer subjective reflections in three contrasting sections titled "(On the Porch:1", "(On the Porch:2", and "(On the Porch:3" [*sic*]. In turn, each of these sections is subdivided into many subsections, some titled and some numbered, with both Roman and Arabic numerals, but some not at all. The writer's plan perhaps is intended as a modernist pastiche on the model of a traditional documentary—one reflexively demonstrating its generic inability to comprehend a subject of such importance, complexity, and urgency. In the execution of that plan, however, Agee's Book Two becomes more an assemblage of individual takes on his subjects and themes, a gathering that ultimately mirrors the montage organization of Evans's photographic Book One.

In my reading of *Let Us Now Praise Famous Men*, its thematic ordering of Agee's multiform reflections on the tenant families is best seen in three focal patterns of material, religious, and photographic imagery. The longest of Agee's three epigraphs is titled "2. Food, Shelter, and Clothing," and it is taken from an introduction in a third-grade geography text belonging to one of the tenant children. Agee's sub-chapters here—"Money," "Shelter," "Clothing," "Education," and "Work"—then document the place of these universal human needs in the lives of the three tenant families. The subtitles recall not just the child's geography textbook, but Thoreau's "Economy" chapter from *Walden*, as in his more documentary chapters Agee depicts the agricultural poor forced to the practice of an involuntary Thoreauvian economics. Unlike the nineteenth-century example, this economic regimen works mostly for the worse; yet, like Thoreau's experiment, it sometimes operates for the better in spiritual if not material terms.

Both the earlier account of a rural retreat by the naturalist Thoreau in *Walden* and this sprawling observation by the Christian humanist Agee are rife with religious imagery. In both books, the allusions prove for the most part Christian, but in Agee's case more specifically Catholic. Several subsections are titled after elements of the Mass including "Gradual," "Reversion," and "Introit"; other sacraments and sacramentals are discovered, and the texts of Christian prayers and scriptural passages are included. These images prove integral to Agee's narrative, as his experience in Alabama is marked by frequent acts of contrition and communion.[21] *Let Us Now Praise Famous Men* likewise is permeated by photography—both as subject when Agee discusses its practice, especially by Evans, and as product when Agee verbally re-creates actual photographs, most importantly those Evans made in the summer of 1936.

Instances of the first sort appear throughout the book, but late in his process of composition Agee added substantial examples near his introduction and conclusion. In the final order of Agee's narration, the subsection "Near a Church" tells how the collaborators interrupted their hunt for white tenants to photograph an empty country church. After Agee "helped get the camera ready," he also considered the best angle for Evans's shot, "searching out and registering within myself all its lines, planes, stresses of relationship" (48). The writer's loving focus on the church's rough façade clearly matches the photographer's care in framing, balance, and lighting. Yet the remainder of this interpellation dramatizes their differences as well. While the two white men wait for the sunlight to strike their subject at its best angle, "a young negro couple came past up the road" (49). Agee pursued them in a self-conscious attempt to secure their consent to enter and photograph the sanctuary. The awkward dialogue which ensues is important as one of the book's few depictions of blacks and also for Agee's consciousness of his subjects' agency. At the same time, he "had no doubt that Walker would do what he wanted whether we had 'permission' or not" (50)—exactly what transpired when Evans was left alone at the church.

Like his introductory example, Agee's concluding one also demonstrates his pervasive patterns of material, religious, and photographic images. It becomes even more subtle and ironic in its evocation of this imagery because it consists of an extensive quotation of several pages. In subsection 3 of Agee's penultimate part, "Notes and Appendices," a substantial article first published in 1937 about the photographer Margaret Bourke-White is reprinted "by courtesy of the New York Post," which Agee notes is "a liberal newspaper" in his only editorial comment (385). Perhaps Agee's appendix was anticipated in his "Preamble," where he asserted that his belief in the camera's centrality to documentary representation during the 1930s also led him to "rage at its misuse, which has spread so nearly universal a corruption of sight that I know of less than a dozen alive whose eyes I can trust" (26). If by implication Evans was numbered among them, Bourke-White surely was not. Along with the exaggerated details endemic to a feature piece on a "Famous Photographer" (382), Agee replicates those parts of the *Post* article concerning her southern excursion with the writer Erskine Caldwell that was published as their *You Have Seen Their Faces* in that same year. Bourke-White is commended for the guile she used to insert herself among the flock of a "Negro preacher" (383) to photograph him from a dramatic angle that emphasizes his emotional oratory. Everything in her account, even allowing for exaggeration by her worshipful interviewer, stands in pointed contrast to the attitudes toward material culture, religious belief, and photographic documentary revealed in the earlier subsection "Near a Church."

∽

> A small octagonal frame surfaced in ivory and black ribbons of thin
> wicker or of straw, the glass broken out: set in this frame, not filling it,
> a fading box-camera snapshot: low, gray, dead-looking land stretched
> back in a deep horizon: twenty yards back, one corner of a tenant
> house, central at the foreground two women.
> —James Agee, *Let Us Now Praise Famous Men*

Agee's narrative line in Book Two of *Let Us Now Praise Famous Men* is ordered by the products of the photographic process as well, for his writing consistently references and recreates actual photographs. The example in my epigraph here is observed on the wall of the Gudgers' front bedroom, and its spatial aspects reinforce the unchanging story of the family's fortunes. Most important are the ones Evans made during their Alabama stay, of course, though other products of photographic practice are found throughout. Examples include allusions to efforts by well-known photographers Agee admired such as Matthew Brady, Henri Cartier-Bresson, and Helen Levitt— as well as those he disparaged such as Margaret Bourke-White, who also is satirized as "maggie berkwitz" (303, 387). Anonymous pictures in publications such as text books, popular magazines, and newspapers are mentioned, as are simple snapshots of the sort found in family albums. These varied types of photographic productions are seen within Evans's pictures as well, most often as details within the frames of his interior shots. Although some of this intertextuality seems unintentional or incidental to other documentary or artistic purposes, the composition of Evans's and Agee's texts makes clear that some of this self-reference is consciously intended.

Most arresting in Book Two are the imprints of Evans's visual images that are to be traced within Agee's verbal ones. Such traces are not mere illustrations of the written text, as in other examples of the photo book. Again, this was one reason that *Let Us Now Praise Famous Men* was divided into the visual Book One and the verbal Book Two. Yet some documentary patterns of visual allusion support the prose; when Agee describes different types of work clothes in his subchapter on "Clothing," he demonstrates his point by telling his reader that "Ricketts in his photograph here, wears such overalls" (235). Likewise, some written passages seem to re-create particular photographs, whether consciously or not. In fact, it seems probable that some of Agee's most detailed descriptions were written with Evans's corresponding picture as an aid to his memory. As the photographer's most recent biographer surmises, "Some descriptions in the book read as though Agee had Evans's detailed photographs in hand while writing the text," with examples such as the coal-oil lamp in "A Country Letter."[22]

The most intriguing correspondences in Book One of *Let Us Now Praise Famous Men*, however, are those where Agee's written depictions contest directly with Evans's photographic ones in a modern variation on the classical literary trope of *ekphrasis*. The rhetorical device of ekphrasis developed as an exercise of ancient orators who paused an argument for an extended description of some aspect of nature or work of art to illustrate a telling point. Ekphrasis then evolved as a literary trope altering narrative progression with a spatial metaphor emphasizing the circularity of time and the universality of human experience. Such a heroic metaphor came to represent all artistic creation for Classical and later poets, as in Homer's "Shield of Achilles" for example. John Keats's "Ode On a Grecian Urn" (1819) presents a salient instance of ekphrasis that the conflicted Agee would have known and appreciated. Here, the poetic persona engages the ancient artwork with creative anxiety, then turns the vase's visual images to his own literary purposes, and finally translates its silent lessons into the universal language of truth and beauty for his audience.[23]

Among Agee's uses of ekphrasis in *Let Us Now Praise Famous Men*, those passages competing with the individual or group portraits seem to me most significant examples, a conclusion that may find support in the writer's frequent agonizing over the inadequacy of his language to capture the full humanity of the Alabama tenants. Evans's iconic portrait of the youngest farmer, Floyd Burroughs, is presented by means of a head and shoulders close-up; his determined, anxious stare is complemented by his worn overalls and work shirt and set against the grainy pine siding of his house. This image of Burroughs introduces the same paired qualities of privation and perseverance in the individual and group portraits that follow it, the very qualities of this collaborative effort that have been most appreciated by cultural historians and art critics.

Agee transforms the youngest of the tenant farmers into George Gudger, picturing him as "a modification of the Leyendecker face, brick red, clean shaven; a medium-height, powerful, football player's body modified into the burlings of oak and into slow square qualities blending those of the lion and the ox" (238). The poetic diction of "burlings" seems especially apt here, as the "burl" or "burr" is the rounded outgrowth of the tree evocative both of Burroughs's sinewy form and of the knotted grain in the unpainted pine wallboards against which Evans posed his subject. In his images of oak, ox, and lion, Agee recalls archetypal legends of human transformation within the natural world. His allusion to other visual art, ironically in "a modification of the Leyendecker face," suggests modern America's myths of social evolution through economic success. For Leyendecker is a visual artist dealing in archetypes as well, though not a photographer but a magazine and advertising illustrator whose images probably were among those decorating the interior walls of the tenant houses. His most enduring creation was the "The Arrow-Collar Man," who seems as good an icon of the 1920s—one reflected in F. Scott Fitzgerald's portrait of Jay Gatsby sporting his beautiful shirts—as Evans's iconic portrait of Burroughs became for the 1930s in the decades following the publication of *Let Us Now Praise Famous Men*.[24]

∾

Agee's descriptions of other tenants—in particular, those he renames Annie Mae and Maggie Louise Gudger, Fred and Sadie Ricketts, and Bud and Ivy Woods—also exist in ekphrastic tension with Evans's pictures of Allie Mae and Lucille Burroughs, Frank and Flora Tengle, and Bud and Lily Fields. Likewise, the visual and verbal texts of *Let Us Now Praise Famous Men* contain literally dozens of additional examples of the photographic practices and products developed above—of documented photo shoots and reframed magazine pictures, of individual portraits from small-town studios and snap-shot contents of family albums. All of these literary images become photographic tropes in some sense, reflecting not just the material culture that produced them, but each other—like a gallery of mirrors. Each reflection reveals aspects of its own time and place, ones then compounded by all of the others to reveal diverse visions before unseen.

The cotton country of Alabama observed by Agee and Evans thus emerges as an artistic microcosm of the human macrocosm, "*The Great Ball on Which We Live*" (14, italics in original), to recall the language of the tenant child's geography text. The record of this exceptional collaboration by writer and photographer becomes nothing less than a Southern masterpiece, one recognized today as recalling those by Thomas Wolfe or William Faulkner that came before it while anticipating those by Richard Wright or Robert Penn Warren which would appear after it. Yet the complementary and conflicting visual and verbal intertexts Agee and Evans created can be appreciated best as providing focus on the dialectical work of cultural representation in the South of the 1930s and after. Rooted in the new documentary realism of the Depression decade, the final record of their Alabama project was influenced by the subterranean modernism that shaped both the writer's and the photographer's artistic programs that evolved under international influences. Thus, the varied texts created by Agee and Evans found their inspiration in a specific reportorial assignment in 1936, but their organization into *Let Us Now Praise Famous Men* in 1941 concluded as a universal instance of modernist montage.

## Notes

1. In *A Staggering Revolution: A Cultural History of Thirties Photography* (2006), John Raeburn notes that by the end of the decade, "More than 50 percent of American families owned a camera and made some six hundred million pictures yearly, spending $100 million doing so. Snapshots marking family and social occasions accounted for much of this, but many who wielded cameras had more artistic goals" (9). Raeburn's valuable study focuses on the creative aspirations of photographic genres, movements, and artists most influenced by modernism in the arts and not just by the documentary realism usually associated with 1930s photography, especially that recorded by key figures such as Edward Steichen, Berenice Abbott, and Edward Weston.

2. Definitive editions of Agee's works have been reconsidered recently, but in the absence of a critical consensus, I believe it is the best course here to use the Library of America editions as the most universally accessible. All references to *Let Us Now Praise Famous Men* will be cited parenthetically from this Library of America (2005) edition.

3. Those recent studies most influential on my formulations here include, in the order of their publication: Paul Hansom, ed. (2002); John Raeburn (2006); Joseph B. Entin (2007); Jeff Allred (2009); Peter Conn (2009); and Morris Dickstein (2009).

4. Belinda Rathbone (1995: 120–21).

5. Laurence Bergreen's *James Agee: A Life* (1984) remains the best biographical source, at least in the absence of a definitive one. A similar situation obtains in regard to the surprisingly large number of critical and scholarly studies that have appeared in the half-century since Agee's death. From my perspective, no fully authoritative reading of the writer's career or canon has emerged as yet, perhaps because the

career was so different, the canon so diverse and difficult, and both so dissimilar from each other. Some important readings include, in chronological order: Alan Spiegel (1998); Michael A. Lofaro, ed. (2007); and Hugh Davis (2008).

6. Perhaps because his career and canon were less varied, Walker Evans has received better biographical, scholarly, and critical treatment than Agee, at least in my judgment. He is the subject of two excellent biographies: Belinda Rathbone (1995) and James R. Mellow (2001). Recent scholarly and critical studies complement rather than displace earlier ones; in chronological order, these works include: John Szarkowski (1971); William Stott (1973); John T. Hill and Jerry L. Thompson, eds. (1982); Alan Trachtenberg (1989); Joel Eisinger (1999); and John T. Hill (2006).

7. In addition to consideration within more general works like those in the preceding notes, *Let Us Now Praise Famous Men* is the particular subject of numerous scholarly and critical studies. Many of them prove more useful for historical, social, or cultural readings of the text, while others focus more directly on its ideas, images, and art. Although my conclusions differ from them in several ways, here are some interesting examples, again in chronological order: Carol Schloss (1987); T. V. Reed (1988); Peter Cosgrove (1995); Janis Bergman-Carton and Evan Carton (2001); Jonathan Raban (2005).

8. Rathbone (1995: 40–42).

9. Ibid., 127.

10. James Agee (1962: 92).

11. Mellow (1999: 331).

12. Rathbone (1995: 111).

13. Raeburn (2006: 34–35).

14. Repr. in Williams (1985: 145). The poem was first published in 1954.

15. It proves interesting in theoretical terms that Evans characterized his own work as "lyric documentary," a formulation that encompasses both genre and style. On the implications of the photographer's depiction of his art, see John T. Hill's introductory essay in his *Walker Evans: Lyric Documentary* (2006).

16. Szarkowski (1971: 13).

17. Raeburn (2006: 182).

18. Quoted in Szarkowski (1971: 15).

19. Quoted in ibid., 16.

20. Bergreen (1985: 126).

21. His description of "James Agee in 1936" serves as the foreword to the 1960 edition of *Let Us Now Praise Famous Men,* and in it Walker Evans reveals his own literary talents through his insightful analysis of his collaborator, including Agee's religious faith: "His Christianity . . . was a punctured and residual remnant but it was still a naked, root emotion. It was an ex-Church, or non-Church, matter, and it was hardly ever in evidence. . . . After a while, in a round-about way, you discovered that, to him, human beings were at least possibly immortal and literally sacred souls" (5).

22. Mellow (1999: 33).

23. In addition to the many examples in *Let Us Now Praise Famous Men*, ekphrasis continued to be significant in much of Agee's later writing—both his fiction, notably the posthumous *A Death in the Family* (1957), and nonfiction, especially his voluminous film criticism. In particular Agee's posthumously published "Foreword" to his friend Helen Levitt's photography collection, *A Way of Seeing* (1965), also proves important both in terms of critical theory and ekphractic practice in describing her photographs of New York street scenes. Also, it is worth mentioning that in his later career Evans produced considerable journalistic and critical writing, most of it quite accomplished and much of it employing ekphrasis in the description of his own or others' pictures.

24. Joseph Christian Leyendecker (1874–1951) mentored Norman Rockwell, and he is the only American illustrator to prove as important to the visual culture of his day. On connections with the modernist classic of 1925, see Thomas Dilworth (2009).

# Works Cited

Agee, James. 1934. *Permit Me Voyage*. New Haven: Yale University Press.

———.1957. *A Death in the Family*. New York: McDowell, Obolensky.

———. 1962. *Letters of James Agee to Father Flye*. New York: Braziller.

———. 1965. "Foreword." In *A Way of Seeing*. By Helen Levitt. New York: Viking Press.

———. 2005. *Let Us Now Praise Famous Men, A Death in the Family, and Shorter Fiction*. New York: Library of America.

Agee, James, and Walker Evans. 1941. *Let Us Now Praise Famous Men*. Boston: Houghton Mifflin Co.

———. 1960 edition. *Let Us Now Praise Famous Men*. New York: Houghton Mifflin Co.

———. 1961 edition. *Let Us Now Praise Famous Men*. Boston: Houghton Mifflin Co.

Allred, Jeff. 2009. *American Modernism and Depression Documentary*. Oxford: Oxford University Press.

Bergman-Carton, Janis, and Evan Carton. 2001. "James Agee and Walker Evans: Tenants in the House of Art." *Raritan* 20.4, 1–20.

Bergreen, Laurence. 1985. *James Agee: A Life*. New York: Penguin.

Caldwell, Erskine, and Margaret Bourke-White. 1937. *You Have Seen Their Faces*. New York: Modern Age Books, Inc.

Conn, Peter. 2009. *The American 1930s: A Literary History*. New York: Cambridge University Press.

Cosgrove, Peter. 1995. "Snapshots of the Absolute: Mediamachia in *Let Us Now Praise Famous Men*." *American Literature* 67.2: 329–57.

Crane, Hart. 1926. *The White Buildings*. New York: Boni & Liveright.

———. 1930. *The Bridge; A Poem*. New York: Horace Liveright. Repr. New York: Liveright, 1970.

Davis, Hugh. 2008. *The Making of James Agee*. Knoxville: University of Tennessee Press.

Dickstein, Morris. 2009. *Dancing in the Dark: A Cultural History of the Great Depression*. New York: W. W. Norton.

Dilworth, Thomas. 2009. "*The Great Gatsby* and the Arrow Collar Man." *The F. Scott Fitzgerald Review* 7.1: 81–93.

Eisinger, Joel. 1999. *Trace and Transformation: American Criticism of Photography in the Modernist Period*. Albuquerque: University of New Mexico Press.

Entin, Joseph B. 2007. *Sensational Modernism: Experimental Fiction and Photography in Thirties America*. Chapel Hill: University of North Carolina Press.

Evans, Walker. 1938. *American Photographs*. New York: Museum of Modern Art.

Hansom, Paul, ed. 2002. *Literary Modernism and Photography*. Westport, CT: Praeger.

Hill, John T. 2006. *Walker Evans: Lyric Documentary*. Göttingen, Germany: Steidl.

Hill, John T., and Jerry L. Thompson, eds. 1982. *Walker Evans at Work*. New York: Harper & Row.

Hurston, Zora Neale. 1937. *Tell My Horse*. Philadelphia: J.B. Lippincott Co.

Keats, John. 1819. "Ode On a Grecian Urn." *The Complete Poems of John Keats*. New York: Modern Library, 1994.

Lofaro, Michael A., ed. 2007. *Agee Agonistes: Essays on the Life, Legend, and Works of James Agee*. Knoxville: University of Tennessee Press.

Maharidge, Dale, and Michael Williamson. 1989. *And Their Children After Them: The Legacy of Let Us Now Praise Famous Men*. New York: Pantheon.

Mellow, James R. 1999. *Walker Evans: A Biography*. New York: Basic Books.

Raban, Jonathan. 2005. "Thinking About Documentary: Notes Toward a Lecture." *Michigan Quarterly Review* 44.4: 554–69.

Raeburn, John. 2006. *A Staggering Revolution: A Cultural History of Thirties Photography*. Champaign: University of Illinois Press.

Rathbone, Belinda. 1995. *Walker Evans: A Biography*. Boston: Houghton Mifflin.

Reed, T. V. 1988. "Unimagined Existence and the Fiction of the Real: Postmodernist Realism in *Let Us Now Praise Famous Men*." *Representations* 24.1: 156–76.

Schloss, Carol. 1987. *In Visible Light: Photography and the American Writer*. New York: Oxford University Press.

Spiegel, Alan. 1998. *James Agee and the Legend of Himself: A Critical Study*. Columbia: University of Missouri Press.

Stott, William. 1973. *Documentary Expression and Thirties America*. New York: Oxford University Press.

Szarkowski, John. 1971. *Walker Evans*. New York: Museum of Modern Art.

Thoreau, Henry David. 1854. *Walden; or, Life in the Woods*. Boston: Ticknor and Fields.

Trachtenberg, Alan. 1989. *Reading American Photography*. New York: Hill and Wang.

Williams, William Carlos. 1938. "Sermon with a Camera." *New Republic* (October 12).

———. 1985. *Selected Poems*. Ed. Charles Tomlinson. New York: New Directions.

Wright, Richard. 1941. *12 Million Black Voices*. New York: Viking Press.

# Contributors

MARGARET WALKER ALEXANDER. (d. 1998). Poet and novelist, author of *For My People* (1942) and *Jubilee* (1966), among other works. Professor of literature, Jackson State University.

ALFRED BENDIXEN. Professor of English, Texas A&M University.

DAVID C. BERRY. Professor emeritus in English, University of Southern Mississippi.

AUGUSTUS M. BURNS. (d. 1999). Professor of history, University of Florida.

JAMES TAYLOR CARSON. Professor of history and department chair, Queen's University, Kingston, Ontario, Canada.

DOUGLAS B. CHAMBERS. Associate professor of history, University of Southern Mississippi. SoQ editor (2005–2011).

THADIOUS M. DAVIS. Geraldine R. Segal Professor of American Social Thought and professor of English, University of Pennsylvania.

SUSAN V. DONALDSON. NEH Professor of English and American Studies, and chair of the English department, College of William and Mary.

DON H. DOYLE. McCausland Professor of History, University of South Carolina.

BARBARA C. EWELL. Dorothy Harrell Brown Distinguished Professor of English, Loyola University, New Orleans.

ROBERT L. HALL. Associate professor of history and African-American Studies, Northeastern University.

WILLIAM H. HATCHER. Professor emeritus in political science, University of Southern Mississippi. *SoQ* editor (1965–1973).

ARTHELL KELLEY. (d. 2009). Professor emeritus in geography, University of Southern Mississippi.

MANNING MARABLE. (d. 2011). M. Moran Weston and Black Alumni Council Professor of African-American Studies and professor of history and public affairs, Columbia University.

JOSEPH MILLICHAP. Professor emeritus in English, Western Kentucky University.

WILLIE MORRIS. (d. 1999). Writer and editor, author of *North Toward Home* (1967), and *My Dog Skip* (1994), among other works.

JOHN SOLOMON OTTO (d. 2006). Research associate, International Center for Development Policy.

HARRIET POLLACK. Professor of English, Bucknell University.

PEGGY WHITMAN PRENSHAW. Millsaps College Humanities Scholar-in-Residence and Fred C. Frey Professor Emerita, Louisiana State University. *SoQ* editor (1974–1991).

KATHRYN L. SEIDEL. Professor of English, University of Central Florida.

JOHN RAY SKATES. Professor emeritus in history, University of Southern Mississippi.

RANDY J. SPARKS. Professor of history, Tulane University.

MARTHA SWAIN. Professor emerita in history, Texas Woman's University.

ANNE BRADFORD WARNER. Director, Cosby Academic Center, and associate professor of English, Spelman College.

# Index